Teacher's Resources for

Contemporary Living

by
Verdene Ryder
Family Life Education Consultant
Houston, Texas

Marjorie B. Harter, Ph.D.
Family Life Education Consultant
Washington, DC

Publisher
The Goodheart-Willcox Company, Inc.
Tinley Park, Illinois

Copyright 2000

by

The Goodheart-Willcox Company, Inc.

Previous Editions Copyright 1995, 1990, 1988

All rights reserved. No part of this book may be reproduced for resale. Manufactured in the United States of America.

Teacher's Resource Guide ISBN 1-56637-643-2

Teacher's Resource Binder ISBN 1-56637-644-0

1 2 3 4 5 6 7 8 9 10   00   03 02 01 00 99

Contents

Teacher's
Resource
Guide/Binder   Text

Introduction

Contemporary Living is a comprehensive text designed to help students explore all aspects of life: personal development, decisions affecting their future, lifestyle options and consequences, relationships with family and friends, marriage, parenting, balancing family and work, dealing with family crises, and managing family living.

In addition to the student text, the *Contemporary Living* learning package includes the *Student Activity Guide, Teacher's Annotated Edition, Teacher's Resource Guide, Teacher's Resource Binder, Test Creation Software,* and *Computer Review Games.* Using these products can help you develop an effective family living program tailored to your students' unique needs.

Using the Text ■ ■ ■ ■ ■ ■

The text, *Contemporary Living,* is designed to help your students learn to deal with the realities of life throughout the entire life cycle. The approach used is not one of telling students what to do. Rather, the information is presented in a factual, objective manner. Once students are aware of the alternatives available to them and the consequences of each alternative, they will be more likely to make wise decisions on their own.

The text is divided into seven parts with a total of 27 chapters. The material is organized and presented in a logical sequence of topics for the study of family living. Although the text was written to be studied in its entirety, individual chapters and sections are complete enough to be studied independently.

The text is straightforward and easy to read. Hundreds of photographs and charts attract student interest and emphasize key concepts. References to the illustrations are included in the copy to help students associate the visual images with the written material. This helps reinforce learning.

The text includes an expanded table of contents to give students an overview of the wide variety of topics they will be studying. The glossary at the back of the book helps students learn terms related to family living. A complete index helps them find information they want quickly and easily.

Each chapter includes several features designed to help students study effectively and review what they have learned.

Objectives. A set of behavioral objectives is found at the beginning of each chapter. These are performance goals that students will be expected to achieve after studying the chapter. Review the objectives in each chapter with students to help make them aware of the skills they will be building as they read the chapter material.

Terms to Know. A list of vocabulary terms also appears at the beginning of each chapter. Terms are listed in the order in which they appear in the chapter. These terms are in bold italic type throughout the text so students can recognize them while reading. Discussing these words with students will help them learn concepts to which they are being introduced. To help students become familiar with these terms, you may want to ask them to

- look up, define, and explain each term.
- relate each term to the topic being studied.
- match terms with their definitions.
- find examples of how the terms are used in current newspapers and magazines, reference books, and other related materials.

Summary. A summary of key points is listed at the end of each chapter. This section will help students review major concepts covered in the text.

To Review. Review questions at the end of each chapter are included to cover the basic information presented. This section consists of a variety of true/false, completion, multiple choice, and short essay questions. It is designed to help students recall, organize, and use the information presented in the text. Answers to these questions appear in the front section of the *Teacher's Annotated Edition* as well as in the *Teacher's Resource Guide,* and the *Teacher's Resource Binder.*

To Do. Suggested activities at the end of each chapter offer students opportunities to increase knowledge through firsthand experiences. These activities encourage students to apply many of the concepts learned in the chapter to real-life situations. Suggestions for both individual and group work are provided in varying degrees of difficulty. Therefore, you may choose and assign activities according to students' interests and abilities.

To Think About. Questions and activities that challenge students to use the higher-level thinking skills of analysis, synthesis, and evaluation are also given at the end of each chapter. These require students to think more about what they have read in the chapter. The questions can be used for group discussions or for personal journal entries.

Using the Student Activity Guide ■ ■ ■ ■ ■ ■ ■ ■

The *Student Activity Guide* designed for use with *Contemporary Living* helps students recall and review material presented in the text. It also helps them apply what they have learned to real-life situations.

The activities in the guide are divided into chapters that correspond to the chapters in the text. The text provides the information students will need to complete many of the activities. Other activities will require creative thinking and research beyond the textbook.

You may want to use the exercises in the *Student Activity Guide* that are directly related to textual material as introductory, review, or evaluation tools. Ask students to do the exercises without looking in the book. Then they can use the text to check their answers and to answer questions they could not complete. The pages of the *Student Activity Guide* are perforated so students can easily turn completed activities in to you for evaluation.

The *Student Activity Guide* includes different types of activities. Some have specific answers related to text material. Students can use these activities to review as they study for tests and quizzes. Answers to these activities appear in the *Teacher's Resource Guide* and *Teacher's Resource Binder.*

Other activities, such as case studies and surveys, ask for students' thoughts or opinions. Answers to these activities cannot be judged as right or wrong. These activities allow students to form their own ideas by considering alternatives and evaluating situations thoughtfully. These thought-provoking exercises can often be used as a basis for classroom discussion by asking students to justify their answers and conclusions.

The use of each activity in the *Student Activity Guide* is described in the *Teacher's Resource Guide* and *Teacher's Resource Binder* as a teaching strategy under the related instructional concept. Activities are identified by name and letter.

Using the Teacher's Annotated Edition ■ ■ ■ ■ ■ ■ ■ ■

The *Teacher's Annotated Edition* for *Contemporary Living* is a special edition of the student text. It is designed to help you more effectively coordinate materials in the *Student Activity Guide* with text concepts. It also provides you with additional suggestions to help you add variety to your classroom teaching.

Annotations are located throughout the text. Numbers are placed in the right and left side margins that correspond with annotations located at the bottom of each page. The accompanying chart on the next page details the annotations used in the annotated edition.

In addition to annotations placed throughout the student text, the *Teacher's Annotated Edition* includes some helpful information in the introductory section. The following aids are included for each chapter of the text:

Chapter Outline. An outline of the chapter's main points is provided to give you an overview of the content and organization of chapter material.

Answer Key. Answers for the "To Review" questions at the end of each chapter are supplied to assist you in clarifying student understanding of chapter concepts.

Annotation Term	Annotation Description
Vocabulary	Suggests vocabulary reinforcement activities such as defining terms, using terms in sentences, looking up terms in the glossary, or comparing important new terms.
Discuss	Discussion questions to reteach or reinforce learning. Questions may also relate to charts in the chapters.
Reflect	Questions to ask students to think about regarding the concepts presented, often by applying the content to their own lives. These questions are often more personal than are the discussion questions.
Activity	Activities related to the chapter that would reteach and reinforce concepts.
Note	Additional points the instructor might want to make regarding the chapter, or to spark student interest in the discussion. Points might include statistics, interesting facts, or historical notes. These may also be notes to the instructor regarding the subject matter.
Example	An example to use in illustrating an important point in the chapter material.
Enrich	Activities that relate to the concept, but are more involved and challenging for students. Examples include role-playing, research topics, debates, surveys, bulletin boards, field trips, or guest speakers.
Resource	An activity from the *Student Activity Guide* that is appropriate for use with this section of the chapter.
Answers	These annotations indicate where answers to questions may be found.

Using the Teacher's Resource Guide

The *Teacher's Resource Guide* for *Contemporary Living* suggests many methods of presenting the concepts in the text to students. It begins with some of the same helpful information found in the *Teacher's Annotated Edition*, including teaching suggestions and a *Scope and Sequence Chart*.

A number of suggestions are given to help you increase the effectiveness of your classroom teaching. This information includes suggestions for teaching students of varying abilities, evaluating students, communicating with students, and promoting your program.

Correlation of National Standards with *Contemporary Living*

In 1998, the National Standards for Family and Consumer Sciences Education were finalized. This comprehensive guide provides family and consumer sciences educators with a structure for identifying what learners should be able to do. This structure is based on knowledge and skills needed for work life and family life, as well as family and consumer sciences careers. The National Standards Components include 16 areas of study, each with a comprehensive standard that describes the overall content of the area. Each comprehensive standard is then broken down into content standards that describe what is expected of the learner. Competencies further define the knowledge, skills, and practices of the content standards and provide the basis for measurement criteria.

By studying the text *Contemporary Living*, students will be prepared to master the competencies listed for the area of study called Interpersonal Relationships and the area of study called Family. To help you see how this can be accomplished, a *Correlation of National Standards for Interpersonal Relationships with Contemporary Living* has been included in the *Teacher's Annotated Edition, Teacher's Resource Guide,* and *Teacher's Resource Binder.* You will also find a *Correlation of National Standards for Family with Contemporary Living.* If you want to make sure you prepare students to meet the National Standards for Family and Consumer Sciences Education, these charts should be of interest to you.

Scope and Sequence Chart

A *Scope and Sequence Chart,* located at the end of this introduction, identifies the major concepts presented in each chapter of the text. This special resource is provided to help you select for study those topics that meet your curriculum needs.

Basic Skills Chart

Another feature of this *Teacher's Resource Guide* is a *Basic Skills Chart*. This chart has been included to identify those activities that encourage the development of the following basic skills: verbal, reading, writing, mathematical, scientific, and analytical. (Analytical skills involve the higher-order thinking skills of analysis, synthesis, and evaluation in problem-solving situations.) The chart includes activities from the *To Do* section of the text, activities from the *Student Activity Guide*, and strategies from the *Teacher's Resource Guide/Binder*. Incorporating a variety of these activities into your daily lesson plans will provide your students with vital practice in the development of basic skills. Also, if you find that students in your classes are weak in a specific basic skill, you can select activities to strengthen that particular skill area.

Pretest

A pretest is included for you to use in planning your program. It can be used to determine what your students already know. It will also identify those areas where your students are likely to encounter difficulty in understanding certain concepts. You can plan to devote more time to these subject areas as you plan your lessons. You can also use the pretest as a post test to determine which topics have been covered effectively and which topics need additional coverage. You may wish to modify this test to tailor the questions to your classroom needs.

The pretest consists of true/false and multiple choice questions representing each chapter in the text. The test should be given during the first few days the class meets. Remind students that they will not be graded on the pretest.

Chapter-by-Chapter Resources

Like the *Student Activity Guide*, the *Teacher's Resource Guide* is divided into chapters that match the chapters in the text. Each chapter contains the following features:

Objectives. These are the objectives that students will be able to accomplish after reading the chapter and completing the suggested activities.

Bulletin Board Ideas. Bulletin board ideas are described for each chapter. One bulletin board idea per chapter is illustrated for you. Putting up bulletin board displays can often be a stimulating student activity.

Teaching Materials. A list of materials available to supplement each chapter in the text is provided. The list includes the names of all the activities contained in the *Student Activity Guide* and all the masters contained in the *Teacher's Resource Guide/Binder*.

Introductory Activities. These motivational exercises are designed to stimulate your students' interest in the chapter they will be studying. The activities help create a sense of curiosity that students will want to satisfy by reading the chapter.

Strategies to Reteach, Reinforce, Enrich, and Extend Text Concepts. A variety of student learning strategies are described for teaching each of the major concepts discussed in the text. Each major concept appears in the guide in bold type. The student learning experiences for each concept follow. Activities from the *Student Activity Guide* are identified for your convenience in planning daily lessons. They are identified with the letters SAG following the title and letter of the activity. (*Environmental Influences*, Activity A, SAG.)

The number of each learning strategy is followed by a code in bold type. These codes identify the teaching goals each strategy is designed to accomplish. The following codes have been used:

RT identifies activities designed to help you *reteach* concepts. These strategies present the chapter concepts in a different way to allow students additional learning opportunities.

RF identifies activities designed to *reinforce* concepts to students. These strategies present techniques and activities to help clarify facts, terms, principles, and concepts, making it easier for students to understand.

ER identifies activities designed to *enrich* learning. These strategies help students learn more about the concepts presented by involving them more fully in the material. Enrichment strategies include diverse experiences, such as demonstrations, field trips, guest speakers, panels, and surveys.

EX identifies activities designed to *extend* learning. These strategies promote thinking skills, such as critical thinking, creative thinking, problem solving, and decision making. Students must analyze, synthesize, and evaluate in order to complete these activities.

Answer Key. This section provides answers for review questions at the end of each chapter in the text, for activities in the *Student Activity Guide,* for the reproducible masters in the *Teacher's Resource Guide/Binder,* and for the chapter tests.

Reproducible Masters. Several reproducible masters are included for each chapter. These masters are designed to enhance the presentation of concepts in the text. Some of the masters are designated as *transparency masters* for use with an overhead projector. These are often charts or graphs that can serve as a basis for class discussion of important concepts. They can also be used as student handouts. Some of the masters are designed as *reproducible masters.* Each student can be given a copy of the activity. These activities encourage creative and critical thinking. They can also serve as a basis for class discussion. Some masters provide material not contained in the text that you may want students to know.

Chapter Test Masters. Individual tests with clear, specific questions that cover all the chapter topics are provided. True/false, multiple choice, and matching questions are used to measure student learning about facts and definitions. Essay questions are also provided in the chapter tests. Some of these require students to list information, while others encourage students to express their opinions and creativity. You may wish to modify the tests and tailor the questions to your classroom needs.

Using the Teacher's Resource Binder ■ ■ ■ ■ ■ ■ ■ ■

The *Teacher's Resource Binder* for *Contemporary Living* combines the *Teacher's Resource Guide* with a set of color transparencies. All of the materials are included in a convenient three-ring binder. Reproducible materials can be removed easily. Handy dividers included with the binder help you organize materials so you can quickly find the items you need.

Color transparencies for *Contemporary Living* are provided to add variety to your classroom lecture as you discuss topics included in the text with your students. You will find some transparencies useful in illustrating and reinforcing information presented in the text. Others will provide you with an opportunity to extend learning beyond the scope of the text. Attractive colors are visually appealing and hold students' attention. Suggestions for how the transparencies can be used in the classroom are included in the *Teacher's Resource Binder.*

Using the GW Test Creation Software ■ ■ ■ ■ ■ ■ ■

In addition to the printed supplements designed to support *Contemporary Living, Test Creation Software* is available. The database for this software package includes all the test master questions from the *Teacher's Resource Guide/Binder* plus an additional 25 percent new questions prepared just for this product. You can choose to have the computer generate a test for you with randomly selected questions. You can also opt to choose specific questions from the database and, if you wish, add your own questions to create customized tests to meet your classroom needs. You may want to make different versions of the same test to use during different class periods. Answer keys are generated automatically to simplify grading.

Using the Computer Review Games for Contemporary Living ■ ■ ■ ■ ■ ■ ■

This software designed for student use provides review questions for each chapter in *Contemporary Living.* Eight game formats are used as challenging, fun methods of reviewing information. One game is provided for each chapter. Each game contains questions that help students review key facts, concepts, and vocabulary terms. Randomized questions make each game different every time it is played. Immediate feedback and an explanation of the correct answer is given for each question.

You may incorporate the review games into your program in a variety of ways. Since the programs are self-guiding, you can have students work at their own pace with minimum supervision. You might allow students to use the software outside of class time as a review for a chapter test. You may find the software useful in reinforcing concepts for lower level or difficult-to-motivate students. The games may also be used as a thought-provoking preview to the chapter.

Using Other Resources ■ ■

Much student learning in your class can be reinforced by allowing students to see, analyze, and work with examples. Your providing pictures and articles related to a variety of family and consumer sciences topics can greatly enhance student learning. Students can use these items in many activities related to the text.

Magazines, catalogs, and sales brochures are excellent sources of photos. Having a large quantity available for clipping and mounting photos will be helpful to students. Students may analyze and discuss the pictures in a variety of activities.

Current magazines and journals are also good sources of articles on various family and consumer sciences topics. Having copies in the classroom will encourage students to use them for research and ideas as they study family and consumer sciences. The following publications may be helpful to you or your students:

Childhood Education
Association for Childhood Education International (ACEI)
11141 Georgia Avenue, Suite 300
Wheaton, MD 20902

Child Health Alert
P O Box 388
Newton Highlands, MA 02161

Child Welfare
Child Welfare League of America, Inc.
440 First Street, NW
Washington, DC 20001

Children Today
Superintendent of Documents
U.S. Government Printing Office
Washington, DC 20402

Developmental Psychology
American Psychological Association
1200 17th Street, NW
Washington, DC 20036

Early Childhood News
330 Progress Road
Dayton, OH 45499

Early Childhood Today
Scholastic
Office of Publication
2931 East McCarty Street
P O Box 3710
Jefferson City, MO 65102-3710

Exceptional Children
Council for Exceptional Children
1920 Association Drive
Reston, VA 22091

Young Children
NAEYC
1509 16th Street NW
Washington, DC 20036-1426

American Health

Choices Magazine

Consumer Reports

Newsweek

Seventeen

Time

What's New in Family and Consumer Sciences

The following is a list of various companies, associations, and government groups that may serve as resources for additional teaching materials. Many provide videos and/or computer software. Most provide printed materials. Contact these organizations for their latest catalogs.*

AAVIM
220 Smithonia Road
Winterville, GA 30683
(800) 228-4689
(software, videos, and publications)

AGC Educational Media
1560 Sherman Ave.
Suite 100
Evanston, IL 60201
(800) 323-9084
FAX: (708) 328-6706

AIDS Action Committee
131 Clarendon Street
Boston, MA 02116
(800) 235-2331

AIDS Action Council
1875 Connecticut Ave., NW
Washington, DC 20009
(202) 986-1300

American Association of Family and Consumer Sciences (AAFCS)
1555 King Street
Alexandria, VA 22314

American Dietetic Association
216 West Jackson Boulevard
Chicago, IL 60606-6995
(800) 366-1655

American Educational Research Association (AERA)
1230 17th Street NW
Washington, DC 20036

*Note: The addresses, phone numbers, FAX numbers, and Web site addresses listed may have changed since the publication of this *Teacher's Resource Guide.*

American Foundation for AIDS Research (AMFAR)
733 Third Ave., 12th Floor
New York, NY 10017
(212) 682-7440

American Montessori Association (AMS)
150 Fifth Avenue
New York, NY 10011

American Red Cross
AIDS Education Office
8111 Gatehouse Road
Falls Church, VA 22042
(202) 737-8300
(703) 206-6000

Association for Career and Technical Education
1410 King St.
Alexandria, VA 22314

Bergwall Productions, Inc.
540 Baltimore Park
PO Box 2400
Chadds Ford, PA 19317
(800) 645-3565

Birthways, Inc.
"The Empathy Belly" Pregnancy Simulator
(educational teaching aid)
Seattle, WA
(800) 882-3559

Bureau for At-Risk Youth
135 Dupont St.
Plainview, NY 11803
(800) 999-6884
(guidance and life skills programs, videos, and handouts)

Cambridge Educational
PO Box 2153
Charleston, WV 25328-2153
(800) 468-4227
(videos, software, CD-ROM, printed materials in all areas of family and consumer sciences)

Center for Science in the Public Interest (CSPI)
1875 Connecticut Ave., NW, Suite 300
Washington, DC 20009
(202) 332-9110

Centers for Disease Control and Prevention (CDC)
Public Inquiries: (404) 639-3534

American Social Health Association
PO Box 13827
Research Triangle Park, NC 27709
National AIDS Hot Line:
(800) 342-AIDS
(800) 344-7432 (Spanish)
(800) 243-7889 (TTY/Deaf Access)
National Sexually Transmitted Diseases Hot Line: (800) 227-8922

Chamber of Commerce of the United States of America
1615 H Street, NW
Washington, DC 20062

Childbirth Graphics
A division of WRS Group, Inc.
PO Box 21207
Waco, TX 76702
(800) 243-2874 ext. 287

Child Welfare League of America
440 First Street, NW
Washington, DC 20001

Children's Defense Fund
122 C Street, NW
Washington, DC 20001

Cocaine Helpline
(800) COCAINE

Concept Media
2493 Dubridge Ave.
Irvine, CA 92606
(800) 233-7078

Consumer Product Safety Commission
1111 18th Street, NW
Washington, DC 20207

Consumer Resource Handbook
Consumer Information Center
Pueblo, CO 81009

Council for Exceptional Children
1920 Association Drive
Reston, VA 22091

Creative Educational Video
PO Box 65265
Lubbock, TX 79464-5265
(800) 922-9965

Cybershopping
Consumer Information Center
Pueblo, CO 81009

Daycare and Child Development Council of America (DCDCA)
   1401 K Street, NW
   Washington, DC 20005

Department of Commerce
   14th St. and Constitution Ave., NW
   Washington, DC 20230

Department of Education
   400 Maryland Avenue, SW
   Washington, DC 20202

Distinctive Home Video Productions
   391 El Portal Rd.
   San Mateo, CA 94402
   (415) 344-7756

Durrin Productions
   1748 Kaorama Rd., NW
   Washington, DC 20009
   (800) 536-6843

ETR Associates
   PO Box 1830
   Santa Cruz, CA 95061-1830
   (408) 438-4060

FHA/HERO
   1910 Association Dr.
   Reston, VA 22091

Films for the Humanities and Sciences
   PO Box 2053
   Princeton, NJ 08543
   (800) 257-5126

Food & Drug Administration (FDA)
   (301) 443-3170

The Health Connection
   55 W. Oak Ridge Drive
   Hagerstown, MD 21740
   (800) 548-8700
   (pamphlets, books, teaching aids, posters, and audiovisual aids)

The Herpes Resource Center
   American Social Health Association
   PO Box 13827
   Research Triangle Park, NC 27709
   (919) 361-8488

Human Relations Media Video (HRM)
   175 Tompkins Ave.
   Pleasantville, NY 10570
   (800) 431-2050
   (family living, guidance, health, drug education, and conflict resolution)

Independent Adoption Center
   319 Taylor Boulevard, Suite 100
   Pleasant Hill, CA 94523
   (800) 877-OPEN

Injoy Videos
   3970 Broadway
   Suite B4
   Boulder, CO 80304
   (800) 326-2082
   (videos on pregnancy, birth, and early parenting)

Internet Fraud Watch
   (800) 876-7060
   www.fraud.org

Karol Media
   350 N. Pennsylvania Ave.
   Wilkes Barre, PA 18773
   (800) 526-4773
   (videos in family and consumer sciences)

The Learning Seed
   330 Telser Road
   Lake Zurich, IL 60047
   (847) 540-8855
   (800) 634-4941
   (videos, software, and audiovisuals for family and consumer sciences)

Mail Order Action Line
   1120 Avenue of the Americas
   New York, NY 10036
   (212) 768-7277

Media International
   5900 San Fernando Rd.
   Glendale, CA 91202
   (800) 477-7575
   (videos on personal, social, and sexual issues, character education, relationships, and substance abuse)

Meridian Education Corp.
   236 E. Front St.
   Bloomington, IL 61701
   (800) 727-5507
   (videos/multimedia for foods/nutrition, clothing, child development, and relationships)

Midwest Agribusiness Services, Inc.
   4565 Highway 33 W.
   West Bend, WI 53095-9108
   (800) 523-3475
   www.hnet.net/midwest
   (software and videos on child development, parenting, and foods)

Nasco
901 Janesville Ave.
Dept. EN701-A
Fort Akinson, WI 53538-0901
(920) 563-2446
(800) 558-9595
FAX: (920) 563-8296

National Adoption Center
(800) 862-3678

National Adoption Information Clearinghouse
PO Box 1182
Washington, DC 20013-1182
(888) 251-0075

National AIDS Hot Line
(800) 342-2437

National AIDS Information Clearinghouse
PO Box 6003
Rockville, MD 20849-6003
(800) 458-5231

National Association for Gifted Children
4175 Lovell Road, Suite 140
Circle Pines, MN 55014

National Association for the Education of Young Children (NAEYC)
1509 16th Street, NW
Washington, DC 20036-1426
(800) 424-8777

National Campaign to Prevent Teen Pregnancy
2100 M Street NW, Suite 300
Washington, DC 20037
(202) 857-8655
e-mail: campaign@teenpregnancy.org
www.teenpregnancy.org

National Clearinghouse for Alcohol and Drug Information,
Center for Substance Abuse Prevention,
U.S. Dept. of Health and Human Services
268-2600 or (800) 729-6686

National Committee for Adoption
1940 17th Street NW
Washington, DC 20009
(202) 328-8072

National Council on Child Abuse and Family Violence
(800) 222-2200

National Foundation for Consumer Credit
8701 Georgia Avenue, Suite 507
Silver Spring, MD 20910

National Fraud Information Center
Consumer Fraud Hot Line
(800) 876-7060
(202) 737-5003

National Organization of Adolescent Pregnancy, Parenting, and Prevention
(301) 913-0378

National Resource Center on Domestic Violence
(800) 537-2238

NIMCO, Inc.
PO Box 9102
Highway 81 North
Calhoun, KY 42327
(800) 962-6662
(502) 273-5844
(textbooks, videos, and slides)

Procter & Gamble
One Procter & Gamble Plaza
Cincinnati, OH 45202
(513) 983-1100

RMI Media Productions
2807 West 47th Street
Shawnee Mission, KS 66205
(800) 821-5480
(educational videos)

Safe and Drug-Free Schools Program,
U.S. Dept. of Education
400 Maryland Ave. SW
Federal Office Building 6
Washington, DC 20202-4101
(202) 260-3954

Sax Family & Consumer Sciences
PO Box 510710
New Berlin, WI 53151
(800) 558-6696
www.artsupplies.com
(a complete line of family and consumer sciences teaching aids)

Students Against Driving Drunk (SADD)
PO Box 800
Marlboro, MA 01752
(508) 481-3568

Sudden Infant Death Syndrome (SIDS) Alliance
(800) 221-7437

Sunburst Communications, Inc.
101 Castleton St.
Pleasantville, NY 10570
(800) 431-1934
www.sunburst.com
(videos on family living, conflict resolution,
sexual education, and anger management)

TARGET
11724 NW Plaza Circle
PO Box 20626
Kansas City, MO 64195-0626
(816) 464-5400
National Resource Center: (800) 366-6666
(A program that trains state high school associations, personnel, students, parents, and
community leaders to help young people
make healthy lifestlye choices.)

Teaching Aids, Inc.
P O Box 1798
Costa Mesa, CA 92628-0798

Teen-Aid
723 E. Jackson
Spokane, WA 99207-2647
(509) 482-2868
FAX: (509) 482-7994
(videos, teaching modules, lesson plans,
pamphlets, overheads, and posters)

Toughlove International
PO Box 1069
Doylestown, PA 18901
(215) 348-7090 or (800) 333-1069
(self-help group emphasizing cooperation,
personal initiative, avoidance of blame, and
action—publishes newsletters, brochures,
and books)

U.S. Food and Drug Administration
5600 Fishers Lane
Rockville, MD 20857
(301) 443-3170
www.fda.gov

U.S. Government Printing Office
Publications Office
(202) 512-1800

USDA Economic Research Service (ERS)
(800) 999-6779

USDA Information
(202) 720-2791

The following Web sites may be of interest to you and your students:

American Association of Family and Consumer Sciences
www.aafcs.org

American Diabetes Association
www.diabetes.org

American Dietetic Association
www.eatright.org

American Heart Association
www.amhrt.org

American Institute for Cancer Research
www.aicr.org

American Medical Association
www.ama-assn.org

Anti-Racism Resources Home Pages
www.efn.org/~dennis_w/race.html

Association of Home Appliance Manufacturers
www.aham.org

Campaign for our Children (teen pregnancy cam-paign)
www.cfoc.org

Center for Food Safety and Applied Nutrition (FDA)
www.vm.cfsan.fda.gov/list.html

Centers for Disease Control and Prevention
www.cdc.gov

Child Abuse Prevention Center
www.capcenter.org

Coalition for Marriage, Family, and Couples Education
www.smartmarriages.com

Consumer Education for Teens
www.wa.gov/ago/youth

Consumer Information Center
www.pueblo.gsa.gov

Council of Better Business Bureaus, Inc.
www.bbb.org

Department of Health and Human Services
aspe.os.dhhs.gov/hsp/97trends/intro-web.htm

Dictionary of Occupational Titles
www.wave.net/upg/immigration
(click on DOT)

Early Childhood Educators' and Family Web Corner
www.nauticom.net/www/cokids

Families USA Foundation
www.familiesusa.org

FDA Center for Food Safety and Applied Nutrition
vm.cfsan.fda.gov/index.html

Federal Trade Commission (FTC)
www.ftc.gov

The Food Allergy Network
www.foodallergy.org

Food and Agricultural Organization of the United Nations
www.fao.org

Food and Drug Administration
www.fda.gov

Food and Nutrition Information Center of the National Agricultural Library
www.nalusda.gov/fnic

Food for the Hungry
www.fh.org/wcn/index.html

Food Safety and Inspection Service/USDA
www.fsis.usda.gov

Fraud on the Internet
www.fraud.org

Grocery Manufacturers of America
www.gmabrands.com

Home and Family Internet Resource Guide
www.homenfamily.com

Internet Fraud Watch
www.fraud.org

International Food Information Council (IFIC) Foundation
ificinfo.health.org

JobWeb
www.jobweb.org

Kidsource OnLine
www.kidsource.com

Mayo Health Oasis
www.mayo.ivi.com

National Academy of Sciences
www.nas.edu

National Association for the Education of Young Children
www.naeyc.org/naeyc

National Association of Home Builders
www.nahb.com

National Black Child Development Institute (NBCDI)
www.nbcdi.org

National Center for Educational Statistics
nces.ed.gov

National Center for Health Statistics of the Center for Disease Control and Prevention
www.cdc.gov/nchswww/nchshome.htm

National Center for Injury Prevention & Control
www.cdc.gov/ncipc

National Child Care Information Center
www.ghententerprises.com

National Consumer League
www.natlconsumersleague.org

National Food Safety Database (NFSD)
www.foodsafety.org

National Information Center for Children and Youth with Disabilities
nichy@aed.org

National Institute for Consumer Education
www.emich.edu/public/coe/nice

National Institute on Aging
www.nih.gov/hia

National Institutes of Health
www.nih.gov/od/odp.whi

National Organization on Fetal Alcohol Syndrome
www.nofas.org

National Pork Producers Council
www.nppc.org

The National Restaurant Association
www.restaurant.org/index.html

Occupational Outlook Handbook
www.espan.com/docs/oohand.html

Occupational Safety and Health Administration (OSHA)
www.osha.gov

Online Career Center
www.occ.com/occ

Partnership for Food Safety Education
www.fightbac.org

Peace Corps
www.peacecorps.gov

Shaken Baby Alliance
www.shakenbaby.com

Small Business Administration
www.sba.gov

The Soap and Detergent Association
www.sdahq.org

Teenager's Guide to the Real World: Money Really Matters
wwws.bygpub.com/books/tg2rw/chap1excerpt.htm

Tufts Nutrition Navigator
navigator.tufts.edu

USDA's School Meals Initiative for Healthy Children
schoolmeals.nalusda.gov:8001

U.S. Dept. of Energy (EREC)
www.eren.doe.gov

U.S. Dept. of Health and Human Services
www.os.dhhs.gov

U.S. House of Representatives
www.house.gov

U.S. Senate
www.senate.gov

World Health Organization
www.who.ch

Teaching Techniques ■ ■ ■ ■

You can make the study of family living exciting and relevant by using a variety of teaching techniques. Below are some principles that will help you choose and use different teaching techniques in your classroom.

- Make learning stimulating. One way to do this is to involve students in lesson planning. When possible, allow them to select the modes of learning that they enjoy most. For example, some students will do well with oral reports; others prefer written assignments. Some learn well through group projects; others do better working independently. You can also make courses more interesting by presenting a variety of learning activities and projects from which students may choose to fulfill their work requirement.

- Make learning realistic. You can do this by relating the subject matter to issues that concern young people. Students gain the most from learning when they can apply it to real-life situations. Case studies, role-playing, and drawing on personal experiences all make learning more realistic and relevant.

- Make learning varied. Try using several different techniques to teach the same concept. Make use of outside resources and current events as they apply to material being presented in class. Students learn through their senses of sight, hearing, touch, taste, and smell. The more senses they use, the easier it will be for them to retain information. Bulletin boards, films, tapes, and transparencies all appeal to the senses.

- Make learning success-oriented. Experiencing success increases self-esteem and confidence. Guarantee success for your students by presenting a variety of learning activities. Key these activities to different ability levels so that each student can enjoy both success and challenge. You also will want to allow for individual learning styles and talents. For instance, creative students may excel at designing projects, while analytical students may be more proficient at organizing details.

- Build in opportunities for individual students to work in ways that let them succeed and shine.
- Make learning personal. Young people become more personally involved in learning if you establish a comfortable rapport with them. Work toward a relaxed classroom atmosphere in which students can feel at ease when sharing their feelings and ideas in group discussions and activities.

Following are descriptions of various teaching techniques you may want to try. Keep in mind that not all methods work equally well in all classrooms. A technique that works beautifully with one group of students may not be successful with another. The techniques you choose will depend on the topic, your teaching goals, and the needs of your students.

One final consideration concerns students' right to privacy. Some activities, such as autobiographies, diaries, and opinion papers, may invade students' privacy. You can maintain a level of confidentiality by letting students turn in unsigned papers in these situations. You may also encourage students to pursue some of these activities at home for personal enlightenment without fear of evaluation or judgment.

Helping Students Gain Basic Information

Many teaching techniques can be grouped according to different goals you may have for your students. One group of techniques is designed to convey information to students. Two of the most common techniques in this group are reading and lecture. Using a number of variations can make these techniques seem less common and more interesting. For instance, students may enjoy taking turns to read aloud as a change of pace from silent reading. Lectures can be energized by the use of flip charts, overhead transparencies, and other visual materials. Classroom

discussions of different aspects of the material being presented get students involved and help impart information.

Other ways to present basic information include the use of outside resources. Guest speakers, whether speaking individually or as part of a panel, can bring a new outlook to classroom material. Guest lectures can be videotaped to show again to other classes or to use for review. In addition to videotapes, students also enjoy films and filmstrips related to material being studied.

Helping Students Question and Evaluate

A second group of teaching techniques helps students develop analytic and judgmental skills. These techniques help your students go beyond what they see on the surface. As you employ these techniques, encourage students to think about points raised by others. Ask them to evaluate how new ideas relate to their attitudes about various subjects.

Discussion is an excellent technique for helping students consider an issue from a new point of view. To be effective, discussion sessions require a great deal of advance planning and preparation. Consider the size of the discussion group and the physical arrangement. Since many students are reluctant to contribute in a large group, you may want to divide the class into smaller groups for discussion sessions. Participation also will be enhanced if the room is arranged so students can see each other.

Discussion can take a number of forms. Generally it is a good idea to reserve group discussions involving the entire class for smaller classes. Buzz groups consisting of two to six students offer a way to get willing participation from students who are not naturally outgoing. They discuss an issue among themselves and then appoint a spokesperson to report back to the entire class.

Debate is an excellent way to explore opposite sides of an issue. You may want to divide the class into two groups, each to take an opposing side of the issue. You can also ask students to work in smaller groups and explore opposing sides of different issues. Each group can select students from the group to present the points for their side.

Helping Students Participate

Another group of teaching techniques is designed to promote student participation in classroom activities and discussion. There are many ways to involve students and encourage them to interact. Case studies, surveys, opinionnaires, stories, and pictures can all be used to boost classroom participation. These techniques allow students to react to or evaluate situations in which they are not directly involved. Open-ended sentences often stimulate discussion. However, it is wise to steer away from overly personal or confidential matters when selecting sentences for completion. Students may be reluctant to deal with confidential issues in front of classmates.

The "fishbowl" can be a good way to stimulate class discussion. An interactive group of five to eight students is encircled by a larger observation group. The encircled students discuss a given topic while the others listen. Observers are not permitted to talk or interrupt. Positions can be reversed at the end of a fishbowl session to allow some of the observers to become the participants.

One of the most effective forms of small group discussion is the cooperative learning group. The teacher has a particular goal or task in mind. Small groups of learners are matched for the purpose of completing the task or goal, and each person in the group is assigned a role. The success of the group is measured not only in terms of outcome, but in the successful performance of each member in his or her role.

In cooperative learning groups, students learn to work together toward a group goal. Each member is dependent upon others for the outcome. This interdependence is a basic component of any cooperative learning group. The value of each group member is affirmed as learners work toward their goal.

The success of the group depends on individual performance. Groups should be mixed in terms of abilities and talents so that there are opportunities for the students to learn from one another. Also, as groups work together over time, the roles should be rotated so that everyone has an opportunity to practice and develop different skills.

The interaction of students in a cooperative learning group creates a tutoring relationship. While cooperative learning groups may involve more than just group discussion, discussion is always part of the process by which cooperative learning groups function.

Helping Students Apply Learning

Some techniques are particularly good for helping students use what they have learned. Simulation games and role-playing allow students to practice solving problems and making decisions under nonthreatening circumstances. Role-playing allows students to examine others' feelings as well as their own. It can help them learn effective ways to react or cope when confronted with similar situations in real life.

Role-plays can be structured, with the actors following written scripts, or they may be improvised in response to a classroom discussion. Students may act out a role as they themselves see it being played, or they may act out the role as they presume a person in that position would behave. Roles are not rehearsed and lines are composed on the spot. The follow-up discussion should focus on the feelings and emotions felt by the participants, and the manner in which the problem was resolved. Role-playing helps students consider how they would behave in similar situations in their own lives.

Helping Students Develop Creativity

Some techniques can be used to help students generate new ideas. For example, brainstorming encourages students to exchange and pool their ideas and to come up with new thoughts and solutions to problems. No evaluation or criticism of ideas is allowed. The format of spontaneously expressing any opinions or reactions that come to mind lets students be creative without fear of judgment.

You also can promote creativity by letting students choose from a variety of assignments related to the same material. For example, suppose you wanted students to develop an understanding of how costly it is to rear a child. You could ask them to contact a government agency to find out the latest statistics in this area. You might give them the choice of writing a story about young parents who discover a number of child-related expenses they hadn't considered before their baby was born. Taking a shopping list of items needed to outfit a nursery to a store and checking actual prices would be an option, too. Any teaching techniques you use to encourage students to develop their own ideas will foster their creativity.

Helping Students Review Information

Certain techniques aid students in recalling and retaining knowledge. Games can be effective for drills on vocabulary and factual information. Crossword puzzles can make the review of vocabulary terms more interesting. Structured outlines of subject matter can also be effective review tools. Open-book quizzes, bulletin board displays, and problem-solving sessions all offer ways to review and apply material presented in the classroom.

Teaching Students of Varying Abilities

The students in your classroom represent a wide range of ability levels. Special needs students who are mainstreamed require unique teaching strategies. Gifted students must not be overlooked. They need to be challenged up to their potential. All of the students in between will have individual needs to consider also. Often you will be asked to meet the needs of all of these students in the same classroom setting. It is a challenge to adapt daily lessons to meet the demands of all your students.

To tailor your teaching to mainstreamed and lower-ability students, consider the following strategies:

- Before assigning a chapter in the text, discuss and define the key words that appear at the beginning of each chapter. These terms are defined in the glossary at the back of the text. Ask students to write out the definitions and to tell what they think the terms mean in their own words. You might want to invite students to guess what they think words mean before they look up the definitions. You also can ask them to use new words in sentences and to find the sentences in the text where the new terms are used.

- When introducing a new chapter, review previously learned information students need to know before they can understand the new material. Review previously learned vocabulary terms they will encounter again.

- Utilize the "Introductory Activities" section in the *Teacher's Resource Guide/Binder* for each chapter. Students who have difficulty reading need a compelling reason to read the material. These introductory activities can provide the necessary motivation. Students will want to read the text to satisfy their curiosity.

- Break the chapters into smaller parts, and assign only one section at a time. Define the terms, answer the *To Review* questions, and discuss the concepts presented in each section before proceeding to the next. It often helps to rephrase questions and problems in simple language and to repeat important concepts in different ways. Assign activities in the *Student Activity Guide* that relate to each section in the book. These reinforce the concepts presented. In addition, many of these activities are designed to improve reading comprehension.

- Ask students, individually or in pairs, to answer the *To Review* questions at the end of each chapter in the text. This will help them focus on the essential information contained in the chapter.

- Use the buddy system. Pair nonreaders with those who read well. Ask students who have mastered the material to work with those who need assistance. It also may be possible to find a parent volunteer who can provide individual attention where needed.

- Select a variety of educational experiences to reinforce the learning of each concept. Look for activities that will help reluctant learners relate information to real-life situations. It helps to draw on the experiences of students at home, in school, and in the community.

- Give directions orally as well as in writing. You will need to explain assignments as thoroughly and simply as possible. Ask questions to be certain students understand what they are to do. Encourage them to ask for help if they need it. You will also want to follow up as assignments proceed to be sure no one is falling behind on required work.

- Use the overhead projector and the transparency masters included in the *Teacher's Resource Guide/Binder.* A visual presentation of concepts will increase students' ability to comprehend the material. You may want to develop your own transparencies to use in reviewing key points covered in each chapter.

- If you have advanced or gifted students in your class, you will need to find ways to challenge them. These students require assignments that involve critical thinking and problem solving. Because advanced students are more capable of independent work, they can use the library and outside resources to research topics in depth. Learning experiences listed in the *Basic Skills Chart* that involve analytical skills are appropriate for gifted students. You may be able to draw on the talents of advanced students in developing case studies and learning activities to use with the entire class.

Evaluation Techniques

A variety of evaluation tools can be used to assess student achievement. Try using the reproducible forms, *Evaluating Individual Participation, Evaluating Individual Reports,* and *Evaluating Group Participation,* included with this introductory material. These rating scales allow you to observe a student's performance and rank it along a continuum. This lets students see what levels they have surpassed and what levels they can still strive to reach.

In some situations, it is worthwhile to allow students to evaluate their own work. When evaluating an independent study project, for example, students may be the best judge of whether or not they met the objectives they set for themselves. Students can think about what they have learned and see how they have improved. They can analyze their strengths and weaknesses.

You may ask students to evaluate their peers from time to time. This gives the student performing the evaluation an opportunity to practice giving constructive criticism. It also gives the student being evaluated the opportunity to accept criticism from his or her peers.

Tests and quizzes are also effective evaluation tools. These may be given in either written or oral form. In either case, however, both objective and subjective questions should be used to help you adequately assess student knowledge and understanding of class material.

Communicating with Students

Communicating with students involves not only sending clear messages, but also receiving and interpreting feedback. Following are some suggestions for productive communication with your students:

- Recognize the importance of body language and nonverbal communication, both in presenting material and interpreting student responses. Eye contact, relaxed but attentive body position, natural gestures, and alert facial expression all make for a presentation of material that will command attention. The same positive nonverbal cues from students are an indication of their response and reactions. Voice is also an important nonverbal communicator. Cultivating a warm, lively, enthusiastic speaking voice will make classroom presentations more interesting. By your tone, you can convey a sense of acceptance and expectation to which your students will respond.

- Use humor whenever possible. Humor is not only good medicine, it opens doors and teaches lasting lessons. Laughter and amusement will reduce tension, make points in a nonthreatening and memorable way, increase the fun and pleasure in classroom learning, and break down stubborn barriers. Relevant cartoons, quotations, jokes, and funny stories all bring a light touch to the classroom.

- Ask questions that promote recall, discussion, and thought. Good questions are tools that open the door to communication. Open-ended inquiries that ask what, where, why, when, and how will stimulate thoughtful answers. You can draw out students by asking for their opinions and conclusions. Questions with yes or no answers tend to discourage rather than promote further communication. Avoid inquiries that are too personal or that might put students on the spot.

- Rephrase students' responses to be sure both you and they understand what has been said. Paraphrasing information students give is a great way to clarify, refine, and reinforce material and ideas under discussion. For example, you might say, "This is what I hear you saying. . . correct me if I'm wrong." Positive acknowledgement of student contributions, insights, and successes encourages more active participation and open communication. Comments such as, "That's a very good point. I hadn't thought of it that way before." or, "What a great idea." will encourage youngsters to express themselves.

- Listen for what students say, what they mean, and what they do not say. Really listening may be the single most important step you can take to promote open communication. As students answer questions and express their ideas and concerns, try not only to hear what they say, but to understand what they mean. What is not said can also be important. Make room for silence and time to think and reflect during discussion sessions.

- Share your own feelings and experiences. The measure of what students communicate to you will depend in part on what you are willing to share with them. Express your personal experiences, ideas, and feelings when they are relevant. Don't forget to tell them about a few of your mistakes. Sharing will give students a sense of exchange and relationship.

- Lead discussion sessions to rational conclusions. Whether with an entire class or with individual students, it is important to identify and resolve conflicting thoughts and contradictions. This will help students think clearly and logically. For example, in a discussion of parent/teen conflicts, young people may want the freedom that comes with adulthood, but not want to accept many of the responsibilities. Pointing out and discussing the inconsistency in these two positions will lead students to more logically consider the consequences of their choices.

- Create a nonjudgmental atmosphere. Students will only communicate freely and openly in a comfortable environment. You can make them comfortable by respecting their ideas, by accepting them for who they are, and by honoring their confidences. It is also important to avoid criticizing a student or discussing personal matters in front of others.

- Use written communication to advantage. The more ways you approach students, the more likely you are to reach them on different levels. Very often, the written word can be an excellent way to connect. Written messages can take different forms—a notice on the chalkboard, a note attached to homework, a memo to parents (with good news as well as bad), or a letter exchange involving class members.

- Be open and available for private discussions of personal or disciplinary problems. It is important to let students know they can come to you with personal concerns as well as questions regarding course material. Be careful not to violate students' trust by discussing confidential matters outside of a professional setting.

Promoting Your Program

You can make family living one of the most important course offerings in your school. You cover material that every student and teacher can use to advantage. It pays to make the student body and faculty aware of your program. With good public relations, you can increase your enrollment, gain support from administrators and other teachers, and achieve recognition in the community. Following are some ways to promote your program:

- Create visibility. It is important to let people know what is going on in family living classes. Ways to do this include announcements of projects and activities at faculty meetings and in school bulletins or newspapers, displays in school showcases or on bulletin boards, and articles and press releases in school and community newspapers. Talk up your program with administrators, other teachers, and students. Invite them to visit your classes.

- Interact within the school. Family living is related to many fields of learning. You can strengthen your program and contribute to other disciplines by cooperating with other teachers. For example, you can work with a science teacher to cover the biology of conception and heredity or a social studies teacher to discuss family structures in society. The more interaction you can generate, the more you promote your family living class.

- Contribute to the educational objectives of the school. If your school follows stated educational objectives and strives to strengthen specific skills, include these overall goals in your teaching. For example, if students need special help in developing verbal or writing skills, select projects and assignments that will help them in these areas. The *Basic Skills Chart* in the *Teacher's Resource Guide/Binder* will give you ideas for activities that strengthen specific skills. Show administrators examples of work that indicate student improvement in needed skills.

- Serve as a resource center. Family living information is of practical use and interest to almost everyone. You can sell your program by making your department a resource center of family living materials. Invite faculty members, students, and parents to tap into the wealth of family living information available in your classroom.

- Generate involvement and activity in the community. You are teaching concepts students can apply in their everyday lives. You can involve students in community life and bring the community into your classroom through field trips, interviews with businesspeople and community leaders, surveys, and presentations from guest speakers. You may be able to set up cooperative projects between the school and community organizations around a variety of topics.

- Connect with parents. If you can get them involved, parents may be your best allies in teaching family living. Let parents know when their children have done good work. Moms and dads have had experiences related to many of the issues you discuss in class. They have watched children grow and develop and dealt with issues such as substitute child care, discipline, and balancing family and work. Call on them to share individually or as part of a panel addressing a specific topic. Parents can be a rich source of real-life experience. Keep them informed about classroom activities and invite them to participate as they are able.

- Establish a student sales staff. Enthusiastic students will be your best salespeople. Encourage them to tell their parents and friends what they are learning in your classes. You might create bulletin boards or write letters to parents that focus on what students are learning in your classes. Ask students to put together a newsletter highlighting their experiences in family living class. Students could write a column from your department for the school paper.

We appreciate the contributions of the following Goodheart-Willcox author to this introduction: "Teaching Techniques" from *Changes and Choices*, by Ruth E. Bragg.

Evaluating Individual Participation

Student Name _________________________________ **Date** _____________ **Period** _____________

The rating scale below shows an evaluation of your class participation. It indicates what levels you have passed and what levels you can continue to try to reach.

Attentiveness

1	2	3	4	5	6	7	8	9	10

Completely inattentive.	Seldom attentive.	Somewhat attentive.	Usually attentive.	Extremely attentive.

Contribution to Discussion

1	2	3	4	5	6	7	8	9	10

Never contributes to class discussion.	Rarely contributes to class discussion.	Occasionally contributes to class discussion.	Regularly contributes to class discussion.	Frequently contributes to class discussion.

Interaction with Peers

1	2	3	4	5	6	7	8	9	10

Often distracts others.	Shows little interaction with others.	Follows leadership of other students.	Sometimes assumes leadership role.	Respected by peers for ability.

Response to Teacher

1	2	3	4	5	6	7	8	9	10

Unable to respond when called on.	Often unable to support or justify answers when called on.	Supports answers based on class information, but seldom offers new ideas.	Able to offer new ideas with prompting.	Often offers new ideas without prompting.

Comments:

____

____

____

____

Evaluating Individual Reports

Name _______________________________________ **Date** _______________ **Period** _______________

The rating scale below shows an evaluation of your oral or written report. It indicates what levels you have passed and what levels you can try to reach on future reports.

Report topic _________________________________ Oral _______________ Written _______________

Choice of Topic

1	2	3	4	5	6	7	8	9	10

Slow to choose topic.	Chooses topic with indifference.	Chooses topic as assigned, seeks suggestions.	Chooses relevant topic without assistance.	Chooses creative topic.

Use of Resources

1	2	3	4	5	6	7	8	9	10

Unable to find resources.	Needs direction to find resources.	Uses limited number of resources.	Uses assigned number of resources from typical sources.	Uses additional resources from a variety of sources.

Oral Presentation

1	2	3	4	5	6	7	8	9	10

No notes or read completely. Poor subject coverage.	Has few good notes. Limited subject coverage.	Uses notes somewhat effectively. Adequate subject coverage.	Uses notes effectively. Good subject coverage.	Uses notes very effectively. Complete coverage.

Written Presentation

1	2	3	4	5	6	7	8	9	10

Many grammar and spelling mistakes. No organization.	Several grammar and spelling mistakes. Poor organization.	Some grammar and spelling mistakes. Fair organization.	A few grammar and spelling mistakes. Good organization.	No grammar or spelling mistakes. Excellent organization.

Evaluating Group Participation

**Group
Members:**
____

_________________________________   _________________________________

_________________________________   _________________________________

_________________________________   _________________________________

The rating scale below shows an evaluation of the efforts of your group. It indicates what levels you have passed and what levels you can try to reach on future group projects.

Teamwork

1	2	3	4	5	6	7	8	9	10

Passive membership. Failed to identify what tasks needed to be completed.	Argumentative membership. Unable to designate who should complete each task.	Independent membership. All tasks completed individually.	Helpful membership. Completed individual tasks and then assisted others.	Cooperative membership. Worked together to complete all tasks.

Leadership

1	2	3	4	5	6	7	8	9	10

No effective leadership.	Group fragmented by several members seeking leadership roles.	Sought leadership from outside group.	One member assumed primary leadership role for the group.	Leadership responsibilities shared by several group members.

Goal Achievement

1	2	3	4	5	6	7	8	9	10

Did not attempt to achieve goal.	Were unable to achieve goal.	Achieved goal with outside assistance.	Achieved assigned goal.	Achieved goal using added materials to enhance total effort.

Members cited for excellent contributions to group's effort are:

_________________________________   _________________________________

Members cited for failing to contribute to group's effort are:

_________________________________   _________________________________

Correlation of National Standards for
Family with
Contemporary Living

In planning your program, you may want to use the correlation chart below. This chart correlates the Family and Consumer Sciences Education National Standards with the content of **Contemporary Living**. It lists the competencies for each of the content standards for **Family**. It also identifies the major text concepts that relate to each competency. Bold numbers indicate chapters in which concepts are found.

After studying the content of this text, students will be able to achieve the following comprehensive standard:

6.0 Evaluate the significance of family and its impact on the well-being of individuals and

Content Standard 6.1 Analyze the impact of family as a system on individuals and society.	
Competencies	**Text Concepts**
6.1.1 Examine the family as the basic unity of society.	**3:** Your family **9:** Adult lifestyle options **14:** Happiness in marriage; adjustments in marriage **15:** What is a family?; the changing family; functions of the family; roles and responsibilities of family members; characteristics of strong families; family structures **16:** Parental roles and responsibilities; sharing parenting responsibilities **19:** Creating a nurturing environment for your child; creating a safe and healthy environment for your child **20:** Types of work and family arrangements; patterns of work and childbearing; impact of work on families; how families are influencing the workplace
6.1.2 Determine the role of family in transmitting societal expectations.	**1:** Forces that shape personality; social growth; your character **3:** Relating to authority figures; cultural patterns; family interactions; influences of birth order **4:** Kohlberg's stages of moral development **9:** Adult lifestyle options **10:** Communicating with parents **12:** Forces affecting mate selection; mixed marriages **15:** The changing family; functions of the family; roles and responsibilities of family members; characteristics of strong families; family structures **19:** Creating a nurturing environment for your child; creating a safe and healthy environment for your child **20:** Changing attitudes; types of work and family arrangements; patterns of work and childbearing
6.1.3 Examine global influences on today's families.	**3:** Your community and world; influence of technology; changing economic conditions; the media **10:** The changing family **16:** Factors to consider in the parenting decision **20:** Why work?; changing attitudes; types of work and family arrangements; impact of work on families **21:** Unemployment **24:** Environmental responsibility

Competencies	Text Concepts
6.1.4 Examine the role of family in teaching culture and traditions across the life span.	**3:** Your family; cultural patterns **10:** Cultural influences on communication **12:** Mixed marriages **15:** Functions of the family; characteristics of strong families
6.1.5 Examine the role of family in developing independence, interdependence, and commitment of family members.	**1:** Becoming a responsible and independent adult; your character **4:** Havighurst's developmental tasks of adolescence **14:** Adjustments in marriage **15:** Roles and responsibilities of family members; characteristics of strong families
6.1.6 Determine the impact of change and transitions over the life course.	**14:** Adjustments in marriage; time as a factor in making adjustments **15:** The changing family; the family life cycle **16:** Parenting as a choice **18:** The newborn; growth and development during the first year **19:** Growth and development during the preschool years; the school years **21:** Coping with crises; seeking stability in crisis; unemployment; frequent moves; addictions to alcohol and other drugs **22:** Divorce trends and issues; legal termination of marriage; remarriage **23:** Young adulthood; middle age; old age; aspects of aging; accepting death as a reality of life; stages of grieving
6.1.7 Explore the ways family and consumer sciences careers assist the works of the family.	**6:** Careers in family and community services **7:** Health and wellness resources **14:** Marriage counseling **21:** Resources to help withstand crises

Content Standard 6.2 **Demonstrate appreciation for diverse perspectives, needs, and characteristics of individuals and families.**

Competencies	Text Concepts
6.2.1 Demonstrate awareness of multiple diversities and their impact on individuals and families.	**3:** Your family; cultural patterns **4:** Attitudes; prejudices; stereotypes **12:** Mixed marriages
6.2.2 Examine the impact of cultural diversity on individuals and families.	**3:** Your family; cultural patterns **12:** Mixed marriages
6.2.3 Examine the impact of empathy for diversity on individuals in family, work, and community settings.	**3:** Your family; cultural patterns **12:** Mixed marriages **15:** Characteristics of strong families **20:** Realities of the workplace
6.2.4 Demonstrate respect for diversity with sensitivity to anti-bias, gender, equity, age, culture, and ethnicity.	**3:** Your family; cultural patterns **4:** Prejudices; stereotypes **10:** Sexual harassment **12:** Mixed marriages **21:** Elder abuse **25:** Young adulthood; middle age; old age
6.2.5 Examine the impact of the global village on the need to appreciate diversity.	**1:** What does it mean to be a good citizen; a citizen of the larger

Correlation of National Standards for
Interpersonal Relationships with
Contemporary Living

In planning your program, you may want to use the correlation chart below. This chart correlates the Family and Consumer Sciences Education National Standards with the content of ***Contemporary Living***. It lists the competencies for each of the content standards for **Interpersonal Relationships**. It also identifies the major text concepts that relate to each competency. Bold numbers indicate chapters in which concepts are found.

After studying the content of this text, students will be able to achieve the following comprehensive standard:

13.0 Demonstrate respectful and caring relationships in the family, workplace, and community.

Content Standard 13.1 Analyze functions and expectations of various types of relationships.	
Competencies	**Text Concepts**
13.1.1 Determine the processes for building and maintaining interpersonal relationships.	**11:** Friendships; dating patterns; developing a relationship; communication of love; physical expressions of affection **13:** Engagement; communication during engagement **14:** Happiness in marriage **15:** Characteristics of strong families
13.1.2 Examine the impact of various stages of the family life cycle on interpersonal relationships.	**4:** Erikson's stages of human development; Havighurst's developmental tasks of adolescence; Maslow's theory of human needs; Kohlberg's stages of moral development **9:** Adult lifestyle options **15:** The family life cycle **23:** Young adulthood; middle age; old age
13.1.3 Compare physical, emotional, and intellectual responses in stable and unstable relationships.	**8:** Dealing with peer pressure **10:** Bullying; gangs **11:** Friendships; dating patterns; developing relationships; ending a relationship; signs a relationship should end; communication of love; physical expressions of affection; date or acquaintance rape **21:** Violent behavior in families **22:** Divorce trends and issues; legal termination of marriage; remarriage
13.1.4 Determine factors that contribute to healthy and unhealthy relationships.	**4:** Defense mechanisms; personal response patterns **8:** Dealing with peer pressure **10:** Levels of communication; using I-messages, you-messages, and we-messages; communicating with parents; bullying; gangs **11:** Friendships; dating patterns; developing relationships; ending a relationship; signs a relationship should end; communication of love; physical expressions of affection; date or acquaintance rape **15:** Characteristics of strong families **21:** Violent behavior in families
13.1.5 Explore processes for handling unhealthy relationships.	**8:** Dealing with peer pressure **10:** What can teens and adults do to stop the violence?; using conflict resolution and mediation; sexual harassment **11:** Ending a relationship **21:** Resources to help withstand crises; legal action in domestic abuse **22:** Divorce trends and issues; legal termination of marriage

Competencies	Text Concepts
13.1.6 Determine stress management strategies for family, work, and community settings.	**7:** Coping with stress; change causes stress; learning to manage stress **24:** Leisure-time decisions

Content Standard 13.2   Analyze personal needs and characteristics and their impact on relationships.

Competencies	Text Concepts
13.2.1 Examine the impact of personal characteristics on relationships.	**1:** Your personality; your self-concept; your character **4:** Personal response patterns **5:** Values; set your standards **6:** Interpersonal skills **9:** Adult lifestyle options **11:** Developing relationships **12:** Forces affecting mate selection; choosing a partner **13:** Communication during engagement **14:** Happiness in marriage **15:** Characteristics of strong families
13.2.2 Consider the effect of personal needs on relationships.	**4:** Maslow's theory of human needs **12:** Forces affecting mate selection; complementary needs; choosing a partner; other factors **24:** What needs must be met?
13.2.3 Examine the effect of self-esteem and self-image on relationships.	**1:** Your self-concept; what is self-esteem?; what is self-worth? **11:** Developing relationships **14:** Importance of self-esteem in marriage
13.2.4 Determine the impact of life span events and conditions on relationships.	**14:** Adjustments in marriage; time as a factor in making adjustments **15:** The changing family; the family life cycle **16:** Parenting as a choice **18:** The newborn; growth and development during the first year **19:** Growth and development during the preschool years; the school years **21:** Coping with crises; seeking stability in crisis; unemployment; frequent moves; addictions to alcohol and other drugs **22:** Divorce trends and issues; legal termination of marriage; remarriage **23:** Young adulthood; middle age; old age; aspects of aging; accepting death as a reality of life; stages of grieving
13.2.5 Examine the impact of personal standards and codes of conduct on interpersonal relationships.	**5:** Set your standards **6:** Follow ethical practices **11:** Physical expressions of affection; sexual decision making; consequences of your decisions

Content Standard 13.3   Demonstrate communication skills that contribute to positive relationships.

Competencies	Text Concepts
13.3.1 Examine communication styles and their effects on relationships.	**10:** Forms of communication; nonverbal communication; levels of communication; using I-messages, you-messages, and we-messages; group behaviors involving violence
13.3.2 Demonstrate verbal and nonverbal behaviors and attitudes that contribute to effective communication.	**10:** Forms of communication; nonverbal communication; body language communicates; your appearance communicates

Content Standard 13.3   (continued)

Competencies	Text Concepts
13.3.3 Demonstrate effective listening and feedback techniques.	**10:** Forms of communication; listening
13.3.4 Examine barriers to communication in family, work, and community settings.	**10:** Levels of communication; communication problems of teens and parents; cultural influence on communication; solving family communication problems; group behaviors involving violence
13.3.5 Practice ethical principles of communication in family, community, and work settings.	**6:** Follow ethical practices
13.3.6 Examine the impact of communication technology in family, work, and community settings.	**3:** The influence of technology **7:** Support groups, hot lines, and help lines; computer-related resources
13.3.7 Examine the roles and functions of communication in family, work, and community settings.	**6:** Strategies for job success; strategies that lead to job advancement **10:** Communicating with parents; solving family communication problems; group communication patterns **13:** Communication during engagement **14:** Communication is vital in marriage

Content Standard 13.4   Evaluate effective conflict prevention and management techniques.

Competencies	Text Concepts
13.4.1 Determine the origin and development of attitudes and behaviors regarding conflict.	**10:** Group behaviors involving violence **12:** Forces affecting mate selection; choosing a partner; other factors
13.4.2 Determine how similarities and differences among people affect conflict prevention and management.	**10:** Using conflict resolution or mediation **14:** Happiness in marriage; realistic expectations; give and take of marriage
13.4.3 Determine the role of decision making and problem solving in reducing and managing conflict.	**5:** The decision-making process; the management process **14:** Conflict can lead to problem solving
13.4.4 Appraise nonviolent strategies to address conflict.	**10:** What can teens and adults do to stop the violence? **14:** Adjustments in marriage; compromise; accommodation; concession; martyrdom; ongoing hostility; time as a factor; functions of conflict
13.4.5 Choose effective responses to harassment.	**10:** Group behaviors involving violence; sexual harassment **20:** Realities of the workplace
13.4.6 Assess community resources that support conflict prevention and management.	**10:** Using conflict resolution or mediation **14:** Marriage counseling **21:** Resources to help withstand crises

Content Standard 13.5 Demonstrate teamwork and leadership skills in the family, workplace, and community.	
Competencies	**Text Concepts**
13.5.1 Create an environment that encourages and respects the ideas, perspectives, and contributions of all group members.	6: Leadership skills; teamwork skills
13.5.2 Demonstrate strategies to motivate and encourage group members.	6: Leadership skills
13.5.3 Create strategies to utilize the strengths and limitations of team members.	6: Leadership skills; teamwork skills
13.5.4 Demonstrate techniques that develop team and community spirit.	1: What does it mean to be a good citizen?; taking a leadership role 6: Leadership skills; teamwork skills
13.5.5 Demonstrate ways to organize and delegate responsibilities.	1: Taking a leadership role 6: Leadership skills; teamwork skills
13.5.6 Create strategies to integrate new members into the team.	
13.5.7 Demonstrate processes for cooperating, compromising, and collaborating.	6: Leadership skills; teamwork skills 14: Compromise

Content Standard 13.6 Demonstrate standards that guide behavior in interpersonal relationships.	
Competencies	**Text Concepts**
13.6.1 Examine types of standards for making judgments about interpersonal relationships.	4: Kohlberg's stages of moral development 5: Values; how values influence decisions; set your standards 9: Lifestyle consequences
13.6.2 Apply guidelines for assessing the nature of issues and situations.	1: Philosophical growth; your character 11: Sexual decision making
13.6.3 Apply standards when making judgments and taking action.	5: Set your standards; making decisions; the management process 11: Saying no to sexual relations
13.6.4 Demonstrate ethical behaviors in family, workplace, and community settings.	1: What does it mean to be a good citizen? 6: Follow ethical practices; honesty; loyalty
13.6.5 Examine the relative merits of opposing points of view regarding current ethical issues.	

Scope and Sequence

In planning your program, you want to use the Scope and Sequence Chart below. This chart identifies the major concepts presented in each chapter of the text. Refer to the chart to find the material that meets your curriculum needs. Bold numbers indicate chapters in which concepts are found.

Part I Personal Development

Personal Development

1: Your personality; Your growth; Your self-concept, self-esteem, and self-worth; Your character; Becoming a responsible and independent adult; Taking a leadership role; Meeting personal expectations; Roadblocks to responsible adulthood.

2: Valuing your uniqueness.

3: Influence of environmental factors; Your family, peers, education, occupation, religion, community, and world.

4: How you respond to your environment; Erikson's stages of human development; Havighurst's developmental tasks of adolescence; Maslow's theory of human needs; Kohlberg's stages of moral development; Defense mechanisms; Personal response patterns.

Interpersonal Relationships

1: Becoming a responsible and independent adult.

2: Family interactions.

3: Relating to authority figures; Your peers; Peer influence during adolescence; Your occupation.

4: Personal response patterns.

Communication and Leadership

1: Taking a leadership role.

3: Peer influence during adolescence.

Family Forms, Functions, Concerns, and Crises

3: Your family; Cultural patterns; Family interactions; Influence of birth order.

Human Reproduction and Sexuality

2: The process of heredity; Twins and multiple births; Inherited characteristics.

Parenting and Child Development

2: Influences of birth order.

Consumer Skills and Information

3: Your community and world; Influence of technology; Changing economic conditions.

Life Management Skills

1: Becoming a responsible and independent adult; Citizenship; Taking a leadership role; Roadblocks to responsible adulthood; Concerns of young adults.

3: Your education; Your occupation.

Contemporary Living Teacher's Resources

Part II The Decisions You Face

Personal Development

5: How values influence decisions; Values change in priority; Setting your goals; Your individual life cycle and time/life line; Identify your resources; Set your standards; Making decisions; Decision-making process; Management process.

6: Deciding on a career; Making a career plan; Careers in family and community services; Decisions about your education; Combining work with education; Developing workplace skills; Getting a job; Strategies for job success; Strategies that lead to advancement on the job; Changing jobs.

7: Coping with stress.

8: Dealing with peer pressure.

9: Responsible behavior.

Interpersonal Relationships

5: Values.

6: Developing workplace skills; Teamwork skills; Developing job contacts; Strategies for job success; Interpersonal skills.

8: Dealing with peer pressure.

9: Marriage; Living together.

Communication and Leadership

5: Values.

6: Leadership skills; Teamwork skills; Developing job contacts; Interpersonal skills; Strategies that lead to advancement on the job.

8: Dealing with peer pressure

Family Forms, Functions, Concerns, and Crises

7: Planning for family wellness; Making time for health; Coping with stress.

8: Tobacco; How smoking affects health; Ways to break the tobacco habit; Alcohol; Health consequences of drinking alcohol; Drugs.

9: Adult lifestyle options; Single life; Marriage; Living together; Lifestyle consequences; Unplanned pregnancy; Alternatives for the pregnant teen; Sexually transmitted diseases; Responsible behavior.

Marriage

9: Marriage; Childless marriage.

Human Reproduction and Sexuality

9: Unplanned pregnancy; Risks involved with teen pregnancies; Sexually transmitted diseases; Responsible behavior.

Consumer Skills and Information

5: Setting your goals; Identify your resources; Set your standards; Making decisions; Management process.

7: Health and wellness resources; Computer-related resources; Government programs; Nonprofit organizations; Consumer choices related to health.

Life Management Skills

5: How values influence decisions; Setting your goals; Your individual life cycle and time/life line; Identify your resources; Set your standards; Making decisions; Decision-making process; Management process.

6: Deciding on a career; Decisions about your education; Developing workplace skills; Getting a job; Strategies for job success.

7: Planning for family wellness; Preventive health practices; Nutrition and your health; Regular exercise; Coping with stress.

Part III Getting Along with Others

Personal Development

11: Friendship; Dating patterns.

Interpersonal Relationships

10: What is communication?; Group behaviors involving violence; Bullying; Gangs; Sexual harassment.

11: Friendship; Developing relationships; Dating patterns; Qualities that characterize a serious relationship; Communication of love.

Communication and Leadership

10: Forms of communication; Listening; Nonverbal communication; Your appearance communicates; Levels of communication; Assertiveness in communication; Using I-messages and We-messages; Communicating with parents; Group communication problems; Using conflict resolution or mediation.

11: Communication of love; Physical expressions of affection.

Family Forms, Functions, Concerns, and Crises

10: Communication with parents; Solving family communication problems; Group behaviors involving violence; Using conflict resolution or mediation; Sexual harassment.

11: Date or acquaintance rape.

Human Reproduction and Sexuality

10: Sexual harassment.

11: Physical expressions of affection; Date or acquaintance rape.

Parenting and Child Development

10: Communicating with parents.

Part IV The Marriage Relationship

Interpersonal Relationships

12: Forces affecting mate selection; Assessing friendships.

13: Engagement; Breaking engagements.

Communication and Leadership

13: Communication during engagement.

14: Communication in marriage; Function of conflict.

Family Forms, Functions, Concerns, and Crises

12: Choosing a partner; Parent approval; Mixed marriages.

14: Function of conflict in marriage.

Marriage

12: Forces affecting mate selection; Choosing a partner; Mixed marriages.

13: Career goals in marriage; Attitudes toward marriage counseling; Marriage laws; Wedding plans; Honeymoon.

14: Happiness in marriage; Realistic expectations; Adjustments in marriage; Marriage counseling.

Human Reproduction and Sexuality

13: Sexual and reproductive expectations.

Consumer Skills and Information

13: Money management in marriage; Obtaining a marriage license; Wedding plans.

14: Finding a marriage counselor; What does the counselor provide?

Part V Dimensions of Families

Family Forms, Functions, Concerns, and Crises

15: Definition of a family; The changing family; Functions of the family; Roles and responsibilities of family members; Functional and dysfunctional families; Characteristics of strong families; Family structures; Two-parent and single-parent families; Blended families; Extended kinship families; Foster families; Adoptive families; Family life cycle.

16: Parental roles and responsibilities; If a couple cannot have children; Genetic counseling.

17: Prenatal care; Medications and exposure to x rays.

18: Parenthood brings new roles; Caring for the newborn; Children with special needs.

19: Creating a nurturing environment for your child; Substitute child care; The school years; Time for family; After-school child care.

Human Reproduction and Sexuality

16: Planning pregnancy; Female and male reproductive systems; Methods for planning or preventing pregnancy; If a couple cannot have children; Genetic counseling.

17: Evidence of pregnancy; Conception; The developing baby; Care of the mother; Miscarriage; Methods of childbirth.

Parenting and Child Development

15: Unwed parents; Single parent by adoption; Support for the single parent.

16: Parenting roles and responsibilities; Parenthood is a choice; Factors to consider in parenting decision.

18: Parenthood brings new roles; The newborn; Planning a schedule; Feeding your baby; Bathing your baby; Clothing your baby; Handling discomforts and problems; Growth and development during the first year; Children with special needs.

19: Creating a nurturing environment for your child; Creating a safe and healthy environment for your child; Food and sleep; Health care; Safety; Growth and development during the preschool years; Discipline; Preschoolers' anxiety, fears, anger; Preparing for another child; Substitute child care; The school years; Your children's friends; Tall tales and lying; Developing responsibility; Money and children; After-school child care.

Consumer Skills and Information

16: Financial considerations of parenthood.

18: Clothing your baby.

19: Creating a safe and healthy environment for your child; Substitute child care; Developing responsibility; Money and children.

Life Management Skills

16: Career considerations involving parenthood; Financial considerations of parenthood.

Part VI Families Face Change

Personal Development

20: Why work; Changing attitudes.

23: Young adulthood; Middle age; Old Age; Aspects of aging; Grandparenting; Retirement.

Family Forms, Functions, Concerns, and Crises

20: Types of work and family arrangements; Dual-worker families; Families with part-time workers; Families with full-time homemakers; Displaced homemakers; Single-parent families; Patterns of work and childbearing; Impact of work on families; How families influence the workplace.

21: Resources to help withstand crises; Coping with crises; Unemployment; Frequent moves; Addictions to alcohol and other drugs; Compulsive gambling; Depression; Suicide; Criminal attack; Rape; Domestic violence; Elder abuse; Child abuse and neglect; Missing children; Runaways.

22: Divorce trends and issues; Adjusting to divorce; Emotional aftermath of divorce; Legal termination of marriage; Remarriage; Blended families.

23: The sandwich generation and intergenerational caregiving; Grandparenting; Retirement; Accepting death as a reality of life; Stages of dying; Stages of grieving.

Marriage

22: Remarriage; Blended families.

Human Reproduction and Sexuality

23: Sexual aspects of aging; Menopause.

Parenting and Child Development

23: Grandparenting; Telling children about death.

Consumer Skills and Information

20: Family and Medical Leave Act; Employer-sponsored child care; Employee-assistance programs.

21: Legal action in domestic abuse.

22: Legal termination of marriage.

23: Impact of growing population of older adults; Financial aspects of aging; Housing arrangements for the aging; Hospice care; Legal issues of death; Living will; Organ banks; Funeral arrangements; The legal will.

Life Management Skills

20: Flexible work schedules; Techniques for managing work and family.

21: Resources to help withstand crises.

Part VII Managing Family Living

Family Forms, Functions, Concerns, and Crises

24: Meeting needs of the family; Time for family.

25: Insurance for the family.

Consumer Skills and Information

24: Factor affecting consumer decisions; Advertising; Consumer protection; Environmental responsibility; Recycling; Food decisions; Understanding food labels; Clothing decisions; Housing decisions; Housing costs; Transportation decisions; Environmental awareness in leisure-time use.

25: Life insurance; Health insurance; HMOs; PPOs; Disability income insurance; Auto insurance; Homeowner's insurance.

26: Your income; Your paycheck; Federal income tax; Social Security; Financial institutions; Financial services; Checking accounts; Saving and investing money.

27: Handling money; Budgeting; Using credit; Types of credit; Sources of credit; Making credit work for you.

Life Management Skills

24: Food decisions; Planning meals; Controlling food costs; Clothing decisions; Housing decisions; Transportation decisions; Leisure-time decisions.

27: Handling your money; Budgeting; Using credit; Making credit work for you.

Basic Skills Chart

The chart below has been designed to identify those activities in the *Contemporary Living* text, *Student Activity Guide,* and *Teacher's Resource Guide/Binder* that specifically encourage the development of basic skills. The following abbreviations are used in the chart:

To Do . . . End of the chapter activities in the text.

SAG . . . Activities in the *Student Activity Guide* (designated by letter).

TRG . . . Strategies described in the *Teacher's Resource Guide/Binder* (referred to by number.

Activities listed as "Verbal" include role-playing, conducting interviews, oral reports, and debates.

Activities listed as "Reading" may involve actual reading in and out of the classroom. However, many of these activities are designed to improve reading comprehension of the concepts presented in each chapter. Some are designed to improve understanding of vocabulary terms.

Activities that involve writing are listed under "Writing." The list includes activities that allow students to practice composition skills, such as letter writing, informative writing, and creative writing.

The "Math/Science" list incldues activities that require students to use computation skills in solving typical problems they may encounter in their everyday living. Any activities related to the sciences are also listed.

The final category, "Analytical," lists those activities that involve the higher order thinking skills of analysis, synthesis, and evaluation. Activities that involve decision making, problem solving, and critical thinking are included in this section.

	Verbal	Reading	Writing	Math/Science	Analytical
Chapter 1	To Do: 2, 3, 5 SAG: A TRG: 1, 2, 3, 4, 9, 11, 12, 13, 16, 19, 21, 22, 23, 24, 25, 26, 29, 30, 31	To Do: 3	To Do: 3, 4, 5 SAG: A, B, C, D, E TRG: 4, 7, 14, 20, 31, 32	To Do: 5 SAG: A, C TRG: 5, 10	To Do: 4, 5 SAG: E TRG: 1, 12, 15, 22, 23, 26
Chapter 2	To Do: 1 TRG: 4, 5, 7, 8, 9, 11, 12, 14, 17, 18, 19, 20, 24, 25	SAG: D TRG: 8, 9, 10, 18, 19, 20	To Do: 1, 2 SAG: A TRG: 18, 19, 20	To Do: 2 SAG: A, B TRG: 2, 3, 4, 5, 9, 10, 12, 13, 18, 19, 20	To Do: 1, 2 TRG: 20
Chapter 3	To Do: 2, 3, 4, 5 TRG: 2, 6, 10, 11, 12, 13, 14, 15, 16, 17, 18, 19, 20, 24, 26, 27, 29, 30, 31, 32, 33, 35	To Do: 4 TRG: 6, 8, 22, 32	To Do: 1, 4 SAG: D TRG: 4, 5, 7, 8, 22, 25, 28		To Do: 4, 5 SAG: A TRG: 1, 4, 7, 31, 36
Chapter 4	To Do: 1, 3, 6 SAG: E TRG: 1, 2, 5, 7, 14, 15, 16, 18, 19, 21, 22, 23, 24, 25, 28, 29, 30, 31, 32, 33, 34	To Do: 1, 2, 5 SAG: D TRG: 4, 11, 26	To Do: 3, 4 SAG: A, B, C, F TRG: 4, 9, 10, 34	To Do: 1 SAG: A, B, C TRG: 3, 4, 6, 7, 8	To Do: 4 SAG: E, F, TRG: 3, 9, 10, 12, 15, 17, 26, 30, 31, 34
Chapter 5	To Do: 1, 3 SAG: B, C, D TRG: 1, 2, 3, 6, 7, 8, 9, 11, 14, 17, 18, 19, 20, 21, 24, 25, 26		To Do: 1, 2, 3, 4, 6 SAG: A, B, C, D, E, F TRG: 5, 7, 9, 14, 16, 23	To Do: 1	To Do: 1, 3, 6 SAG: A, C, F TRG: 9, 10, 14, 15, 17, 23

(Continued)

	Verbal	Reading	Writing	Math/Science	Analytical
Chapter 6	To Do: 2, 3, 4, 5, 6, 7 SAG: D TRG: 6, 8, 9, 11, 12, 14, 16, 18, 20, 21, 22, 23, 26, 29	To Do: 1, 5 TRG: 5, 11, 13, 20, 22	To Do: 1, 5, 6, 7 SAG: A, B, D TRG: 2, 3, 11, 13, 20, 22, 23, 24, 30	SAG: C	To Do: 1, 2 SAG: A, B, C TRG: 3, 7, 19, 24, 25, 30
Chapter 7	To Do: 3, 4, 7, 8 SAG: E TRG: 1, 6, 7, 9, 11, 15, 16, 18, 19, 20, 23, 24, 25, 29, 30, 32, 33, 34	To Do: 7 SAG: C TRG: 10, 17	To Do: 1, 2, 4, 6, 7, 8 SAG: B, D, E TRG: 5, 10, 12, 17, 21, 26, 27, 28	To Do: 1, 2 SAG: A, B, C, D, E TRG: 4, 5, 6, 7, 8, 9, 10, 11, 12, 14, 19, 26	To Do: 2, 3, 6, 8 SAG: B, C TRG: 4, 8, 18, 30, 32
Chapter 8	To Do: 1, 2, 3, 4, 5, 6, 7 SAG: B, C, F, H TRG: 1, 2, 3, 4, 5, 6, 7, 9, 10, 11, 12, 13, 14, 15, 16, 17, 18, 19, 20, 21, 22, 24, 25, 26, 27, 29, 32, 33, 34, 35, 36	To Do: 3, 5, 8 SAG: A, G TRG: 14, 23, 28, 29, 30	To Do: 1, 5, 8 SAG: A, D, E, F, H, I TRG: 30, 35, 36	To Do: 5, 6 SAG: A, I TRG: 4, 5, 7, 8, 22, 28, 32	To Do: 4, 7 SAG: A, C, D, F, H, I TRG: 11, 12, 17, 20, 31, 35, 36
Chapter 9	To Do: 1, 2, 3, 4, 5, 6, 8, 9, 11 TRG: 1, 2, 3, 4, 5, 7, 8, 9, 10, 11, 12, 15, 16, 17, 18, 20, 21, 22, 24, 25, 26, 28, 30, 31, 32, 33, 34	To Do: 7, 10 SAG: D TRG: 5, 10, 23, 27	To Do: 7, 10 SAG: A, B, C TRG: 5, 7, 13, 14, 20, 23, 26	To Do: 5, 9 SAG: D, E TRG: 18, 28, 29, 30, 31, 32	To Do: 4, 8, 11 SAG: A, B, C TRG: 1, 3, 10, 14, 17, 19
Chapter 10	To Do: 1, 3, 4, 5, 6, 7 SAG: A TRG: 1, 2, 3, 4, 6, 7, 8, 11, 13, 14, 15, 16, 18, 19, 22, 23, 24, 26, 29, 30, 31, 33, 34, 36, 37, 38, 39, 40	SAG: D TRG: 12, 14, 39	To Do: 2, 7 SAG: A, B, D, F TRG: 4, 5, 7, 17, 18, 22, 23, 32, 35	SAG: A, E TRG: 4	To Do: 3, 4, 6 SAG: C, E, F TRG: 4, 6, 9, 13, 15, 25, 27, 28, 30, 32, 36, 38
Chapter 11	To Do: 1, 2, 4, 5, 6, 7 SAG: A, E, F, G TRG: 3, 4, 6, 7, 9, 10, 12, 13, 17, 19, 20, 21, 23, 24, 25, 30, 31, 32, 33, 34, 35, 39, 41, 42, 43, 45, 46	To Do: 5 SAG: C TRG: 28	To Do: 3 SAG: A, B, D, F, G TRG: 1, 2, 5, 10, 15, 18, 22, 24, 26, 33, 37	SAG: A TRG: 10	To Do: 3, 4, 6 SAG: A, B, D, E, F, G TRG: 3, 8, 10, 11, 12, 14, 16, 20, 30, 37, 43, 45
Chapter 12	To Do: 2 SAG: A, B TRG: 2, 3, 4, 5, 7, 8, 9, 11, 12, 15, 16, 17, 18, 19	To Do: 2, 3 SAG: D TRG: 13	To Do: 1, 2, 3 SAG: A, B, C TRG: 1, 5, 9, 40		To Do: 1, 3 SAG: B, C TRG: 4, 10, 12, 15, 19

(Continued)

Contemporary Living Teacher's Resources

	Verbal	Reading	Writing	Math/Science	Analytical
Chapter 13	To Do: 1, 2, 4 SAG: A, D TRG: 1, 3, 4, 5, 8, 10, 11, 12, 13, 14, 15, 17, 19, 20, 21, 22, 25, 26	To Do: 3, 5, 7 SAG: C, D TRG: 4, 16, 17, 20, 22, 23, 24	To Do: 6 SAG: B, D TRG: 17, 20, 22	SAG: D TRG: 22	To Do: 5, 6 SAG: B, D TRG: 2, 6, 7, 18, 22
Chapter 14	To Do: 1, 2, 3 SAG: B, C TRG: 1, 3, 4, 5, 6, 7, 8, 9, 10, 12, 14, 16, 18, 21, 22	To Do: 3 TRG: 19, 20	SAG: C TRG: 11, 14, 15		To Do: 1, 2 TRG: 8, 9, 10, 16, 20, 21
Chapter 15	To Do: 1, 2, 4, 5, 6 SAG: B, C TRG: 1, 2, 4, 6, 7, 8, 9, 10, 11, 12, 15, 16, 17, 18, 19, 20, 21, 22, 23, 24, 25, 26, 27, 30, 31, 32	To Do: 1 TRG: 18	To Do: 1 SAG: A, B, C, D TRG: 1, 3, 5, 9, 14, 15, 16, 18, 24		To Do: 1, 6 SAG: B TRG: 7, 9, 18, 22, 28, 29, 31
Chapter 16	To Do: 1, 2, 4 SAG: A, B TRG: 1, 3, 4, 5, 6, 7, 8, 9, 10, 12, 13, 14, 15, 16, 17, 18, 19, 20, 21, 22, 25, 27, 33, 34, 35, 36	To Do: 3 SAG: C, D TRG: 23, 24, 26, 30, 31, 32	To Do: 3 TRG: 2, 10, 18, 28, 29, 32	To Do: 4 SAG: A, C TRG: 4, 20, 23, 24, 26, 30, 32, 33, 35, 36	To Do: 2, 4 TRG: 1, 8, 16, 19, 27
Chapter 17	To Do: 1, 2, 4 SAG: B TRG: 1, 2, 3, 4, 5, 6, 7, 8, 9, 10, 13, 17, 19, 20, 21, 22, 23, 24, 25, 26, 27, 28, 29, 30, 33, 34, 35, 36, 38	To Do: 3, 4 SAG: B TRG: 11, 15, 19, 23, 25, 37	SAG: B, D TRG: 11, 19, 27, 32	To Do: 1, 3 SAG: A, B, C TRG: 2, 3, 4, 6, 11, 12, 16, 18, 19, 24, 28, 31, 36, 38	To Do: 3 SAG: A, B, D TRG: 18, 19, 32, 39
Chapter 18	To Do: 1, 2, 3, 4, 6 SAG: B, C TRG: 1, 3, 4, 5, 6, 9, 10, 11, 12, 13, 14, 15, 16, 18, 21, 22, 23, 25, 27, 29, 30, 31, 32, 33, 34, 35, 36, 37, 39	To Do: 3, 5 SAG: D TRG: 38	To Do: 3 TRG: 2	SAG: A TRG: 26	TRG: 6, 20, 22, 26
Chapter 19	To Do: 1, 2, 6 SAG: B, D, E TRG: 1, 2, 3, 4, 5, 6, 7, 9, 10, 11, 12, 13, 14, 15, 16, 17, 18, 19, 21, 22, 23, 25, 26, 27, 30, 31, 32, 33, 34, 35, 36, 37, 39, 40	To Do: 1, 3, 4, 7 TRG: 7, 22, 28, 29, 30, 40	To Do: 3, 7 SAG: A, B, C, D TRG: 8, 20, 24, 29, 33, 38		To Do: 1, 2, 4, 5 SAG: D TRG: 2, 14, 18, 23, 32, 36, 38
Chapter 20	To Do: 2, 3, 4 SAG: A, C TRG: 1, 2, 3, 4, 5, 6, 7, 8, 9, 10, 11, 12, 13, 15, 16, 17, 18, 19, 20, 21, 24, 25, 26, 27, 29, 30	To Do: 1 TRG: 22	To Do: 3 SAG: D TRG: 29	TRG: 14	To Do: 1, 4 SAG: C, D TRG: 4, 8, 10, 13, 15, 23, 28

(Continued)

	Verbal	Reading	Writing	Math/Science	Analytical
Chapter 21	To Do: 2, 3, 4, 5, 6 SAG: A, C, E TRG: 1, 2, 3, 4, 5, 8, 9, 10, 11, 12, 13, 14, 15, 16, 18, 19, 20, 21, 23, 24, 25, 26, 27, 28, 29, 30, 31, 32, 35, 36, 38, 39, 40, 41, 42, 44, 45, 46, 47, 48, 49, 50, 51, 52, 54, 55, 56, 57, 59, 60, 61, 64, 65, 66, 67	To Do: 2 SAG: B TRG: 2, 6, 7, 11, 14, 17, 22, 24, 26, 27, 33, 37, 43, 45, 48, 53, 54, 62, 63, 64	To Do: 1, 2, 5 SAG: A, C, D, E TRG: 2, 14, 34	To Do: 5 TRG: 7	To Do: 3, 6 SAG: C, E TRG: 1, 2, 4, 20, 24, 27, 28, 42, 45, 55, 60, 67
Chapter 22	To Do: 2, 4 SAG: A, C, D TRG: 1, 2, 3, 4, 5, 6, 8, 9, 10, 11, 12, 13, 14, 15, 17, 19, 20, 21, 22, 23, 24, 25, 27, 28, 29, 30, 31, 32, 33	To Do: 1, 3 SAG: B TRG: 8, 16	To Do: 3, 5 SAG: C, D TRG: 7, 8, 10, 30		To Do: 5 SAG: A, C, D TRG: 4, 7, 9, 10
Chapter 23	To Do: 1, 2, 3, 4, 5, 6, 8 SAG: D TRG: 1, 2, 3, 4, 5, 6, 7, 8, 9, 10, 11, 13, 14, 16, 17, 18, 19, 22, 23, 27, 28, 29, 30, 32, 33, 34, 35, 38, 40, 41, 44, 46, 47, 48, 49	To Do: 7 SAG: C, D TRG: 12, 15, 21, 22, 24, 25, 26, 27, 31, 36, 40, 42, 45, 48	To Do: 5 SAG: B, D TRG: 1, 3, 15, 16, 22, 27, 39, 43, 48	SAG: A, D TRG: 20, 27, 48	To Do: 1, 2, 3, 5, 6 SAG: D TRG: 3, 8, 16, 29, 30, 35
Chapter 24	To Do: 1, 2, 3, 4, 5, 6 SAG: C, D TRG: 1, 2, 4, 6, 7, 8, 9, 14, 15, 17, 18, 20, 22, 23, 24, 25, 26, 27, 30, 32, 34, 36, 38	To Do: 1, 2, 6 SAG: A, C, D TRG: 2, 6, 11, 12, 31, 32, 33, 35, 36, 37	SAG: C, D TRG: 1, 3, 5, 12, 32, 39, 40	To Do: 3, 5, 6 SAG: B, C TRG: 2, 21, 22, 26, 33, 34, 35, 37	To Do: 3, 4, 6 SAG: B, C TRG: 3, 7, 19, 20, 28, 29, 35, 37
Chapter 25	To Do: 1, 2, 3, 4 SAG: A, C TRG: 1, 2, 3, 4, 5, 6, 7, 8, 9, 10, 12, 13, 14, 15, 16, 17, 18, 19, 20	To Do: 2 SAG: B TRG: 6, 11, 13, 20, 21	To Do: 2 TRG: 12, 20		To Do: 1, 2 SAG: A, C TRG: 3, 7
Chapter 26	To Do: 4, 5, 6, 7 SAG: A, D TRG: 1, 2, 3, 4, 5, 6, 8, 10, 11, 12, 13, 14, 16, 17, 18, 19, 22, 23, 25	To Do: 1, 2, 3 SAG: A, B TRG: 20	SAG: C, D TRG: 25	To Do: 2, 3 SAG: A, C TRG: 4, 7, 9, 11, 15, 19, 24	To Do: 1, 2, 3, 4 SAG: A, D TRG: 7, 9, 23, 24, 25
Chapter 27	To Do: 3, 4 SAG: D TRG: 1, 4, 6, 7, 8, 15, 16, 17, 18	TRG: 9, 13, 14, 15	To Do: 1 SAG: A, D TRG: 11, 12	To Do: 1, 2 SAG: C TRG: 10, 11, 12, 13, 15	To Do: 1, 2 SAG: A, B, C, D TRG: 2, 3, 11, 12, 14, 15

Contemporary Living Teacher's Resources

Contemporary Living

Pretest

Multiple Choice: Read each of the following questions and choose the best response. Write your answers on a separate sheet of paper.

1. The force that guides your conduct and behavior into acceptable standards of right and wrong is known as _____.
   A. self-concept
   B. personality
   C. character
   D. environmental response
2. The basic unit of heredity is the _____.
   A. gene
   B. chromosome
   C. sperm
   D. egg
3. A family structure where either or both spouses may have been married before and have one or more children from the previous marriage is known as _____.
   A. traditional
   B. blended
   C. nuclear
   D. extended kinship
4. When you use a substitute method to achieve a desired goal, you are using the defense mechanism of _____.
   A. projection
   B. displacement
   C. compensation
   D. regression
5. A _____ is a belief that all members of a group share the same characteristics.
   A. bigot
   B. stereotype
   C. scape goat
   D. defense mechanism
6. According to Maslow, _____ needs must be at least partially fulfilled before other needs can be addressed.
   A. safety
   B. physical
   C. esteem
   D. love
7. A condition in which a person eats an inade-

quate diet because they fear becoming obese is known as _____.
   A. bulimia
   B. dyslexia
   C. anemia
   D. anorexia nervosa
8. A disease affecting the air sacs of the lungs causing breathing difficulties, is known as _____.
   A. bulimia
   B. asthma
   C. diabetes
   D. emphysema
9. How does the body react to stress?
   A. Pulse quickens, blood pressure rises, muscles tense.
   B. Muscles relax, pulse quickens, blood pressure goes down.
   C. Muscles tense, pulse slows, blood pressure rises.
   D. Pulse slows, blood pressure goes down, muscles relax.
10. Studies show that teenagers obtain most of their information about their sexuality from _____.
    A. their parents
    B. their peers
    C. the media
    D. both b and c
11. The AIDS virus can be transmitted by _____.
    A. homosexuals
    B. heterosexuals
    C. intravenous injections
    D. All of the above.
12. A person who displays empathy in communication is one who _____.
    A. demonstrates anger because they disagree with the other person
    B. shares the feelings of the other person
    C. sees things from another person's viewpoint
    D. questions why the other person feels as they do

(Continued)

13. The tendency to sometimes hate those you love is called _____.
   A. ambivalence
   B. infatuation
   C. anguished love
   D. hostile love
14. The tendency to choose a mate who lives close to you is called _____.
   A. homogamy
   B. role compatibility
   C. complementary needs
   D. propinquity
15. When a person enters into a second marriage before the first one has been dissolved, it is known as _____.
   A. polygamy
   B. monogamy
   C. bigamy
   D. breach of promise
16. Which of the following is true concerning dual-career families?
   A. Being employed helps both spouses develop their personal identities.
   B. When both spouses are employed, husbands share the responsibility for home and family matters half and half.
   C. Finding adequate child care is a primary concern of dual-career families.
   D. Both A and C.
17. A form of adjustment in marriage in which the couple agrees to disagree is called _____.
   A. martyrdom
   B. accommodation
   C. concession
   D. compromise
18. Advertising that offers an item at an extremely low price to get you into the store is known as _____.
   A. bait advertising
   B. puffery advertising
   C. pseudo-truth advertising
   D. subliminal advertising
19. Amounts of money subtracted from your wages before you receive them are called _____.
   A. exemptions
   B. fringe benefits
   C. gross income
   D. deductions
20. The type of credit you are using when you agree to pay for a purchase in several regular payments is _____.
   A. revolving credit
   B. non-installment credit
   C. installment credit
   D. credit card
21. The most ideal spacing between the birth of children should be _____.
   A. one to two years
   B. two to three years
   C. three to four years
   D. at least five years
22. A method of childbirth based on the theory that the pain of childbirth can be controlled by the woman is known as _____.
   A. the Leboyer method
   B. the Lamaze method
   C. the traditional method
   D. the family-centered method
23. When newborns are touched on one of their cheeks, they turn their heads in that direction and open their mouths. This is called the _____ reflex.
   A. Babinski
   B. grasp
   C. startle
   D. rooting
24. When young children play next to their friends, but not with them, it is called _____.
   A. cooperative play
   B. social play
   C. on-looker play
   D. parallel play
25. In the U.S. today, substitute child care is most likely to be provided in _____.
   A. the home of a caregiver
   B. the child's own home
   C. a day care center
   D. an employer-sponsored center
26. Which of these tactics is recommended for family members of an alcoholic?
   A. Bribe the alcoholic to stop drinking by making a deal with him or her.
   B. Handle the responsibilities the alcoholic is unable to fulfill.
   C. Call in sick for the alcoholic if he or she is unable to go to work.
   D. Stop any enabling behaviors and get professional help.

   Contemporary Living Teacher's Resources

27. If you have a friend who is threatening suicide, you should _____.
   A. express your concern to the person directly
   B. listen quietly and let your friend talk about the problem
   C. never ignore the threat of a suicide attempt
   D. All of the above.
28. Select the true statement concerning domestic violence.
   A. Most domestic violence is committed by husbands.
   B. Verbal abuse is not considered a form of domestic violence.
   C. Anger and frustration are the emotions that form the core of most domestic violence.
   D. Experts agree that violence at home does not lead children to act violently outside the home.
29. The problem most elderly persons worry about concerns _____.
   A. finances
   B. isolation
   C. poor health
   D. crime
30. In adjusting to the death of a loved one, you should _____.
   A. try to keep your grief under control
   B. spend time with friends and talk out your grief
   C. take a long, expensive vacation to try to forget your problems
   D. stay away from others until you have dealt with your grief

True/False: Read each of the following statements. Write *true* if the statement is true. Write *false* if the statement is false.

31. Self-esteem is how you feel about your self-concept.
32. Fraternal twins result when one egg splits to form two babies.
33. A mutation is a chemical change that occurs in a gene.
34. The mother determines the sex of the child.
35. A family structure that includes several generations of one family living together is called the extended kinship family system.
36. Most boys reach puberty two years ahead of girls.
37. When people place blame on other people or things for their own failures they are using the defense mechanism of rationalization.
38. Making no decision is actually making a decision.
39. Peer pressure is harmful.
40. A breakdown in family communication is usually cited as the cause for a young person running away from home.
41. Alcohol is a stimulant and can make you feel more energetic.
42. Positive as well as negative changes in your life can cause stress.
43. An active listener indicates to the sender that a message is heard and understood.
44. Assertiveness in communication means you express your feelings in a forceful, hostile, or destructive manner.
45. When a person shows jealousy, it is a good indication of positive love.
46. When you break up with someone, it is *not* a good idea to seek another serious relationship immediately.
47. Homogamy in mate selection means you choose a mate who is interested in home and family.
48. In an annulment, the court rules that the couple were never legally married.
49. Productive quarreling can actually strengthen a marriage.
50. Habit is the largest motivating reason for buying.
51. Term insurance provides both savings and protection.
52. Women—but not men—can experience gender-based discrimination in the workplace.
53. You can borrow from yourself with a passbook loan or by borrowing against your life insurance policy.
54. Changes in the breasts may be one of the first symptoms noted by a woman who suspects she may be pregnant.
55. Children gain large muscle control before they gain small muscle control.
56. When children have temper tantrums, it is best to ignore them as long as they are not doing something that will harm themselves or others.
57. Most authorities feel the practice of paying children for small jobs they do is the best method for teaching money management.

58. Investigators report that children are more often abducted by people the children do not regard as strangers.

59. Physically the body reaches its maximum size and strength by about 35 years.

60. Some food labels contain terms implying healthfulness, such as "lite," but there are no government regulations setting up criteria for the use of these terms.

Pretest Answer Key

Multiple Choice

1.	C	16.	D
2.	A	17.	B
3.	B	18.	A
4.	C	19.	D
5.	B	20.	C
6.	B	21.	C
7.	D	22.	B
8.	D	23.	D
9.	A	24.	D
10.	D	25.	A
11.	D	26.	D
12.	C	27.	D
13.	A	28.	C
14.	D	29.	A
15.	C	30.	B

True/False

31.	T	46.	T
32.	F	47.	F
33.	T	48.	T
34.	F	49.	T
35.	T	50.	T
36.	F	51.	F
37.	F	52.	F
38.	T	53.	T
39.	F	54.	T
40.	T	55.	T
41.	F	56.	T
42.	T	57.	F
43.	T	58.	T
44.	F	59.	F
45.	F	60.	F

Part I
Personal Development

Chapter 1 ■ ■ ■ ■ ■ ■ ■ ■ ■ ■ ■ ■ ■ ■ ■
You: Growing and Changing

Objectives

After studying this chapter, students will be able to
- identify the three forces that shape personality.
- describe six patterns of growth.
- define self-concept, self-esteem, and self-worth.
- explain how a person's character is revealed by his or her behavior.
- describe what it means to be a responsible adult.
- identify possible roadblocks to responsible adulthood.

Bulletin Boards

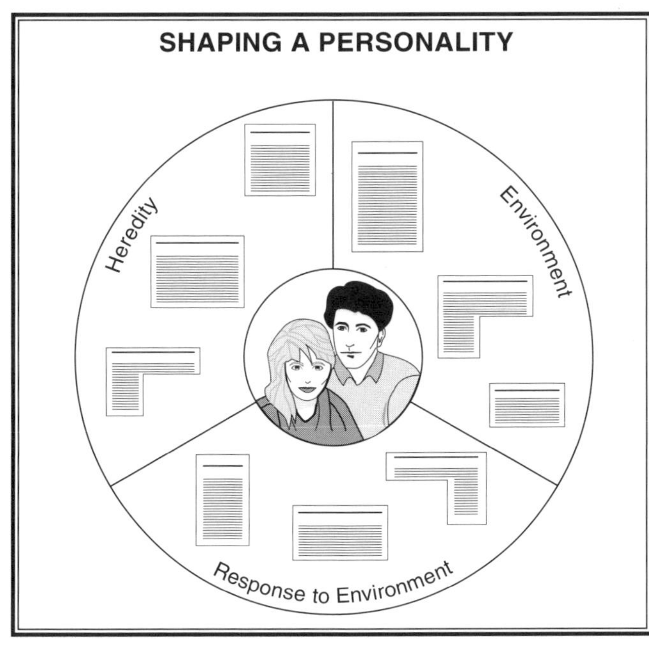

I. Title: "Shaping a Personality"

Draw a large circle and divide into thirds. Cover each third with a different color of paper. Attach a magazine picture of teenagers in the center. Find pictures and news articles dealing with each of the three factors that influence personality and place them on the board in the appropriate sections. Have students bring in additional articles and pictures.

II. Title: "Connectedness"

Cut out a large circle of colored shelf paper to represent a globe and cut out or sketch the two hemispheres. At the top place the words *You Function*, on the left side place the words *In a Family*, on the right side place the words *In a Community*, and at the bottom *In a Society and World*. On the left side place figures representing a family and on the right side place silhouettes of buildings representing a community. Have students discuss their roles in each area.

Teaching Materials

Text, pages 18-41

Terms to Know, To Review, To Do, and *To Think About*

Student Activity Guide
    A. *Personality Test*
    B. *Understanding Growth Patterns*
    C. *Your Self-Concept*
    D. *How Is Your Self-Esteem?*
    E. *Character Traits*

Teacher's Resource Guide/Binder
Influences That Shape Personality, reproducible master, 1-1

Which Shoe Fits You? reproducible master, 1-2
Developing Self-Esteem, reproducible master, 1-3
Character-Building Virtues Help You in Your Pathways of Life, transparency master, 1-4
Responsibility in a Cooperative Venture, reproducible master, 1-5
Chapter 1 Test

Teacher's Resource Binder
I Have Positive Possibilities! color transparency, CT-1

Software for Contemporary Living
Chapter Review Game

Introductory Activities

1. *Influences That Shape Personality*, reproducible master, 1-1. Have students, individually or in groups, think about how personalities are influenced by persons and events. Use the activity to stimulate student interest in how personalities are shaped.
2. Ask each student to think of a famous person they admire, and to list at least six personal characteristics that they think contributed to that person's success. Discuss the meaning of the terms "heredity" and "environment" and ask the students to decide which characteristics on their lists might have been the result of heredity and which might have been the result of environmental influences. Share with the class.
3. *Which Shoe Fits You?* reproducible master, 1-2. Have a shoe of each type described in this master and show to the class. Students are asked to select their favorite shoe. They can then read the descriptions of personality types based on shoe selections. Indicate that shoes come in different shapes and styles just as people are all different. Shoes are also chosen for different circumstances, just as people make choices based on circumstances in their lives. This activity is not to be taken seriously, but it gives students an opportunity to get acquainted with other class members. As an extension of this activity, ask all students who selected the same shoe type to get into a small group. Ask them to get acquainted with each other and discuss why they chose this shoe type.
4. See if your students can identify the six different areas in which people grow. Then ask them to list these categories on a sheet of notebook paper and describe how they think they have grown in these six areas over the past year. Ask if anyone would care to share what they have written with the class.

Strategies to Reteach, Reinforce, Enrich, and Extend Text Concepts

Your Personality

5. **EX** *Personality Test,* Activity A, SAG. Students will record responses to the personality test and compute average scores. They will list the five highest and five lowest average scores and then explain how they could further strengthen their high scores and improve their low scores.
6. **ER** Have students design a "shield" of their personalities by drawing and cutting a shield out of heavy paper or cardboard. Cover the shield with words and pictures they feel describe their personalities. Have students compare their shields with those of their classmates.
7. **ER** Have students write a short paper explaining which of the three forces they feel contributes most to personality development. Ask them to refer back to their papers after studying Chapters 2, 3, and 4 to see if they still feel the same way.

Your Growth

8. **RT** Ask students to list the six ways people grow and give examples of each.
9. **RT** Discuss the importance of a positive attitude toward chronological growth (aging) in our youth-oriented culture.
10. **RT** Using a physical growth chart, which you can obtain from a school nurse or a local physician, point out growth spurts in developmental stages of children and teenagers.
11. **RT** Discuss how heredity, environment, and responses to environment work together to determine intellectual growth.
12. **RF** Discuss the pros and cons of not having a set pattern of social growth as some cultures do. Cite and compare cultures which have set patterns of social growth.

13. **RT** Discuss the changes that take place as a person grows philosophically. How does this growth affect choices in high school and college years?

14. **RF** *Understanding Growth Patterns*, Activity B, SAG. Students are asked to define the six patterns of growth using their own words. Additional questions are asked regarding the six patterns of growth.

Your Self-Concept

15. **EX** *Your Self-Concept*, Activity C, SAG. Students are asked to evaluate their self-concepts by completing the exercise. The student is then asked to describe what a person could do to improve his or her self-concept.

16. **RT** A failure should be viewed as a learning experience instead of a personal defeat. Cite examples of well-known figures who have turned a failure into a positive challenge.

17. **EX** *Developing Self-Esteem*, reproducible master, 1-3. One of the best ways to feel good about yourself is to help others appreciate their strengths. In this exercise, students are asked to check ways they can increase their own self-esteem, as well as others.

18. **EX** *How Is Your Self-Esteem?* Activity D, SAG. Students are to circle sentences that indicate how they feel most of the time in order to evaluate their own self-esteem. They are to then answer questions concerning their self-esteem.

19. **RT** *I Have Positive Possibilities!* color transparency, CT-1. Discuss how teens do not always like who they are now, but with feelings of self-worth, they can look ahead and see their positive possibilities. This transparency lists the steps to this feeling of empowerment discussed on pages 29-30 of the text.

Your Character

20. **EX** *Character Traits*, Activity E, SAG. Students are asked to identify character traits that they think are important. They are to then answer questions about one of the traits of their choosing.

21. **RT** Cite examples in recent news events where people showed character. Describe other situations that showed a lack of character.

22. **RF** Cite decisions students in high school often have to make that show character, or a lack of it. Discuss character development pressures in the teen years. How does the phrase, "Everybody's doing it," compare with the phrase, "I know it's wrong and I choose not to do it." Which phrase indicates the person is developing character?

23. **RF** Discuss how parents help their children develop character. Compare how over-protective parents, permissive parents, and caring and trusting parents influence character formation in their children.

24. **EX** *Character-Building Virtues Help You in Your Pathways of Life*, transparency master, 1-4. Have students ask themselves the following questions: "What do I believe in?" "What kind of person should I become?" Ask students to refer to the chart on page 31 of the text. Discuss each of the virtues given on the transparency. What tends to enhance character development? What tends to impede character development? Discuss how enhancing these virtues can assist a person in achieving their goals.

Becoming a Responsible and Independent Adult

25. **EX** *Responsibility in a Cooperative Venture*, reproducible master, 1-5. In small groups, have students review the scenarios involving four young people as they attempt to work cooperatively on several club projects. They are to then answer questions concerning responsibility and character-building virtues.

26. **RT** Divide the class into two groups. Have one group of students list rights of citizenship. Have the other group list responsibilities of citizenship. Have each group share their lists with the class. Compare the two lists.

27. **RT** Discuss the benefits of volunteering and see if students can add to the list of benefits given on pages 36-37 of the text. Ask students to describe any volunteering that they have done and to explain how they learned about these opportunities. Discuss any problems they might have encountered.

28. **RT** Ask students what it means to be a citizen of the larger community. Has this changed today as compared to two centuries ago?

29. **RT** Ask students to state some goals they hope to achieve in the next five years. Discuss how setting goals can give people a sense of promise as they look to the future.

Roadblocks to Responsible Adulthood

30. **ER** Have each student interview an adult about the roadblocks young people faced when they were teenagers. Share their findings with the class.
31. **EX** In small groups, have students make a list of roadblocks teens may face today. Then have the groups discuss how teens might be able to move past these roadblocks. Have the groups share their findings with the rest of the class. List the roadblocks on the chalkboard. Then have each student rank the roadblocks in the order of importance to them. Tabulate the results to determine what the class feels is the greatest roadblock facing teens today. Ask each student to write a paper describing what could be done by a teen to overcome this roadblock.
32. **ER** Ask each student to choose one of the points listed on page 39 of the text and to write a paper discussing how it might help them as they prepare for responsible adulthood.

Answer Key for Chapter 1

Text
To Review, pages 40-41.

1. A. self-esteem
   B. growth pattern
   C. environment
   D. character
   E. self-worth
   F. personality
   G. self-concept
   H. heredity
2. (Name two:) Two eyes, two ears, a nose, a mouth, two arms, two legs, etc.
3. (Name two:) Color of eyes, shape of ears, length of arms, mental attitude, intelligence, behavior, etc.
4. (Shared parts of environment. List two:) School, classes, teachers, activities, etc. (Unique parts of environment. List two:) Family situation, neighborhood, religion, friends, etc.
5. A. philosophical
   B. chronological
   C. physical
   D. social
   E. intellectual
   F. emotional
6. At puberty. (Age 12 for girls; age 14 for boys.)
7. A sense of right and wrong that guides behavior.
8. Fulfilling responsibilities is the way you become more independent. Independence is something you earn by proving you can handle responsibility.
9. (Student response for two rights and two responsibilities.)
10. (Student response for three roadblocks.)

Teacher's Resource Guide

Chapter 1 Test

1. K	12. T	23. F
2. G	13. F	24. D
3. E	14. F	25. A
4. F	15. F	26. B
5. D	16. T	27. C
6. J	17. T	28. C
7. H	18. T	29. C
8. I	19. T	30. A
9. A	20. T	31. D
10. B	21. T	32. A
11. C	22. F	33. D

34. (Student response.)
35. (Student response.)
36. (Student response for three rights and three responsibilities.)
37. (Student response.)

Influences That Shape Personality

Name _______________________________________ **Date** _______________ **Period** _______________

The traits that make up your personality are influenced in part by persons and events in your environment. These influences occur everyday throughout your life. Typical traits are listed in the left-hand column below. Give examples of how certain persons and particular events might influence the formation of these traits or attitudes.

Traits	Person	Events
Love		
Fear		
Optimism		
Self-esteem		
Trust		
Joy		
Other:		

Which Shoe Fits You?

Name ____ **Date** _____________ **Period** _____________

Shoes come in many styles. Which style would you choose, or do you prefer going barefoot? Circle your choice below. Then read the descriptions at the bottom of this page to learn what your choice may reveal about your personality.

Dress Shoe   **Tennis Shoe**   **Work or Hiking Boot**

Loafer   **Earth or Nature Shoe**   **Barefoot**

Dress Shoe: You are probably a good manager; dependable; able to lead, but you know when to be a part of a group to get things done; careful; you work quietly, but may speak out if necessary.

Tennis Shoe: You are probably a comfortable person; you fit in most places and with most people; you like sports, both as a participant and as a spectator; you're flexible and adaptable; help out when needed; friendly.

Work or Hiking Boot: You are probably a hard worker; can take getting dirty; like a challenge; like to be active and don't like to sit around; will do unpleasant jobs if they need to be done; can do many things.

Loafer: You are probably calm and relaxed most of the time; you complete your work before pursuing personal interests; you cope well in stressful situations; a practical person; you enjoy being with the opposite sex.

Earth or Nature Shoe: You are probably creative, arty, and a little different; not always aware of what day it is; may not relate well to others at times; you like to try out new ideas and funky things; you have special talents; can really produce when motivated.

Barefoot: You are probably a nature lover; you enjoy the physical aspects of life, such as eating and sleeping; you like to be outdoors; enjoy animals.

Does the shoe you selected (along with its personality profile) match your personality? Explain your answer. ____

____

____

Five years from now, you may choose a different shoe to fit your changing personality. What shoe might that be and why? ____

____

Adapted from: Shirley Slater and Lee Cibrowski, *What Do You Like about Yourself?* (Washington, D.C.: HEEA, 1982), p. 22.

Developing Self-Esteem

Name _______________________________ **Date** _____________ **Period** _____________

Your feeling of self-esteem will increase as you are able to help others appreciate their strengths. Place a check in the column that shows how often you say and do the following to increase self-esteem in others.

I say to others:	Often	Sometimes	Never
1. I like the way you did that.			
2. Thanks for understanding.			
3. I'm glad you're my friend.			
4. You look great today.			
5. Thanks for listening.			
6. I really missed you.			
7. I heard something nice about you.			
8. You were a big help to me.			
9. If you need someone to talk to, call me.			
10. You're good at this.			
11. You make me feel good.			
12. You have a lot to offer.			
I do for others:			
1. Help them with a chore they have to do.			
2. Write a note to say "Thanks" or "I think you're great!"			
3. Share something that you enjoy.			
4. Suggest that you do something together that they enjoy.			
5. Make a special gift for someone.			

*Think about how good you feel when you
help someone else to feel good about themselves!*

Character-Building Virtues Help You in Your Pathways of Life

Responsibility in a Cooperative Venture

Group Members: _________________________ **Date** ____________ **Period** ____________

____

____

____

Four members of a high school FHA/HERO chapter are working together on several club projects. Read about the projects and how each club member handled his or her responsibilities. Then answer the questions below.

Club Project:	Joshua	Cary	Jason	Elisa
Volunteered to clean home of an elderly invalid.	Said he would bring stepladder, rags, and buckets. Result: Brought all items; worked all day.	Would bring old rags and cleaning solutions. Result: Brought all items; worked hard.	Would bring garbage can and trash bags. Result: Brought garbage can, but forgot trash bags.	Would bring lunch for everyone. Result: Forgot lunch; collected money to pick up lunch. Did no work.
Tutor a small group of children in math.	Brought his math books; arrived on time and worked with children.	Arrived late. Said she didn't know much about math herself; left early.	Arrived on time. Worked with Joshua to help students.	Called 1/2 hour late–had lost directions. Admitted later she went to a movie.
Sell ads for community helpline booklet their chapter is sponsoring.	Got list of possible contributors. Called to make appointments. Sold 26 ads out of 30 contacts.	Said her dad knew all the people with money. After two weeks, had contacted only four people; sold two ads.	Got list to call. Waited until last weekend. Brought in four ads, but they were too late for the deadline.	Got list to call. Called four prospects and sold two ads.

1. Who was the most responsible in fulfilling the tasks that needed to be done? _________________

2. Who was the least responsible? ____

3. Who lied to cover up the real reason for his or her actions? _______________________

4. How did the individual performances affect the total group effort? ____________________

____

5. Refer to the chart on page 31 of your text and evaluate each student on the virtues that help build character.

   Joshua____

   ____

   Cary ____

   ____

   Jason____

   ____

   Elisa ____

   ____

You: Growing and Changing

Name ____

Date _________________________________ **Period** __________ **Score** ______________

Chapter 1 Test

Matching: Match the following terms and identifying phrases.

______ 1. Force that guides your behavior into acceptable standards of right and wrong.

______ 2. Sum of the traits that are passed from ancestors to you.

______ 3. You know yourself and accept yourself as you are.

______ 4. The unique way a person grows.

______ 5. Includes your family, your community, and the world around you.

______ 6. The group of behavioral and emotional traits that distinguishes an individual.

______ 7. Time when the body first becomes capable of reproducing sexually.

______ 8. Type of growth that is the same for everyone.

______ 9. A sense of adequacy and belonging.

______ 10. Gives direction to a person's decision making.

______ 11. The picture you have of yourself.

A. self-worth
B. goal
C. self-concept
D. environment
E. self-esteem
F. growth pattern
G. heredity
H. puberty
I. chronological
J. personality
K. character

True/False: Circle *T* if the statement is true or *F* if the statement is false.

T F 12. Your personality is the sum of your inherited and acquired traits.

T F 13. All authorities agree about how the forces of heredity and environment affect personality.

T F 14. Males generally reach puberty at the same age as females.

T F 15. A person with a high potential for intelligence will always develop a sharp mind.

T F 16. How you control your emotions will be an indication of your emotional maturity.

T F 17. As they grow older, children's behavior is shaped by approval or disapproval by others.

T F 18. How people react to your behavior influences your self-concept.

T F 19. Practicing positive self-talk can improve your feeling of self-worth.

T F 20. Being responsible means you not only perform tasks assigned to you, but you also admit if you have done something wrong.

T F 21. Traits developed as a result of environmental factors are called acquired traits.

T F 22. Citizens have rights, but they are not required to fulfill any responsibilities.

T F 23. Goals have little to do with the decisions you make from day to day.

(Continued)

                                Contemporary Living Teacher's Resources

Name ____

Multiple Choice: Choose the best response. Write the letter in the space provided.

_______ 24. A force that helps shape your personality is _______.
A. heredity
B. environment
C. your response to your environment
D. All of the above.

_______ 25. Self-esteem is _______.
A. the way you feel about yourself
B. the way you see yourself
C. the promise of what you think you can become
D. None of the above.

_______ 26. Self-concept is _______.
A. the way you feel about yourself
B. the way you see yourself
C. the promise of what you think you can become
D. None of the above.

_______ 27. Self-worth is _______.
A. the way you feel about yourself
B. the way you see yourself
C. the promise of what you think you can become
D. None of the above.

_______ 28. When you have self-esteem, you _______.
A. may be reluctant to take reasonable risks
B. worry about weaknesses that may be a problem for you
C. know yourself and accept yourself as you are
D. are certain you will make no mistakes

_______ 29. Learning to express your feelings in a way that is acceptable to others is an example of _______ growth.
A. chronological
B. social
C. emotional
D. philosophical

_______ 30. Virtues _______.
A. are traits that indicate character
B. are things you want to achieve or have
C. give you a purpose for making the most of every day
D. All of the above.

_______ 31. Being responsible _______.
A. means you are ready for greater independence
B. is one of the tasks of adolescence
C. means you take responsibility for your conduct
D. All of the above.

_______ 32. A leader should be able to _______.
A. lead the group in finding ways to solve problems
B. handle all the work of the group
C. solve problems for the group
D. keep communication with group members to a minimum

(Continued)

_______ 33. Goals _______.
A. begin as expectations
B. are things you want to achieve or have
C. give you a sense of promise for your future
D. All of the above.

Essay Questions: Provide complete responses to the following questions or statements.

34. Identify an environmental factor that might influence a person's personality. Explain how the personality might be affected.

35. Discuss when and how character formation occurs.

36. Give three examples of citizens' rights. Give three examples of citizens' responsibilities.

37. Identify a roadblock to responsible adulthood that your parents may have faced. Is this still a roadblock for young people today? Explain your answer.

Chapter 2
Your Heredity

Objectives

After studying this chapter, students will be able to

- explain the process of heredity.
- describe how twins and multiple births occur.
- identify the characteristics that a person inherits.
- explain the role of heredity as only one of many factors influencing life success.

Bulletin Boards

I. Title: "Octogenarians: Secrets of a Long Life"

Capture students' attention with this bulletin board when people ask, "What's an octogenarian?" Ask students to interview octogenarians (persons at least 80 years old). Ask them to find out the older person's secrets for living a long life. Bring in photos of the octogenarians and write their "secrets" on index cards. Place the photos and cards on the bulletin board. Students may also bring in magazine and newspaper articles about octogenarians or other older people who are featured.

II. Title: "Inherited Traits...Environment Altered"

Bring to class pictures from magazines showing various physical traits. On one side of the bulletin board, mount pictures of traits that are determined by heredity. On the other side, mount pictures that show how environment can change inherited traits. (For example, brunette hair can be changed to blonde, some birth defects can be corrected, and some fat people can become thin.)

Teaching Materials

Text, pages 42-59

Terms To Know, To Review, To Do, and *To Think About*

Student Activity Guide

A. *Inheritance of Chromosomes*
B. *Inheritance of Dominant and Recessive Genes*
C. *Your Family Heritage*
D. *Heredity Crossword*

Teacher's Resource Guide/Binder

Heredity–Truths and Myths, reproducible master, 2-1

Twins and Multiple Births, transparency master, 2-2

Inherited Conditions/Environment Altered, reproducible master, 2-3

Venture Game, reproducible master, 2-4

Chapter 2 Test

Teacher's Resource Binder

Multiple Births, color transparency, CT-2A

Transmission of Sex-Linked Characteristics, color transparency, CT-2B

Software for Contemporary Living

Chapter Review Game

Introductory Activity

1. *Heredity–Truths and Myths,* reproducible master, 2-1. Have students test their beginning knowledge of heredity by completing the checklist. Then either go over the checklist as a class or have students correct their own papers as they read the chapter. After completing the chapter, ask them to report how many questions they originally answered correctly.

Strategies to Reteach, Reinforce, Enrich, and Extend Text Concepts

The Process of Heredity

2. **EX** *Inheritance of Chromosomes,* Activity A, SAG. Have students complete the chart tracing the inheritance of chromosomes. Then ask them to explain the importance of knowing their genetic background when planning their future families.

3. **RF** *Inheritance of Dominant and Recessive Genes,* Activity B, SAG. Have students complete the chart indicating the inheritance of dominant and recessive genes.

4. **EX** Medical research has shown that outside influences can cause mutations, such as occurred after the explosion of the atomic bomb in Japan. Have students cite other examples in which mutations have resulted from environmental events.

Twins and Multiple Births

5. **ER** *Twins and Multiple Births,* transparency master, 2-2. Use this transparency to discuss the rising incidence of twins and multiple births due to older women having babies and the use of fertility drugs.

6. **RT** *Multiple Births,* color transparency, CT-2A. Use this transparency to illustrate examples of various types of multiple births. Cite current examples of multiple births.

7. **RF** Discuss the difference between fraternal and identical twins.

8. **ER** Discuss, or have students research, unusual cases of multiple births such as quintuplets (Dionne, Fischer, or Kienast).

9. **ER** Discuss, or have students research, unusual cases of Siamese (conjoined) twins, such as Chang and Eng. Cite medical advances that have allowed surgeons to separate Siamese (conjoined) twins.

Inherited Characteristics

10. **ER** Explain how gender is determined by heredity. Ask students to investigate recent medical reports that indicate that couples may be able to select the sex of their child.

11. **EX** Discuss ways in which heredity affects intellectual ability and ways in which environment can positively affect intelligence. Ask students how this information can be used to advantage in children's education.

12. **RT** *Inherited Conditions/Environment Altered,* reproducible master, 2-3. This master may be used as an overhead transparency to facilitate class discussion, or it may be duplicated for each student to use as a chapter review or study guide. Inherited physical characteristics and diseases are listed in the left-hand column. Ask students to identify the cause of each characteristic or disease. Causes might be: dominant genes, recessive genes, sex-linked chromosomes, abnormal chromosomes, or other factors. Then have them indicate whether or not each condition can be altered by the environment, and if so, in what way.

13. **RT** *Transmission of Sex-Linked Characteristics,* color transparency, CT-2B. Use this transparency to illustrate examples of how sex-linked characteristics, such as hemophilia, can be passed from one generation to another.

14. **RT** Discuss how persons may blame their obesity on heredity, when, in fact, environmental factors may be to blame. Also discuss how knowledge of a poten-

tial weight problem may encourage a person to use environmental factors (such as diet and exercise) to control a possible problem.

15. **RF** Refer to the spectrum of inherited traits in the text. Ask students to pick out the traits their families exhibit and note their tendencies to be recessive or dominant.

16. **EX** *Your Family Heritage,* Activity C, SAG. Have students trace the inheritance of certain characteristics in their families.

17. **EX** Divide the class into small groups and ask them to discuss the following question: What would you do if you were planning to marry and you learned that your future mate may be carrying a gene for an inheritable disease?

18. **ER** Special project. Have students research the following hereditary disorders and report to the class any recent medical advances being made: color blindness, Tay-Sachs disease, thalassemia, congenital heart defects, spina bifida, hemophilia, Rh factor disease, achondroplasia (small stature).

19. **ER** Special project. A chart on inherited defects and diseases can be found in Chapter 2. Have students research additional hereditary defects and determine their symptoms, causes, and treatments. Report findings to the class. Possible research topics: Marfan's syndrome, Alzheimer's disease, hemophilia, spina bifida, clubfoot, achondroplasia (small stature).

20. **ER** Have students research the following topics and report back to class, giving brief descriptions of the processes. Ask students to indicate both the positive and negative results that could develop if these technologies were adopted.
    a. Gene mapping or genetic fingerprinting. (DNA is used in identifying inherited characteristics.)
    b. Genetic testing. (Screening of individuals for hereditary diseases.)
    c. Choosing the sex of a child. (Chromosome screening can reveal the sex of a child early in pregnancy.)
    d. Gene therapy. (Inserting a healthy gene into cells containing damaged genes.)

21. **ER** Invite a genetic counselor or obstetrician to speak to the class. Ask students to prepare a list of questions to ask the speaker concerning the topics presented in the chapter.

22. **RT** *Heredity Crossword,* Activity D, SAG. Use the puzzle to help students review vocabulary terms found in Chapter 2.

23. **RT** *Venture Game,* reproducible master, 2-4. Have students play the game to review vocabulary terms found in Chapter 2.

Valuing Your Uniqueness

24. **ER** Ask a mental health professional to address the class on the topic, "Learning to Accept Yourself–Warts and All."

25. **ER** Ask a rehabilitation professional to address the class on the topic, "Self-Esteem and Disability."

Answer Key for Chapter 2

Text
To Review, page 58.

1. 23.
2. true
3. A. Genes are strands of thousands of chromosomes.
4. Yes.
5. Yes.
6. The person will exhibit the trait of the dominant gene.
7. Fraternal twins are the products of two eggs fertilized by two sperm. Identical twins are the products of a single fertilized egg that divides and develops into two separate persons.
8. false
9. Males.
10. Mental; chronological.
11. Blood type O.
12. During the birth process, some of the baby's blood enters the mother's bloodstream. The mother produces antibodies against the Rh factor. If the mother carries another Rh-positive baby, her antibodies will enter the baby's system and attack the red blood cells.
13. Dominant genes (list four:) Long, full eyelashes; high and narrow nose; kinky hair; black or brown hair; brown eyes; full lips. Recessive genes (list four:) Blue eyes; short, thin eyelashes; straight hair; blonde hair; thin lips; low and broad nose.
14. (Describe two. Student response. See Chart 2-16 on page 55 of the text.)

Student Activity Guide

Activity A, Inheritance of Chromosomes.

Each person has 46 chromosomes and passes 23 to an offspring.

Knowing your hereditary background is important because if your family has a history of a particular disease, you can receive genetic counseling to determine the possibility of your future children inheriting the disease. If the possibility is great, you may choose to adopt children (or remain childless) rather than to have your own.

Activity B, *Inheritance of Dominant and Recessive Genes.*

●● ●○ ●○   ○○

1. A. three
   B. brown eyes
   C. blue eyes
   D. brown eyes
2. Kinky hair. Long eyelashes. Brown eyes. High, narrow nose. Free earlobes. Dimples. Black hair.

Activity D, *Heredity Crossword.*

A crossword puzzle grid with the following answers:

Across:
4. LINKED
8. HEMOPHILIA
9. CHROMOSOME
10. IMAGING
11. MUTATION
15. RECESSIVE
17. GENIUS
18. FRATERNAL
19. OBESITY

Down:
1. RECEIVE
2. IDENTICAL
3. PUD
5. DOMINANT
6. AUTOSOME
7. GENE
12. DIABETES
13. DONOR
14. DION
16. CELL

Teacher's Resource Guide

Heredity–Truths and Myths, reproducible master, 2-1.

1. Truth.	8. Truth.	15. Truth.
2. Myth.	9. Myth.	16. Truth.
3. Truth.	10. Truth.	17. Truth.
4. Myth.	11. Truth.	18. Myth.
5. Myth.	12. Myth.	19. Myth.
6. Myth.	13. Truth.	20. Truth.
7. Truth.	14. Truth.	

Chapter 2 Test

1. D	11. T	21. B
2. A	12. F	22. A
3. J	13. T	23. C
4. I	14. F	24. B
5. C	15. T	25. B
6. B	16. F	26. C
7. E	17. T	27. B
8. G	18. T	28. D
9. F	19. T	29. C
10. H	20. T	30. B

31. Each male child has a 50-percent risk of being color-blind. Each female has a 50-percent risk of being a carrier, but no chance of being color-blind.

32. Within certain limits, the life span of humans seems to be set by heredity. However, environment can lengthen the expected life span through improved scientific and medical knowledge. Environment can also shorten the expected life span through accidents, wars, and natural catastrophes.

33. If genetic counseling shows that a child of the couple would have a high risk of hereditary defects, the couple may decide to adopt a child. If the doctor finds little risk of hereditary defects, the couple may decide to have a child of their own.

Heredity–Truths and Myths

Name ____ **Date** ______________ **Period**______________

Read the following statements concerning heredity. Indicate whether you think each statement is a truth or a myth by checking the appropriate column.

	Truth	**Myth**
1. If a recessive gene and a dominant gene are paired, the dominant gene will mask the recessive gene.	________	________
2. The genes for one trait will have an effect on the genes of other traits.	________	________
3. Once a woman has had twins, her chances for having twins again are three to ten times greater.	________	________
4. Identical twins result when two identical eggs are fertilized by two identical sperm.	________	________
5. Mirror imaging often occurs in identical twins. This means that the same body details will always appear in exactly the same place on both twins.	________	________
6. Siamese twins are identical twins who are linked at some place on their bodies. It is impossible to ever separate them.	________	________
7. The Dionne quintuplets were the result of one fertilized egg splitting to form five individuals.	________	________
8. Fraternal twins are no more alike than any two siblings.	________	________
9. The female determines the sex of a child because the embryo develops in her body.	________	________
10. More males than females are color-blind.	________	________
11. Though your intellectual potential is inherited, it is greatly influenced by your environment and your response to environment.	________	________
12. More people in our country have blood type AB than any other type.	________	________
13. You may inherit the tendency to live a long life, but environment sometimes shortens it.	________	________
14. The average life span of the first American colonists was about 35 years.	________	________
15. Wavy hair is dominant over straight hair.	________	________
16. College students today are over two inches taller than college students 50 years ago.	________	________
17. A person's potentials for height and bone structure are inherited.	________	________
18. If a disease is inherited, it will appear at birth.	________	________
19. The best time to seek genetic counseling is when a woman is certain that she is pregnant.	________	________
20. Down syndrome is more likely to occur when the mother is over age 45.	________	________

Twins and Multiple Births

1982: One in 50 births was a twin or multiple birth.
1992: One in 41 births was a twin or multiple birth.

Experts recommend that parents:

Dress them differently.

Give them nonrhyming names.

Ask that they be put in different classes.

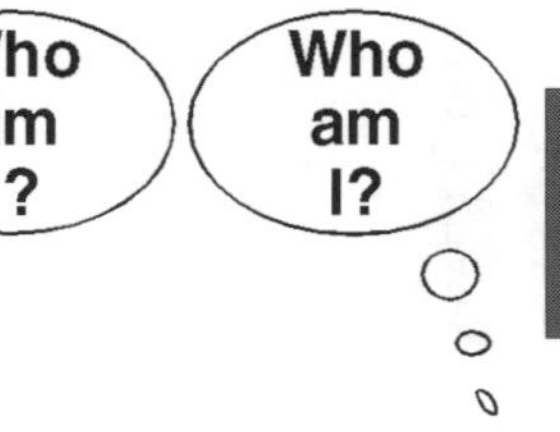

Encourage their development as individuals.

Inherited Conditions/Environment Altered

Name _______________________________ **Date** _______________ **Period**_______________

Characteristic or disease:	Cause:	Altered by environment:
1. Black hair		
2. Blonde hair		
3. Straight hair		
4. Kinky hair		
5. Brown eyes		
6. High, narrow nose		
7. Dark skin		
8. Light skin		
9. Obesity		
10. Hemophilia		
11. Color blindness		
12. Down syndrome		
13. Cystic fibrosis		
14. Muscular dystrophy		
15. Sickle cell anemia		
16. Diabetes		

Venture Game

Pregame procedure:

Choose three terms from Chapter 2. Write the terms with their definitions on index cards. On the blank side of the index cards, write the "value" of the terms. For instance, a simple term would have a value of 10 points. A more difficult term would have a value of 30 points. The most difficult terms would have a value of 50 points.

Game cards:

| 10 | 30 | 50 |

front

| term definition |

back

Game procedure:

Divide into four groups and select a team captain for each group. Each team will have the same opportunity to answer. Only team captains should raise their hands indicating their teams' ability to answer the questions. Once committed, the captain will have to answer. If the answer is correct, the team will be awarded the point value of the card. If the answer is wrong, the team will have that number of points deducted from their total. If no one can answer the question, the card is placed in a separate stack. When all other cards have been used, these cards may be used as "double win" cards. At this point (but not before) students may use their texts. As before, the team captains will raise their hands when their teams want to try to answer. If correct, they win double point value. If they answer incorrectly, double point value is deducted from their total.

After each question is answered, record the score on the following chart. For example, write "+10" if 10 points are won by a team, or "-30" if 30 points are lost. At the end of the game, total the number of points scored by each team. The team with the most points wins.

Team 1   **Team 2**   **Team 3**   **Team 4**

Your Heredity

Name ____

Date ____ **Period** _____________ **Score** _______________

Chapter 2 Test

Matching: Match the following terms and identifying phrases.

_______ 1. Gene whose effect is noticed when combined with any other gene.

_______ 2. Basic unit of heredity.

_______ 3. Twins born physically linked.

_______ 4. Products of a single fertilized egg.

_______ 5. Chemical changes in genes

_______ 6. A string of many genes.

_______ 7. Gene that will manifest itself only when paired with a similar gene.

_______ 8. The chromosomes that are alike in both the male and female.

_______ 9. Type of blood that can be given to anyone because it is "universal."

_______ 10. Products of two eggs fertilized by two sperm.

A. gene
B. chromosome
C. mutations
D. dominant
E. recessive
F. type O
G. autosomes
H. fraternal twins
I. identical twins
J. Siamese twins
K. type A

True/False: Circle *T* if the statement is true or *F* if the statement is false.

T F 11. Exposure to radiation can result in defective offspring.

T F 12. The recessive gene will exert its influence regardless of the other gene in a pair.

T F 13. The Dionne quintuplets, who were born in Canada, were all identical.

T F 14. Every person born normally has 48 chromosomes in every cell.

T F 15. A mother who has twins has a greater chance of having twins again than a mother who has not had twins.

T F 16. The average life expectancy of the early American colonists was over 70 years.

T F 17. An inherited characteristic that is determined by genes on the X chromosome is called a sex-linked characteristic.

T F 18. Heredity can cause differences in the way food is utilized by the body.

T F 19. A mother and father contribute equal amounts to the genetic background of their baby.

T F 20. Genetic counseling can provide important information for couples who desire to know more about the hereditary potentials they could pass on to their offspring.

(Continued)

Multiple Choice: Select the best response. Write the letter in the space provided.

______ 21. Sometimes one identical twin will have physical characteristics on one side of the body that are exactly opposite those of the other twin. This is called ______.
A. Siamese twins
B. mirror imaging
C. reverse images
D. oppositeness

______ 22. Humans have 22 pairs of ______.
A. autosomes
B. sex chromosomes
C. X chromosomes
D. Y chromosomes

______ 23. The "bleeding" disease, which is sex-linked, is called ______.
A. diabetes
B. sickle cell anemia
C. hemophilia
D. muscular dystrophy

______ 24. ______ founded the laws of dominant and recessive genes.
A. Lou Gehrig
B. Gregor Mendel
C. John Huntington
D. Chang and Eng

______ 25. The three races in the world today are ______.
A. Negroid, Mongoloid, and American
B. Caucasoid, Negroid, and Mongoloid
C. Mongoloid, Caucasoid, and European
D. African, European, and American

______ 26. Which of the following statements is true?
A. More girl babies than boy babies are born.
B. Men on average live longer than women.
C. More boys than girls die during childhood.
D. The number of male and female young adults is about even.

______ 27. The Rh factor ______.
A. is inherited by about 5 percent of all humans
B. may be a problem when an Rh-negative mother carries an Rh-positive fetus
C. may be a problem when an Rh-positive mother carries an Rh-negative fetus
D. is a problem for all expectant mothers

______ 28. The test in which the fluid surrounding the developing fetus is studied for chromosomal abnormality is called ______.
A. a Shick test
B. a skin test
C. a chromosome
D. amniocentesis

(Continued)

_____ 29. Intelligence-test scores reflect the _______.
     A. influence of heredity but not of environment
     B. influence of environment but not of heredity
     C. influences of both heredity and environment
     D. role of motivation and interpersonal skills in attaining success

_____ 30. If a person's I.Q. score is between 90 and 110, the person is in the _______ range of intelligence.
     A. genius
     B. normal
     C. below normal
     D. superior

Essay Questions: Provide complete responses to the following questions or statements.

31. Color blindness is a sex-linked trait. Suppose a woman is a carrier of the trait, and a man is normal. What are the odds that each of their male children will be color-blind? What are the odds that each of their female children will be color-blind?

32. Explain how both heredity and environment affect longevity.

33. How can genetic counseling assist a couple in making the decision to adopt a child or to have their own child?

Chapter 3 ▪ ▪ ▪ ▪ ▪ ▪ ▪ ▪ ▪ ▪ ▪ ▪ ▪ ▪ ▪ ▪ ▪
Your Environment

Objectives

After studying this chapter, students will be able to

- describe environmental influences on personality development.
- explain the role of the family in the development of the child's personality.
- summarize the role of peers in personality development.
- analyze ways in which education, occupation, religion, changing economic conditions, and the mass media may influence personality development.

Bulletin Boards

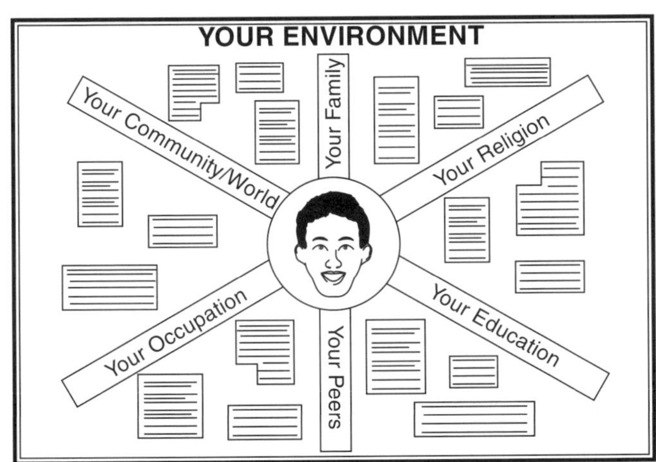

I. Title: "Your Environment"

Place a magazine picture of a teenager in the middle of a bulletin board. List the environmental factors covered in this chapter around the picture like spokes on a wheel. Within the spaces display pictures and news stories that show how these factors affect people.

II. Title: "Your Work Environment: Where Are You Headed?"

Make a signpost from brown construction paper. Add a vertical row of directional signs (pointed on one side to resemble a "directional" sign and set at slight angles so they are not exactly parallel). Label the signs as follows: *Medical Work, Food Service, Legal Work, Sales, Administration, Business, Education, Data Processing,* and *Other.*

Teaching Materials

Text, pages 60-77

Terms to Know, To Review, To Do, and *To Think About*

Student Activity Guide

    A. *Environmental Influences*
    B. *Influence of Birth Order*
    C. *Family and Peer Influence*
    D. *Media Watch*

Teacher's Resource Guide/Binder

    Your Environment, reproducible master, 3-1
    Roots and Wings, reproducible master, 3-2
    Siblings, transparency master, 3-3
    Birth Order, transparency master, 3-4
    Chapter 3 Test

Teacher's Resource Binder

    Kwanzaa, color transparency, CT-3A
    Hanukkah, color transparency, CT-3B

Software for Contemporary Living
Chapter Review Game

Introductory Activities

1. To introduce the concept of various types of environment, ask students to respond to the following questions:
   My family environment is . . .
   My peer group influences my choice of . . .
   I study best when . . .
   Someday, I would like to become . . .
   Religion is . . .
   I think my community and world would be improved if . . .
2. *Your Environment*, reproducible master, 3-1. Have students complete the introductory activity and compare their results with other class members. Discuss their responses to the questions at the end of the activity. Also ask how the media influences decision making. Do people sometimes blame their environment for adversely influencing their decisions?

Strategies to Reteach, Reinforce, Enrich, and Extend Text Concepts

3. **RF** *Environmental Influences*, Activity A, SAG. Have students rank the environmental factors that influence their lives in the order of their importance. Then project how these will change in the next five years.
4. **ER** Ask students to write a paper describing the factors in their environment that have affected their personality development the most. Cite both positive and negative aspects of these factors.

Your Family

5. **EX** *Roots and Wings*, reproducible master, 3-2. Students are asked to list family traditions and customs. They are then to describe those traditions and customs they would like to continue or create to give their future children "wings."
6. **RT** *Kwanzaa*, color transparency, CT-3A, and *Hanukkah*, color transparency, CT-3B. Refer to these transparencies to illustrate spe-cial holiday traditions in a culturally diverse society. Students may wish to do further research on these and other holidays and report their findings to the class.
7. **ER** Have each student write a paper describing family customs and traditions and how they feel about them.
8. **ER** Have students research the history of families and write papers expressing their views on how today's family roles and functions have changed from those of families of the past. Predict how families may change in the future.
9. **EX** Ask students to list all of the roles they have in their families. Some students may have longer lists than others. Ask what factors contribute to increased role assignments, such as number of siblings, birth order, death of relatives, etc.
10. **EX** Write on the board: "Your son's your son 'till he takes a wife, but your daughter's your daughter all her life." Ask students their interpretation of the meaning of this adage and whether they agree with it. Why are daughters more likely to serve as the primary caretakers of elderly parents?
11. **RT** *Siblings*, transparency master, 3-3. Use this transparency to introduce a brief discussion of what siblings can mean to one another presently and throughout life.
12. **RF** Ask students to accept or reject this statement: "Sibling rivalry can be a good thing." Cite examples.
13. **EX** Ask each student to select a family-oriented situation comedy to view on television. Note the relationships within the family, citing examples of rivalry, siblings helping each other, sibling-to-sibling and parent-child interactions, and communication. Ask if the students feel these shows depict normal family interactions. Why or why not?
14. **RF** Discuss happenings in the local community that tend to strengthen family relationships (religious activities, recreational programs, school functions, etc.). Can family members become too involved in individual activities to the detriment of the entire family (e.g., activities that frequently keep family members from sharing mealtimes)?
15. **ER** Ask a psychologist to speak to your class on the subject of family relationships and sibling interactions in families. Ask students to prepare questions to use in the discussion.

16. **RT** *Birth Order,* transparency master, 3-4. Use this transparency to introduce a brief overview of traits characteristic of oldest, middle, and youngest siblings. Explain that these traits are only tendencies and should not necessarily be viewed as preordaining the person to any certain set of personality characteristics.

17. **RF** *Influence of Birth Order,* Activity B, SAG. Students are asked to discuss sibling relationships in families and to indicate characteristics that are apparent in oldest, middle, and youngest children.

Your Peers

18. **RF** *Family and Peer Influence,* Activity C, SAG. Given a list of activities that can be shared, ask students if they would rather share the activities with their parents or peers. Use as a basis for class discussion.

19. **EX** Ask several students from your school to serve on a panel to discuss the topic, "The Influence of Peers–Good or Bad?" Ask a counselor to be moderator. Solicit questions from students.

20. **ER** Bring in examples of news stories indicating the positive influence of peers, such as peer drug counseling, etc. In addition, find examples of negative peer influence (drug involvement because of peers, etc.). Use as a basis for class discussion.

Your Education

21. **ER** To help students focus on getting the most from their educational environment, ask an educational specialist or a school guidance counselor to address the class on the topic, "Positive Study Skills."

22. **EX** Ask students to choose a culture different from their own and to research and write a brief report on educational methods in this culture.

23. **ER** To help students understand the importance of the educational environment for individuals, ask an educational specialist to address the class on the topic, "Common Learning Disabilities and How to Overcome Them." Allow time for questions and answers.

24. **EX** As part of a class discussion on educational environments, list on the board the basic factors that provide for a positive learning environment (e.g., a trusting environment free from threat of ridicule; an environment that provides freedom to make mistakes as part of learning; freedom to ask even "dumb" questions; and an atmosphere conducive to thought and focused discussion). Solicit student contributions on particular ways they believe they learn best (e.g., reading, discussion, research projects, etc.).

25. **EX** Ask students to write a paragraph describing their ideal educational environment–one in which the learning process is both efficient and enjoyable. Ask them to address various learning modalities (self-paced learning, lecture, discussion, small group work, cooperative learning, independent research) and to discuss which they like best and why.

Your Occupation

26. **EX** Discuss how a person's work identity can influence his or her personality. Identify some careers and list characteristics that people need to succeed in those careers.

27. **EX** A question often asked when you meet someone new is, "What kind of work do you do?" Have students discuss ways in which education and career decisions affect a person's identity and lifestyle.

28. **EX** Have students write a few paragraphs describing a career they might like and the education they would need for that career. Also have them explain how the career would influence their environment.

Your Religion

29. **RF** Religious freedom is one of the basic freedoms we enjoy in this country. Discuss how this applies to education, to taxation, and to politics. Ask students if they feel this basic freedom is being preserved.

30. **ER** Ask leaders of various religions to come to class to discuss religious subjects of interest to class members. Prepare a list of questions about trends in the growth or decline of religion in the lives of individuals and families.

Your Community and World

31. **EX** List the following categories across the top of the board: communications; transportation; entertainment; shopping and banking; household equipment; health and fitness; safety and security. Ask students to cite examples of new technology in each category. Then discuss the positive as well as negative impacts that each of these technologies has had on families.
32. **ER** Have students research how the nation's economy affects us. Find news stories dealing with events in the economy and post them on a bulletin board. Discuss.
33. **RF** Discuss the effects of affluence and recession on individuals and families.
34. **ER** Collect advertisements that are aimed specifically at the teenage market. Ask students if these advertisements do, in fact, influence their spending. Will their current buying habits influence future spending?
35. **RF** Ask students how laws act as a factor of environment. Consider laws related to driving, drinking, working, credit, etc. Do laws today give young people more privileges and responsibilities than in the past?
36. **EX** *Media Watch,* Activity D, SAG. Use this activity to raise students' awareness of values transmitted through the media. Ask them to appraise these values critically. Which values are helpful in building strong families? Which are destructive?

Answer Key for Chapter 3

Text
To Review, page 76.

1. The family.
2. Our society is made up of families representing many different cultures. Successive generations incorporate and blend these cultural characteristics into their current way of life.
3. (Describe three characteristics for each age position: Student response. See pages 66-67 of the text.)
4. The family will continue to be a strong influence, but peers will also emerge as an impor-

tant force. As family ties grow weaker, peer influence becomes stronger.
5. An appreciation for learning will equip you to seek information to help you solve problems throughout life.
6. As students perform their jobs, they can evaluate their assets and their liabilities. Their later career choices will probably reflect this self-knowledge.
7. Psychologically secure, able to handle crises, trusting, tolerant, humble.
8. The teen market is one of the most lucrative in the economy. Teens are establishing new buying habits, and businesses want teens to establish the habit of buying their products.
9. Teens can learn how to manage money wisely, how to adapt to changing economic conditions, and how to pull together as a family through difficult times.
10. (Name one negative and one positive influence: Student response. See pages 73-74 of the text.)

Student Activity Guide
Activity B, Influence of Birth Order.

1. Youngest.	9. Youngest.
2. Oldest.	10. Oldest.
3. Oldest.	11. Middle.
4. Middle.	12. Oldest.
5. Oldest.	13. Youngest.
6. Youngest.	14. Oldest.
7. Youngest.	15. Youngest.
8. Middle.	16. Middle.

Teacher's Resource Guide
Chapter 3 Test

1. C	11. F	21. D
2. G	12. T	22. D
3. D	13. T	23. A
4. B	14. F	24. C
5. A	15. T	25. B
6. J	16. T	26. D
7. K	17. F	27. D
8. F	18. F	28. A
9. E	19. T	29. B
10. H	20. F	30. A

31. (Student response.)
32. (Student response.)
33. (Student response.)

Your Environment

Name _______________________________________ **Date** _______________ **Period** _______________

There are many factors in your environment that influence your decisions. Some of these factors are listed across the top of the following chart. Decisions teens often have to make are listed in the left column. For each decision, rank the influence of the various environmental factors from 1 to 6, with 1 being the most influential. Total each column. Then answer the questions below.

Decisions	Peer Group	Boy/Girl Friend	Family	School/ Religion	Other Adults	Media
Choice of clothes						
Hair style						
Food preferences						
Choice of friends						
Dates						
Curfew						
Movies						
Reading material						
Part-time work						
Career goals						
College plans						
Sports and recreation						
Leisure activities						
Standards of behavior						
Other:						
Totals						

1. Which environmental factor seems to influence your decisions the most (received lowest total)?

   ____

2. Which environmental factor influences your decisions the least (received the highest total)?

   ____

3. Which environmental factors will become more influential as you get older? Explain your answer.

   ____

   ____

4. Which environmental factors will be less likely to influence your decisions as you get older? Explain your answer. ____

   ____

   ____

Roots and Wings

Name _______________________________________ **Date** _______________ **Period** _______________

Cultural traditions and customs provide "roots" that express your family's heritage. These traditions and customs were meaningful in the lives of your ancestors, and continue to be important to you and your parents. They may become meaningful in the lives of your future children, providing them with "wings." Describe below those family traditions and customs that have served as "roots" for your family. In the second column, indicate the "roots" you would like to become "wings" for your future children.

"Roots" **Present family traditions and customs:**	"Wings" **Traditions and customs you would like to continue, or new "roots" you would like to create for your future children:**
Family heirlooms:	
Holiday customs:	
Stories of ancestors:	
Traditional foods:	
Family vacations:	
Family photo albums:	
Family genealogy:	
Religious traditions:	

Siblings

Siblings offer:

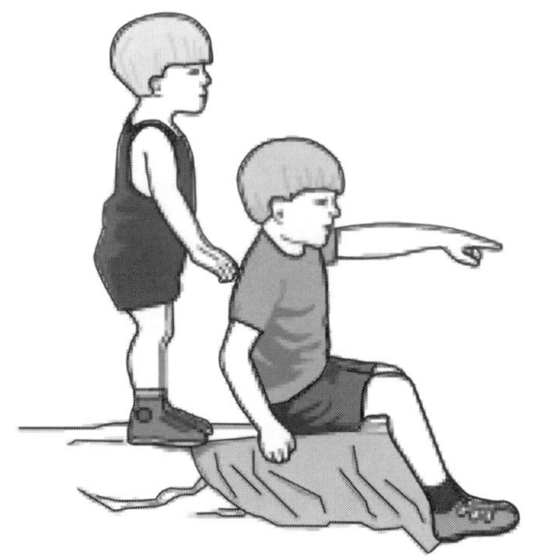

Birth Order

Oldest Child

* Responsible
* Motivated to achieve
* Independent

Middle Child

* Resilient
* Peacemaker
* May feel "overshadowed"

Youngest Child

* Gets a lot of attention
* May be pampered
* May have difficulty becoming independent

Your Environment

Chapter 3 Test

Matching: Match the following terms and identifying phrases.

_______ 1. This child may receive a lot of attention but also tends to receive more bossing from family members.

_______ 2. The total social environment of a people or group.

_______ 3. People who make final decisions.

_______ 4. Sense of competition with brothers or sisters.

_______ 5. This child usually grows up rapidly and tends to have more responsibilities than other children.

_______ 6. People who are about your own age.

_______ 7. Age of each child in relationship to the other children in a family.

_______ 8. This child does not have the advantage of individual attention from parents and has the advantage of being the youngest child for only a limited time.

_______ 9. A socially expected behavior pattern.

_______ 10. Brothers or sisters.

A. oldest child
B. sibling rivalry
C. youngest child
D. authority figures
E. role
F. middle child
G. culture
H. siblings
I. peer pressure
J. peer group
K. birth order

True/False: Circle *T* if the statement is true or *F* if the statement is false.

T F 11. The United States is not a culturally diverse country.

T F 12. Each member of a family fulfills certain roles.

T F 13. Middle children often become particularly good at dealing with the ups and downs of human relationships.

T F 14. Relationships with peers tend to be unimportant during adolescence.

T F 15. Almost everyone is accountable to someone.

T F 16. Freedom of religious choice is a basic right in the United States.

T F 17. True friends will admire you less if you stick to your convictions.

T F 18. A person's career has no influence on his or her salary or place of residence.

T F 19. Technological advances such as satellite TV have brought about a new awareness of global conditions.

T F 20. Each generation faces the same economic and environmental conditions as each of the generations that comes after it.

(Continued)

Name ____

Multiple Choice: Select the best response. Write the letter in the space provided.

_____ 21. For most people, the most influential factor affecting personality development is their _____.
  A. peers
  B. community
  C. school
  D. family

_____ 22. Which of the following is a basic function of families in our society?
  A. To provide physical care for children.
  B. To nurture the personality growth of children.
  C. To meet the emotional needs of all members.
  D. All of the above.

_____ 23. Children can acquire a healthy level of self-esteem _____.
  A. by being raised in a positive, nurturing environment where they feel loved and valued
  B. by being praised even if they are misbehaving
  C. if they are never disciplined
  D. by learning that others are unworthy of love and trust

_____ 24. Discipline in the family should be administered _____.
  A. to boys but not to girls
  B. in an abusive manner
  C. in a loving, consistent, and fair manner
  D. All of the above.

_____ 25. A culturally diverse society is made up _____.
  A. of families who have nothing in common with one another
  B. of families representing the influence of many different cultures
  C. only of families whose ancestors originated in Northern Europe
  D. only of families whose ancestors originated in Africa

_____ 26. A person's siblings can _____.
  A. offer companionship
  B. help a person develop an understanding of sharing and compromise
  C. provide a source of emotional support throughout life
  D. All of the above.

_____ 27. The way you interact with other family members _____.
  A. has no effect on their happiness
  B. has no effect on their personality development
  C. has no effect on your personality development
  D. affects their personality development as well as your own

_____ 28. In general, adolescents tend to _____.
  A. be especially vulnerable to peer pressure
  B. be unaffected by peer pressure
  C. make decisions independent of family and friends
  D. need no one

_____ 29. Mature spending behavior emphasizes _____.
  A. spending the bulk of your earnings on soft drinks and CD players
  B. saving for a rainy day as well as spending for necessities and recreation
  C. being easily swayed by advertisements
  D. refusal to adapt to changing economic conditions

(Continued)

 Contemporary Living Teacher's Resources

_______ 30. Computers are most likely to help people _______.
    A.   gather and exchange information
    B.   become more physically fit
    C.   develop trust, tolerance, and humility through the practice of a religious faith
    D.   learn to live with scarcity

Essay Questions: Provide complete responses to the following questions or statements.

31. Select the two most influential factors in your environment and explain how they affect your personality development.

32. Summarize possible positive and negative effects of peer influence during adolescence.

33. Why will an understanding of various cultures be useful to you when you enter the workforce?

Chapter 4
Your Response to Your Environment

Objectives

After studying this chapter, students will be able to
- explain the theories of Erikson, Havighurst, Maslow, and Kohlberg concerning personal development.
- describe the use of defense mechanisms in responding to their environment.
- explain various types of personal response patterns.

Bulletin Boards

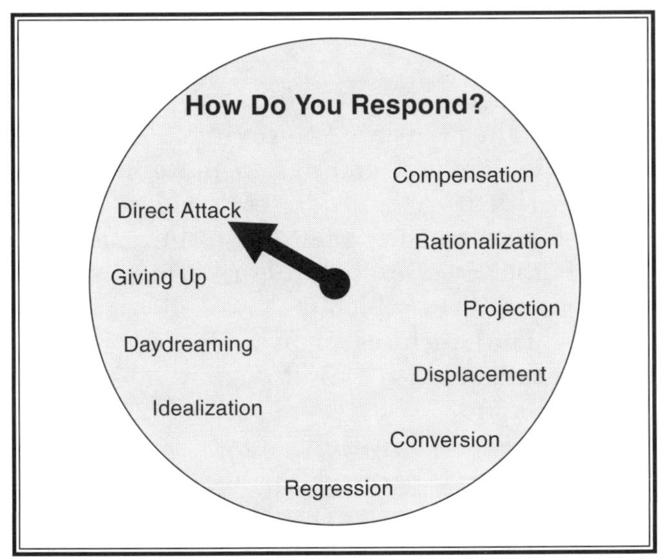

I. Title: "How Do You Respond?"

Draw a large circle and place the defense mechanisms so that they radiate from the center. Cut an arrow out of stiff cardboard and attach the blunt end to the center of the circle using a large brass brad. The pointed end can then be moved around the circle as the various defense mechanisms are discussed in class.

II. Title: "What Do You Tell Yourself?"

Draw a hand mirror and mount aluminum foil in the center to simulate the mirror's surface. Cut out a profile of a person looking into the mirror. In bubbles depicting statements the person might be making, post positive and negative self-talk such as, "I know I can't," "I know I can!" "I'm going to make it," "I might as well give up now," etc.

Teaching Materials

Text, pages 78-107

Terms to Know, To Review, To Do, and *To Think About*

Student Activity Guide
- A. *Erikson's Stages of Human Development*
- B. *Havighurst's Developmental Tasks*
- C. *Maslow's Theory of Human Needs*
- D. *Defense Mechanisms*
- E. *Depression*
- F. *Attitudes*

Teacher's Resource Guide/Binder

The Developmental Tasks of Teens, transparency master, 4-1

Defense Mechanisms—A Case Study, reproducible master, 4-2

How Do You Handle Anger in Your Daily Life? reproducible master, 4-3

How Do You Talk to Yourself? transparency master, 4-4

Chapter 4 Test

Teacher's Resource Binder

Maslow's Theory of Human Needs, color transparency, CT-4A

A Positive Attitude Wins Every Time! color transparency, CT-4B

Software for Contemporary Living

Chapter Review Game

Introductory Activities

1. Ask students what they think the title of this chapter means. How do people respond to their environment? What might influence how a person responds to his or her environment? Do these response patterns change as people grow and mature?
2. Ask students to indicate the different ways people respond in different environments by citing several instances, such as people in shopping malls; "cruising" activities of teens.

Strategies to Reteach, Reinforce, Enrich, and Extend Text Concepts

How You Respond to Your Environment

3. **RF** *Erikson's Stages of Human Development,* Activity A, SAG. Students are asked to complete a chart giving the approximate age of each stage and the name of each stage. They are to then describe the expected behavior changes that should occur at each stage in the development of a healthy personality.
4. **EX** Ask each student to choose one of Erikson's stages of human development and write a three-page paper about its influence on personality. Indicate the sources of information used.
5. **RF** *The Developmental Tasks of Teens,* transparency master, 4-1. Use this master to present and discuss the developmental tasks of teens.
6. **EX** *Havighurst's Developmental Tasks,* Activity B, SAG. Students are asked to describe each of the tasks and to give two examples of behaviors that might indicate

successful achievement of each developmental task.

7. **RF** *Maslow's Theory of Human Needs,* color transparency, CT-4A. Use this transparency to present and discuss Maslow's theory. Discuss how the lower levels of needs must be at least partially fulfilled before higher-level needs can be met.
8. **RF** *Maslow's Theory of Human Needs,* Activity C, SAG. Students will complete a chart using Maslow's theory to name human needs in order of their priority and to describe each level of need.
9. **EX** Have students write a paper indicating how they feel they are progressing toward reaching the need for self-actualization. Ask them to cite strengths in their personalities that are helping them and weaknesses that are hindering them. Examine how personal relationships have helped them progress toward self-actualization.
10. **EX** Ask students to write a paper on the moral and ethical climate of our society, citing examples of persons who respect human rights and democratic principles. Ask students to indicate if they feel our society needs to improve in this area and, if so, how these improvements could be made.

Defense Mechanisms

11. **RF** *Defense Mechanisms,* Activity D, SAG. Students will complete a crossword puzzle using terms related to defense mechanisms.
12. **RF** *Defense Mechanisms–A Case Study,* reproducible master, 4-2. Ask students to read the episode involving Renee and Daniel. Several endings to the episode are described. Ask students to identify the defense mechanisms used and indicate whether they are helpful or harmful in coping with the problem.
13. **RF** Find pictures of people using defense mechanisms. Label and display on the bulletin board.
14. **RF** Discuss how direct attack can be both a helpful and harmful method of solving a problem. Give examples.
15. **EX** Discuss the feature article on page 98 of the text, asking how rules protect freedoms and provide security and protection. Compare with instances where there are no boundaries, no structure, and no rules. Cite

sports games where there are specific boundaries, structure, and rules.

Personal Response Patterns

16. **RF** *How Do You Handle Anger in Your Daily Life?* reproducible master, 4-3. (Note: This is the same chart as found on page 99 of the text.) Ask students to indicate how they handle anger and then answer the questions at the end of the activity. Ask class members to share what they have learned about anger.

17. **RF** Ask students to make a list of verbal and physical expressions they have exhibited when they were angry. Then have them project these expressions to future stages in their lives as career persons, married persons, and parents. Decide if these expressions are constructive now, and if they will be in the future.

18. **RF** Ask students to accept or reject the statement, "Getting mad is quite OK." Discuss the reasons why expressions of anger may be helpful. Consider also that there are consequences when anger is repressed, such as psychosomatic disorders (headaches, for example). Repressed anger can also suddenly explode into violence. Discuss episodes in the news when anger is possibly the basis of violent reactions.

19. **RF** Have the class make a list of the positive effects of fear in childhood, adolescence, young adulthood, middle age, and old age. Cite instances when fear gave added strength to a person or saved a person from a harmful situation.

20. **RF** Cite the negative effects of fear. Recall examples of real life or fictional stories or movies where fear produced harmful personalities.

21. **EX** Exaggerated fears are called phobias. Discuss instances when phobias caused persons to have difficulty with everyday living.

22. **RF** *Depression*, Activity E, SAG. Students are to read the statements concerning depression in this activity in order to identify their feelings about depression. Discuss responses in class.

23. **RF** Discuss the statement, "It is important that you give yourself permission to have low feelings." Ask students what they do when they are feeling low.

24. **RF** Form small groups and ask students to answer these questions: "If I was very depressed, what would I like my family and friends to do to help me? What would I do to help myself?"

25. **RF** The following is a list of resources available for teens who become depressed. Ask students to describe how the resource can be used and how it can benefit the young person.
    - Parent or other family member.
    - Close friend.
    - Counselor or therapist.
    - Religious leader.
    - Personal philosophy of life.

26. **ER** Have students research the incidence of depression among children and teens. Is it more common today than in previous generations? Why or why not?

27. **EX** *Attitudes*, Activity F, SAG. The situations depicted in this activity reveal typical negative attitudes. Students are to explain how these same teens might respond in each situation if they had more positive attitudes.

28. **RT** Discuss how people form and express their attitudes.

29. **RF** *A Positive Attitude Wins Every Time!* color transparency, CT-4B. Use this transparency to discuss the impact a positive attitude can have on a person's life. Ask students to identify characteristics of persons who display positive attitudes. These might include such characteristics as cooperation, optimism, and perseverence. Ask what areas of life a positive attitude can impact, i.e., family relationships, friendships, school, and work. Then discuss how it might influence each of these areas, such as job promotions.

30. **EX** *How Do You Talk to Yourself?* transparency master, 4-4. Ask students to think about the different messages they give themselves, from negative to positive, and to cite messages they have heard or used themselves. Have students consider the following statement: "Everything you tell yourself about yourself becomes a powerful directive for your subconscious mind, programming you to become the person you describe." Ask students to think about something they really want to do, and formulate a positive self-talk statement. Write it down in a prominent spot in the student's notebook. Ask students if they have ever defeated themselves with negative attitude self-talk messages.

31. **RF** Have the class make a list of prejudices that are common in our society. Discuss how these might have been formed and how they might be changed. (Refer to steps for overcoming prejudices listed on pages 102-103 of text.)

32. **RF** Discuss how the various media, such as television, movies, and music, can promote prejudices that may create problems in society. During election years, how do political candidates attempt to "prejudice" the voting public through various campaign strategies?

33. **RF** List the following words on the board and ask students to respond with a statement that indicates a stereotype, such as, "All teens are irresponsible." List the following: older persons, men, women, feminist, blue-collar worker, business executive, teachers, athletes. Discuss how stereotyping groups of people can be harmful.

34. **ER** Ask students to write a short paper stating their views concerning heredity, environment, and your response to environment. Ask them to state which of the three contributes the most to personality development. Ask students to compare this paper with the paper they wrote after studying Chapter 1. Are there changes in their views? Read several of the papers in class.

Answer Key for Chapter 4

Text
To Review, pages 105-106.

1. Initiative: A. Trust: B. Identity: G. Autonomy: E. Intimacy: D. Accomplishment: C. Generativity: H. Integrity: F.

2. Success in each task leads to happiness and success in other developmental tasks they will perform later in life. Failure leads to unhappiness, disapproval by society, and difficulty with later developmental tasks.

3. physical

4. B

5. What the consequences (punishment or rewards) will be.

6. false

7. A. direct attack B. compensation
   C. rationalization D. displacement
   E. regression F. daydreaming
   G. idealization H. conversion
   I. Giving up J. Projection

8. (Student response.)

9. (Student response.)

10. attitude

11. False or insufficient information.

12. (Student response.)

Student Activity Guide

Activity A, Erikson's Stages of Human Development.

Stage One: Infancy. Trust versus mistrust. Basic sense of trust is established; children develop confidence and trust in themselves, in other people, and in their environment; they become secure and optimistic.

Stage Two: Ages 1-4. Autonomy versus shame and doubt. Children begin to experience autonomy or the freedom of self-direction; assert themselves; begin to make decisions; learn social lessons.

Stage Three: Ages 4-5. Initiative versus guilt. Children develop imagination and begin to do things on their own; learn to cooperate, lead, and follow.

Stage Four: Ages 6-12. Accomplishment and industry versus inferiority. Children learn that work is worthwhile and meaningful; learn self-discipline and more about getting along with peers.

Stage Five: Adolescence. Identity versus identity confusion. Establish a sense of identity–knowing who you are and what your roles are in society.

Stage Six: Young adulthood. Intimacy versus isolation. Young adults establish a sense of intimacy, accepting themselves as worthwhile persons and giving of themselves to others.

Stage Seven: Adulthood. Generativity versus self-absorption. Adults begin to be concerned with others beyond their immediate families and especially with future generations.

Stage Eight: Adulthood. Integrity versus despair. Adults develop a sense of integrity–a state of being complete; the person is satisfied with his or her life.

Activity B, Havighurst's Developmental Tasks.

Task One: To achieve new and more mature relations with peers of both sexes.

Task Two: To adopt socially approved masculine or feminine adult roles.

Task Three: To accept your physical self and to use your body effectively.

Task Four: To achieve emotional independence.

Task Five: To develop your personal attitude toward marriage and family living.

Contemporary Living Teacher's Resources

Task Six: To select and prepare for an occupation.

Task Seven: To acquire a set of standards as a guide to behavior.

Task Eight: To accept and adopt socially responsible behavior. (Students should give two examples of behaviors that indicate successful achievement of each task.)

Activity C, Maslow's Theory of Human Needs.

Needs in order of priority (from base of chart upward): Physical; Safety and security; Love and acceptance; Esteem; Self-actualization. (For a description of each level of need, see pages 90-93 of text.)

Activity D, Defense Mechanisms.

<table>
<tr><td></td><td></td><td></td><td></td><td></td><td></td><td></td><td></td><td></td><td></td><td></td><td></td><td></td><td></td><td></td><td></td><td>[1]C</td><td></td></tr>
<tr><td></td><td></td><td></td><td></td><td></td><td></td><td></td><td></td><td>[2]P</td><td>[3]R</td><td>O</td><td>J</td><td>E</td><td>[4]C</td><td>T</td><td>I</td><td>O</td><td>N</td></tr>
<tr><td></td><td></td><td></td><td></td><td></td><td></td><td></td><td></td><td></td><td>E</td><td></td><td></td><td></td><td>O</td><td></td><td></td><td>M</td><td></td></tr>
<tr><td></td><td></td><td></td><td></td><td></td><td></td><td></td><td></td><td></td><td>G</td><td></td><td></td><td></td><td>N</td><td></td><td></td><td>P</td><td></td></tr>
<tr><td></td><td></td><td></td><td></td><td></td><td>[5]R</td><td></td><td></td><td></td><td>R</td><td></td><td></td><td></td><td>V</td><td></td><td></td><td>E</td><td></td></tr>
<tr><td>[6]D</td><td>I</td><td>S</td><td>P</td><td>L</td><td>A</td><td>C</td><td>E</td><td>M</td><td>E</td><td>N</td><td>T</td><td></td><td>E</td><td></td><td></td><td>N</td><td></td></tr>
<tr><td>A</td><td></td><td></td><td></td><td></td><td>T</td><td></td><td></td><td></td><td>S</td><td></td><td></td><td></td><td>R</td><td></td><td></td><td>S</td><td></td></tr>
<tr><td>Y</td><td></td><td></td><td></td><td></td><td>I</td><td></td><td></td><td></td><td>S</td><td></td><td></td><td></td><td>S</td><td></td><td></td><td>A</td><td></td></tr>
<tr><td>D</td><td></td><td></td><td></td><td></td><td>O</td><td></td><td></td><td></td><td>I</td><td></td><td></td><td></td><td>I</td><td></td><td></td><td>T</td><td></td></tr>
<tr><td>R</td><td></td><td></td><td></td><td></td><td>N</td><td></td><td></td><td></td><td>O</td><td></td><td></td><td></td><td>O</td><td></td><td></td><td>I</td><td></td></tr>
<tr><td>E</td><td></td><td></td><td></td><td></td><td>A</td><td></td><td></td><td></td><td>N</td><td></td><td></td><td></td><td>N</td><td></td><td></td><td>O</td><td></td></tr>
<tr><td>A</td><td></td><td>[7]G</td><td></td><td></td><td>L</td><td></td><td></td><td></td><td></td><td></td><td></td><td></td><td></td><td></td><td></td><td>N</td><td></td></tr>
<tr><td>M</td><td></td><td>I</td><td></td><td>[8]D</td><td>I</td><td>R</td><td>E</td><td>C</td><td>T</td><td>A</td><td>T</td><td>T</td><td>A</td><td>C</td><td>K</td><td></td><td></td></tr>
<tr><td>I</td><td></td><td>V</td><td></td><td></td><td>Z</td><td></td><td></td><td></td><td></td><td></td><td></td><td></td><td></td><td></td><td></td><td></td><td></td></tr>
<tr><td>N</td><td></td><td>[9]I</td><td>D</td><td>E</td><td>A</td><td>L</td><td>I</td><td>Z</td><td>A</td><td>T</td><td>I</td><td>O</td><td>N</td><td></td><td></td><td></td><td></td></tr>
<tr><td>G</td><td></td><td>N</td><td></td><td></td><td>T</td><td></td><td></td><td></td><td></td><td></td><td></td><td></td><td></td><td></td><td></td><td></td><td></td></tr>
<tr><td></td><td></td><td>G</td><td></td><td></td><td>I</td><td></td><td></td><td></td><td></td><td></td><td></td><td></td><td></td><td></td><td></td><td></td><td></td></tr>
<tr><td></td><td></td><td>U</td><td></td><td></td><td>O</td><td></td><td></td><td></td><td></td><td></td><td></td><td></td><td></td><td></td><td></td><td></td><td></td></tr>
<tr><td></td><td></td><td>P</td><td></td><td></td><td>N</td><td></td><td></td><td></td><td></td><td></td><td></td><td></td><td></td><td></td><td></td><td></td><td></td></tr>
</table>

Teacher's Resource Guide

Defense Mechanisms—A Case Study, reproducible master, 4-2.

1. Regression
2. Projection
3. Conversion
4. Idealization
5. Giving up
6. Rationalization
7. Daydreaming

Chapter 4 Test

1. I	11. T	21. C
2. B	12. F	22. D
3. H	13. F	23. D
4. A	14. T	24. B
5. E	15. F	25. B
6. C	16. T	26. D
7. J	17. F	27. A
8. F	18. T	28. C
9. G	19. F	29. C
10. D	20. T	30. D

31. (Student response.)
32. (Student response.)
33. Fear, guilt, frustration, or feelings of inferiority are the basis for some prejudices. Others result from attitudes expressed by family members, television shows, and peers. Sometimes personal experiences can create prejudices. To change prejudices, people need to recognize their prejudices, refrain from saying things that are not based on facts, learn more about the subjects of their prejudices, be aware of the prejudices of other people, and be cautious of statements regarding common areas of strong prejudices.
34. (Student response for one example of each type of stereotype.)

The Developmental Tasks of Teens

Task One:

To develop mature relations with peers of both sexes.

Task Two:

To adopt a socially approved sex role.

Task Three:

To accept your physical self as it is, and to use your body effectively.

Task Four:

To become emotionally independent from parents and other adults.

Task Five:

To prepare for marriage and family life.

Task Six:

To select and prepare for an occupation.

Task Seven:

To acquire a set of standards as a guide to behavior.

Task Eight:

To accept and adopt socially responsible behavior.

Defense Mechanisms–A Case Study

Name _______________________________ **Date** _____________ **Period** _____________

Read the following episode involving Renee and Daniel.

> Renee and Daniel had been dating all during their senior year. Renee had not even looked at another boy. She had not even gone out many times with girlfriends, because she wanted to devote her time to Daniel. Now he suddenly announced that he wanted to date other girls, and not go out with Renee any longer. He said, "I think we both need to see other people, but we'll still be friends."
>
> Renee was mad. The senior prom was only one month away and she had assumed she would be going with Daniel. She was hurt, angry, and upset. She didn't know what to do.

Renee could choose to respond to this event in her environment in many ways. Several possibilities are described below. See if you can identify a defense mechanism she has used in each response. Then circle the word to indicate whether the response would be either a *healthy* or *unhealthy* way of coping with the problem. Explain your answer.

1. Renee went home, locked herself in her room, pounded her pillow, and had a good cry.
   Defense mechanism: ____

   Healthy or unhealthy: ____

   ____

   ____

   ____

2. Renee called Melissa and told her she had stolen Daniel away from her, and blamed Melissa for making her feel so bad.
   Defense mechanism: ____

   Healthy or unhealthy: ____

   ____

   ____

   ____

   ____

3. During her last period class, Renee had to ask her teacher for a permit to go to the nurse. She had a splitting headache.
   Defense mechanism: ____

   Healthy or unhealthy: ____

   ____

   ____

   ____

   ____

(Continued)

Name ____

4. Renee told herself, "Daniel was nobody. He knew he wasn't good enough for me. That's why he didn't want to go out with me anymore."
   Defense mechanism: ____

   Healthy or unhealthy: ____

   ____

   ____

   ____

5. Renee's friends worried about her because she suddenly seemed to be afraid to try anything. She was fearful of going out with anyone else, and she started staying in her room for long periods of time.
   Defense mechanism: ____

   Healthy or unhealthy: ____

   ____

   ____

   ____

   ____

   ____

6. Renee told everyone she was glad she and Daniel had broken up. They really didn't like doing the same things anyway.
   Defense mechanism: ____

   Healthy or unhealthy: ____

   ____

   ____

   ____

   ____

7. Renee started fantasizing that she met this really spectacular guy. She didn't really care what happened to Daniel now because she believed she would meet someone even better.
   Defense mechanism: ____

   Helpful or harmful: ____

   Healthy or unhealthy: ____

   ____

   ____

   ____

8. What would you advise Renee to do that would be a healthy response to the breakup?

   ____

   ____

   ____

   ____

How Do You Handle Anger in Your Daily Life?

Name ___________________________ **Date** ___________ **Period** ___________

Read each of the following reactions to anger. Place a check in the blank that indicates how often the statement describes your response to anger. Then answer the questions that follow.

	USUALLY	SOMETIMES	NEVER
When you are frustrated, do you . . .			
go for a walk?	_______	_______	_______
listen to music?	_______	_______	_______
go somewhere to be alone?	_______	_______	_______
talk to a good friend?	_______	_______	_______
* throw things or hit things?	_______	_______	_______
When you have a disagreement with your family, do you . . .			
find information to back up your argument?	_______	_______	_______
ask family members to discuss the problem calmly?	_______	_______	_______
ask a third party to discuss the problem with you?	_______	_______	_______
#refuse to talk to anyone?	_______	_______	_______
#argue loudly with family members?	_______	_______	_______
* throw things or hit a family member?	_______	_______	_______
When you have a disagreement with a friend, do you . . .			
find information to back up your argument?	_______	_______	_______
discuss the problem calmly with the friend?	_______	_______	_______
arrange another time to discuss the problem calmly?	_______	_______	_______
bring in a third party?	_______	_______	_______
#refuse to talk with anyone?	_______	_______	_______
#argue loudly, shout, and insult your friend?	_______	_______	_______
* throw things, or physically abuse your friend?	_______	_______	_______

* Physical aggression
#Verbal aggression

(Continued)

Name _______________________________

1. Do your responses follow a pattern? Explain your answer. _______________________

    ____

    ____

    ____

2. Do you often respond with verbal aggression? _______________________________

    ____

    ____

3. Do you often respond with physical aggression? _____________________________

    ____

    ____

4. Are you satisfied with the ways you respond to anger? Explain your answer. _______

    ____

    ____

    ____

    ____

5. How could you improve your response to anger? _____________________________

    ____

    ____

    ____

    ____

    ____

    ____

    ____

(Continued)

How Do You Talk to Yourself?

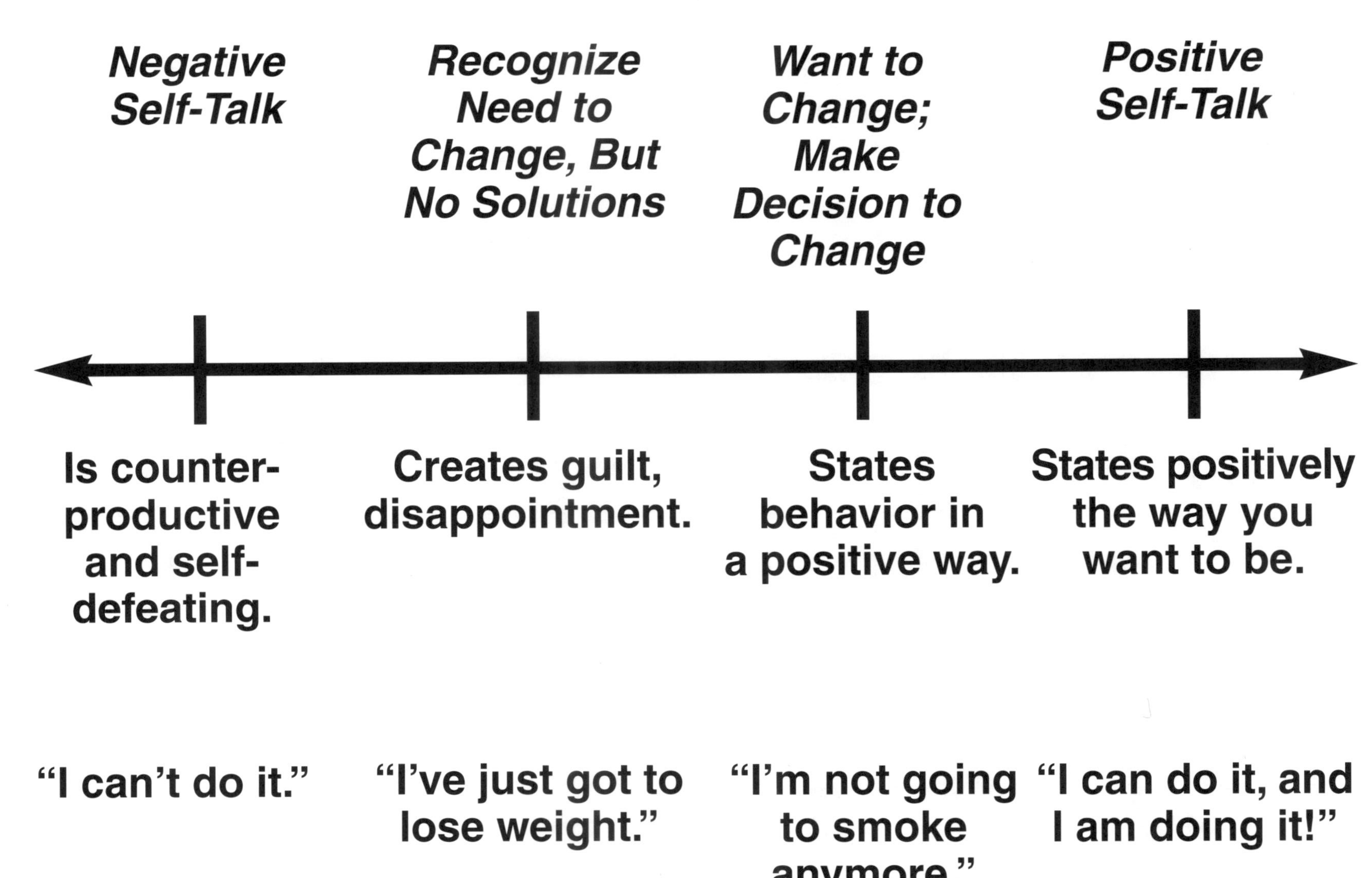

Your Response to Your Environment

Name _______________________________________

Date _________________________________ **Period** ___________ **Score** _____________

Chapter 4 Test

Matching: Match the following terms and identifying phrases.

		A. Direct attack
		B. Compensation
		C. Regression
		D. Rationalization
		E. Projection
		F. Daydreaming
		G. Idealization
		H. Displacement
		I. Conversion
		J. Giving up

______ 1. Transferring the energy of a desire you cannot express into a physical symptom or complaint.

______ 2. Using a substitute method to achieve a desired goal.

______ 3. Transferring an emotion connected with one person or thing to an unrelated person or thing.

______ 4. Recognizing the heart of a problem and striving to solve it.

______ 5. Blaming other people or things for your failures.

______ 6. Turning back to a less mature stage of development.

______ 7. Feeling discouraged and refusing to face any more situations in which failure may occur.

______ 8. Trying to accomplish in fantasy what you cannot accomplish in reality.

______ 9. Valuing something far beyond its real worth.

______ 10. Explaining weaknesses or failures y giving excuses that are socially acceptable but that hide the real reason for failure.

True/False: Circle *T* if the statement is true or *F* if the statement is false.

T F 11. Erikson's theory of personality development states that a person confronts certain crises that must be resolved at each of eight stages of life.

T F 12. Children who are not allowed to explore their world may have difficulty in establishing a sense of trust.

T F 13. According to Erikson, an important stage of development is establishing a sense of shame and doubt.

T F 14. Adolescents who are not able to establish stable roles for themselves become preoccupied with their identities in the eyes of others.

T F 15. Integrity means that adults learn to be concerned with others beyond their immediate families and also with future generations.

T F 16. According to Havighurst, adopting socially approved masculine or feminine roles is an important task for adolescents.

(Continued)

Contemporary Living Teacher's Resources

T F   17. According to Maslow's theory of human needs, safety and security have first priority.

T F   18. The first step in overcoming fear is to discover the cause of the fear.

T F   19. A prejudice is a feeling that causes a person to choose one type of behavior in place of another.

T F   20. If you believe a stereotype, you are likely to prejudge people before you ever know them.

Multiple Choice: Choose the best response. Write the letter in the space provided.

______   21. According to Kohlberg, beliefs about right and wrong behavior are known as ______.
   A. phobias
   B. attitudes
   C. morals
   D. stereotypes

______   22. A ______ is a belief that all members of a group share the same characteristics.
   A. defense mechanism
   B. scapegoat
   C. bigot
   D. stereotype

______   23. Children make moral decisions based on ______.
   A. rewards they might receive
   B. punishment they might receive
   C. consequences of their behavior
   D. All of the above.

______   24. When you transfer the energy of a desire you cannot express into a physical symptom or complaint, you are using the defense mechanism of______.
   A. displacement
   B. conversion
   C. regression
   D. idealization

______   25. Which of the following statements is true?
   A. Repressing anger helps people overcome their angry feelings.
   B. Anger is a normal human reaction to a stressful situation.
   C. Expressions of anger are always destructive.
   D. All of the above.

______   26. Which of the following statements is true?
   A. Fear can give people the added strength they need in dangerous situations.
   B. Fear can be harmful when it prevents people from facing their problems.
   C. Exaggerated fears are called phobias.
   D. All of the above.

______   27. Defense mechanisms are ______.
   A. usually automatic
   B. completely voluntary
   C. used with total awareness
   D. healthy ways of dealing with problems.

(Continued)

_______   28. Only women can be family and consumer sciences teachers is an example
of _____ stereotype.
A. a racial
B. a gender
C. an occupational
D. a socio-economic

_______   29. Attitudes based on false or insufficient information are known as _____.
A. scapegoats
B. ambiverts
C. prejudices
D. values

_______   30. A feeling or mental position about something is called _____.
A. a bigot
B. a defense mechanism
C. a conversion
D. an attitude

Essay Questions: Provide complete responses to the following questions or statements.

31. Give a brief description of Kohlberg's theory of moral development.

32. Describe a situation in which you or someone you know used a defense mechanism to deal with an anxiety-producing event or threat. Identify the defense mechanism used.

33. How do people acquire prejudices? How can people change the prejudices they have?

34. Give an example of each of the following:

A.   A gender stereotype.
B.   An age stereotype.
C.   An occupational stereotype.

Part 2
The Decisions You Face

Chapter 5 ■ ■ ■ ■ ■ ■ ■ ■ ■ ■ ■ ■ ■ ■ ■ ■ ■ ■
It's Your Decision

Objectives

After studying this chapter, students will be able to

- define values and explain how they influence decisions.
- give examples of short-term and long-term goals.
- plot goals based on the stages of an individual's life cycle using a time/life line.
- identify types of human and nonhuman resources.
- establish standards for measuring goal achievement.
- explain the steps in the decision-making process.
- describe the four steps in the management process.

Bulletin Boards

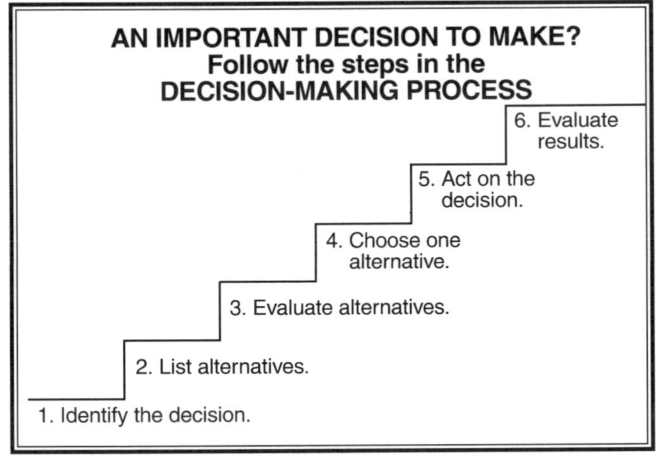

I. Title: "An Important Decision to Make?"

Use colored construction paper to create stair steps. List the six steps in the decision-making process on the stairs.

II. Title: "How Do Values Translate into Goals?"

Label two columns on the bulletin board: *Values* and *Goals*. Under the first column, list various values. Under the second column, list a goal that might relate to each value. Draw an arrow from each value to its corresponding goal. Ask students to add other possible values and goals to the lists.

Teaching Materials

Text, pages 110-130

Terms to Know, To Review, To Do, and *To Think About*

Student Activity Guide

    A. *Personal Values*

    B. *Understanding Your Values*

    C. *How Values Influence Decisions*

    D. *Your Time/Life Line*

    E. *Managing Time*

    F. *Using the Decision-Making Process*

Teacher's Resource Guide/Binder

Forces that Influence Values, transparency master, 5-1

Understanding Goals, reproducible master, 5-2

Ways to Make a Decision, reproducible master, 5-3

The Decision-Making Process, transparency master, 5-4

Case Studies for Decision Making, reproducible master, 5-5

The Management Process, transparency master, 5-6

Chapter 5 Test

Teacher's Resource Binder

Values: The Keys to "Unlock" Decisions, color transparency, CT-5

Software for Contemporary Living

Chapter Review Game

Introductory Activities

1. Introduce the topic of decision making to your class using this decision story chain. Explain to the students that events in their lives often initiate the need for making decisions that will affect them as individuals, and which will influence their families as well. Events occur in chains, leading from one decision-making event to another. In this activity, students will reassemble a chain to complete a story involving many decisions.

   Print each of the following sentences on individual poster board placards, large pieces of construction paper, or sheets of newsprint paper. Distribute the placards to ten different students. Ask students to complete the decision story chain by raising the placard that they think comes next in the story. (Ask the students to come to the front of the room and face the class.) As each placard is raised, discuss the event as it affects the continuing story and the decisions that must be made. Identify decision-making steps as the story unfolds. When the last placard is raised, the story should be complete.

   Set the story line by saying, "Brad is a graduating senior. Both his mother and father have careers. He has a sister in junior high. He has enrolled and paid deposits on tuition and room at a state college about 75 miles away. His parents are both very anxious that he follow these plans."

   Then continue with the events written on the individual placards in the following order:

   - "Right before Brad's graduation, Brad's father suffers a ....

   - sudden heart attack. Father is in the hospital, Mother continues to work, and Brad keeps ....

   - a summer job. Father comes home, recovery proceeds slowly. A family conference is held. Should Brad keep his plans for college or ....

   - get a job to help the family? Brad continues with his plans, but readjusts his schedule to come home ....

   - Friday to Sunday to help the family. Father is partially recovered, and goes back to work part-time. Brad continues in college, maintains his grades, and comes home on weekends to ....

   - help Mother and sister care for Dad. Dad recovers, working full-time. Brad finishes college, and Mother and Dad are proud of his record ....

   - at school and of his assistance at home. Brad chooses a job in the city near his home and continues to assist the family."

2. Discuss the following approaches to decision making and evaluate their effectiveness.

   a. The ostrich approach: hoping the decision will go away if you ignore it.

   b. The bulldozer approach: what you decide is your own business, and you don't have to consider anyone else.

   c. The speed demon approach: decisions are made fast, without considering alternatives or consequences.

   Ask students to give examples of the ways they have made decisions. Do they fit any of these patterns? Were they successful ways to make decisions? End the discussion by telling the class that they will learn a better approach to decision making in this chapter.

Strategies to Reteach, Reinforce, Enrich, and Extend Text Concepts

Values

3. **RT** *Forces that Influence Values*, transparency

master, 5-1. Use this master to discuss the various factors that influence the formation of values.

4. **EX** *Personal Values*, Activity A, SAG. Using a checklist, students are asked to indicate the values that they consider to be the most important. They will rank them in order of priority and then explain how their values have changed since their childhoods and how they may change as they get older.

5. **EX** Ask students to write short essays discussing what influences they feel have had the greatest impact on their personal values up to now.

6. **RF** Making value choices involving relationships may be hard during the teen years. Discuss how feelings of loyalty, wanting to belong, and sensing right and wrong behavior may confuse value choices when you want to please a friend. Ask the class to suggest typical scenarios where teens may have a difficult time making choices for which they can be responsible.

7. **EX** *Understanding Your Values*, Activity B, SAG. Students will answer questions related to personal values in this activity. Form small groups and have students share their responses with each other.

8. **RF** *Values: The Keys to "Unlock" Decisions*, color transparency, CT-5. Use this transparency to discuss how beliefs, concepts, ideals, feelings, activities, and attitudes are all a part of a person's values. Continue the discussion by indicating how values influence the decisions people make. Many decisions relate to the goals people set for themselves.

9. **EX** *How Values Influence Decisions*, Activity C, SAG. Students are to write their reactions to situations that show how values influence decisions. Then have students role-play the situations described in this activity. Small groups can be formed and each group can decide how they will portray one of the situations.

Setting Your Goals

10. **ER** *Understanding Goals*, reproducible master, 5-2. Use this activity to help students to identify three different types of goals: interpersonal, intrapersonal, and material. They are then asked to list their top five goals in each category and to prioritize them.

11. **RF** Ask students to consider the statement, "Life is not either work or marriage or family. These goals, if chosen, have to be combined and balanced." Refer to the points to remember in planning goals on page 119 of text. Discuss the special challenges involved when combining marriage and family with work in a mutually beneficial arrangement. Ask students if they feel this is easier to do today than in former years.

12. **RF** Review possible goal sequences as shown on page 119 of the text. Ask students to select sequences they feel might work for them, giving reasons for their selections.

13. **RF** Ask students to refer to the case study about Jesse on page 120 of the text. Review how his goals are plotted on a time/life line.

14. **ER** *Your Time/Life Line*, Activity D, SAG. Students are to complete the time/life line chart. They will plot the goals for their lives on the chart, and then write a summary of their goals. Discuss how decisions they make today can affect their entire lives.

Identify Your Resources

15. **RF** Ask students to list human and nonhuman resources. Ask them to evaluate how effectively these resources are used–by themselves and by people in your community.

16. **ER** *Managing Time*, Activity E, SAG. Students are asked to analyze their use of time in this activity. They are to then describe how they might improve their time management skills.

17. **ER** Working in small groups, ask students to identify some projects that they might undertake to make their community a better place in which to live. Then have them identify both human and nonhuman resources available to help with the project. As a class or club activity, you might undertake one of the projects. Keep track of all of the resources used.

18. **RF** Discuss the wide variety of human resources that are evidenced by the special skills and talents of the members of the class, as well as by members of the entire student body, and members of the community. Project how these human resources might be used for some special holiday event, to assist in a community project, or used in a time of crisis.

Set Your Standards

19. **RF** Discuss the importance of including standards when setting education or career goals. Also discuss problems that might occur if standards are set either too low or too high. Ask students to discuss any job experiences they may have had where standards were not established or maintained and how this affected their work.
20. **RF** Discuss standards of dress as they affect job performance. Ask students to determine a standard for clothing and grooming for sales positions in a department store.

Making Decisions

21. **RF** *Ways to Make a Decision*, reproducible master, 5-3. Six different resources for decision making are listed. Students are to check which method they would use for typical decisions they make daily. Discuss why different students use different resources for the same decision. Use this activity as a lead-in to a discussion of the decision-making process–a process that can be used when none of the other resources will suffice.
22. **EX** *The Decision-Making Process*, transparency master, 5-4, and *Case Studies for Decision Making*, reproducible master, 5-5. Demonstrate the use of the six steps of decision making in solving problems. Sample problems are given on the reproducible master. Use the transparency of the decision-making process throughout the course whenever topics requiring difficult decisions are discussed.
23. **ER** *Using the Decision-Making Process*, Activity G, SAG. Students are asked to think of a decision they must make and to follow the steps of the decision-making process to determine the best alternative.
24. **EX** Ask a school counselor to speak to the class about the important decisions juniors and seniors in high school have to make before they graduate. Ask the counselor to cite resources that are available to help in making these decisions.
25. **ER** Set up a panel of parents and students to discuss how parents can help students make important decisions.

The Management Process

26. **RF** Discuss the meaning of the term *manage*—to direct, control, or administer. If you were asked to be the chairperson for the turnabout dance, would you be required to "manage" the work that would need to be done? If so, could the management process help you in this assignment?
27. **RF** *The Management Process*, transparency master, 5-6. Use this master to review the steps in the management process. Ask students to give examples of situations at home, at school, and at work where the management process could be used to manage tasks.
28. **EX** Divide the class into small groups. Ask each group to write a case study showing how the management process could be used to help an individual, group, or family to reach a goal. Have them identify each of the four steps in the process. Use the example given on pages 126-128 of the text as a guide.
29. **EX** Ask each student to write a paper citing a time when he or she could have used the management process to better accomplish a task. Describe the task, what happened, and what could have happened had the management process been used.

Answer Key for Chapter 5

Text
To Review, page 129.

1. (Student response.)
2. (Student response.)
3. (Student response for three examples of short-term goals and three examples of long-term goals.)
4. Birth, infancy, childhood, young adulthood, adulthood, middle age, aging, death.
5. This gives you an idea of how your future goals will fit into your life. It also lets you see how decisions you make today will have an effect on your entire life.
6. (Name three human resources): Personal characteristics, character traits, time, talents and skills, other people. (Name three nonhuman resources): Money, material possessions, community resources and facilities, government services.
7. (Student response for two examples of school standards.)

Contemporary Living Teacher's Resources

8. The result of habits, using common sense, using intuition, referring to past experiences, applying lessons learned from parental guidance.
9. Identify the decision to be made, gather and examine information, identify possible alternatives, evaluate the consequences of each alternative, choose the best alternative and act on it, evaluate the results.
10. Making no decision is deciding not to act. It is accepting whatever happens or whatever other people decide for you. It is giving up a chance to manage your own life.
11. Setting a goal, making a plan, carrying out the plan, evaluating.

Teacher's Resource Guide

Chapter 5 Test

1. J	11. F	21. A
2. C	12. T	22. D
3. B	13. F	23. A
4. G	14. F	24. D
5. I	15. T	25. D
6. H	16. T	26. D
7. A	17. T	27. C
8. E	18. T	28. C
9. K	19. T	29. B
10. D	20. F	30. A

31. (Student response. List three examples each of human and nonhuman resources.)
32. (Student response.)
33. 1. Identify the decision to be made.
    2. Gather and examine information.
    3. Identify possible alternatives.
    4. Evaluate consequences of each alternative.
    5. Choose the best alternative and act on it.
    6. Evaluate the results.

Forces that Influence Values

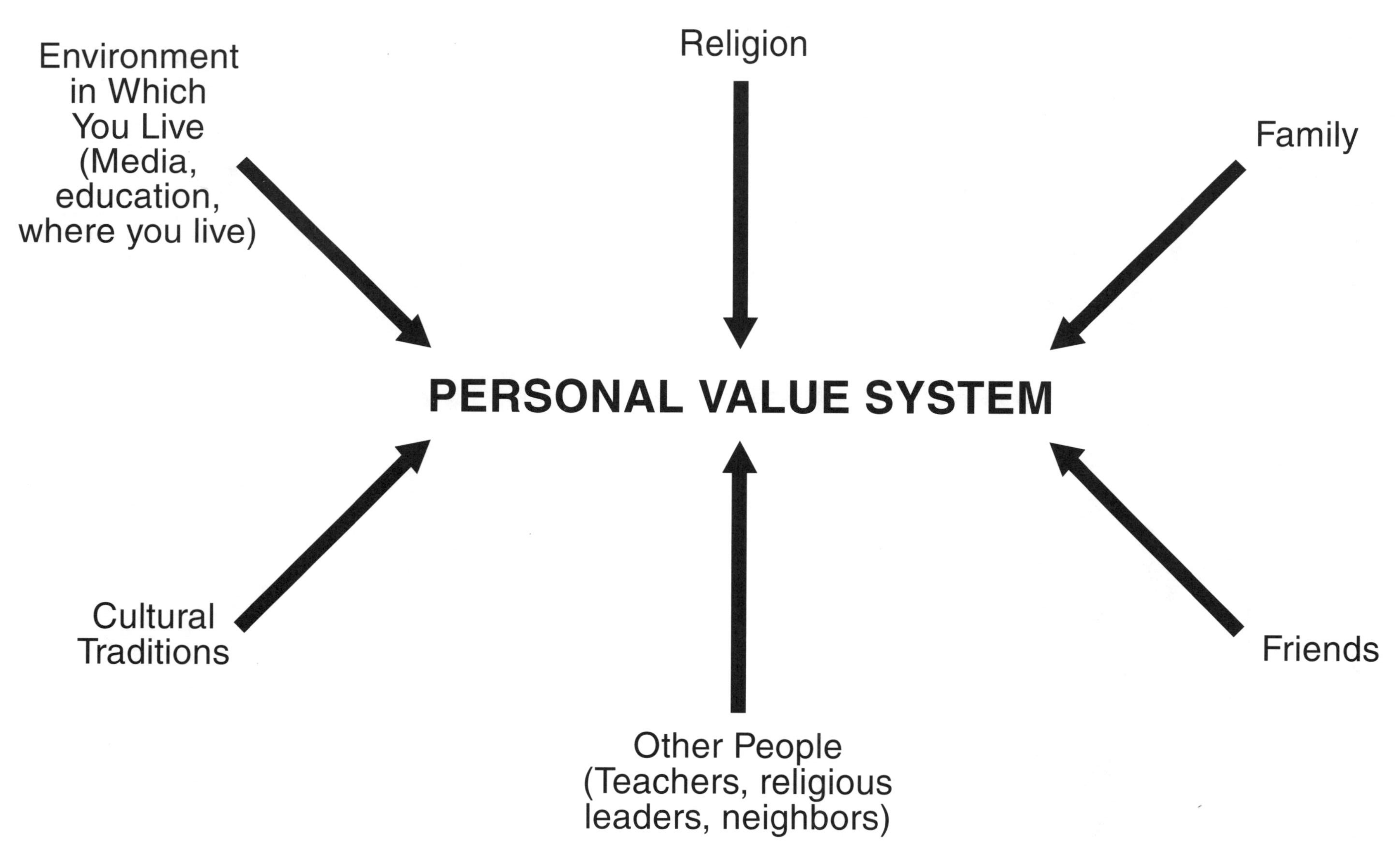

Understanding Goals

Name ______________________________ **Date** ______________ **Period** ______________

Goals can be divided into three categories. *Interpersonal goals* are those that involve relationships with others. *Intrapersonal goals* are personal concerns. *Material goals* include concrete or professional goals. Examples of each of these three types of goals are listed below. Add examples of your own to the lists.

Interpersonal Goals	**Intrapersonal Goals**	**Material Goals**
• To be a good friend to others.	• To be well-liked by others for who I am.	• To have a good job I enjoy.
• To be close to my family.	• To respect myself.	• To work to make money.
• To marry someone I love.	• To be able to think on my own.	• To advance in my job.
• To have children when I am able to be responsible for them.	• To be able to try new things.	• To have a good car to meet my needs.
• To be a good example for my children.	• To be able to do exciting things.	• To have enough money to help others.
• To be a good listener.	• To develop my strengths and ideals.	• To keep my home in good condition.
• To communicate easily with others.	• To exercise for good health.	• To have many possessions.
• To do volunteer work.	• To eat the right foods for good health.	• To own my own home.
• To have leadership qualities.	• To be an attractive person.	• To collect interesting possessions.

___________________________   ___________________________   ___________________________

___________________________   ___________________________   ___________________________

___________________________   ___________________________   ___________________________

List below your top five goals in each category at this stage in your life. (These may or may not be included on the lists above.)

Interpersonal Goals	**Intrapersonal Goals**	**Material Goals**
1. _______________	_______________	_______________
2. _______________	_______________	_______________
3. _______________	_______________	_______________
4. _______________	_______________	_______________
5. _______________	_______________	_______________

What can you do now to help reach one of your top goals?_______________________________

____

Ways to Make a Decision

Name_______________________________________ **Date**_______________ **Period**_______________

You use different methods to make decisions every day of your life. Typical decisions you might make daily are listed below. The six different resources to use in making decisions are also listed. Place the letter in the blank that indicates which resource you would use in making each decision.

Resources

A. Habit

B. Common sense

C. Intuition (instincts or feelings)

D. Past experience

E. Parental guidance or religious training

F. Decision-making process

______ 1. When to get up.

______ 2. What to wear.

______ 3. Grooming choices.

______ 4. What to eat.

______ 5. Outer garment for weather.

______ 6. When to get to school.

______ 7. How to get to school.

______ 8. What classes to attend.

______ 9. Who to talk to.

______ 10. What friends to be with.

______ 11. Where to go after school.

______ 12. What activity to attend.

______ 13. What to do after school.

______ 14. What TV shows to watch.

______ 15. What friends to call.

______ 16. When to go to bed.

______ 17. Other:____

______ 18. Other:____

Which resources would you call upon to make a decision in the following situations?

______ 19. At lunch hour, your friend suggests you go out to lunch in his van. You know he has a cooler of beer. School officials would not allow him to drive to school if they knew this.

______ 20. In your math class, one of your friends asks you to give her the answers to several questions when the teacher is not looking.

______ 21. After school, two friends walk home with you and suggest they come into your house and "hang out." You know your parents have said not to have friends in when they are gone.

______ 22. Your younger sister wants you to drive her to the library to get a needed book. Your friends want you to stay and play basketball with them.

The Decision-Making Process

Step 1: Identify the decision to be made.

Step 2: Gather and examine information.

Step 3: Identify possible alternatives.

1. ____

____

____

____

____

____

2. ____

____

____

____

____

3. ____

____

____

____

____

Step 4: Evaluate the consequences of each alternative.

1. ____

____

____

____

____

____

2. ____

____

____

____

____

3. ____

____

____

____

____

Step 5: Choose the best alternative and act on it.

Step 6: Evaluate the results.

Case Studies for Decision Making

Alan's Decision

Sam and Alan were high school friends. Sam wanted a medical career so he enrolled in a state university. Alan wanted to work with sports cars, hoping to eventually set up his own shop. Alan would like to go with his best friend to the university. He knows they'd have a lot of fun together. Alan's parents said he could choose any college or training program he wanted. His high school grades were above average. What should Alan do?

Senior Skip Day

This decision faced members of a senior class in a typical high school. Every year senior skip day was a part of the senior activities. The date for this event was set on the school calendar before school even began. This year, with no exception, senior skip day was awaited with eager anticipation by all members of the class.

About two months before the awaited day, the school board announced that a very special test was to be administered to all graduating seniors. It was mandatory that it be taken, and the scores could have a bearing on whether or not they would receive a diploma. The test was also mandated by the state legislature. The day set for the test was the day after senior skip day. However, a special review session had been set for 4:00 p.m. *on* senior skip day.

All senior class members had to make a decision. Julie and Tony had plans for college and knew they had to make good scores on their tests. Jonas and Dominique were applying for a special apprenticeship program. They knew this test would have a bearing on whether or not they would be accepted. Hector and Zoe had to work for a year before they could go to college, but the scores on this test would be important when they applied next year. Their families were counting on them to fulfill these plans, and each of them wanted to succeed in college and in their careers. Kevin and his friends had no set plans and wanted the skip day to stay as it was. Other students in the class had similar decisions to make.

Use the steps in the decision-making process to reach a decision concerning senior skip day. First consider the options the class as a whole could consider. Then consider the decisions individual members of the class would have to make if no changes were made in the schedule.

The Management Process

1. Set a goal.
- Base it on your values.
- Assess your resources.
- Consider your criteria for success.

2. Make a plan.
- List steps to take.
- Gather information to help you succeed.
- Ask someone to review your plan.

3. Carry out the plan.
- Be prepared to make adjustments as needed.
- Watch for ways to improve.

4. Evaluate at each step of the process.
- How well were your evaluation criteria met?
- What criteria would you add or omit next time?
- What would you do differently next time?

It's Your Decision

Name ____

Date ____ **Period** ____________ **Score** _______________

Chapter 5 Test

Matching: Match the following terms and identifying phrases.

_______ 1. Help that comes from within yourself and from other support people.

_______ 2. When you make a choice or judgment.

_______ 3. Goal for the next hour, day, or week.

_______ 4. Something you want to achieve next year or later.

_______ 5. To direct, control, or administer.

_______ 6. Ways and means you have for reaching your goals.

_______ 7. Steps include setting a goal, making a plan, carrying out the plan, and evaluating.

_______ 8. Shows how you are doing in reaching goals.

_______ 9. These include your posessions as well as community facilities.

_______ 10. Beliefs, ideals, and concepts that you consider very important to you.

A. management process
B. short-term goal
C. decision
D. values
E. standards
F. decision-making process
G. long-term goal
H. resources
I. manage
J. human resources
K. nonhuman resources

True/False: Circle *T* if the statement is true and *F* if the statement is false.

T F 11. Your peers were the first to influence your values.

T F 12. Your values may change as you mature.

T F 13. Values influence your goals, but not your decisions.

T F 14. Marriage and family are different goals than work, and they cannot be combined successfully.

T F 15. You may choose different goal sequences, but you will ultimately reach some of the same goals as your peers.

T F 16. Some goals continue for a lifetime.

T F 17. Your resources include all of the ways you have to achieve your goals.

T F 18. By not making a decision, you are letting someone else make the decision for you.

T F 19. Some decisions you make are simply habits.

T F 20. Unconventional standards are those commonly accepted by society.

(Continued)

Contemporary Living Teacher's Resources

Name ____

Multiple Choice: Choose the best response. Write the letter in the space provided.

______ 21. Nonhuman resources include ______.
     A. items such as money and possessions
     B. time
     C. energy
     D. All of the above.

______ 22. Human resources include ______.
     A. compassion
     B. self-discipline
     C. skills
     D. All of the above.

______ 23. Measures or levels of achievement are called ______.
     A. standards
     B. resources
     C. goals
     D. values

______ 24. Good health is an example of a ______.
     A. value
     B. resource
     C. decision
     D. Both A and B above.

______ 25. Getting an A on your next science test is an example of ______.
     A. a long-term goal
     B. a short-term goal
     C. a standard
     D. Both B and C above.

______ 26. Plotting your life on a time/life line ______.
     A. gives you an idea of how your future goals will fit into your life
     B. will help you to avoid making wrong decisions
     C. will allow you to see how decisions made today can affect your entire life
     D. Both A and C above.

______ 27. The first step of the decision-making process is to ______.
     A. gather and examine information
     B. identify the alternatives
     C. identify the decision to be made
     D. evaluate the consequences

______ 28. The last step of the decision-making process is to ______.
     A. consider the consequences
     B. choose the best course and act on it
     C. evaluate the results
     D. consider the alternatives

______ 29. When using the management process, set goals that ______.
     A. are based on the values of other people
     B. include criteria for evaluating the sucess of the project
     C. are beyond the scope of your available resources
     D. Both A and B above.

(Continued)

______ 30. Evaluation occurs ______.
    A. in each step of the management process
    B. in the last step of the management process
    C. when a plan is being carried out
    D. when a goal is being determined

Essay Questions: Provide complete responses to the following questions or statements.

31. List three examples of human resources and three examples of nonhuman resources.

32. Explain how your values, goals, resources, and standards relate to decision making. You may want to give an example of a decision to explain your answer.

33. List the six steps in the decision-making process.

Chapter 6
Decisions Concerning Your Future Career

Objectives

After studying this chapter, students will be able to
- identify career decisions that need to be made.
- describe education and training options related to career preparation.
- explain the importance of developing workplace skills.
- summarize strategies for job success and advancement.
- list points to keep in mind when changing jobs.

Bulletin Boards

I. Title: "Steps to Landing a Job"

Put up a set of brightly-colored construction-paper stairs on the bulletin board. Label each step as follows: Education/Training, Resume/Cover Letter, Job Application, Job Interview, Job Offer. Use pictures from magazines to illustrate each step.

II. Title: "Make a Career Match"

Under the title, write "If you like to work with...." Place these three words under the incomplete sentence: *people, things, ideas*. Attach magazine pictures randomly on the board of people working in a variety of careers. Using pieces of yarn, match the careers to the appropriate categories. Ask students to bring in pictures of careers of interest to them and mount the pictures on the board.

Teaching Materials

Text, pages 132-157
Terms to Know, To Review, To Do, and *To Think About*

Student Activity Guide
- A. *Clues to Your Career Choice*
- B. *Combining Work with School*
- C. *Workplace Skills*
- D. *Write Your Resume*

Teacher's Resource Guide/Binder
Job Research Data Sheet, reproducible master, 6-1
My Career Plan, reproducible master, 6-2
What Does It Take to Lead? transparency master, 6-3
Write a Cover Letter, transparency master, 6-4
Chapter 6 Test

Teacher's Resource Binder
Qualities that Count with Employers, color transparency, CT-6A

Steps in Job Advancement, color transparency, CT-6B

Software for Contemporary Living
Chapter Review Game

Introductory Activities

1. Ask students to complete the following statements:
    *   I am interested in the career fields of ...
    *   When I graduate from high school, I plan to ...
    *   When I am 24 years old, I plan to be ...
    *   When I am 44 years old, I would like to be ...
    *   I feel that I am or could be a good leader in ...

2. Show a video on the life of a famous person who has been very successful in his or her career. Ask students to note the number and type of jobs this person held. How did this person use one opportunity to create other opportunities? What role did hard work play in his or her success? Did luck play a role as well? Did this person benefit from having a mentor? What obstacles or setbacks had to be overcome? What lessons does this person's life offer to students today?

Strategies to Reteach, Reinforce, Enrich, and Extend Test Concepts

Deciding on a Career

3. **RF** *Clues to Your Career Choice,* Activity A, SAG. This activity helps students identify careers of interest to them based on their personal aptitudes and interests.
4. **RF** Discuss different types of careers available for those who like to work with people (sales, social work, education), things (machinery, sewing machines, automobiles), or ideas (writing, advertising, bookkeeping).
5. **RF** *Job Research Data Sheet,* reproducible master, 6-1. Students can use this data sheet to organize the information they gather as they research various job options. Ask students to research five jobs of interest to them using this data sheet.

6. **RT** Ask students to look at the chart on pages 139-140 of the text. Discuss the following:
    *   Which careers deal with people, things, and ideas?
    *   What personal qualifications and aptitudes would be needed for a person to succeed in this field?
    *   Which careers, if any, sound most interesting and why?
7. **ER** *My Career Plan,* reproducible master, 6-2. After students have researched several careers, have them each choose a possible career and complete a career plan using this form. They are to choose long-term career goals and then list activities, jobs, and education that will help them achieve their long-term goals.
8. **ER** Assemble a panel of professionals in careers involving personal/family relations skills (e.g., a marriage and family college instructor, mental health professional, social worker, preschool teacher, extension worker, and entrepreneur). Ask each to outline the following in relation to their work: training, challenges, satisfactions, and special aptitudes that make for success. Conclude with a question-and-answer session.

Decisions About Your Education

9. **ER** Interview successful vocational school graduates. How did their training help them succeed in their chosen occupations? What skills did they have to learn on the job?
10. **ER** Collect brochures describing various kinds of education and training available to high school students when they graduate. Keep the brochures in a file that will be available to all students.
11. **ER** Have students research different types of training and education available in or near their community, using the six areas that are discussed in the text. Share results with the class.
12. **ER** Ask admissions officers from area community colleges, four-year colleges, and universities to visit the class to discuss academic offerings, job placement programs for graduates, requirements for admission, etc.
13. **ER** Ask students to identify three areas of further education or training in which they may be interested. Ask them to research these options and summarize their findings in a report

14. **ER** Conduct a class poll to determine how many students have part-time jobs as well as the types of jobs they have. Ask students to describe to the class what they believe they have learned from their jobs that will benefit them in later life.
15. **EX** *Combining Work with School,* Activity B, SAG. This activity will help students make decisions concerning part-time work while in school.

Developing Workplace Skills

16. **RT** *What Does It Take to Lead?* transparency master, 6-3. Lead the class in a discussion of leadership qualities using this transparency on an overhead projector. Begin by revealing only the left-hand column. Go through the list of leadership qualities and ask students to explain what each means and why it is an important quality in a leader. Then reveal the column titled "In School" and ask students to identify what is meant by a leader in school. Then go through the list of qualities and check those that students think school leaders should possess. Do the same for the other two categories. Also ask:
    - Do all leadership roles require the same qualities?
    - Which qualities seem to be needed in any leadership role?
    - Does the size and makeup of the group affect the kind of leadership needed?
    - Do the physical characteristics of a leader affect their ability to lead?
    - How can experience gained in leadership during the school years affect future roles?
    - What negative qualities might affect a person's ability to be a good leader?
17. **RF** *Workplace Skills,* Activity C, SAG. Have students evaluate their workplace skills by responding to the statements in the activity. They are then asked to describe how they could improve their workplace skills.
18. **RT** Refer to illustration 6-10 of the text. Discuss the leadership skills that are listed there. Why are these behaviors valued in a leader? How can students develop these behaviors?
19. **EX** Have students brainstorm a list of teamwork skills. Write these on the chalkboard. Ask what skills workers need to be successful team players on the job.

20. **ER** Have students research the changes that have occurred in the workplace since W.W. II that have caused this new emphasis on teams. Prepare a report for the class.
21. **ER** Ask students to locate and interview local employers who utilize teams in the workplace.

Getting a Job

22. **ER** Divide the class into groups based on their interest in the following career areas: medical work, food service, legal work, sales, administration, business, education, social work, data processing, or other. Ask each person to research an individual profession within his or her chosen career area and to share this information with a reporter chosen for each group. Ask each reporter to summarize the information his or her group gathered in a brief report to the class.
23. **EX** *Write Your Resume,* Activity D, SAG. After students have completed this resume-writing exercise, ask them to exchange their documents with at least two other people in the class and to make any necessary revisions based on this critique.
24. **EX** *Write a Cover Letter,* transparency master, 6-4. Refer to this transparency as part of a brief discussion of the basic elements of a standard cover letter. Ask students to write sample cover letters and then exchange them with other students for their comments and suggestions.
25. **EX** Role-play the following job interview situations:
    - Female applicant applying for position in business; chauvinistic male interviewer who thinks she is not qualified for the job because she is a woman.
    - Applicant who is asked "tricky" or hostile questions (e.g., What makes you think you are qualified for this position? What are your faults? How much pay do you expect?)
    - Female applicant who is asked illegal questions (e.g., Are you married? Do you have children? How can you take care of a spouse and children and work at the same time?)
    - Interviewer goes on and on about the company and the requirements for the job and does not ask applicant any questions.

Applicant must try to remain calm and pleasant and find ways to politely state why he or she is qualified for the job.

Strategies for Job Success

26. **RF** *Qualities that Count with Employers,* color transparency, CT-6A. This transparency reports the results of a 1994 Census Bureau survey in which 3,000 employers nationwide were asked, "When you consider hiring a new nonsupervisory or production worker, how important are the following in your decision to hire?" The employers' ratings are listed in descending order of importance, with attitude topping the list as most important, followed by communication skills. Ask students:
    - What interview behaviors encourage a prospective employer to believe that you have a good attitude and good communication skills?
    - What behaviors will encourage them to decide that you do not? Point out that in many homes, children are taught that good behavior means keeping quiet and not communicating. How can noncommunicative behavior hold people back in the workplace?

27. **RF** Ask students who work to relate some of the problems they have had on the job and how they handled them. Can they think of instances where they made mistakes or were criticized? Have they worked with difficult coworkers or supervisors? How did they deal with these situations?

28. **RF** Have students list practices that would be considered dishonest by employers including copying software programs for home use. Discuss how even small instances of theft can lead to enormous costs to a company.

Strategies that Lead to Advancement on the Job

29. **RF** *Steps in Job Advancement,* color transparency, CT-6B. Refer to this transparency as you briefly describe the hierarchical nature of most employment environments. Point out that a worker's education and experience are key factors in deciding which level is appropriate for him or her at any given time in the worker's career.

Changing Jobs

30. **RF** Divide the class into small groups. Have each group compose lists containing the do's and don'ts of leaving a job. Share lists and make one list of the best suggestions. Use these to write an article for the school paper.

31. **RT** Discuss why people should not criticize former employers when interviewing for new jobs.

Answer Key for Chapter 6

Text
To Review, page 156.

1. The work must satisfy your needs. The work you do must satisfy your employer's needs.
2. (Student response for an aptitude and a related career.)
3. (Student response for an example of a short-term career goal and a long-term career goal.)
4. Its application to your family roles.
5. An apprenticeship is a formal, registered program for a skilled craft or trade. It combines classroom instruction with on-the-job training and includes a written agreement with an employer and/or a union.
6. (Name three advantages and three disadvantages. Student response.)
7. (Student response for two leadership skills and two teamwork skills.)
8. Develop a list of potential employers whose organizations have entry-level positions in the field in which you have an interest.
9. Your name, address, and telephone number; your educational background; your work experience; and your memberships in work-related associations or organizations.
10. (List three. Student response.)
11. (Student response. Name three ethical practices.)
12. Two weeks.

Chapter 6 Test

1. H	11. T	21. A
2. J	12. F	22. D
3. B	13. F	23. A
4. G	14. T	24. D
5. A	15. F	25. B
6. K	16. T	26. B
7. D	17. F	27. D
8. C	18. T	28. C
9. E	19. F	29. B
10. I	20. F	30. C

31. Pros: Gain work experience. Challenging jobs may allow students to learn new skills, practice cognitive skills, and learn skills in interacting with others. Income can help student meet family expenses, pay for personal needs and wants, and learn money management. Cons: Work experience may be menial and of questionable value, leading to poor work habits and negative attitudes. Time devoted to work competes with time for studies, household chores, and family activities.

32. (Student response. Discuss three.)

33. Resume: Name, address, telephone number, educational background, work experience, memberships. Sometimes one's career objective and a list of areas of expertise are included. Cover letter: States job for which applicant is applying and provides brief summary of qualifications. Refers to enclosed resume. States date applicant would be available for employment, and thanks addressee for considering applicant's qualifications.

Job Research Data Sheet

Name _________________________________ **Date** _____________ **Period** ___________

Job: ____

Education/training required for

    entry-level position: ____

    senior-level position: ____

Typical hours (normal business week, shifts, etc.): __________________________

____

Typical fringe benefits: ____

____

Tasks in a typical day: ____

____

____

Expected future demand for job: _______________________________________

____

Number of positions nationwide: _______________________________________

Professional associations: ____

____

Salary or other type of compensation for

    entry-level position: ____

    senior-level position: ____

Where are position vacancies advertised? _________________________________

____

Additional notes: ____

____

____

____

____

____

____

Source(s) of information: ____

____

____

My Career Plan

Name ____ **Date** ______________ **Period** ______________

If my long-term career goal is to be a ____,
I can prepare myself by working on the following short-term goals.

While in high school, I can:

Extracurricular and Volunteer Activities	Part-time Jobs That Can Provide Experience	Education and Training

After high school, I can:

Extracurricular and Volunteer Activities	Part-time Jobs That Can Provide Experience	Education and Training

What Does It Take to Lead?

Leadership Qualities:	In School	At Work	In Your Community
Positive Self-Concept			
Decision-Making Skills			
Courage of Convictions			
Communication Skills			
Has Empathy			
Delegates Responsibility			
Puts Group Success above Personal Success			

Write a Cover Letter

Your address

Date

Name and address
of potential employer

Dear Mr. or Ms.________:

Paragraph 1: State job for which you are applying.

Paragraph 2: Briefly summarize your qualifications and refer to enclosed resume.

Paragraph 3: State the date when you would be available for employment (unless you are already available). You may also wish to express an interest in an interview at the employer's convenience.

Paragraph 4: Thank the potential employer for considering your qualifications.

Sincerely,

Your name

Decisions Concerning Your Future Career

Name ____

Date ____ **Period** _____________ **Score** _______________

Chapter 6 Test

Matching: Match the following terms and identifying phrases.

_______ 1. The ability to lead and influence others.

_______ 2. Potential for special talents.

_______ 3. The worldwide network of computers.

_______ 4. Information sheet containing information about a person's educational and job background.

_______ 5. Formal, registered program for training an individual in a skilled craft or trade.

_______ 6. A group of people who rely on each other in achieving success.

_______ 7. A list of short- and long-term goals for reaching a long-range job goal.

_______ 8. Making professional contacts.

_______ 9. A location you can access on a computer that provides information, services, or products.

_______ 10. Starting and owning your own business.

A. apprenticeship
B. Internet
C. networking
D. career plan
E. Web site
F. cover letter
G. resume
H. leadership
I. entrepreneurship
J. aptitude
K. team

True/False: Circle *T* if the statement is true or *F* if the statement is false.

T F 11. Students who drop out of high school usually encounter problems as they attempt to compete in the job market.

T F 12. It is a good idea to admit your weaknesses in a job interview.

T F 13. An employee can learn nothing from a poor supervisor.

T F 14. After an interview, it makes a good impression if the interviewee sends the interviewer a brief letter thanking him or her for the opportunity to learn more about the company.

T F 15. If you have been healthy and have not taken any medical leave for six months, most supervisors would understand if you faked an illness and took the unused leave.

T F 16. People who do like people tend to find careers in family relations and child development fulfilling.

T F 17. If a job interviewer asks an interviewee for an entry-level job what salary is desired, it is best for the interviewee to name a figure promptly.

(Continued)

    Contemporary Living Teacher's Resources

T F   18. If you have an appointment for a job interview and are not sure how to find the building in which it will be held, it is a good idea to find a map and rehearse the route ahead of time.

T F   19. If you know that under normal circumstances it takes exactly 15 minutes to reach the building in which you have a job interview, there is nothing to be gained by starting out any earlier than that on the day of the interview.

T F   20. If you have superb qualifications for a position, most interviewers will excuse sloppy grooming and a "smart-aleck" attitude.

Multiple Choice: Select the best response. Write the letter in the space provided.

______ 21. Which of the following statements is NOT true?
    A. Once people choose a career, they usually stay with it throughout their working lives.
    B. Part-time jobs can help people learn about their strengths and weaknesses.
    C. The hours you work, the salary you earn, and the place you live are all influenced by your job.
    D. Most students who work spend their money to satisfy their personal needs and wants.

______ 22. Factors likely to affect career choice include ______.
    A. personal preferences
    B. aptitudes and abilities
    C. knowledge of career opportunities
    D. All of the above.

______ 23. A first step in ______ is to learn as much as possible about the issue or situation.
    A. problem solving
    B. making a career plan
    C. writing a resume
    D. applying for a job

______ 24. Examples of ethical practices include ______.
    A. principles and values
    B. cooperation and teamwork
    C. optimism and persistence
    D. honesty and loyalty

______ 25. In a job interview, discussion of your dissatisfaction with your current job or supervisor ______.
    A. is important in creating a good impression
    B. usually works against you
    C. helps your interviewer understand what a gifted person you are
    D. will help you get a better job and supervisor

______ 26. In a job interview, you will tend to be more successful if you emphasize ______.
    A. what the company can do for you
    B. what you can do for the company
    C. your faults
    D. your interest in making as much money as possible rather than doing the best possible work

(Continued)

_____ 27. If, after interviewing for a job, you are not offered a position, _____.
    A. there is no point in ever applying for another job with the company again
    B. this proves that you will never get a job
    C. you should make up bad things to tell others about the company in order to make yourself feel better
    D. you can still try to position yourself for favorable consideration for future job openings with the company

_____ 28. If an employee wakes up feeling ill and decides to miss a day of work, _____.
    A. it is unnecessary to call the supervisor
    B. it is unnecessary to call the supervisor until much later in the day
    C. it is important to call the supervisor by the time the employee is expected at work
    D. it is important to spend at least 10 minutes telling the supervisor how bad the employee feels in order to receive as many expressions of sympathy as possible

_____ 29. Associations whose members hold the kind of job you would like to hold _____.
    A. guarantee you the job of your choice
    B. can be valuable sources of networking opportunities and career information
    C. are made up of people who have no interest in answering your questions
    D. cannot help you until you already have your dream job

_____ 30. If you make a serious mistake on the job, it is usually best to _____.
    A. try to blame the mistake on someone else
    B. keep quiet and hope no one notices the mistake
    C. inform your supervisor immediately
    D. pretend that the mistake did not occur

Essay Questions

31. Discuss the pros and cons of combining work with education.

32. Name and discuss three strategies for success on the job.

33. What information should be included in a resume and cover letter?

Chapter 7
Decisions Affecting Your Health

Objectives

After studying this chapter, students will be able to

- choose nutritious foods that promote good health.
- describe the benefits of regular exercise.
- adopt an appropriate exercise program.
- describe causes of stress and ways to deal effectively with stress.
- identify community and other resources that promote health and wellness
- make informed consumer choices related to health.

Bulletin Boards

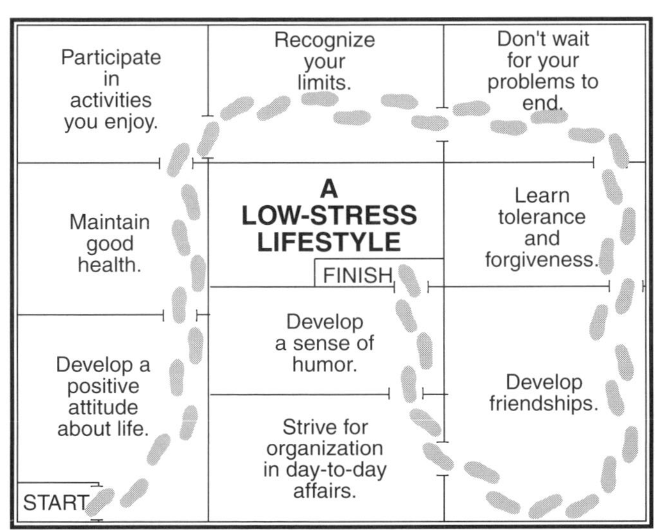

I. Title: "Path to a Low-Stress Lifestyle"

Draw a maze on the bulletin board and fill in the spaces with guidelines for a low-stress lifestyle. (See Chart 7-11 in the text.) Cut out or draw small footprints on the maze to indicate the path to follow.

II. Title: "What Is Your Nutrition Score?"

Assemble a bulletin board illustrating the food groups in the Food Guide Pyramid. Find pictures of various foods and place them in the appropriate category on the board. Have students refer to the bulletin board as they keep track of the foods they eat as part of *Nutrition Log, Activity B, SAG*. Also refer to the board as you discuss the nutrients supplied by each food group.

Teaching Materials

Text, pages 158-181

Terms to Know, To Review, To Do, and *To Think About*

Student Activity Guide

A. *Your Nutrition/Exercise Inventory*
B. *Nutrition Log*
C. *Weight Control*
D. *My Exercise Inventory*
E. *Stress Rating Scale*

Teacher's Resource Guide/Binder

What's True About Diet and Exercise? reproducible masters, 7-1A and 7-1B

Pyramid of Healthy Eating, reproducible master, 7-2

Calories in Fast-Food Favorites, transparency master, 7-3

Burn Those Fast-Food Calories! transparency master, 7-4

Reducing Stress, reproducible master, 7-5

Chapter 7 Test

Teacher's Resource Binder

Food Guide Pyramid, color transparency, CT-7A

Managing Stress, color transparency, CT-7B

Software for Contemporary Living

Chapter Review Game

Introductory Activities

1. Ask students to complete the following sentences:
   - I take care of my health by ...
   - I could take better care of my health if I ...
   - To get some exercise, I enjoy ...
   - I feel "stressed to the max" when ...
   - To deal with stress, I ...

2. *What's True About Diet and Exercise?* reproducible master, 7-1A. Students can check their knowledge of diet and exercise using this pretest. Go over their responses using the answer sheet, reproducible master, 7-1B. You may reproduce the answer sheet on the back of each pretest, or read the answers to the class yourself.

Strategies to Reteach, Reinforce, Enrich, and Extend Text Concepts

Planning for Family Wellness

3. **RF** Review the definition of wellness. Then ask students to list key elements in a commitment to family wellness, such as regular exercise, getting needed sleep, avoiding smoking, etc.

Preventive Health Practices

4. **RF** *Your Nutrition/Exercise Inventory,* Activity A, SAG. Using this inventory, have students analyze their current health practices. You will need to provide height/weight charts for them to use. At the end of the month, have them score themselves again to see if they have improved their health practices.

Nutrition and Your Health

5. **EX** *Nutrition Log,* Activity B, SAG. Using the chart, students will record everything they eat for three days. They are then asked to write a summary of what they have learned concerning their eating habits.

6. **RT** *Food Guide Pyramid,* color transparency, CT-7A. Use this transparency to illustrate the Food Guide Pyramid. Ask students to give examples of foods they have eaten at various meals and determine to which group in the Food Guide Pyramid the foods belong.

7. **RF** *Pyramid of Healthy Eating,* reproducible master, 7-2. Use this exercise to review your students' understanding of the Food Guide Pyramid. Ask students to fill in the pyramid with the appropriate food groups and the correct range of recommended daily servings for each group.

8. **RF** *Weight Control,* Activity C, SAG. Students will analyze their eating habits and goals for weight control. Remind students that assuming their weight is stable, one pound of weight can be lost in seven days by cutting back by 500 calories per day. Also, a pound can be lost by increasing activity to burn an extra 500 calories a day. How can students apply this information? (Note: You will need to provide calorie charts for students to use for this activity.)

9. **RF** Contrast good and poor methods of weight loss. Ask students to list characteristics of a healthy weight-loss program. Then list characteristics of an unhealthy weight-loss program that could lead to malnutrition, serious illness, or even death. Discuss fad diets students have heard of and decide whether these diets are healthy or unhealthy. Follow up with a review of the eating disorders of bulimia and anorexia nervosa.

10. **ER** Have students research the latest findings concerning bulimia and anorexia nervosa. Discuss possible causes of emotional stress that often trigger these eating disorders.

11. **EX** Ask students to bring examples of food ads to class. Do any of these ads provide nutrition information? Do the ads emphasize the "social function" of food? Have students revise ads or write their own in order to provide nutrition information for the consumer. Post and discuss in class.

Regular Exercise

12. **RF** *My Exercise Inventory*, Activity D, SAG. Students are asked to keep a record of their exercise for a week and to describe how they could improve their exercise plans.

13. **RF** *Calories in Fast-Food Favorites*, transparency master, 7-3. This master can be used as a transparency with the overhead projector, or it can be used as a basis for class discussion of the eating habits of teens. Ask students to keep track of the number of times they eat food items from this list for three days or a week.

14. **RF** *Burn Those Fast-Food Calories!* transparency master, 7-4. This master can be used as a transparency, or it can be used as a basis for class discussion concerning the exercise habits of teens. Ask students to keep track of the number of times they engage in the types of exercise listed for three days or a week. Are students burning as many calories as they are consuming?

15. **RT** Walking is regarded as one of the best forms of exercise. Discuss ways in which walking can be included in a daily exercise plan for children, young adults, adults, and elderly persons. Is this activity encouraged in your community by public parks, designated walking trails, etc.?

16. **RT** Discuss aspects of a good exercise program for teens. When can teens fit exercise into their schedules? What facilities for exercise are available? What kinds of exercise are appropriate? Why are the warm-up and cool-down periods important?

17. **ER** Ask students to research the exercise programs available in your community, such as the YWCA, YMCA, health clubs, park district programs, programs sponsored by community groups, etc. What are the costs of these programs? Are the instructors adequately trained?

18. **ER** Ask a health and fitness specialist to talk to your class on the benefits of exercise and on the pros and cons of various forms of exercise that are popular today.

19. **ER** Ask a specialist in sports medicine to discuss health problems related to exercise. The discussion should include procedures to follow (e.g., seek medical attention) when pain is experienced and injuries occur.

Rest and Sleep

20. **EX** Discuss the importance of relaxation in maintaining good mental health. Ask students to volunteer examples of hobbies or other leisure-time activities that they believe contribute to their own happiness and mental health.

21. **EX** Ask students to keep track of the amount of sleep they get for three days or a week. How much sleep does each student think he or she needs? What activities interfered with getting a full night's rest? How did the amount of sleep they got on any given night affect how they felt the next day?

Making Time for Health

22. **RF** Discuss the importance of making time for health today to avoid significant health problems in the future. Ask students to give examples of practices that can lead to long-term health problems, such as failure to brush teeth leading to dental cavities. Then have them think of ways they can make time for health in their busy lives.

Coping with Stress

23. **RT** Form buzz groups to list and discuss stressful events that occur in the lives of teens. Have each group share its list with the class.

24. **RF** *Managing Stress*, color transparency, CT-7B. Use this transparency to review ways to manage stress. Ask students to name other techniques that they have found helpful in managing stress.

25. **RT** Discuss resources teens have for coping with stress, such as parents, friends, counselors, and religion. If they have a stressful problem, to whom would they turn for help? How can they provide help to friends who are under stress? When should they advise friends to get professional help?

26. **RF** *Stress Rating Scale*, Activity E, SAG. Students are asked to determine the amount of stress they have been under during the past year using a chart similar to the one on page 173 of the text. They are then asked to describe how they managed the stress created by an event in their lives.

27. **EX** *Reducing Stress,* reproducible master, 7-5. Students are to try the relaxation techniques discussed in the text and to report on the effectiveness of each.

28. **ER** Ask each student to write a paper discussing how he or she reacts to stress, and what can be done to reduce this stress.

Health and Wellness Resources

29. **ER** Ask a public health nurse or social worker to address the class on the topic, "Health Resources in Our Community."

30. **EX** Ask students to suggest a community health resource that could be recommended to people with the following problems:
    - A homeless person with suspected tuberculosis.
    - A young teenager who thinks she may be pregnant.
    - A person who needs gall bladder surgery.
    - A teenager who thinks he may have AIDS.
    - A person who has just been diagnosed with cancer and who needs support.
    - A person whose spouse has Alzheimer's disease and who is looking for support.

31. **ER** Have a few students visit several stores that sell computer software, and have them list all of the titles that deal with health, nutrition, and fitness. Report back to the class.

32. **ER** Have several students visit computer Web sites that provide information on health, nutrition, and fitness. Have them print off samples of information available at these sites and tell which sites they would recommend as providing reliable information.

Consumer Choices Related to Health

33. **RT** Ask students to list two or three new or improved food items (e.g., reduced-fat products) that they believe would enhance their physical health. Use students' responses as the basis for discussion.

34. **RT** Ask students to list two or three improved public policies (e.g., universal health insurance, free or low-cost mental health services, smoke-free public places) that they believe would enhance their physical or mental health. Use students' responses as the basis for discussion.

Answer Key for Chapter 7

Text
To Review, page 180.

1. Bread, cereal, rice, and pasta group: 6-11 servings. Fruit group: 2-4 servings. Vegetable group: 3-5 servings. Meat, poultry, fish, dry beans, eggs, and nuts group: 2-3 servings. Milk, yogurt, and cheese group: 3 or more servings. Fats, oils, and sweets group: Eat sparingly.

2. Saturated fats tend to be solid at room temperature and come from animal sources. Unsaturated fats tend to be liquid at room temperature and come from plant sources.

3. Eat a variety of foods. Balance the food you eat with physical activity; maintain or improve your weight. Choose a diet low in fat, saturated fat, and cholesterol. Choose a diet with plenty of vegetables, fruits, and grain products. Choose a diet moderate in sugars. Choose a diet moderate in salt and sodium. If you drink alcoholic beverages, do so in moderation.

4. false

5. (List five. Student response.)

6. C

7. false

8. (Describe three. Student response.)

9. (List three with an example for each. Student response.)

10. (Give two examples. Student response.)

Teacher's Resource Guide

Pyramid of Healthy Eating, **reproducible master, 7-2.**

Fats, Oils, and Sweets: Use sparingly.
Milk, Yogurt, and Cheese Group: 2-3 servings.
Meat, Poultry, Fish, Dry Beans, Eggs, and Nuts Group: 2-3 servings.
Vegetable Group: 3-5 servings.
Fruit Group: 2-4 servings.
Bread, Cereal, Rice, and Pasta Group: 6-11 servings.

Chapter 7 Test

1. F	11. T	21. B
2. I	12. T	22. D
3. D	13. T	23. C
4. A	14. F	24. B
5. G	15. T	25. A
6. J	16. F	26. B
7. H	17. T	27. A
8. K	18. F	28. D
9. E	19. T	29. C
10. B	20. F	30. C

31. Student response. (See discussion of Dietary Guidelines for Americans in text, pages 163-164.)
32. Three of the following: increased muscle strength, stamina, and coordination; increased lung capacity; improved blood circulation; greater flexibility and improved posture. Weight is more easily managed. Stress, boredom, and depression are less likely to occur.
33. Two of the following: take deep breaths; tense and release muscles in different parts of the body; use biofeedback to distinguish between feelings of relaxation and tension and thus relax more easily; stretch, hold, and release various parts of the body; exercise.

What's True About Diet and Exercise?

Name ____ **Date** _______________ **Period** _______________

Read the following statements and decide if they are true or false.

T F 1. If you are running a marathon race or taking a long bike ride, eat plenty of pasta, potatoes, and bread at least 2 to 3 hours before the activity.

T F 2. Eating meat, fish, and poultry is the only way to get protein in your diet.

T F 3. Breads and cereals are the only sources of fiber in our diets.

T F 4. There are more calories per gram of carbohydrate than per gram of protein.

T F 5. For exercise to be effective, your muscles should be sore and stiff afterward.

T F 6. A tablespoon of butter has more calories than a tablespoon of margarine.

T F 7. You should try to eliminate all fat from your diet.

T F 8. Once you reach adulthood, your body no longer needs calcium because your bones have stopped growing.

T F 9. When exercising, it is better to drink soda than water to replace fluids.

T F 10. Snacking between meals should be avoided.

T F 11. Drinking water before you feel thirsty is a good idea.

T F 12. If you are on a 1500 calorie diet, it is alright if all the calories come from the same food, such as ice cream.

T F 13. Your body needs vitamin A for good vision and healthy skin. If a little vitamin A is good for you, a large amount is even better.

T F 14. To lose weight, you have to use up more energy than you take in through food.

T F 15. One pound of body weight is equal to 3500 calories. Thus, a pound can be lost in a week by cutting back 500 calories a day.

T F 16. The pregame meal is more important to an athlete's performance than the athlete's regular diet.

T F 17. Exercise increases the body's need for energy and water.

T F 18. If you want to lose extra pounds, you should stop eating starchy foods like potatoes, bread, and rice.

T F 19. You get an equal amount of calcium from one cup of ice cream and one cup of milk.

T F 20. Exercise increases your appetite, thus preventing weight loss.

What's True About Diet and Exercise?

Check your responses with these answers:

1. True. If you are participating in strenuous activities or are an athlete in training it is important to follow the Food Guide Pyramid. Also add more carbohydrates to your diet right before a long, strenuous event. Pasta, potatoes, and bread will give your body extra energy.
2. False. Other sources of protein are dried beans and peas, nuts, cereals, and even peanut butter.
3. False. All plant foods, including fruits and vegetables, are good sources of fiber.
4. False. Fat contains 9 calories per gram compared to 4 calories per gram of protein and carbohydrate.
5. False. Sore, stiff muscles usually mean that you are overdoing things.
6. False. A tablespoon of butter and margarine both have 100 calories, but butter has more saturated fat.
7. False. Some fat is necessary for the absorption of fat-soluble vitamins in the body.
8. False. Your body continues to need calcium throughout your lifetime. Years of calcium deficiency may lead to a condition called osteoporosis. Bone mass is lost and bones become weaker.
9. False. Carbonated drinks contain salt and caffeine. These cause your body to lose fluids. Water quenches thirst and replaces body fluids.
10. False. Snacks can be good for your health. Fresh fruits and vegetables make good nutritious snacks. Some packaged snacks, however, are high in calories and low in nutrients. These snacks should be avoided.
11. True. You should get in the habit of drinking water, even before you feel thirsty. Your body needs eight glasses of fluids a day.
12. False. Getting all your calories from one source, especially food high in fat, is not good nutrition. You should choose foods from all the food groups to meet your nutritional needs.
13. False. Vitamin A can be stored in the body. Too much vitamin A can cause fatigue, headaches, and nausea.
14. True. To lose weight, you must either eat less or exercise more. A combination of the two is best.
15. True. A pound can also be lost by increasing activity to burn up an extra 500 calories a day.
16. False. Maintaining a high quality diet consistently is more important than the one meal right before an athletic event.
17. True. Exercise burns fat in the body. If not resupplied, protein will be used for energy instead of for body growth and maintenance. Water lost during exercise must be resupplied to avoid dehydration.
18. False. These foods are low in calories. It's the butter, sour cream, and cheese commonly used with them that are high in calories.
19. False. You would have to eat at least 1 3/4 cups of ice cream (233 calories) to get the same amount of calcium as in 1 cup of milk (150 calories).
20. False. Exercise may reduce the appetite while the body continues to burn calories at a higher rate following the exercise period.

Pyramid of Healthy Eating

Name ____ **Date** ________________ **Period** ________________

Label the outline of the Food Guide Pyramid below with the name of each food group. Then indicate the correct range of recommended daily servings for each group.

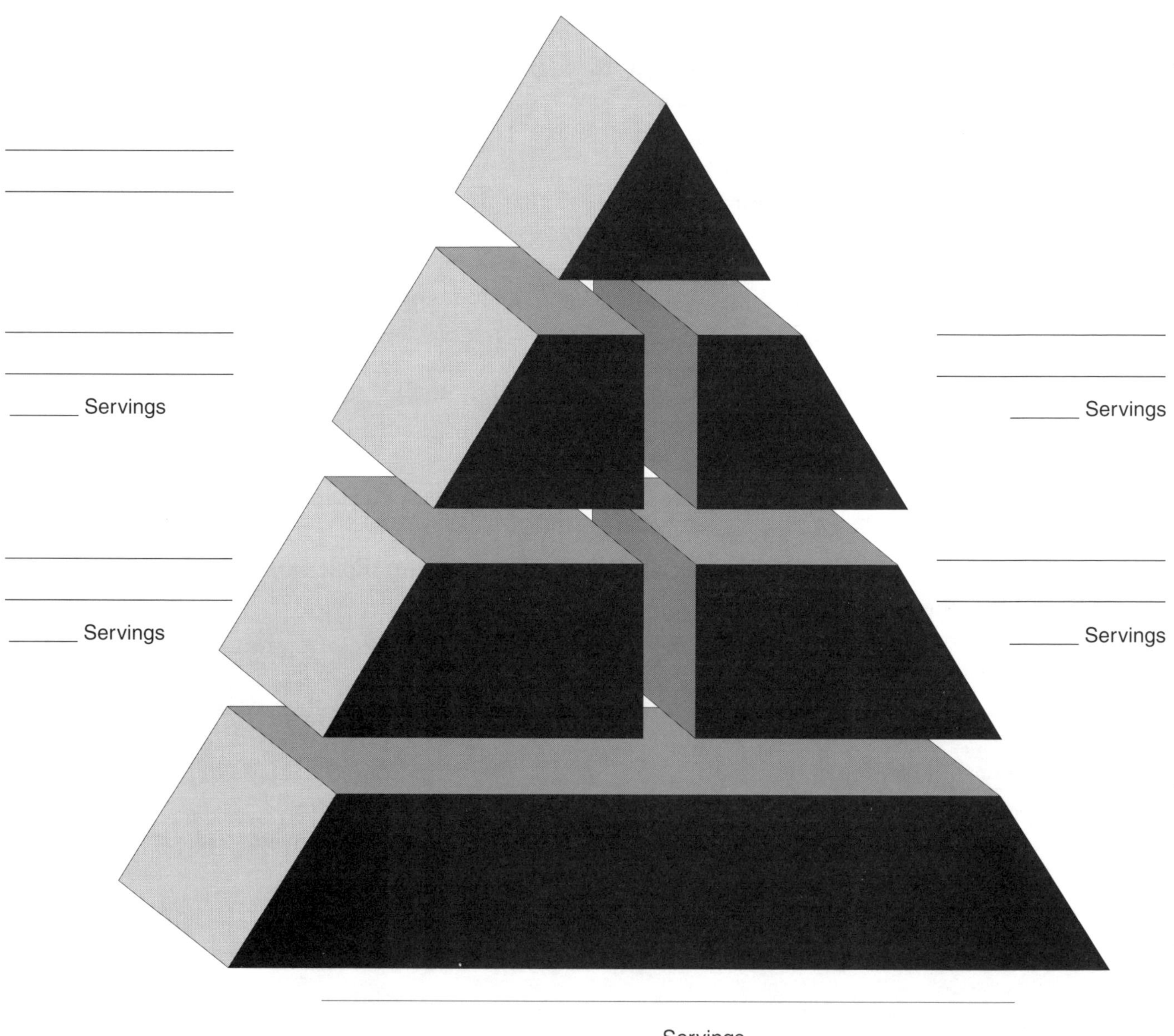

____

____

____

____

______ Servings

____

____

______ Servings

____

____

______ Servings

____

____

______ Servings

____

______ Servings

Calories in
Fast-Food Favorites

Hamburger (regular size)	240	Hot dog with bun	291
Hamburger (medium size)	420	Beef taco	216
Cheeseburger	307	Fish sandwich	432
French fries	220	Bean burrito	343
Milk shake	350	Fried chicken, one piece	250
Roast beef sandwich	400	Potato chips (10)	114
Pizza (1/4 of 13"), cheese	340	Cake donut	125
pepperoni	370	Milk chocolate candy bar	147
deluxe	400	Soft drink, cola	96

Burn Those Fast-Food Calories!

Activity	Female	Male
Lying quietly	72*	85
Sitting; studying	75	110
Walking slowly	143	230
Walking quickly	230	315
Light work or exercise (shopping, cleaning, office work)	143	250
Moderate work or exercise (cycling, jogging, tennis, dancing, skiing)	226	400
Hard work or exercise (aerobic dancing, basketball, running, freestyle swimming, shoveling snow)	410	625

*Typical calories burned per hour of activity.

Reducing Stress

Name ____ **Date** _______________ **Period**_______________

Reducing stress is not always easy! Try using three of the techniques suggested in your text during the next week. Describe each technique briefly. Then report on the effectiveness of each in dealing with a specific event.

1. Describe the technique: ____

____

____

   When did you use this technique? ____

____

   How effective was this technique in helping to reduce stress?___________________________

____

____

____

2. Describe the technique: ____

____

____

   When did you use this technique? ____

____

   How effective was this technique in helping to reduce stress?___________________________

____

____

____

3. Describe the technique: ____

____

____

   When did you use this technique? ____

____

   How effective was this technique in helping to reduce stress?___________________________

____

____

____

4. Which technique was the most effective in helping you reduce your stress?___________________

____

____

Decisions Affecting Your Health

Name ____

Date ____**Period**______________ **Score** ________________

Chapter 7 Test

Matching: Match the following terms and identifying phrases.

_______ 1. A state of physical, mental, and emotional health.

_______ 2. A guide developed by the federal government to help people make healthful food choices.

_______ 3. A guide to good nutrition that includes food groups and recommended servings.

_______ 4. A fat-like substance in blood.

_______ 5. The component in blood that carries oxygen to all the cells of the body.

_______ 6. A physical condition caused by a lack of calcium.

_______ 7. An eating disorder characterized by eating large amounts of food, followed by purging (vomiting or taking laxatives).

_______ 8. Fats that tend to be liquid at room temperature and come from plant sources.

_______ 9. Fats that tend to be solid at room temperature and come from animal sources.

_______ 10. An eating disorder characterized by an intense fear of being obese, leading to a refusal to eat.

A. cholesterol

B. anorexia nervosa

C. blood pooling

D. Food Guide Pyramid

E. saturated fat

F. wellness

G. hemoglobin

H. bulimia

I. Dietary Guidelines for Americans

J. osteoporosis

K. unsaturated fat

True/False: Circle *T* if the statement is true or *F* if the statement is false.

T F 11. Three or more servings daily from the milk and milk products group are recommended for teenagers.

T F 12. Good sources of vitamin A include vegetables such as spinach, carrots, and sweet potatoes.

T F 13. The human body needs protein for the growth and repair of body tissues.

T F 14. Snacks are not nutritious.

T F 15. Stress can result from positive as well as negative events.

T F 16. Treatment for eating disorders should address physical problems but not the underlying emotional problems.

T F 17. A health-conscious consumer can help shape a society that promotes optimal health for its members.

T F 18. Athletes in training should disregard the Food Guide Pyramid.

T F 19. Insufficient sleep can have negative effects on a person's health, appearance, ability to concentrate on schoolwork, and overall feeling of well-being.

T F 20. Individuals who experience chest pain during exercise have no cause for medical concern.

(Continued)

Contemporary Living Teacher's Resources

Multiple Choice: Select the best response. Write the letter in the space provided.

_____ 21. What condition can occur later in life from years of calcium deficiency?
A. Cancer.
B. Osteoporosis.
C. Bulimia.
D. Anemia.

_____ 22. A diet high in saturated fat can lead to _____.
A. high blood cholesterol levels
B. heart disease
C. weight gain
D. All of the above.

_____ 23. The healthiest approach to weight loss is to _____.
A. lose as much weight as quickly as possible
B. confine your eating to one type of food
C. use up more calories than you consume by following a sensible diet and exercise plan
D. eliminate all carbohydrates from your diet

_____ 24. People who are obsessed with being thin may develop _____.
A. cancer
B. anorexia nervosa
C. hemophilia
D. Down's syndrome

_____ 25. In general, authorities recommend that a person exercise vigorously for at least _____.
A. 30 minutes four days a week
B. 60 minutes once a week
C. 60 minutes every day
D. 10 minutes every day

_____ 26. Which of the following statements concerning stress is NOT true?
A. Stress results from change.
B. Stress is unrelated to mental and physical health.
C. Crying can be a good, healthy way to relieve stress.
D. Using drugs and alcohol does not remove the condition causing stress.

_____ 27. Binge-purge syndrome is a symptom of _____.
A. bulimia
B. anorexia
C. sleep deficit
D. conditioning

_____ 28. To avoid blood pooling, _____.
A. eat a healthful diet
B. do not eat fats, oils, or sweets
C. be sure to get enough sleep
D. do not stop vigorous exercise abruptly

_____ 29. Which of the following is NOT a major group in the Food Guide Pyramid?
A. Fruit.
B. Milk, yogurt, and cheese.
C. Soda pop, crackers, and potato chips.
D. Fats, oils, and sweets.

(Continued)

_______ 30. A high-fiber diet is believed to be a significant factor in avoiding _____.
  A. heart disease
  B. some types of cancer
  C. Both of the above.
  D. None of the above.

Essay Questions: Provide the answers that you feel best show your understanding of the subject matter.

31. List and briefly discuss four recommendations from the Dietary Guidelines for Americans.

32. Describe three benefits of regular exercise.

33. Describe two stress-reduction techniques.

Chapter 8
Avoiding Harmful Substances

Objectives

After studying this chapter, students will be able to

- explain the health hazards of smoking.
- describe the consequences of drinking alcohol.
- define various terms related to drug use and abuse.
- describe various kinds of drugs and how they affect the body.
- explain how peer pressure influences behavior.

Bulletin Boards

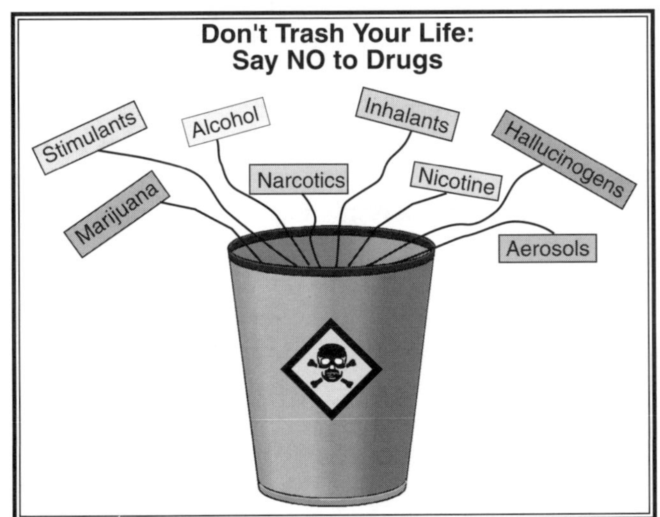

I. Title: "Don't Trash Your Life: Say NO to Drugs"

Draw a construction paper trash can with a skull and crossbones on it, or use a plastic trash bag. Mount on bulletin board. Above the trash can, arrange brightly colored pieces of paper labeled *Stimulants, Narcotics, Hallucinogens, Aerosols, Marijuana, Inhalants, Nicotine,* and *Alcohol.* Use pieces of yarn to connect labels and top of trash can.

II. Title: "How Many Ways to Say No!"

How to say no to peer pressure concerning the use of tobacco, alcohol, and drugs is discussed frequently in this chapter and will also be referred to again in later chapters. Help students remember these techniques by printing them on cards and placing them on the bulletin board. Under the title, place an explanatory sentence that reads, "When pressured to do something you do not feel is right for you, try these techniques:"

- Don't give reasons or excuses that just cause arguments.
- Say no like you mean it!
- Say no without becoming angry, calling names, or adding insults.
- After you say no, suggest another activity.
- Get away from the person (or persons) as soon as you can after saying no.

Invite students to add other ideas.

Teaching Materials

Text, pages 182-205

Terms to Know, To Review, To Do, and *To Think About*

Student Activity Guide
   A. *Smoking*
   B. *Drinking and Driving*
   C. *Alcohol's Effect on Personal Relationships*
   D. *The Use of Alcohol*
   E. *How Alcohol Is Portrayed on Television*
   F. *Saying No to Alcohol*
   G. *Drugs*
   H. *Saying No to Drugs*
   I. *The Use of Drugs*

Teacher's Resource Guide/Binder
   How Alcohol Kills, transparency master, 8-1
   Combining Drugs and Alcohol, transparency master, 8-2
   Legal Consequences of Alcohol and Drug Abuse, reproducible master, 8-3
   How to Say No to Peer Pressure, reproducible master, 8-4
   Chapter 8 Test

Teacher's Resource Binder
   Smoking and Health Problems, color transparency, CT-8A
   Alcoholism and Health Problems, color transparency, CT-8B

Software for Contemporary Living
   Chapter Review Game

Introductory Activity

1. Ask students to respond to the following incomplete sentences:
    *   If I were offered alcohol, I would . . .
    *   If I were offered a cigarette, I would . . .
    *   If I were offered drugs, I would . . .
    *   Using illegal substances is . . .
    *   The best way to withstand peer pressure to use illegal substances is . . .

    Ask students to share responses as a basis for discussion.

Strategies to Reteach, Reinforce, Enrich, and Extend Text Concepts

Tobacco

2. **RF** *Smoking,* Activity A, SAG. Have students complete the activity and use their responses as a basis for class discussion.

3. **RF** Discuss the reasons for not using tobacco that are given in the text. Ask students for additional reasons for not using tobacco.

4. **RT** *Smoking and Health Problems,* color transparency, CT-8A. Refer to this transparency in discussing the health problems related to smoking. Point out that despite the glamorous figures depicted in tobacco advertising, there is nothing glamorous about the health problems associated with tobacco and smoking.

5. **RF** Discuss the use of smokeless tobacco and the health problems that can result. Talk about the effects of prominent sports figures using smokeless tobacco.

6. **ER** Discuss new laws concerning the rights of nonsmokers in public places. How have these changed offices, restaurants, public buildings, etc.? Do students foresee increased restrictions on smokers? What is your school's policy on smoking? Poll the student body for their opinions about smoking restrictions.

7. **ER** Ask a physician to speak to your class about health problems related to smoking.

Alcohol

8. **RF** *Alcoholism and Health Problems,* color transparency, CT-8B. Refer to this transparency to emphasize the contrast between the glamorous images presented by alcohol advertising and the stark reality of alcohol-caused health problems.

9. **RT** *How Alcohol Kills,* transparency master, 8-1. Refer to this transparency in discussing the many societal problems in which alcohol plays a major role.

10. **RF** *Drinking and Driving,* Activity B, SAG. Ask students to respond to the statements on drinking and driving. Go over the statements and discuss.

11. **RF** *Alcohol's Effect on Personal Relationships,* Activity C, SAG. Students are to write their reactions to situations depicting relationship problems caused by drinking. Have them discuss their responses in small groups.

12. **RF** *The Use of Alcohol,* Activity D, SAG. Ask students to complete the activity and discuss their reactions to the statements.

Contemporary Living Teacher's Resources

13. **RF** *How Alcohol Is Portrayed on Television,* Activity E, SAG. Assign students to watch TV for two hours and note the number of times alcohol is shown or mentioned. Discuss the impact this may have on persons making decisions about alcohol use.

14. **RF** Ask students to look up the definition of "drug" in the dictionary. Ask if alcohol is a drug. Also look up "depressant." Discuss how alcohol acts as a depressant.

15. **RF** Ask students to make their own list of "Reasons for Not Drinking." Share and discuss.

16. **RF** Ask students what noticeable behavioral changes occur when a person has been drinking, such as slurred speech, clumsiness, short temper, etc. Ask why these changes occur. Are these behavioral changes appealing to other people?

17. **EX** *Saying No to Alcohol,* Activity F, SAG. Students are asked to write ways to say no to alcohol and to role-play selected situations, followed by discussion.

18. **ER** Ask a speaker from Alcoholics Anonymous to talk to your class about the problems faced by alcoholics and their families.

19. **ER** Ask a speaker from MADD (Mothers Against Drunk Driving) to talk to your class.

Drugs

20. **RF** Compare the meanings of the terms "drug use," "drug misuse," and "drug abuse." Give examples of each.

21. **RF** Go over reasons for saying no to drugs. Discuss the consequences of drug abuse and the use of illegal drugs.

22. **RF** *Combining Drugs and Alcohol,* transparency master, 8-2. Refer to this transparency in emphasizing the dangers of combining drugs and alcohol.

23. **RF** *Drugs,* Activity G, SAG. Review terms related to drugs using this crossword puzzle.

24. **RF** *The Use of Drugs,* Activity I, SAG. Ask students to complete the activity and discuss their responses as a class.

25. **RF** Ask class members to respond to the open-ended statement, "I think people should not use illegal drugs because...." Share responses.

26. **RF** Many people mistakenly believe that marijuana is a "safe" drug. Ask students if they feel this attitude is common among teens. Discuss ways to overcome this misinformation.

27. **EX** Ask volunteers to debate whether or not schools have the right to test student athletes for drug use.

28. **ER** Ask students to research the use of anabolic steroids by athletes, citing the physical and mental side effects of the drug.

29. **ER** *Legal Consequences of Alcohol and Drug Abuse,* reproducible master, 8-3. Ask students to research the legal consequences of drug use in your local area, or ask a law enforcement officer to speak to your class. Determine the legal consequences of the activities described in the duplicating master.

30. **ER** Ask the class to research and develop a list of resources available to persons who have a drug problem. Write or call organizations for brochures and information. Organize a file in your classroom with names, addresses, phone numbers, costs, etc.

31. **EX** Use *The Decision-Making Process* transparency master from Chapter 5 to help students make a decision concerning the use of tobacco, alcohol, and drugs. You can also make copies of this master for each student to use individually to work through a decision concerning the use of these substances. Remind students to consider both long- and short-term consequences, including effects on family and friends.

32. **ER** Ask a physician or psychiatrist to speak to your class about the problems of drug abuse. Prepare a list of questions about the unknown quality of drugs, the tendency to evade problems with drugs, and the wide scope of effects that drugs have on people.

33. **ER** Assemble a panel consisting of a male student, a female student, a physician, a psychologist, and a parent. Ask the panel to discuss the topic, "Drug Misuse is a Process–A Chain of Events." Cite the reasons why persons start to use drugs and how they are pressured to continue using drugs. Discuss the various community resources young people and their families can use when help is needed.

34. **ER** Crack is a dangerous drug, and because it is relatively inexpensive, it is available to many. Ask a drug enforcement officer to speak to your class and discuss the problems involved in the use of crack.

Dealing with Peer Pressure

35. **ER** *Saying No to Drugs,* Activity H, SAG. Have students write responses to statements commonly used to persuade young people to try drugs. Ask students to share their responses with other class members.

36. **RF** *How to Say No to Peer Pressure,* reproducible master, 8-4. Students are asked to read tips for saying no and to apply them to various situations by role-playing, discussion, and writing their own reactions.

Answer Key for Chapter 8

Text
To Review, page 204.

1. true
2. (Describe five. Student response.)
3. false
4. (Describe three. Student response.)
5. A, C, D, G.
6. Drug use is the taking of a drug for its intended purposes, in the appropriate amount, frequency, strength, and manner. Drug misuse is taking a substance for its intended purpose but not in the appropriate amount, frequency, strength, or manner. Drug abuse is deliberately taking a substance for other than its intended purpose, and in a manner that can result in damage to the person's health or his or her ability to function.
7. The effects of crack are far more intense, much quicker, and far more addictive. Crack greatly multiplies the danger of cocaine use.
8. They neglect work and adopt a "drop-out" personality.
9. Inhalants can cause death due to suffocation as the oxygen in the body is replaced with the chemicals. Sniffing inhalants can also cause brain damage, as well as serious damage to the liver or kidneys. Inhaling certain aerosol spray products can kill in seconds by freezing the larynx and respiratory system.
10. true
11. (Student response.)

Activity G, *Drugs.*

The completed crossword puzzle:

					H					L		H		U		
				D	E	P	R	E	S	S	A	N	T	S		
M					R				D		L			E		D
A					O						L					E
R					I		S	T	I	M	U	L	A	N	T	S
I					N						C					I
J							P	H	Y	S	I	C	A	L		G
U											N					N
A		C								C	O	C	A	I	N	E
N	A	R	C	O	T	I	C	S			G					R
A		A									E					
	P	C	P		S	N	I	F	F	I	N	G				
		K									S					

Across: 5. DEPRESSANTS 8. STIMULANTS 9. PHYSICAL 11. COCAINE 12. NARCOTICS 13. PCP 14. SNIFFING

Down: 1. HEROIN 2. LSD 3. HALLUCINOGENS 4. USE 6. MARIJUANA 7. DESIGNER 10. CRACK

Teacher's Resource Guide

Chapter 8 Test

1. J	11. T	21. D
2. H	12. F	22. C
3. I	13. F	23. A
4. F	14. F	24. C
5. A	15. T	25. B
6. G	16. T	26. D
7. K	17. T	27. C
8. C	18. F	28. A
9. D	19. F	29. D
10. B	20. T	30. A

31. (List four:) Chronic cough; cancer of the lung, lips, mouth, larynx, and esophagus; emphysema; heart disease; dangers during pregnancy.
32. (See discussion on page 192 of the text.)
33. (Describe three. Student response.)

How Alcohol Kills

Alcohol is involved in more than half of . . . .

accidental deaths,

homicides,

suicides,

. . . and just under half of . . . .

traffic fatalities.

Combining Drugs and Alcohol

Can cause

- Impaired memory
- Confusion
- Harmful chemical interactions
- Death

Drugs + Alcohol = A Deadly Combination

Legal Consequences of Alcohol and Drug Abuse

Name _______________________________ **Date** _____________ **Period** _____________

Research the legal consequences of drug and alcohol abuse in your state.

1. What is the penalty if a minor is arrested and convicted of alcohol use? _______________________
____
____

2. What is the liability of the seller if alcohol is sold to a minor? _______________________________
____
____

3. What is the liability of a buyer if alcohol is used by a minor?________________________________
____
____

4. What is the liability of a person who serves too much alcohol to an individual who is then involved
in a drunk-driving accident? ____
____
____

5. What is the liability of a host who serves alcohol to guests who are drinking too much? ___________
____
____

6. What driving restrictions are levied when a person is convicted of DWI (driving while intoxicated)?
____
____

7. What are the penalties if convicted of marijuana possession? ________________________________
____
____

8. What are the penalties if convicted of selling marijuana? __________________________________
____
____

9. Is a drug arrest a misdemeanor or a felony? ____

10. What is being done in your local community to combat the drunk driving and other drug abuse
problems? ____
____
____

How to Say No to Peer Pressure

Name_______________________________________ **Date** _______________ **Period**_______________

Some tips for saying no to peer pressure are described below. Relate each tip to the situation then described. Role-play the situations in class using the techniques for saying no. Discuss the effectiveness of each technique. Then write your reaction.

Tips for saying no	Situation	Reaction
Don't give reasons or excuses for your decision–just say no. It's your right to make the decision of your choice. Reasons and excuses can bring an argument.	Your friends want you to go riding with them. You know they have beer in the car, which they will be drinking.	
Say no like you mean it. Look straight at the person pressuring you, keep your voice steady, and watch your body movements. Be firm and don't worry about what to say next.	You walk up to a group of friends you see outside the local mall. They are passing around a marijuana cigarette and someone hands it to you.	
Say no without becoming angry, calling names, or adding insults. You have a right to make your own decisions. You don't need to argue in order to convince the other person.	Your friends have come over to your home when your parents are gone. They look in your parents' liquor cabinet and say, "If we took a little bit from a couple of bottles, they would never know!"	
After you say no, suggest another activity. Then the other person has to resist your suggestion.	Your date suggests the two of you go to your house since no one is at home, and you can be alone. Your date says he wants to start on the six-pack he has with him.	
Get away from the person as soon as you can after saying no. Don't give him or her a chance to question your decision to say no.	You are at a party with several of your friends. A girl you met at school starts up a conversation with you. You are having a good time when she whispers that she has something in her purse that will really make the party fun.	

Avoiding Harmful Substances

Name

Date ___________ **Period** _______ **Score** _______

Chapter 8 Test

Matching: Match the following terms and identifying phrases.

_____   1. Psychological dependence on a drug.

_____   2. Synthetic testosterone-like drug that has tissue-building properties.

_____   3. Behavior involving neglect of work and adoption of a "drop-out" personality.

_____   4. Substances that give off fumes that are sniffed for a quick "high."

_____   5. Taking a substance for its intended purpose but not in the appropriate amount, frequency, strength, or manner.

_____   6. Drugs that speed up the central nervous system.

_____   7. Addictive drug that induces sleep or stupor and relieves pain.

_____   8. Contains nicotine, is habit-forming, and can lead to a number of health problems.

_____   9. Drugs that slow down the central nervous system.

_____   10. Mind-altering drugs.

A. drug misuse
B. hallucinogens
C. smokeless tobacco
D. depressants
E. glaucoma
F. inhalants
G. stimulants
H. anabolic steroid
I. amotivational syndrome
J. habituation
K. narcotic

True/False: Circle *T* if the statement is true or *F* if the statement is false.

T F   11. A drug is a substance, other than food, that has an effect on one or more systems of the body, especially the central nervous system.

T F   12. Alcohol is a stimulant.

T F   13. Marijuana is also known as "scag," "smack," and "junk."

T F   14. National sports organizations have taken a strong stand in favor of the use of steroids by athletes.

T F   15. Time and space distortion, impairment of judgment, and loss of motor skills may occur when using marijuana.

T F   16. Physicians believe that it is best for the fetus if pregnant women do not drink at all.

T F   17. Pregnant women who smoke have a greater chance of having premature deliveries and smaller babies than pregnant women who do not smoke.

T F   18. Second-hand smoke does not affect the health of nonsmokers.

T F   19. Drugs secured illegally are consistent in quality and potency.

T F   20. People have died from alcohol poisoning after drinking one pint of liquor all at once.

(Continued)

Multiple Choice: Select the best response. Write the letter in the space provided.

_______ 21. People who smoke have a greater chance of developing ____.
A. lung cancer
B. lip cancer
C. larynx cancer
D. All of the above.

_______ 22. Which of the following statements concerning alcohol is true?
A. The effects of alcohol do not vary with body size.
B. The absorption of alcohol into the bloodstream occurs more rapidly when there is food in the stomach.
C. Alcohol is sometimes used as a main food source by people who drink to excess.
D. Drinking coffee speeds up the elimination of alcohol from the bloodstream.

_______ 23. Drug abuse is _____.
A. deliberately taking a substance for other than its intended purpose in a manner that can damage a person's health
B. taking a substance for its intended purpose but not in the appropriate amount or manner
C. physical rather than psychological dependence on a drug
D. not a problem for young people today

_______ 24. Which of the following is NOT a problem that can be caused by alcohol consumption?
A. Brain damage.
B. Pancreatitis.
C. Cystic fibrosis.
D. Cirrhosis of the liver.

_______ 25. Addiction refers to _____.
A. the taking of a drug for its intended purpose
B. physical dependence on a drug
C. psychological dependence on a drug
D. drugs that induce resistance to infection

_______ 26. Use of inhalants can damage _____.
A. the brain
B. the liver
C. the kidneys
D. All of the above.

_______ 27. _____ is a drug that is sometimes used to help heroin addicts by serving as a substitute for heroin.
A. Marijuana
B. Hashish
C. Methadone
D. Cannabis sativa

_______ 28. Crack is a form of _____.
A. cocaine
B. amphetamine
C. narcotic
D. methamphetamine

(Continued)

_____ 29. The effects of alcohol on the body are influenced by _____.
     A. the amount of alcohol consumed
     B. the speed with which alcohol is consumed
     C. the amount of food in the stomach
     D. All of the above.

_____ 30. Alcoholic mothers or mothers who drink heavily are more likely to give birth to babies with _____.
     A. fetal alcohol syndrome
     B. Rh factor
     C. Tay sachs disease
     D. Sickle cell anemia

Essay Questions: Provide complete responses to the following questions or statements.

31. List four ways in which smoking affects health.

32. Discuss effective and ineffective ways to try to help an alcoholic.

33. Describe three ways to say no to peer pressure to use tobacco or drugs.

Chapter 9 ■ ■ ■ ■ ■ ■ ■ ■ ■ ■ ■ ■ ■ ■ ■ ■
Lifestyle Options and Consequences

Objectives

After studying this chapter, students will be able to

- define lifestyle and identify adult lifestyle options as they exist today.
- describe reasons and circumstances people cite for choosing a single lifestyle, marriage, childless marriage, or living together.
- identify an unplanned pregnancy as a lifestyle consequence.
- evaluate alternative options available when an unplanned pregnancy occurs.
- identify sexually transmitted diseases and explain the health crises they pose.
- assess the role of responsible behavior concerning lifestyle options and consequences.

Bulletin Boards

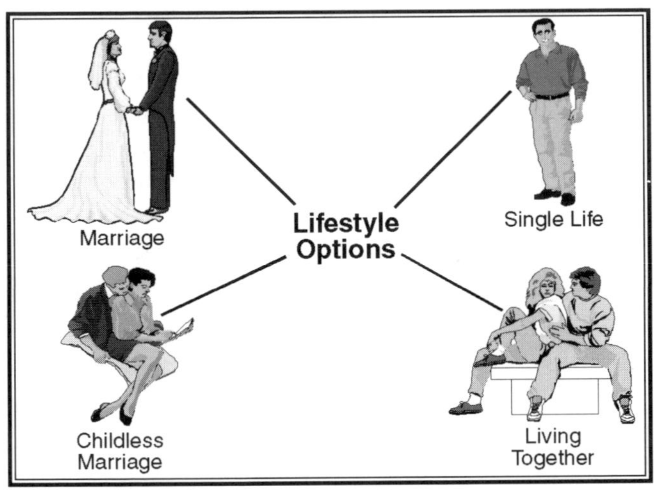

I. Title: "Lifestyle Options"

Place the title in the center of a bulletin board and list the four options under magazine pictures that depict each lifestyle. As the various lifestyles are studied, ask students to list the pros and cons of each lifestyle on 3 x 5 inch index cards. Post these under the appropriate lifestyles.

II. Title: "Adoption Is An Option"

Place newspaper and magazine articles about adoption on the bulletin board. Also post brochures from various adoption agencies. Pictures of adoptive families can also be added (with their permission), as well as any photos of class members who might wish to let the class know that they are adopted. (Many adopted teens are very open about their adoptions and might welcome an opportunity to share their thoughts about adoption.)

Teaching Materials

Text, pages 206-231
Terms to Know, To Review, To Do, and *To Think About*

Student Activity Guide
- A. *Lifestyles*
- B *Premarital Pregnancy*
- C. *A Look at the Adoption Options*
- D. *Lifestyles and Health*
- E. *Sexually Transmitted Diseases–Myths and Truths*

Teacher's Resource Guide/Binder
Lifestyle Choices, reproducible master, 9-1
Teenage Pregnancies–The Risks, the Results, transparency master, 9-2

A Look at the Alternatives, transparency masters, 9-3A and 3B

An Unplanned Pregnancy, reproducible master, 9-4

Pregnancy Decisions, transparency masters, 9-5A, 5B, 5C, and 5D

A Typical Case of STD, transparency master, 9-6

Chapter 9 Test

Teacher's Resource Binder

Adult Lifestyle Options, color transparency, CT-9A

Aids–Leading Killer of Young Men, color transparency, CT-9B

Software for Contemporary Living

Chapter Review Game

Introductory Activities

1. *Lifestyle Choices,* reproducible master, 9-1. Use this activity to encourage students to begin thinking about various lifestyle options, and the issues these lifestyles raise. Have students indicate whether they agree or disagree with the statements. Compare and discuss in class.

2. Introduce the study of lifestyle options and consequences by using a fishbowl structure to stimulate discussion. Ask the question, "What do we mean by the term lifestyle?" Have those students who raise their hands form a circle with their chairs in the front of the classroom. Ask them to share freely their reactions to the question for five minutes. The remaining class members should only watch and listen. After five minutes, ask the students to exchange places. The new group members respond, clarify, evaluate, accept, or reject what was previously said. The groups can continue to change positions and share. The following incomplete sentences can also be used to stimulate discussion:

   • Some lifestyles mean...

   • The biggest problem in the______________ lifestyle is...

Strategies to Reteach, Reinforce, Enrich, and Extend Text Concepts

Adult Lifestyle Options

3. **RF** *Adult Lifestyle Options,* color transparency, CT-9A. Use this transparency to discuss the three adult lifestyle options, as well as marriage with and without children. Students can discuss the pros and cons of each option, as well as some of the consequences of each choice. Ask students which option they would choose now and which they might choose five or ten years from now.

4. **RF** Cite the increase in the number of persons choosing the single lifestyle. Ask for possible reasons for this increase. Discuss reasons why many people today feel single life may be more attractive.

5. **EX** Divide the class into groups to research how the increasing trend toward single living is affecting your community. Contact each of the following: real estate agents about singles buying homes, financial institutions about credit and saving trends of singles, apartment managers about rentals to singles, religious organizations about programs for singles, and community agencies about the special needs of singles. Ask each group to report back to class.

6. **EX** Ask students to develop a list of new food products and small appliances specifically designed for singles.

7. **EX** Ask students to write papers explaining why marriage is the most popular lifestyle in our country, or discuss the topic with the class.

8. **RF** Form buzz groups to discuss the reasons why couples may choose to remain childless. What criticism might they face from relatives and friends?

9. **EX** Have students complete the statement, "I view parenthood as a (duty/right/privilege)." Give reasons for their answers.

10. **EX** Ask students to debate the pros and cons of couples living together before marriage. Ask them to indicate if the male or the female has greater risk. Consider property rights and living expenses. Research the legality of social security benefits, health care expenses, and inheritance rights if children are born.

11. **ER** Ask a judge or lawyer to talk on legal and financial matters relating to the living together lifestyle. Consider property rights, inheritance rights of children, claims to income, social security, income taxes, child custody, insurance claims, and other legal and financial issues.

12. **RF** Ask students to discuss how the living together arrangement might be viewed by parents. What happens when the couple visits parents and how might parental views influence the young couple?

13. **EX** *Lifestyles*, Activity A, SAG. Students are asked to read the statements concerning various lifestyles and give their opinions.

Lifestyle Consequences

14. **EX** *Premarital Pregnancy*, Activity B, SAG. Students are asked to evaluate the four options available to unmarried, pregnant teens, listing the pros and cons of each alternative. Students will select the best options in their opinion and give reasons for their choices.

15. **RT** *Teenage Pregnancies–The Risks, the Results*, transparency master, 9-2. Use this transparency when discussing the risks involved with teen pregnancies. Results or consequences facing young parents are also given.

16. **RT** Review the myths about pregnancy listed on page 215 of the text. Discuss why these are referred to as myths.

17. **EX** Ask students to pretend they are parents of a teenage son or daughter. Have them write letters to their sons or daughters expressing their views concerning sexual priorities. Discuss the following: Does you letter reveal a more permissive or a traditional attitude? Did you adopt the attitudes your own parents expressed to you?

18. **ER** Ask a doctor associated with a teenage clinic to discuss the risks involved with teen pregnancies. Ask students to list questions before the speaker arrives.

19. **EX** *A Look at the Alternatives*, transparency masters, 9-3A and 9-3B. Use these transparencies to identify the pros and cons of each alternative for a pregnant teen. The masters can also be duplicated for each student to use individually.

20. **EX** *An Unplanned Pregnancy*, reproducible master, 9-4. This activity allows students to see the many questions that must be answered when an unplanned pregnancy occurs. You can use the questions as a basis for class discussion, or you can have your students discuss the questions in small groups. This activity can also be used as a writing assignment with each student answering the questions individually, or you can ask them to read through and think how they would answer all the questions, then choose one alternative, and write out the answers to only the questions for that alternative. By using this type of activity, your students are more likely to understand the many aspects of each alternative.

21. **EX** *Pregnancy Decisions*, transparency masters, 9-5A to 9-5D. These four transparencies are to be used together as overlays, or you can use a blank transparency and ask your students to give responses to create your own. The transparencies are based on a future wheel, a teaching technique that begins with a central issue or problem. Brainstorming results in various possibilities that are placed like spokes on the wheel. Ask your students to think through the decisions facing a teenage girl when she discovers she is pregnant. In transparency 9-5A, she decides to tell her parents and the father. In transparency 9-5B, two possible responses from these parties are shown. In 9-5C, the girl considers single parenting, and two of the possible outcomes are shown. Also shown are possible responses by the father. In 9-5D, the option of the couple choosing to parent together is shown, with possible outcomes. (Note: The two alternatives of adoption and abortion are not considered in this scenario, but they could be added. Students may think of other possible outcomes that could be added to the transparencies, or you could ask them to create their own future wheels beginning with the central problem–an unplanned pregnancy.)

22. **ER** Invite a panel of young parents who married because of a pregnancy, or who are single parents, to talk to the class about the difficulties they faced. Also have them share the positive aspects of their decision to parent.

23. **EX** *A Look at the Adoption Options*, Activity C, SAG. Students are to research and describe agency adoptions, independent adoptions, open adoptions, closed adoptions, and to state which options they think a woman should select and why.

24. **ER** Ask a case worker from an adoption agency to speak to the class about adoption, explaining the positive factors, the procedures, and the resources available for

adoption. Ask the speaker to bring pamphlets and other information about adoption that can be kept on file in the classroom.

25. **RT** In class discussions, use phrases such as "making an adoption plan," "placing the child in an adoptive home," and "arranging for an adoption" rather than negative phrases such as "giving away your child." Other terms to use are "birthmother or biological mother" rather than "real mother or natural mother." Discuss why many young people have a negative attitude concerning adoption.

26. **EX** Discuss how both agency and independent adoptions may be either "open" or "closed" adoptions. Then have students write short papers indicating what their choice would be should they make the decision to place a child in an adoptive home.

27. **RF** *Lifestyles and Health*, Activity D, SAG. Use this activity to review vocabulary terms introduced in the chapter.

28. **RF** *A Typical Case of STD*, transparency master, 9-6. Use this transparency to help students understand how quickly STDs can spread (1) if they remain untreated, (2) if sexual partners are numerous, (3) if the presence of an STD is not revealed to a sexual partner, and (4) if the identity of sexual partners is not revealed, preventing medical treatment from being obtained.

29. **RF** *Sexually Transmitted Diseases–Myths and Truths*, Activity E, SAG. Students are asked to read the statements concerning sexually transmitted diseases and to indicate if they are myths or truths. Answers are given on the back of the page. Read through the answers together to clarify any questions students may have.

30. **ER** Ask a health counselor, health care professional, or a speaker from the local public health department to speak to the class about sexually transmitted diseases. Have students prepare a list of questions concerning STDs. Ask the speaker to bring pamphlets and other information on STDs to keep on file in your class.

31. **RF** *AIDS–Leading Killer of Young Men*, color transparency, CT-9B. This transparency shows the leading causes of death of men ages 24 to 44. Note that in ten years, AIDS as a cause of death went from last place to first place. In 1993 AIDS was responsible for about 36,500 of the 2.18 million deaths in the U.S. For all people aged 25-44, HIV dropped from the leading cause of death in 1995 to fifth-leading in 1997. Since 1996, the number of AIDS deaths has decreased sharply due to the availability of improved medical treatments. Emphasize that despite the decrease in AIDS deaths, the number of people infected with HIV each year has not declined, and the total number of people living with HIV—and potentially able to infect others—is still increasing. An estimated 40,000 new HIV infections occur each year.

32. **ER** Ask a health care professional to speak to the class about AIDS, the preventive measures to take, the health consequences to the patient, the impact on family and friends, as well as society, the costs involved in care and treatment, etc.

Responsible Behavior

33. **RF** Discuss the word *abstinence* and what it means. If abstinence is chosen, what positive feelings can result (i.e., no guilt feelings, no clash with values, no self-destruction, no unplanned pregnancy, and no worry about STDs)?

34. **RF** The only 100 percent effective method of escaping sexually transmitted diseases and preventing unplanned pregnancies is to practice abstinence. Ask students to discuss the most effective way to teach young people the truth of this statement.

Answer Key for Chapter 9

Text
To Review, page 228.

1. Behaviors; choice.
2. (Describe three. Student response.)
3. false
4. (Cite three. Student response.)
5. Social Security survivor benefits are denied. The right of interspousal protection, important in criminal cases, is denied. Joint income tax returns cannot be filed. When one partner of an unmarried couple leaves or dies, the question of ownership of property arises. In most cases, the remaining partner has no legal claim to the property. If an unmarried

couple have a child, custody problems arise when and if the partners separate or when one dies and children have no inheritance rights.

6. (Describe two. Student response.)
7. (Describe three. Student response.)
8. false
9. In an open adoption, the birthparents and adoptive parents meet or know each other. In a closed adoption, the birthparents do not meet or know the adoptive parents.
10. Placing a baby in an adoptive home is putting the welfare of the baby first. Sometimes young teens cannot provide the best home for a child at this time in their lives. In an adoptive home, the needs of the child can more readily be met.
11. false
12. A woman with an active case of genital herpes may infect her baby during delivery. If the infection is severe, the baby may not survive. With a cesarean delivery, the baby does not pass through the infected birth canal.
13. The bacteria begin to damage the heart, brain, or spinal cord. Mental illness, blindness, paralysis, heart disease, and eventually death may result.

Student Activity Guide

Activity D, *Lifestyles and Health.*

1. F	9. E
2. M	10. N
3. P	11. L
4. C	12. O
5. A	13. G
6. D	14. H
7. I	15. B
8. K	16. J

Teacher's Resource Guide

Chapter 9 Test

1. C	11. T	21. B
2. I	12. T	22. C
3. D	13. F	23. D
4. G	14. T	24. B
5. H	15. F	25. A
6. F	16. F	26. D
7. E	17. F	27. D
8. A	18. T	28. B
9. F	19. F	29. B
10. T	20. T	30. C

31. (Give three:) Young adults working full-time; death of a spouse; separation and divorce; preference for the single lifestyle.
32. Marriage. (Student response for why it is popular.)
33. (Student response.)
34. (State two differences:) In an agency adoption, the birthmother relinquishes the child to the agency; in an independent adoption, the child may be given directly to the adoptive family. In an agency adoption, a counselor works with the birthparents; in an independent adoption, there is no counselor. In an agency adoption, the birthmother and the adoptive family do not generally meet; in an independent adoption, the birthparents may work directly with adoptive parents.
35. (Student response.)

Lifestyle Choices

Name_______________________________________ **Date**_______________ **Period**_______________

The following statements relate to the various lifestyles present in our society today. Decide whether you agree or disagree with each of the statements. Compare your responses with your classmates.

Agree   Disagree

_______ _______ 1. A single person is usually someone who has been rejected or has never considered marriage.

_______ _______ 2. Today, more persons are remaining single longer or are deciding never to marry.

_______ _______ 3. Some careers accommodate the single lifestyle better than a married lifestyle.

_______ _______ 4. It is easier today for single persons to adopt children, to buy homes, and to otherwise function in our society.

_______ _______ 5. Marriage provides the most ideal setting for raising children.

_______ _______ 6. Marriage means entrapment and stagnation for one of the partners.

_______ _______ 7. For a marriage to be vital and successful, there must be room for both individual and mutual growth.

_______ _______ 8. If either spouse places more importance on individual goals than on the mutual relationship, the marriage will probably deteriorate.

_______ _______ 9. In dual-career families, the birth of children will mean greater sharing of roles.

_______ _______ 10. Today parenthood is considered by most people to be a privilege, not a duty.

_______ _______ 11. Partners should discuss their feelings about having children before marriage.

_______ _______ 12. Children are a necessary and vital part of a marriage.

_______ _______ 13. Couples who remain childless are ignoring the "natural" purpose of marriage.

_______ _______ 14. Parenthood is irreversible even if a couple should become divorced.

_______ _______ 15. Men and women who live together are happier than those who choose the single or married lifestyle.

_______ _______ 16. A couple who avoids making deep personal commitments may be setting themselves up for a mediocre relationship.

_______ _______ 17. Couples who live together tend to follow traditional roles in the division of labor and power much the same as married couples.

_______ _______ 18. Couples who live together are denied social security survivor benefits and the right to file a joint income tax return.

_______ _______ 19. Living together is often a method people use to avoid responsibility.

_______ _______ 20. A couple who live together may be settling for too little. They could have a richer, more meaningful relationship if they were married.

Teenage Pregnancies–The Risks, the Results

The risks:

- Young girls' bodies may not be fully developed. The added strain of pregnancy may create health risks for the young mothers and their babies.

- Teens are twice as likely to have low-birthweight babies or premature babies compared to older mothers.

- The risk of infant death is twice as high for teenage mothers as it is for older mothers.

- The risk of maternal death is much greater for young teens than for women in their 20s.

- Poorly nourished teens are more likely to get toxemia and more likely to become anemic during pregnancy.

- Many teenage girls do not get adequate prenatal care.

The results:

- 70 percent of teenage mothers never finish high school.

- Teenage fathers who accept the responsibilities of their parenthood are less likely to graduate from high school.

- Teenage parents, who may lack adequate job skills, are more likely to have low-paying jobs or to be unemployed and on welfare.

- Teenage marriages are three times more likely to end in divorce.

A Look at the Alternatives

Alternative: Single Parenting

PROS	CONS

Alternative: Marriage

PROS	CONS

Alternative: Adoption

PROS	CONS

Alternative: Ending the Pregnancy

PROS	CONS

An Unplanned Pregnancy

Nancy became pregnant when she was a junior in high school and Brad was a senior. Suddenly they found themselves faced with a very difficult decision. They considered several alternatives and discovered many questions had to be answered concerning each option. Many of those questions are listed below. Read each question through and think how Nancy and Brad might answer each one.

Keeping the baby:

1. Will they be able to continue to attend high school?
2. Will they be able to go on to college after they graduate?
3. Will they be able to handle the 24-hour-a-day responsibilities of raising a child?
4. Where will they live?
5. Will they be able to afford the extra expense of raising a child?
6. Where can they obtain financial assistance in rearing a child?

How would you answer the previous questions if Brad decided to have nothing to do with Nancy and the baby? Go through the questions again, and answer them as Nancy would have to if she were alone.

Marriage:

1. Should Nancy insist that Brad marry her?
2. Would Nancy wonder, "Did Brad marry me because I was pregnant, or because he really loved me?"
3. How will marriage affect their education and career goals?
4. How will marriage and parenthood affect their relationships with their friends?
5. Are Nancy and Brad too young to have a successful marriage?
6. Can a new marriage succeed when combined with instant parenthood?

Adoption:

1. Will a couple that has been carefully selected by an agency be better able to provide for the needs of a baby?
2. Will a couple that Nancy and Brad select through an independent adoption arrangement be better able to provide for the needs of the baby?
3. Will Nancy and Brad be able to handle the emotional trauma of placing their baby for adoption?
4. Can one parent choose to place a baby for adoption without the consent of the other?
5. Can Nancy get any housing and financial assistance during her pregnancy prior to adoption?
6. Can Nancy and Brad indicate any preferences as to the type of family they would like selected for their baby?
7. How will an adoption affect their education and career goals?

Ending the pregnancy:

1. How might Brad and Nancy feel emotionally following an abortion?
2. What are the medical risks of an abortion?
3. How much time do Nancy and Brad have to make a decision concerning abortion?
4. Must the parents of Nancy and Brad give their permission or be notified of a decision to seek an abortion?
5. Should Nancy and Brad seek counseling prior to an abortion?

Pregnancy Decisions
(Future Focus Wheel)

Parents may offer emotional/ financial help.

Parents may refuse or be unable to help.

He may feel trapped and abondon the girl.

He may accept responsibility.

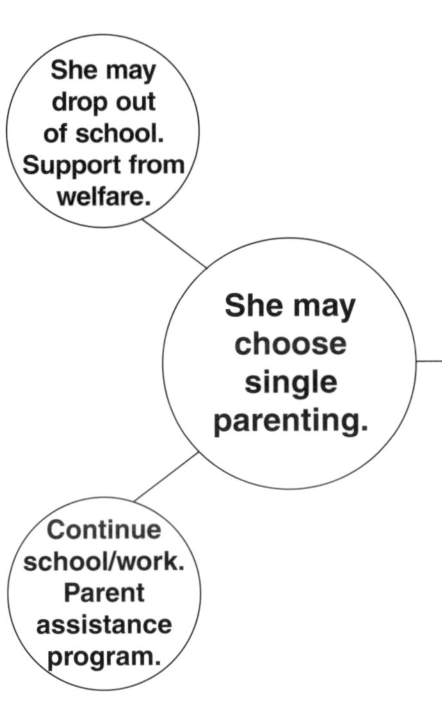

She may drop out of school. Support from welfare.
She may choose single parenting.
Continue school/work. Parent assistance program.

Court may seek paternity testing.
May continue school/work with assistance.
May seek custody if mother abondons child.
May drop out of school to work.

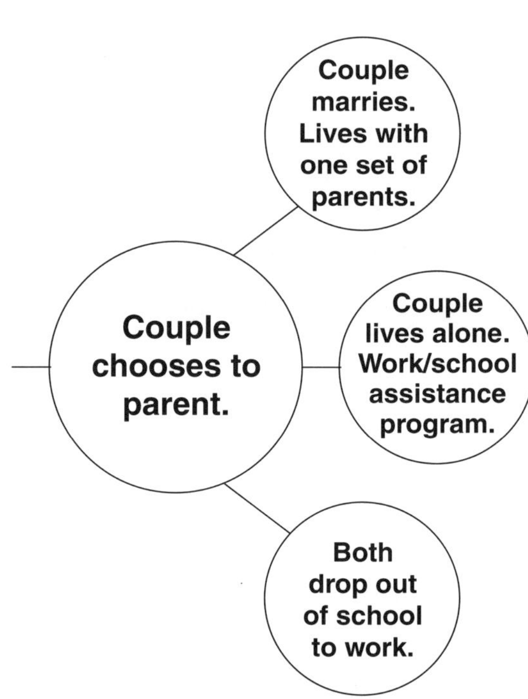
Couple marries. Lives with one set of parents.
Couple chooses to parent.
Couple lives alone. Work/school assistance program.
Both drop out of school to work.

A Typical Case of STD

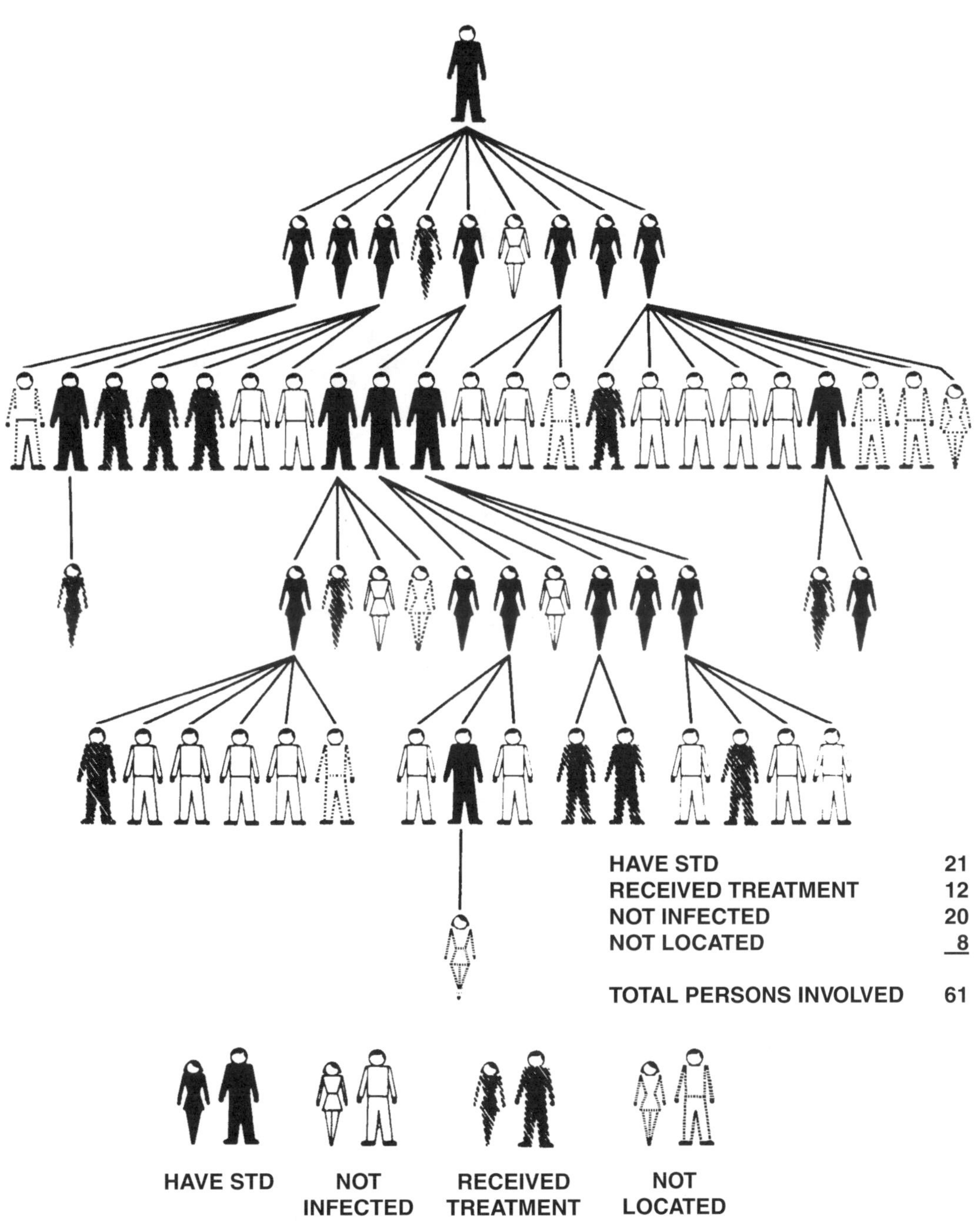

Lifestyle Options and Consequences

Chapter 9 Test

Matching: Choose the best response. Write the letter in the space provided.

_______ 1. STD that goes through two stages before entering a latent stage where the victim is no longer infectious.

_______ 2. STD that stays in the body, flaring up at irregular intervals. It cannot be cured.

_______ 3. Results in fluid retention during pregnancy.

_______ 4. STD that causes infection in the lining of the genital and urinary tracts.

_______ 5. A widespread STD that often causes no symptoms, but is a major cause of urinary tract infections.

_______ 6. A condition caused by the breakdown of the body's immune system.

_______ 7. An STD that causes flat or raised bumps to appear in the genital area.

_______ 8. A low level of hemoglobin in the blood.

A. anemic
B. HIV
C. syphilis
D. toxemia
E. genital warts
F. AIDS
G. gonorrhea
H. chlamydia
I. herpes

True/False: Circle *T* if the statement is true or *F* if the statement is false.

T F 9. The number of adults living alone is decreasing in our society.

T F 10. The percentage of married-couple households in the U.S. is decreasing.

T F 11. The division of labor within households where couples live together tends to follow traditional patterns.

T F 12. Legally, a family must be bonded by either a common ancestor or a marriage contract.

T F 13. Pregnancy cannot occur the first time sexual intercourse takes place.

T F 14. Compared to older women, teenage mothers are twice as likely to have low birth-weight babies or premature babies.

T F 15. Failing grades is the number one cause of female high school dropouts.

T F 16. In an adoption, the birthparents do not meet or know the adoptive parents.

T F 17. Once you have been cured of an STD, you cannot get it again.

T F 18. Gonorrhea can cause infertility in women.

T F 19. Syphilis cannot be detected and diagnosed by a blood test during any of its stages.

T F 20. Genital herpes cannot be cured.

(Continued)

Name ____

Multiple Choice: Choose the best response. Write the letter in the space provided.

_______ 21. _______ is defined as a set of behaviors adopted by personal choice.
   A. Options
   B. Lifestyles
   C. Parenthood
   D. Being single

_______ 22. Married couples who choose not to have children _______.
   A. are selfish
   B. are ignoring the "natural" purpose of marriage
   C. often view parenthood as a difficult and demanding task
   D. should discuss this decision after they marry

_______ 23. According to the judicial system, the legal family provides _______, which cannot be served by another lifestyle.
   A. a protective environment for raising and educating children
   B. an economic support system
   C. a legal outlet for sexual expression
   D. All of the above.

_______ 24. Which of the following statements is true about adoption?
   A. The pregnant mother has no say in the selection of the adoptive parents.
   B. In an agency adoption, a counselor works with the pregnant mother to help her with her problems and concerns.
   C. The birthfather has no legal rights in the adoption decision.
   D. The birthparents have one year after the baby is born to reclaim their child.

_______ 25. Which of the following statements is true concerning teenage pregnancy?
   A. The risk of an infant death is twice as high for teenage mothers as it is for older mothers.
   B. Teenagers are less likely to suffer from toxemia.
   C. Teenage girls are more likely to get good prenatal care.
   D. Most pregnant teens give birth.

_______ 26. Which of the following statements is true concerning sexually transmitted diseases?
   A. There are no vaccines for immunization against STDs.
   B. Every time you have sexual contact with another person without knowing the health of the other person, you run the risk of getting an STD.
   C. If you have been cured of an STD, you cannot get it again.
   D. Both A and B above.

_______ 27. Which of the following statements is true about AIDS?
   A. HIV may exist in the body for several years before AIDS develops.
   B. Teens may contract HIV during their teen years, but they may not develop AIDS until their twenties.
   C. HIV attacks the immune system, creating a weakness to other infections that the body cannot fight.
   D. All of the above.

_______ 28. You can contract AIDS _______.
   A. by donating blood
   B. through intravenous drug use
   C. through sexual contact only
   D. by shaking hands

(Continued)

Name ____

_______ 29. ______ is a sexually transmitted disease that causes a small, firm sore or chancre to appear after exposure.
    A. Gonorrhea
    B. Syphilis
    C. Genital warts
    D. Herpes

_______ 30. A pregnant woman with an active case of ______ may infect her baby during delivery.
    A. chlamydia
    B. syphilis
    C. genital herpes
    D. genital warts

Essay Questions: Provide complete responses to the following questions.

31. Give three reasons why a person might choose or have a single lifestyle.

32. What is the most popular lifestyle in our society? Why do you think this lifestyle continues to be so popular?

33. Briefly discuss the social, educational, and financial risks a pregnant teenager may face.

34. State two differences between an agency adoption and an independent adoption.

35. Explain some of the reasons AIDS is considered to be one of the biggest health risks of our time.

Part 3

Getting Along with Others

Chapter 10

Communicating with Others

Objectives

After studying this chapter, students will be able to

- recognize the many ways people communicate with others.
- evaluate the importance of good listening skills.
- judge the importance of communicating a positive image of themselves to others.
- identify five levels of communication.
- describe assertive behavior and its effect on communication.
- analyze communication skills that work well with parents.
- describe group behaviors that involve violence.
- define sexual harassment.

Bulletin Boards

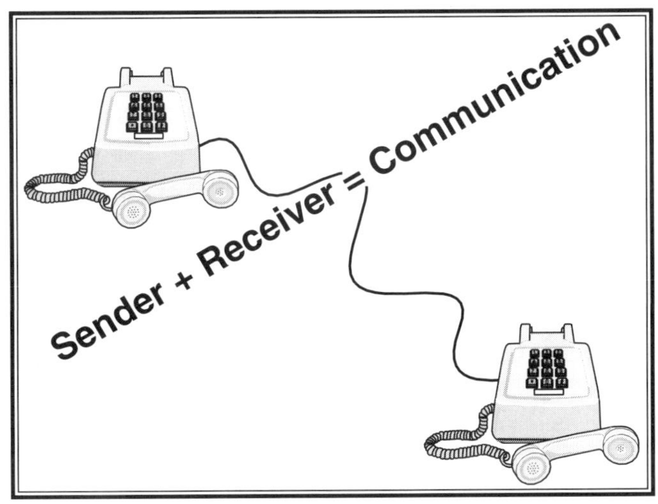

I. Title: "Sender + Receiver = Communication"

Mount this equation in large letters on the bulletin board. Mount a toy telephone on the board, or make a child's telephone out of two cans and a string. Arrange the cord or string across the board.

II. Title: "The Body Speaks"

Find pictures of people in magazines who are expressing various messages through body language. Examples might be: "I'm angry," "I'm in control," "I'm scared," "I could care less," "Back off," or "Let's talk." Mount the pictures on the bulletin board along with the nonverbal messages they depict.

III. Title: "The Communication Generation"

Mount newspaper and magazine articles as well as brochures that describe the latest developments in communication technology. Ask students to bring in additional articles to add to the bulletin board display.

Teaching Materials

Text, pages 234 to 259

Terms to Know, To Review, To Do , and To Think About

Student Activity Guide

A. *Communication Survey*
B. *Communication–Helping or Hindering?*
C. *Sympathy vs. Empathy*
D. *Levels of Communication*
E. *Communication Checklist*

F.   *Family Communication*

Teacher's Resource Guide/Binder

Verbal and Nonverbal Expressions, reproducible master, 10-1

Is Anybody Listening? reproducible master, 10-2

Communication Charades, reproducible master, 10-3

Communicating to Bring About Change, transparency master, 10-4

Word Choice in Communication, reproducible master, 10-5

Negotiating with Parents, reproducible master, 10-6

The Conflict Resolution Process, reproducible master, 10-7

Stay Alert to Sexual Harassment, transparency master, 10-8

Chapter 10 Test

Teacher's Resource Binder

Levels of Communication, color transparency, CT-10

Software for Contemporary Living

Chapter Review Game

Introductory Activities

1. *Verbal and Nonverbal Expressions*, reproducible master, 10-1. Use this activity to introduce the concept of verbal and nonverbal communication. Students are asked to indicate how they would respond, both verbally and nonverbally, to various situations. Ask for volunteers to share some of their sentences. After discussing the sentences, explain that the students will learn about various forms and methods of effective communication in this chapter.

2. Introduce the topic of nonverbal communication to your class. Ask students how they feel on an elevator when no one talks. How close can you get when talking to other people before they start to back away? Show magazine ads that have the written messages eliminated and see if students can identify what the people in the ads are trying to say. Ask students to watch a television program with the sound turned off. See if they can follow the story line by watching the nonverbal communication.

Strategies to Reteach, Reinforce, Enrich, and Extend Text Concepts

What Is Communication?

3. **RT**   Ask students to describe the various ways people communicate. Look around the class to see different ways depicted.

4. **EX**   *Communication Survey*, Activity A, SAG. Have students use the survey to determine communication patterns in their school environment. Tabulate the results and write a story for the school paper. Discuss the findings.

Forms of Communication

5. **EX**   *Is Anybody Listening?* reproducible master, 10-2. Students are asked to write three reactions to behaviors commonly exhibited during communication. They are to describe how they would feel, and then how each behavior would influence further communication.

6. **ER**   Ask students to do role-playing showing how careless listening, narrow listening, and defensive listening can prevent good communication between a parent and a child, a teacher and student, and dating partners. Evaluate in class.

7. **EX**   *Communication–Helping or Hindering?* Activity B, SAG. Students are asked to classify personal characteristics that either help or hinder communication. Discuss how using the helpful characteristics could help solve communication problems.

8. **EX**   Ask students to work in pairs to try this listening activity. Have one student discuss a problem while the other "listens" by interrupting, looking away, asking unrelated questions, or just distracting. Have each take a turn. Then discuss with each other how it felt not to have the other person really listen to them. Then repeat the activity and have the listener listen carefully using eye contact, acknowledging statements, and giving feedback. Compare the two exchanges.

9. **RF**   *Sympathy vs. Empathy*, Activity C, SAG. Students are asked to differentiate between sympathetic and empathetic statements.

Nonverbal Communication

10. **EX** *Communication Charades*, reproducible master, 10-3. Have students play the game of charades to see how body language can be used to communicate.
11. **EX** The following activities can be used to illustrate nonverbal communication:
    a. Divide the class into small groups. Ask students to remain silent for five minutes while watching other members of the group. Do they see the nonverbal messages they are constantly sending and receiving?
    b. Have each student draw a card on which is written a single word, such as happy, sad, angry, frightened, aggressive, nervous, seductive, tired, bored, disgusted, depressed, loving, hostile, superior, frustrated, possessive, conceited, excited, helpless, stubborn. Show the card to no one else. Then, using nonverbal communication, have each student act out the word. As the activity proceeds, the other students will write down the words they think are being portrayed, along with the nonverbal clues. Discuss their observations.
12. **ER** Have students find books and magazine articles about body language. Make a list of messages, and show how body language could be used to communicate these messages.
13. **ER** Role-play, or indicate by discussion, how important first impressions can be in various situations, such as a first date, meeting parents of a friend, a job interview, etc.
14. **EX** Ask students to read the feature article, "Communicating Socially," on page 242 of the text. Discuss how knowing what to do socially is an effective way to communicate in a positive manner.
15. **EX** Role-play different social situations involving rules of etiquette.

Levels of Communication

16. **RT** *Levels of Communication*, color transparency, CT-10. Use this transparency as you review the five levels of communication. Ask students to give examples of each level.
17. **RF** *Levels of Communication*, Activity D, SAG. Students are asked to write examples of verbal exchanges that could take place at the five levels of communication.
18. **RF** Have students keep a record of the different levels of communication they use during one day. Have them make note of the levels, the type of communication, and a brief description of the communication that took place. Discuss the results in class.
19. **RF** Discuss the importance of complete openness and honesty in establishing meaningful communication. Does this make a person vulnerable?

Assertiveness in Communication

20. **RT** Ask students to compare the descriptions of assertiveness and aggressiveness in communication given in the text. How can assertiveness help young people feel good about themselves? How can aggressiveness sometimes get them into trouble?
21. **ER** Ask students to watch television shows and political events to see how assertiveness helps communication and how aggressiveness tends to defeat good communication. Watch for examples of how assertiveness helps young people feel good about themselves.
22. **ER** *Communicating to Bring About Change*, transparency master, 10-4. This transparency presents assertive techniques to get people to change their behaviors or attitudes. Review the suggestions and examples given with the class. Then divide the class into three groups and give each group one of the following situations. Ask the students to write down how they could use each of the suggestions in their case situations.
    a. Rick has asked Sam to help him set up the booth at the fun fair. Sam has turned on Rick and has said Rick only seeks him out when he needs help—and he doesn't want to help.
    b. Janis would like her friend Ricky to work with her on a volunteer project this weekend. Ricky says he has better things to do, and that Janis has only asked him because she couldn't get anyone else.
    c. Jennifer's dad would like for her to go with him to visit his mother who has been ill. Jennifer says her dad never does

anything with her, so why should she do this.

Using I-messages, You-messages, and We-messages

23. **RF** *Word Choice in Communication,* reproducible master, 10-5. Discuss how the choice of words may interfere with effective communication by comparing the examples in this activity. Students are then asked to write their own sentences. Have them note the many I-messages in the right column and the you-messages in the left column.
24. **EX** Divide the class into small groups. Have each group brainstorm lists of you-messages, I-messages, and we-messages that might be used when communicating with family members and friends. Then have them discuss which messages are most likely to bring about positive feelings and cooperation.
25. **RT** Have students compare the I-messages and you-messages given in 10-12 on page 246 of the text.
26. **ER** Have your students compare various verbal communication patterns and discuss the effectiveness of each technique. Working in pairs, ask your students to use each of these methods for two minutes each. Then discuss how they felt.
    a. Students will talk with their partners using only the word "it." (Result: Students will feel disassociated with each other.)
    b. Students will talk with their partners using only statements that begin with "you." (Result: Little is revealed about oneself.)
    c. Students will talk with their partners using only statements that begin with "we." (Result: Students will feel closer to each other.)
    d. Students will talk with their partners using only statements that begin with "I." (Result: A nonthreatening exchange that allows people to reveal feelings, and reasons for those feelings.)
    e. Students will ask questions that begin with "why" and give answers that begin with "because." Then ask questions that begin with the words "how" and "what." (Result: Questions that begin with the words "how" and "what" are

more effective when you want to obtain information.)
27. **RF** *Communication Checklist,* Activity E, SAG. Students can use this checklist to evaluate their communication skills.

Communicating with Parents

28. **EX** *Family Communication,* Activity F, SAG. Students are asked to try some of the suggestions for improving family communication that are given in the text. They are to evaluate how effective each technique was in aiding communication.
29. **RF** List the many ways families influence the communication patterns of their members. Discuss how these learned communication patterns may affect future marriage relationships.
30. **ER** Role-play situations involving communication problems between teens and parents. Show how the problem can be solved and how communication can be improved.
31. **RF** Lack of trust is often a complaint teens have about their parents. Discuss how teens can help assure their parents they can be trusted (i.e., completing chores, respecting curfews, caring for siblings, etc.)
32. **EX** *Negotiating with Parents,* reproducible master, 10-6. Situations that can be negotiated between parents and teens are described. Students are to indicate typical teen and parent responses. They are to then decide on a solution that might be acceptable to both parties. This solution might be arrived at through the process of negotiation.

Group Communication Patterns

33. **RF** Have students give examples of how certain personal traits–trust, honesty, kindness, optimism, generosity, patience, and courage can help the development of good communication and good relationships.
34. **RF** Discuss groups and cliques. Is being a part of a group of peers important in your school? At what age do cliques begin to form? Is it hard to get in or out of a group?

Group Behaviors Involving Violence

35. **RF** Ask students to list examples of bullying behavior. Have they seen any instances of bullying in your school?

Contemporary Living Teacher's Resources

36. **RF** Discuss the following reasons young people join gangs:
   - Seeking a sense of family.
   - Wanting to be respected and admired.
   - Protection from other gangs.
   - Gives them status.
   - Gives them friends who will care about them.
   - Gives them something to do.
   - Can make money selling drugs.

   Ask students the following: If a friend wanted to join a gang for one of these reasons, what could you say to your friend to counteract the reason given?
37. **RF** Review the list of suggestions given on page 254 to avoid being a victim of bullies and gangs. Ask students if they feel these suggestions would help. Ask them to add their suggestions to the list.
38. **ER** *The Conflict Resolution Process*, reproducible master, 10-7. This is a more detailed version of the conflict resolution process described on page 254 of the text. Review the steps for resolving conflict. Then use the conflict resolution process to resolve a typical conflict situation. Ask students to role-play the parties involved.
39. **EX** Discuss the legal consequences that may occur if a conflict cannot be settled and it escalates into violence. Ask students to research the legal ramifications of a misdemeanor (such as disorderly conduct), a simple assault (attack without weapon), an aggravated assault (attack with weapon), and a felony (rape, murder, kidnapping, armed robbery, arson, or narcotic sales).

Sexual Harassment

40. **RF** *Stay Alert to Sexual Harassment*, transparency master, 10-8. Use this master to review points young people need to keep in mind regarding sexual harassment. Ask students to brainstorm how they can protect themselves.

Answer Key for Chapter 10

Text
To Review, page 257.

1. (Student response for three ways people communicate.)
2. Passive listeners: E. Feedback: D. Active listening: F. Careless listeners: B. Defensive listeners: A. Narrow listeners: C.
3. Empathy means understanding how the other person feels and why. Sympathy means sharing someone else's feelings and this is sometimes resented.
4. (Describe three:) Thumping fingers and swinging legs is a sign of tenseness. Touching nose may mean disapproval. Steepling fingers show you feel you have authority. Face-to-face contact shows interest in communicating. Turning your body, moving away, folding your arms, or crossing your legs sets up barriers to communication. Using hands and arms to emphasize speech allows people to read each other more clearly. Facial expressions can indicate enthusiasm.
5. (Student response.)
6. Level five: No involvement, cliché level which is weakest level. Level four: No commitment, you will not invest any of yourself in the conversation. Level three: You indicate some willingness to share ideas or judgments with another person but you carefully restrict them. Level two: You become increasingly open to another person as you expose your feelings and emotions. Level one: Complete openness and honesty, desire to share and understand.
7. false
8. (Student response for examples.) I-messages will improve communication.
9. (1) Ask for permission. (2) If your parents deny you permission, find out their objections. (3) Propose a compromise that might overcome their objections.
10. Name calling, theft, extortion of money, physical intimidation, harsh pranks, and imposed territorial bases.
11. Step 1: Gather information. Each party tells what is causing the conflict. Step 2: Define the problem. The mediator restates facts and issues. Step 3: Alternative solutions are identified. Step 4: A possible solution is identified. Step 5: An agreement is reached.
12. Unwelcome sexual advances, requests for sexual favors, or other verbal or physical conduct of a sexual nature.

Student Activity Guide

Activity B, *Communication—Helping or Hindering?*

Helpful characteristics are: Encourages talk; Smiles; Willing to listen; Nods head; Shows interest in what others have to say; Makes others feel good about themselves; Gives feedback; Cheerful; Explains reasons for doing things; Optimistic; Makes eye contact.

Activity C, *Sympathy vs. Empathy.*

Statements 1, 3, and 6 are sympathetic.
Statements 2, 4, 5, and 7 are empathetic.

Teacher's Resource Guide
Chapter 10 Test

1. D	4. E	7. G
2. B	5. K	8. I
3. A	6. J	9. F

10. C	17. T	24. D
11. T	18. F	25. B
12. F	19. F	26. D
13. T	20. T	27. D
14. F	21. A	28. B
15. T	22. C	29. A
16. F	23. B	30. C

31. (Student response.)
32. (Student response.)
33. Step 1. Gather information. Step 2. Define the problem. Step 3. Identify alternative solutions. Step 4. Identify a possible solution. Step 5. Reach an agreement.
34. (Student response.)

Verbal and Nonverbal Expressions

Name ____ **Date** _______________ **Period** _______________

Complete the sentences below, indicating what you might say (verbal) and what you might do (nonverbal).

1. If someone hurts me deeply, I express my feelings
   a. verbally, by saying ____
   b. nonverbally, by doing____

2. When someone I like does something to annoy me, I express my feelings
   a. verbally, by saying ____
   b. nonverbally, by doing____

3. If I find out that someone has lied to me, I express my feelings
   a. verbally, by saying ____
   b. nonverbally, by doing____

4. When someone destroys something that belongs to me, I express myself
   a. verbally, by saying ____
   b. nonverbally, by doing____

5. When someone interrupts me when I am speaking, I express myself
   a. verbally, by saying ____
   b. nonverbally, by doing____

6. When I am unsure about whether someone likes me or not, I express myself
   a. verbally, by saying ____
   b. nonverbally, by doing____

7. When someone asks me if they can copy from my test, I express myself
   a. verbally, by saying ____
   b. nonverbally, by doing____

8. If I feel that I am not able to do a task someone has asked me to do, I express myself
   a. verbally, by saying ____
   b. nonverbally, by doing____

Is Anybody Listening?

Name _______________________________ **Date** _____________ **Period** _____________

One of the important ingredients of good communication is good listening by both parties. Behaviors commonly used during communication are listed below. Write how you would feel if a person with whom you were speaking exhibited each of these behaviors. Then describe what your reaction would be to each.

The Listener	Your Feeling	Your Reaction
1. Gives advice you didn't ask for.		
2. Starts walking around while you are talking.		
3. Interrupts and prevents you from finishing your statement.		
4. Nods and seems to be interested.		
5. Tries to top your story with a better one.		
6. Puts you down.		
7. Compliments you.		

(Continued)

Name ____

The Listener	Your Feeling	Your Reaction
8. Fails to answer you.		
9. Laughs when you are being serious.		
10. Seems shocked or offended by something you've said.		
11. Talks to someone else while you are still talking.		
12. Keeps good eye contact and follows what you say.		
13. Changes the subject.		
14. Becomes defensive.		
15. Repeats back to you parts of what you said.		
16. Lightly touches your hand.		

Communication Charades

Many messages can be communicated through gestures and body movements. Play this game of charades to find out! Divide the class into two to four teams. Cut the following messages into strips and place them in a container. Each team member will take turns pantomiming the message they draw from the container. Their fellow team members must try to guess the nonverbal message being portrayed. One person should act as a timer counting the number of seconds it takes for the team members to identify the message. The team with the lowest number of total seconds is the winner.

I'm bored with the whole thing.

- -

You really blew it!

- -

I really don't want to be bothered.

- -

You really think you are something, don't you?

- -

I'm tired.

- -

I can't hear you.

- -

I am so embarrassed!

- -

I'm disgusted.

- -

It's time to stop.

- -

Communicating to Bring About Change

Suggestions	Examples
• Offer help.	• "Do you need something from me? Maybe I can help."
• Register how you feel.	• "I feel angry when you criticize what I am saying."
• Offer a wish.	• "I wish you would tell me what you want."
• Give directions.	• "Tell me what you want me to do–I am having trouble understanding you."
• Offer two options.	• "Should we discuss this now, or would you rather wait until morning?"
• Offer a reminder.	• "Remember that we agreed not to criticize each other."
• State your expectation.	• "You are my friend. You are important to me. Let's find an easier way to solve this."
• Offer three options.	• "You can write me a note stating what you want, tell me now what you want me to do, or let me know when I do please you."
• Issue a demand with consequences.	• "Find a way to tell me what you want without criticizing me, or I will avoid

Word Choice in Communication

Name ___________________________________ **Date** _______________ **Period** _______________

Often the words we use convey the wrong message. Note the poor choice of words in the left-hand column below. See how slight changes can produce more effective communication as illustrated in the right-hand column. See if you can identify why these changes might lead to more effective communication. Then write sentences that you would use to convey a message to parents, a brother or sister, a good friend, and a dating partner. First write an ineffective message, then change it to improve communication.

Ineffective Message	**More Effective Message**
1. You probably won't have the time, but I need help with my homework.	1. I need some help with my homework and I am wondering if you could work with me.
2. You are going to be angry when I tell you why I wasn't home on time.	2. I want to tell you why I wasn't home on time.
3. I know it's dinnertime, but I want a minute of your time.	3. Could I have a minute of your time before dinner?
4. It's a sure bet that you're not going to like what I'm going to tell you.	4. I need you to listen to what I am about to tell you.
5. Don't take it personally, but I'm riding to the party with some friends.	5. Thanks for the offer. I've already made arrangements to get to the party.
6. You never call.	6. I wish you would call more often.
7. You're always late.	7. I would like you to be on time.
8. That's a stupid idea.	8. I disagree with you because...
9. You shouldn't do that.	9. I would prefer that you do ______________ instead of ______________.
10. It's not really important, but I wanted to talk to you.	10. Could I talk with you for a few minutes?
11. Your statement to a parent:	
12. Your statement to a sibling:	
13. Your statement to a good friend:	
14. Your statement to a dating partner:	

Negotiating with Parents

Name _________________________________ **Date** _____________ **Period** _____________

Negotiation is an important communication tool for teens and parents. The following are typical concerns that may be negotiated between parents and their teenagers:

grooming and clothes	homework
grades	household chores
social activities	money/allowance
curfews	watching TV

The following situations can benefit from negotiation. Read each situation. In the first column, describe how a parent might respond. In the second column, describe how a teenager might respond. Then, in the third column, describe how they could negotiate and arrive at a win/win solution for both parties.

Suzanne's (age 13) grades dropped from a B to a D- in math. She has been invited to a party the weekend before midterm exams. She wants to go, but her parents say she needs to study.

Parent response:	**Teen response:**	**Solution:**

Bettina (age 13) wants to wear a skirt that her parents say is too short—in fact does not comply with suggested school attire in the handbook. She says other girls are wearing them.

Parent response:	**Teen response:**	**Solution:**

(Continued)

Name ____

Jennifer's (age 14) parents have set a curfew of 11:00 p.m. on Friday and Saturday nights. The school play is Friday, and the cast wants to have a party afterwards, which would be later than the curfew hour.		
Parent response:	**Teen response:**	**Solution:**

Scott (age 15) mows the family lawn. He has put off mowing it for a week, and now a friend has invited him to go camping over the weekend. This means the lawn will not be mowed for another four days. His parents are demanding that he complete his task.		
Parent response:	**Teen response:**	**Solution:**

Shaunna (age 16) wants to be picked up by her friend, Andy, who has just gotten his driver's license. Her parents say they are not sure of his driving ability. They would prefer to take her to the party.		
Parent response:	**Teen response:**	**Solution:**

The Conflict Resolution Process

The following are detailed steps for using the conflict resolution (mediation) process. This process creates an open, nonjudgmental atmosphere for airing problems and resolving them.

Before beginning the process, make introductions. Only the people involved in the conflict should be present.

Ask the individuals if they want to solve the problem. Get agreement to five ground rules:

1. One person speaks at a time (no interruptions allowed).
2. Show courtesy and respect (no name calling or put-downs).
3. Be as honest as you can.
4. Keep everything confidential.
5. Agree to try to solve the problem.

Step 1: Gather information.
- Decide who will talk first.
- Ask #1 what happened.
- Mediator will say, "Let me be sure I understand this is what happened." Restate. If mediator does not understand, tell the person you are confused and ask him or her to explain it again.
- Ask person #1 how he or she feels.
- Ask person #2 what happened.
- Mediator will say, "Let me be sure I understand this is what happened." Restate. If mediator does not understand, tell the person you are confused and ask him or her to explain it again.
- Ask person #2 how he or she feels.
- Allow each involved person to speak.
- Have each one repeat what the other person(s) said.

Step 2: Define the problem.
- Summarize. The mediator restates the facts and issues that were presented by each party. The mediator asks each person if he or she understands what the other person is saying.
- Look for points of agreement.

Step 3: Identify alternative solutions.
- Brainstorm solutions, accepting all ideas at first. Write down all possible solutions.
- Get ideas from both persons or parties.
- Mediator will not offer suggestions unless it is necessary.

Step 4: Identify a possible solution.
- Which solution would work for both parties?
- Is the solution fair to both?
- Is it a win/win solution?
- Can both persons or parties do what they promise?
- Do both persons or parties think the problem is solved?

Step 5: Reach an agreement.
- Write down the agreement. Be specific. Use who, what, when, how, and where.
- Have both parties sign the agreement.
- Ask each person what he or she would do differently if the problem happened again.
- Ask participants to tell their friends that the conflict has been solved to prevent rumors from spreading.
- Shake hands and thank everyone for using mediation to reach an agreement.
- Congratulate the participants for their hard work!

Stay Alert to Sexual Harassment

Sexual harassment can happen anywhere–at school, at work, or at social gatherings.

- Trust your feelings and your instincts. If you feel uncomfortable with someone, try not to be around or alone with that person.

- Don't be afraid to talk to someone if you feel you are being sexually harassed. Many young people are embarrassed to accuse someone, or they don't want to cause problems. Talk to a parent or trusted adult if you are in doubt.

- Don't feel that you have to handle a problem alone. If an offender senses you will not involve anyone else, the harassment may continue. If the offender knows you have reported the harassment, it will probably end.

- Use common sense. Sometimes behavior is misunderstood and may be interpreted as sexual harassment. Also be sure that you have not misinterpreted someone's reactions to your nonverbal messages–body language, tone of voice, clothing, etc. Talk to the person and state how you feel.

- Clearly state how you feel, what you mean, and what you want. Many problems stem from a person's inability to communicate clearly and honestly. Continue to improve your communication skills.

Communicating with Others

Name ____

Date ____ **Period** _____________ **Score** _______________

Chapter 10 Test

Matching: Match the following terms and identifying phrases.

_______ 1. Using words to send and receive messages.

_______ 2. Using body movements to communicate inner feelings.

_______ 3. Any means by which you share a message with another person.

_______ 4. Expressing your feelings directly–asking for what you want and refusing what you don't want.

_______ 5. Offering no sign of hearing or understanding a message.

_______ 6. A form of violence that inflicts physical, verbal, or emotional abuse on another person.

_______ 7. Using factors other than words to communicate.

_______ 8. A way of resolving problems in a positive way.

_______ 9. Indicating in various ways that you have received a message.

_______ 10. Communicating to another person how you feel about what was said.

A. communication
B. body language
C. feedback
D. verbal communication
E. assertive
F. active listening
G. nonverbal communication
H. aggressive
I. conflict resolution
J. bullying
K. passive listening

True/False: Circle *T* if the statement is true or *F* is the statement is false.

T F 11. Sympathy means that you feel as another person feels when he or she is upset or sad.

T F 12. Communication involves only a sender of messages.

T F 13. When you cross your arms across your chest, you are setting up barriers to further communication.

T F 14. I-messages are usually accusing and blaming, and they can hinder communication.

T F 15. Employers have the right to demand certain standards of grooming as they evaluate job applicants.

T F 16. You-statements are good to use when problems exist in a group or relationship.

T F 17. Violence is negative communication that is a learned behavior.

T F 18. Teens often join gangs because they seek freedom from structure and discipline.

T F 19. Sexual harassment seldom occurs in schools.

T F 20. Boys sometimes misinterpret girls' behavior as sexual even though this is not intended.

(Continued)

Multiple Choice:Choose the best response. Write the letter in the space provided.

_______ 21. Writing a letter is an example of _____.
   A.   verbal communication
   B.   nonverbal communication
   C.   feedback
   D.   body language

_______ 22. Listeners who read meanings into what is being said and feel like they are being attacked are known as _____ listeners.
   A.   careless
   B.   narrow
   C.   defensive
   D.   good

_______ 23. The process of seeing things from another person's view is known as _____.
   A.   sympathy
   B.   empathy
   C.   trust
   D.   sarcasm

_______ 24. Which of the following statements is true?
   A.   Thumping fingers is a sign of tenseness.
   B.   Steepling fingers shows you are hiding something.
   C.   Touching your nose is a sign of acceptance.
   D.   All of the above.

_______ 25. An example of the weakest level of communication, which is often called the cliché level, is _____.
   A.   "Let's get together and get to the bottom of this."
   B.   "How are you?"
   C.   "I love you."
   D.   "I heard you were running for a class office."

_______ 26. Assertiveness in communication means you _____.
   A.   are forceful, hostile, or destructive
   B.   put other people down
   C.   never say no
   D.   express your feelings honestly and directly

_______ 27. Lack of trust is often mentioned as a problem between parents and teens. Teens can help solve this problem by _____.
   A.   demonstrating that they can be trusted by fulfilling everyday obligations
   B.   reminding parents that teens have to be trusted
   C.   being honest with their parents
   D.   Both A and C above.

_______ 28. If you want to improve communication with your parents, you should _____.
   A.   use you-messages so you won't appear to be self-centered
   B.   use I-messages as you take responsibility for the feelings you are stating
   C.   talk to them as soon as they come home, even if they are busy
   D.   not talk to them, for they won't understand anyway

(Continued)

______ 29. Conflict resolution includes ______.
    A. active listening in a risk-free environment
    B. a mediator who will provide a solution to the conflict
    C. a meeting that is open to anyone who wants to attend
    D. the finding of a solution that one party can accept

______ 30. Sexual harassment ______.
    A. only happens to women
    B. only happens at work
    C. is sometimes confused with flirting or teasing
    D. occurs when the sexual comment or action is welcomed

Essay Questions: Provide complete responses to the following questions or statements.

31. Describe five things you can do to improve family communication.

32. Describe one typical communication problem between teens and their parents and explain how the problem can be solved.

33. List the steps involved in the conflict resolution process.

34. Discuss what young people should do if they think they are experiencing sexual harassment.

Chapter 11
Developing Close Relationships

Objectives

After studying this chapter, students will be able to
- identify friendships that involve important, close relationships.
- describe the informal and formal dating choices of teens.
- describe the qualities that characterize a serious relationship with a member of the opposite sex.
- discuss the issues involved in ending a relationship.
- recognize the many different types of love.
- differentiate between love, infatuation, and sexual gratification.
- analyze the issues involved in sexual decision making.
- practice techniques for saying no to sexual relations.
- define acquaintance rape and identify ways to prevent it.

Bulletin Boards

I. Title: "What Makes Love Grow?"

Cover a bulletin board with white paper. Make large flowers out of yellow and green construction paper. Place a gray cloud at the top of the board under the title. Draw large raindrops on the board and write the following words inside the drops: *concern, sharing, acceptance, giving, patience, unselfish, trust, openness, "we" feeling, time.*

II. Title: "What Is Love?"

Write the title on a large red heart placed in the center of a bulletin board. Write positive aspects and types of love on smaller hearts and place them randomly around the large heart. Also write the negative aspects and types of love on small hearts, but cut these hearts in half with a jagged edge. Place these randomly around the bulletin board, as well.

Teaching Materials

Text, pages 260-285

Terms to Know, To Review, To Do, and *To Think About*

Student Activity Guide
- A. *Dating Survey*
- B. *Positive and Negative Types of Love*
- C. *Love Match*
- D. *Your Attitudes About Sex*
- E. *Communicating Affection*
- F. *Just Say No*
- G. *Acquaintance/Date Rape*

Teacher's Resource Guide/Binder

A Bill of Rights for Those Who Date, transparency master, 11-1

Developing Relationships, reproducible master, 11-2

The Do's and Don't's of Breaking Up, transparency master, 11-3

What Does Love Mean? reproducible master, 11-4

Is It Love or Infatuation? reproducible master, 11-5

Should I Have Premarital Sexual Experiences? transparency master, 11-6

Questions to Ask Yourself Before Entering a Sexual Relationship, reproducible master, 11-7

Acquaintance Rape: A Case Study, reproducible master, 11-8

Chapter 11 Test

Teacher's Resource Binder

What Is a Friend? color transparency, CT-11

Software for Contemporary Living

Chapter Review Game

Introductory Activities

1. Ask students to write responses to the following incomplete sentences:
   Group dating is....
   Steady dating is....
   Love is....
   You know you are in love when....
   You know someone loves you when....
2. Ask each student to write a definition of love. Refer to these again after students have read the chapter. Would they change their definitions of love?
3. Identify past and present dating practices in our culture. Point out differences in formality, curfews, pair and group activities, restrictions, activities available, cost, transportation, etc. Predict future dating patterns. Ask students representing different ethnic groups to discuss dating practices in their culture.

Strategies to Reteach, Reinforce, Enrich, and Extend Text Concepts

Friendship

4. **RF** Ask students to respond to the statement, "No man is an island." What does this mean? Are there times when friends are needed more than at other times? Are friends most important during the teen years?

5. **RF** Discuss the meaning of the statement, "You will have different sets of friends." Reflect on your "best friend" during elementary school, middle school, and now.
6. **RT** Discuss the positive experience of "just friend" relationships, and cross-gender friendships. How can these be a testing ground for honesty, truth, respect, and communication?
7. **RF** *What Is a Friend?* color transparency, CT-11. Review the phrases listed on this transparency that describe the roles friends play. Have students add other phrases that describe a friend. Ask them to complete the following sentence: A friend is someone who....

Dating Patterns

8. **ER** *A Bill of Rights for Those Who Date*, transparency master, 11-1. Review the rights and responsibilities listed in this master. Ask students to indicate whether they agree or disagree with each "right."
9. **RF** Discuss the differences between informal group dating and formal pair dating patterns.
10. **ER** *Dating Survey*, Activity A, SAG. Have students conduct a survey of dating practices in their school. Tabulate the results and discuss. Share the results in an article in the school paper.
11. **EX** Ask students to consider their future role as parents. Would they set more restrictions or fewer restrictions on dating practices of their children?
12. **ER** Analyze the casualness of dating today compared to the structured dating of the past. Discuss the pros and cons of each form of dating.
13. **ER** Arrange chairs in two circles, one inside the other. Divide the class by sex and have one group sit in the inner circle and the other in the outside circle. Use an incomplete sentence to begin a free discussion of the topic. Only the persons in the inner circle can participate–the others must only listen. Ask the group to react to these incomplete sentences:
    I like to date girls (guys) who....
    When I go on a date, I like to....
    I think it (is/is not) okay for girls to ask guys for dates....
    A teen should be allowed to start pair dating at age....

Reverse the positions and have the second group react to the statements made by the first group, then have them discuss the incomplete sentence topics.

14. **EX** Write each of the following characteristics of dating partners on separate sheets of paper: attractive; similar religious beliefs; similar leisure interests; intelligent; similar economic background; easy to talk to; popular; fun to be with; emotionally supportive; liked by family; etc. Post them on a bulletin board. Ask each student to rank the characteristics as to their importance in a dating partner. Compile the results and arrange them in order of class preference.

15. **RF** The trend today is for young people to marry at a later age. How might this impact dating practices? How might this impact marriage?

Developing Relationships

16. **EX** *Developing Relationships,* reproducible master, 11-2. This master lists qualities that often characterize a deepening relationship. Students are asked to indicate how important they feel each quality is in a relationship.

17. **EX** Ask students to explain what intimacy means to them. Discuss the importance of developing a feeling of intimacy in a relationship. Have them interpret the meaning of the following quotation:
"If I am I, because I am I, and
You are you, because you are you,
Then I am I, and you are you.
But, if I am I, because I am you,
And you are you, because you are me,
Then I am not, and you are not."

18. **RF** Ask students to list ways a couple can communicate affection without sexual intimacy.

Ending a Relationship

19. **RT** Discuss the cycle of dating and why it is important for teens to realize breaking up is part of the dating cycle. Review the signs that indicate a relationship should end.

20. **ER** *The Do's and Don't's of Breaking Up,* transparency master, 11-3. Review the suggestions to follow if it appears that a relationship is headed toward a breakup. Then read the following case study. Divide the class into four groups and ask each group to role-play a version of how the breakup could be handled. Have some groups role-play poor ways to break up and some groups role-play ways to break up without pain. Ask class members to evaluate which version was the best.
Case Study: Caitlin and Tyler have been going steady for two years. About two months before their high school graduation, their relationship began to change. They argued more, often hurting each other's feelings. Finally, one night Tyler said, "I think we should each start seeing other people. We are having too many problems." Caitlin was devastated. The senior prom was just one month away. She had been looking forward to sharing all of the end-of-the-year activities with Tyler. What should they do?

Communication of Love

21. **RF** *What Does Love Mean?* reproducible master, 11-4. Cut along the dotted lines and place the cards in a basket. If there are more than 20 students in your class, add blank cards so each student will have a card to draw. Have your students sit in a large circle. Introduce *love* as the topic. Ask each student to select a card from the basket, read the statement, and give a brief explanation of what it means to them. Students who draw blank cards are to write their own statements about love to share with the class.

22. **RF** Have students refine the definitions of love they wrote in the introductory activity. Then develop a group definition of love. Also develop a list of characteristics of love. Are there differences between the boys' and girls' descriptions of love?

23. **RF** Discuss the importance of parental love for children. What happens when love is withheld from a child?

24. **ER** Ask students to write a paper on the topic of *love.* They may write about the topic in any manner they choose–a story, a poem, a narrative, etc. Ask volunteers to read their papers to the class.

25. **RF** Discuss the negative types of love described on pages 271-272 of the text. How can these emotions damage a relationship?

26. **EX** *Positive and Negative Types of Love,* Activity B, SAG. Students are asked to distinguish between statements describing positive and negative types of love.

27. **ER**   Ask students to bring tapes or CDs of popular "love" songs to class and listen to the words. How do the songs define love? Is it love, infatuation, or sexual gratification? Bring in words to songs that were popular ten or more years ago. Have the messages changed?

28. **EX**   *Love Match*, Activity C, SAG. Students are to match terms related to love with their definitions.

29. **RF**   *Is It Love or Infatuation?* reproducible master, 11-5. Students are asked to distinguish between characteristics of love and infatuation.

Physical Expressions of Affection

30. **RF**   Discuss the trend in our society toward the more explicit portrayal of sexual intimacy on TV, in movies, and in advertising. Discuss the pros and cons.

31. **RF**   The expression of emotions and affection is often different for males and females. Discuss the differences and how they might affect a relationship between two persons.

32. **EX**   *Your Attitudes About Sex*, Activity D, SAG. This activity can be used to help students identify their own attitudes concerning sexual behavior. Students can share their responses in small groups or with the class.

33. **EX**   *Communicating Affection*, Activity E, SAG. Students are to write their reactions to situations involving the communication of affection, and then share their ideas in small groups. The groups will then combine their best ideas and write group solutions for each situation.

34. **RF**   *Should I Have Premarital Sexual Experiences?* transparency master, 11-6. This is a copy of the decision-making chain found on page 277 of the text. Have students follow through the chain of decisions. Discuss the consequences resulting from a decision concerning premarital sexual relations. Discuss the differences in the decisions and their results for both boys and girls.

35. **EX**   *The Decision-Making Process*, transparency master, 5-4. This was first used in Chapter 5. It can be used again to reach a decision concerning premarital sexual relations. The transparency can be used as a basis for class discussion, or copies of the master can be made so that each student can work through his or her own decision.

36. **EX**   *Questions to Ask Yourself Before Entering a Sexual Relationship,* reproducible master, 11-7. Ask students to answer these questions for themselves before entering a sexual relationship.

37. **RF**   *Just Say No*, Activity F, SAG. Students are asked to write responses to typical arguments used to persuade dating partners to have sex. Have students compare their responses with their classmates.

38. **RF**   Across the country, many students are signing pledges stating they will practice abstinence until they are married. They feel this is a moral commitment as well as a health commitment. Ask if your students would consider signing such a pledge.

39. **RF**   One of Maslow's human needs is for love and acceptance–a need to be liked and valued by someone. Discuss how the desire to fulfill this need can sometimes lead to sexual involvement. Have students identify ways the need can be fulfilled without sexual expressions. Is sex necessary in order to feel loved? Also discuss how feelings of loneliness and a desire to act grown up can mistakenly lead to sexual involvement.

40. **ER**   Ask students to write a short paper responding to the following: Somewhere in the world there is a person who may become your future marriage partner. How would you like him or her to respond to pressures for sexual involvement?

Date or Acquaintance Rape

41. **RF**   Discuss what acquaintance rape is, how it can be prevented, and what can be done if a date is pressuring a person to have sex. Also discuss signs to look for in situations which are getting out of control and how to avoid situations which may become troublesome.

42. **EX**   Parents may prefer that teens go to parties or on group dates instead of single dates, but group events have their own hazards. Discuss how teens can protect themselves in group situations. Have students list their own suggestions, or discuss the following:

- Maintain your option to leave by having your own transportation, or knowing you can call your parents.

- Pay attention to the mood changes within the group. A situation may seem alright at first, but then become uncomfortable.

- Decide what you will do if others in the group engage in sexual activities.
- Decide what you will do if you are pressured to participate in sexual activities.

43. **EX**   The public's sympathy for rape victims is often determined by the conduct of the victim prior to the assault. These behaviors are often brought out during a trial. Ask your students to list these behaviors and discuss if they should, in fact, be allowed to influence the verdict in a rape case. The following behaviors might be discussed:
- Did the boy spend a lot of money on the girl expecting a form of repayment?
- Did the girl often have sex with other boys?
- Was the girl drunk or on drugs?
- Did the girl get the boy sexually excited?
- Did the girl say she would have sex, and then change her mind?
- Did the girl fight back?
- Did the girl dress provocatively?
- Did the girl willingly go to where she knew they would be alone?
- Did the girl know the boy had a reputation for trying to "score" with every girl he dated?

44. **ER**   *Acquaintance Rape: A Case Study,* reproducible master, 11-8. This master can be used to help students identify the feelings and emotions that can lead to, and result from, an acquaintance rape. It can be used in small groups or as an individual assignment.

45. **EX**   *Acquaintance/Date Rape,* Activity G, SAG. The strategies to prevent acquaintance rape that were discussed in the text are listed in this activity. Students are asked to personalize these strategies for their own use. Then have students share their responses with classmates.

46. **EX**   Ask a speaker from a Rape Crisis Center to speak to the class.

Answer Key for Chapter 11

Text
To Review, page 283.

1. Dating helps you learn about interpersonal relationships; it encourages good peer relationships and helps you learn to evaluate personalities; you discover those personality traits that appeal to you and those that do not; dating makes you aware of the demands and restrictions involved in getting along with members of the opposite sex.
2. (Student response.)
3. out; steady
4. (1) Trust: A feeling that the person would not betray you or cause you any harm. (2) Self-disclosure: A willingness to share significant information about yourself with the other person. (3) Communication: Expressing their beliefs, values, goals, and concerns. (4) Intimacy: A sense of familiarity; a feeling of warm friendship.
5. Conflicting values, withdrawal from other friends, overemphasis on physical involvement, frequent arguments and fights.
6. Choose an appropriate time and place, try to remember the good times you spent together, share the blame for the failure of the relationship, be honest about the reason for the break up.
7. Passionate love: D. Infatuation: G. Hostile love: E. Unreturned love: F. Friendly love: B. Jealous love: C. True love: A.
8. (List five:) Know yourself, accept yourself, and believe in yourself. Develop a healthy self-concept and learn to deal with your strengths and weakness. Refine your decision-making skills. Recognize your values, and set goals for your future. Learn to communicate honestly with others. Think ahead about what you will do if you are with someone who is pressuring you. Think about how you can communicate your feelings for someone without getting involved sexually.
9. (Student response. See pages 278-279 of the text.)
10. Rape is any sexual intimacy forced on one person by another. The victim may or may not know the assailant. Acquaintance rape is rape committed by someone the person knows.
11. (Describe four. Student response. See page 281 of the text.)

Student Activity Guide

Activity B, *Positive and Negative Types of Love.*

Statements 1, 2, 5, 6, 7, and 10 describe positive types of love. Statements 3, 4, 8, and 9 describe negative types of love. Student response for five statements describing love relationships in today's society.

Activity C, *Love.*

1. D
2. C
3. E
4. J
5. F
6. A
7. I
8. H
9. G
10. B

Teacher's Resource Guide

Is It Love or Infatuation? reproducible master, 11-5.

1. Infatuation
2. Love
3. Infatuation
4. Love
5. Love
6. Infatuation
7. Love
8. Infatuation
9. Infatuation
10. Infatuation
11. Love
12. Love
13. Love
14. Infatuation
15. Love
16. Infatuation
17. Love
18. Love
19. Love
20. Infatuation

Chapter 11 Test

1. E	12. T	22. A
2. G	13. F	23. B
3. B	14. T	24. B
4. F	15. F	25. B
5. I	16. T	26. C
6. J	17. F	27. D
7. D	18. T	28. C
8. H	19. T	29. D
9. C	20. T	30. C
10. F	21. F	31. A
11. T		

32. (Student response for five characteristics of a good friend.)
33. (Student response.)
34. (Student response.)
35. (Student response. List five.)

A Bill of Rights for Those Who Date

1. I have the right to refuse a date without feeling guilty.

2. I can ask for a date without feeling rejected if I am turned down for a date.

3. I have the right to start a relationship slowly.

4. I have the right to be myself without changing to please a date.

5. If I do not want physical closeness, I have the right to say no.

6. I have the right to change a relationship when my feelings change.

7. If I am told a relationship is changing, I have the right not to blame or change myself to keep it going.

8. If I feel uncomfortable, I have the right to express my feelings without being criticized or blamed.

9. If I feel that I no longer wish to continue a relationship, I have the right to express why I feel that way.

10. If I no longer wish to continue a relationship, I have the right to express my desire to end it. I also have the responsibility of being honest and respectful to the other person.

Developing Relationships

Name______________________________________ **Date**_______________ **Period**______________

The following are qualities that often characterize a deepening relationship. Indicate how important you feel each quality is in a relationship by checking the appropriate column. Then choose one statement with which you strongly agree or disagree and explain your reasoning.

Very Important	**Somewhat Important**	**Not Important**	
_____	_____	_____	1. The individuals trust each other knowing the other person would not betray them or cause them harm.
_____	_____	_____	2. The individuals feel free to talk about their deepest concerns and feelings.
_____	_____	_____	3. The individuals are able to sustain a give and take attitude.
_____	_____	_____	4. The individuals feel free to share significant information about themselves with the other person.
_____	_____	_____	5. The individuals are not afraid to reveal their idiosyncrasies, which are peculiar to them.
_____	_____	_____	6. The individuals feel comfortable with each other, sharing what they have in common.
_____	_____	_____	7. The individuals feel free to express their beliefs, values, goals, and concerns.
_____	_____	_____	8. The individuals are able to share their lives while still retaining their own individuality.
_____	_____	_____	9. The individuals are able to accept each other's varying moods.
_____	_____	_____	10. Each person may dislike some things the other does, but this does not diminish their affection for each other.

I strongly agree/disagree with statement ______ because ______________________________________

____

____

____

____

____

____

____

____

____

The Do's and Don't's of Breaking Up

The Don't's:

- Don't use angry and degrading remarks.

- Don't blame the other person.

- Don't begin dating someone else right away as a form of revenge.

- Don't break up without an explanation.

- Don't lead the other person on.

The Do's:

- Do choose an appropriate time and place.

- Do recall some good times and good qualities.

- Do share responsibility for the failed relationship.

- Do recognize that a failed relationship does not mean either person is inadequate.

- Do be honest about the reason for the break up.

What Does Love Mean?

Reproduce this page. Cut along the dotted lines to form cards. Directions for using this activity are given on page 189.

LOVE ISN'T LOVE UNTIL YOU GIVE IT AWAY.	LOVE MAKES THE WORLD GO AROUND.
LOVE CONQUERS ALL.	LOVE IS A TRADE — WE GIVE, BUT IF WE DON'T GET A FAIR RETURN, LOVE WITHERS.
YOU CAN LOVE AND HATE SOMEONE AT THE SAME TIME— THEY ARE DIFFERENT FORMS OF THE SAME STRONG EMOTION.	TRUE LOVE SAYS I NEED YOU BECAUSE I LOVE YOU — UNTRUE LOVE SAYS I LOVE YOU BECAUSE I NEED YOU.
LOVE IS SO IMPORTANT TO AN INFANT THAT HE OR SHE MAY DIE FROM LACK OF IT, EVEN IF THERE IS NO PHYSICAL ILLNESS.	MATURE LOVE IS THE LOVE THAT COMES WHEN YOU'VE LEARNED TO GIVE AND CARE DEEPLY AND UNSELFISHLY FOR ANOTHER.
LOVE MEANS YOU NEVER HAVE TO SAY "I'M SORRY."	LOVE IS LIKE AN ITCHING IN YOUR HEART.
ALL YOU NEED IS LOVE.	WHEN YOU ARE MORE IN LOVE WITH THE IDEA OF LOVE THAN WITH A PERSON, YOU ARE EXPERIENCING INFATUATION.
TO BE LOVED, BE LOVABLE.	LOVE IS A CANVAS FURNISHED BY NATURE AND EMBROIDERED BY IMAGINATION.
HOW DO I LOVE THEE? LET ME COUNT THE WAYS . . .	LOVE MEANS YOU DO MORE GIVING THAN TAKING.
LOVE MEANS YOU ACCEPT YOURSELF AND YOUR PARTNER AS YOU ARE.	PARENTS' LOVE FOR THEIR CHILD IS UNCONDITIONAL.
LOVE AND MARRIAGE GO TOGETHER LIKE A HORSE AND CARRIAGE.	LOVE INCLUDES PHYSICAL ATTRACTION, BUT IT DOES NOT DEPEND ON THIS ALONE.

Is It Love or Infatuation?

Name _______________________________________ **Date** _____________ **Period** ___________

Can you distinguish between relationships that are based on love and those that are based on infatuation? Read the following descriptions. Indicate whether they characterize relationships based on love or on infatuation by checking the appropriate column. Then answer the questions that follow.

Love   Infatuation

Love	Infatuation	
_____	_____	1. Concerned for own welfare.
_____	_____	2. Unselfish in actions.
_____	_____	3. Physical attraction often is the major factor in the relationship.
_____	_____	4. Grows slowly and steadily.
_____	_____	5. Exhibits a "we" feeling.
_____	_____	6. Tends to destroy purpose and ambition.
_____	_____	7. Concerned for the welfare of the other person.
_____	_____	8. Overlooks undesirable traits and pretends they don't exist.
_____	_____	9. Very selfish in actions.
_____	_____	10. Exhibits an "I" feeling– "How do I feel?"
_____	_____	11. Trusting and accepting of others.
_____	_____	12. Makes a person feel proud and confident.
_____	_____	13. Indicates "I care how you feel."
_____	_____	14. Emotions flow at a fast pace.
_____	_____	15. Increases ability to relate to others.
_____	_____	16. Engulfing, selfish feelings.
_____	_____	17. Both partners give generously of themselves.
_____	_____	18. Aware of other person's faults, but accepts them as part of total personality.
_____	_____	19. Physical attraction is only one aspect of the relationship.
_____	_____	20. Likes only a few friends and tends to be moody and indifferent.

1. What additional characteristics would you use to describe a relationship based on love? _________

____

____

2. What additional characteristics would you use to describe a relationship based on infatuation? _____

____

____

3. What role does sexual gratification sometimes play in relationships based on infatuation? _________

____

____

4. Is sexual gratification a necessary part of a relationship based on true love?___________________

____

Should I Have Premarital Sexual Experiences?

No

Yes

Virginity until marriage

Abstinence assures:

No exploitation of another individual

No guilt feelings concerning premarital experiences

No risk of loss of reputation

No premarital pregnancy

No risk of AIDS

No risk of STDs

— Possible exposure to AIDS

— Possible exposure to STDs

— Possible pregnancy

Keep child, stay single
  parenting difficult alone
  may limit education
  financial pressures
  additional pregnancies
    often follow

Forced marriage
  immature parenting
  financial pressures
  emotional tensions
  may end in divorce

Adoption
  give up child
  emotionally difficult

Abortion
  possible guilt feelings
  many in society
    disapprove
  health risks

Questions to Ask Yourself Before Entering a Sexual Relationship

Young people make many decisions that can impact the rest of their lives. Some of these decisions have to do with sexual relationships. To help you make the right decision, answer the following questions:

1. Why am I doing this? Am I doing this for me or my partner? Am I doing this to prove I am an adult?

2. Am I feeling pressured to have sex? Is my partner pressuring me? If my partner is not pressuring me, where is the pressure coming from?

3. Am I believing my friends when they say, "Everyone is doing it!" Do I really believe this?

4. How do I feel about my partner? Do I really love him/her? Do I respect him/her? Do I trust him/her? Could our relationship go on if I decided not to have sex?

5. What are my religious and moral values concerning sex before marriage? How will I feel if I go against my beliefs?

6. Have we talked about these decisions? Do I really know what my partner is thinking? Does my partner really know what I am thinking?

7. Do I really believe sex is safe with birth control? Do I want to risk STDs, including AIDS, or pregnancy?

8. Is having sex just a payoff for having a good time? Don't I put more importance on myself than that?

9. Am I being honest with myself? Are we really ready to go this far in our relationship? Am I trying to make it more serious than it is?

10. My sexuality is mine–my partner's sexuality is his or hers. Are we ready to give our sexuality to each other if we are not married and in a committed relationship?

Acquaintance Rape: A Case Study

Debbie arrived at the party when it was in full swing. She knew some of the people there, but she wanted to meet some new people. As she moved around the room, she saw a guy looking at her. He seemed to be watching her as he talked to some other people.

Debbie decided to be daring. She went over and started a conversation with him. He was nice looking, and as they talked she learned more about him. She found she was enjoying their conversation, and she felt she wanted to get to know him better. She was really enjoying the party and thought it was probably because of him. When he asked if he could take her home, she was flattered and surprised, but it sounded like a good idea. She wasn't ready to say good-bye.

Write down three feelings that you think Debbie is having at this point.

1. ____

2. ____

3. ____

When they got in his car, he suggested they stop by his apartment for a few minutes. That's where the evening began to change. He put on some quiet music. They talked, and then they danced. He kissed Debbie, and she didn't mind that, but when he started pulling at her blouse she became upset. He kept saying, "Just relax–you know you will enjoy this." Debbie was really scared and tried to get away. He grabbed her arms and forced her down. Debbie started to cry and kept begging him to stop. He just ignored her, and forced himself on her. Debbie couldn't believe what was happening.

He raped her. She felt terrible. She got herself together, and he took her home. Debbie was horrified. What should she do?

Write down three feelings that you think Debbie is having at this point.

1. ____

2. ____

3. ____

What should Debbie do now? ____

____

____

____

____

What could Debbie have done to possibly avoid being raped? ______________________

____

____

____

____

Developing Close Relationships

Name ____

Date ____ **Period** _____________ **Score** _______________

Chapter 11 Test

Matching: Match the following terms and identifying phrases.

_______ 1. You are willing to share significant information about yourself with another person.

_______ 2. Total communication and commitment between two people.

_______ 3. Any sexual intimacy forced on one person by another.

_______ 4. A foolish, extreme attraction that does not last.

_______ 5. Being attracted to and repelled by someone at the same time.

_______ 6. The belief that boys will always behave differently than girls in sexual matters.

_______ 7. A sense of familiarity that develops over a long and close association.

_______ 8. A possessive love that cuts the loved one off from other people.

_______ 9. Saying no to any sexual relations.

A. trust
B. rape
C. abstinence
D. intimacy
E. self-disclosure
F. infatuation
G. true love
H. jealous love
I. ambivalence
J. double standard

True/False: Circle *T* if the statement is true or *F* if the statement is false.

T F 10. Your friendships will not vary through the years.

T F 11. People who have dated are likely to be more successful marriage partners.

T F 12. Most young people begin dating in informal group settings.

T F 13. "Going out" is not the same as steady dating.

T F 14. People today are marrying at a later age.

T F 15. One of the best things to do when you break up with someone is to start dating others immediately.

T F 16. Most people would rather know the reason for a breakup even though it might hurt to find out.

T F 17. Jealous love is a positive type of love.

T F 18. Unreturned love can become a form of harassment if the person persists on forcing unwanted expressions of love on another.

T F 19. Physical attraction is a component of love.

T F 20. The most common reason people give for having had premarital sex is, "We thought we were in love."

T F 21. Risk taking is never harmful as it helps you grow and learn.

(Continued)

Name ____

Multiple Choice: Choose the best response. Write the letter in the space provided.

_______ 22. Group dating _______.
  A. can involve any number of people
  B. is planned by the females
  C. limits cross-gender friendships
  D. All of the above.

_______ 23. A relationship may need to end if _______.
  A. the couple spends time with other people
  B. the couple differ on personal values
  C. the couple occasionally argue
  D. All of the above.

_______ 24. When you break up, it is best to _______.
  A. end the relationship with no explanation
  B. share the blame for the breakup
  C. lead the other person on so the breakup won't be so painful
  D. break up in front of friends so everyone will find out about it at the same time

_______ 25. Select the statement that is *not* true.
  A. True love is sharing and giving.
  B. True love shows no anger.
  C. True love is lasting and protective.
  D. Physical attraction is a component of love.

_______ 26. Infatuation _______.
  A. takes time to grow and develop
  B. is steady and secure
  C. inspires selfish thoughts and actions
  D. All of the above.

_______ 27. Which of the following is true concerning intimacy?
  A. Intimacy does not necessarily mean sexual intimacy.
  B. Intimacy means you accept another person as he or she is.
  C. Intimacy is a feeling of warm friendship.
  D. All of the above.

_______ 28. Which of the following is true concerning physical expressions of affection?
  A. All teens are ready to accept the responsibilities of a sexual relationship.
  B. A relationship can be sustained on physical expressions alone.
  C. Some people seek physical expressions of affection from others to prove their femininity or masculinity.
  D. Physical expressions are the only way to show you really care about a person.

_______ 29. Which of the following causes confusion for teens concerning sexual feelings?
  A. They may not know the facts about teenage sexual behavior.
  B. They may not have correct information concerning sexual development.
  C. They receive mixed messages from the media, their parents, and others in authority.
  D. All of the above.

_______ 30. Rape _______.
  A. is only committed by strangers
  B. is always reported to the authorities
  C. victims sometimes feel they are to blame
  D. is not likely to occur if you are with a group

(Continued)

                                        Contemporary Living Teacher's Resources

_____ 31. When you need to say no to sex, it is helpful if you _____.
      A. do so firmly, but with respect
      B. show anger in your voice
      C. give excuses
      D. stay around for awhile

Essay Questions: Provide complete responses to the following questions or statements.

32. Give five characteristics of a good friend.

33. Discuss the differences between informal group dating and formal pair dating.

34. Discuss what young people can do to prepare themselves for sexual decision making.

35. List five things a person can do to try to avoid date rape.

Part 4

The Marriage Relationship

Chapter 12 ■ ■ ■ ■ ■ ■ ■ ■ ■ ■ ■ ■ ■ ■ ■ ■ ■
Choosing to Marry

Objectives

After studying this chapter, students will be able to
- list social and psychological forces involved in choosing a spouse.
- describe other personal factors people use to evaluate possible spouses.
- identify issues related to mixed marriages.

Bulletin Boards

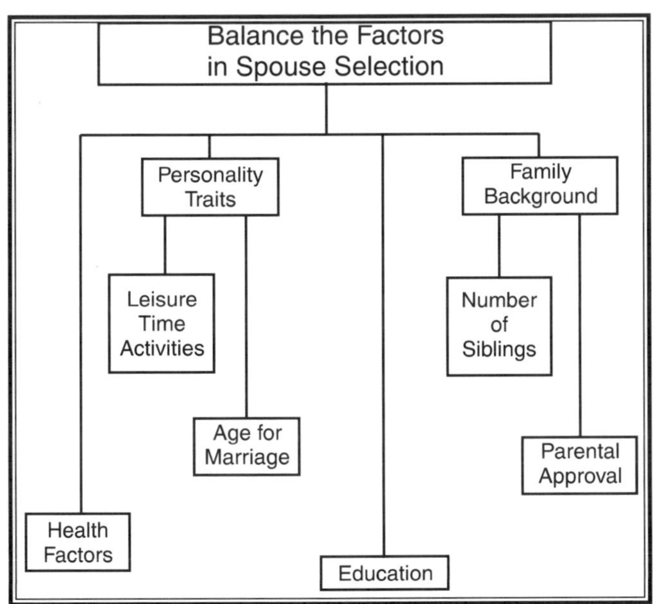

I. Title: "Balance the Factors in Spouse Selection"
Create a mobile on the bulletin board using cards, marking pens, and/or yarn. Print the factors to consider when selecting a spouse on cards of various sizes and secure them to the mobile.

II. Title: "What Can You Bring to a Marriage?"
Place a magazine picture of a young person or a young couple in the center of the bulletin board. Ask students to brainstorm a list of desirable characteristics a person seeks in a mate. Have students print the characteristics on the cards, then place them randomly around the picture. (You may refer to Chart 12-3 on page 292 of the text.)

Teaching Materials

Text, pages 288-301
Terms to Know, To Review, To Do, and *To Think About*

Student Activity Guide
    A. *Role Expectations in Marriage*
    B. *Statements About Spouse Selection*
    C. *Mixed Marriages*
    D. *Mate Selection Puzzle*

Teacher's Resource Guide/Binder
Finding Mr./Ms. Right, reproducible master, 12-1
Spouses' Educational Backgrounds, reproducible master, 12-2
Men's Age at First Marriage, 1890-1998, transparency master, 12-3
Women's Age at First Marriage, 1890-1998, transparency master, 12-4
Chapter 12 Test

Teacher's Resource Binder
Forces Affecting Mate Selection, color transparency, CT-12

Software for Contemporary Living
Chapter Review Game

Introductory Activities

1. Ask students to write their reactions to the following incomplete sentences:
   Engagement is . . .
   People get married because they . . .
   The person I choose to marry must be . . .
   I would make a good marriage partner because . . .
   I would make a better marriage partner if . . .
2. *Finding Mr./Ms. Right,* reproducible master, 12-1. Ask students to express their opinions about engagement and marriage issues. Briefly discuss student responses in class. Remind students that they may change their minds on some issues after studying the chapter.

Strategies to Reteach, Reinforce, Enrich, and Extend Text Concepts

Forces Affecting Mate Selection

3. **RT** *Forces Affecting Mate Selection,* color transparency, CT-12. Use this transparency to review these concepts and to foster discussion.
4. **EX** Ask students to compare the force of similarity to the force of complementary needs. Which force do students feel is more likely to foster a stable marriage?
5. **RF** *Statements About Spouse Selection,* Activity B, SAG. Instruct students to write their reactions to statements concerning mate selection. Students should compare their answers in small groups and discuss opinions.
6. **RF** *Role Expectations in Marriage,* Activity A, SAG. Instruct students to indicate whether they agree or disagree with the statements concerning spousal roles in marriage.

Choosing a Partner: Other Factors

7. **RT** Discuss with students the statement "Happiness runs in families." Cite two exceptions to the rule. (See text discussion.)
8. **RF** Discuss with students couple relationships that do not receive parental approval.

Ask students to identify the three potential problems such marriages face. Do parents have an obligation to express their disapproval? Are parents obligated to continue to show love? Ask students whether parental disapproval would cause them to postpone marriage.

9. **RF** *Spouses' Educational Backgrounds,* reproducible master, 12-2. Students should respond to statements, then compare results and discuss in class.
10. **EX** Achieving educational goals can sometimes be difficult for married couples. Ask students to evaluate each of the following options Jean and Charles might consider:
    - Both Jean and Charles could work part-time, complete their education, then marry.
    - Both could complete their education, work to pay back loans, then marry.
    - The couple could marry, Charles could work full time to put Jean through school, then Jean could work full time to put Charles through school.
    - Jean and Charles could marry, Jean could work full time to put Charles through school, then Charles could work full time and put Jean through school.
    - The couple could marry and neither could complete their education.
    - They could complete their education and never marry.
11. **RT** *Men's Age at First Marriage, 1890-1998,* transparency master, 12-3 and *Women's Age at First Marriage, 1890-1998,* transparency master, 12-4. Today people marry at a later age than they did in the 1950s. Point out that the average age for a first marriage today is closer to the norm of more than 100 years ago than to the norm of the 1950s. Discuss the roles societal attitudes and the expanding national economy played in encouraging younger marriages in the 1950s. Discuss reasons why women tend to marry at a younger age than men. Explain that these graphs provide only a "big picture" and that a more detailed graph would show more ups and downs between the 30-year points than these graphs show.
12. **ER** Ask students what age they feel is the ideal age to marry. Discuss with students the pros and cons of marrying as a teenager.

13. **RF** *Mate Selection Puzzle*, Activity D, SAG. Students should complete the word puzzle using terms defined in the chapter.

Mixed Marriages

14. **RF** *Mixed Marriages*, Activity C, SAG. Ask students to react to statements concerning mixed marriages.
15. **RT** Discuss with students particular problems each type of mixed marriage may foster. Ask students to discuss possible solutions for couples in each situation.
16. **RF** Discuss with students alternatives for church attendance for an interfaith couple. Also, explore various ways in which couples could work out differences concerning child rearing, birth control, and abortion. Emphasize the importance of discussing religious differences when contemplating marriage.
17. **ER** Invite foreign exchange students to discuss spouse selection, engagement, and marriage customs in their countries. Discuss similarities and differences in class.
18. **ER** Invite a marriage counselor to talk to the class about problems international, interfaith, and interracial married couples face.
19. **ER** Students representing different religions should form a panel and discuss issues related to interfaith marriages.

Answer Key for Chapter 12

Text
To Review, page 300.

1. Proximity: B. Complementary needs: D. Parent image: A. Similarity: E. Role expectations: C.
2. In a happy home you learn how spouses who love and respect one another behave in marriage relationships. Also, a child raised in a happy home is more likely to be emotionally secure and to build fulfilling relationships.
3. A, B, and C.
4. (Student response.)

5. Meet with one or more local spiritual leaders. Take an instructional class to help non-Catholics become familiar with the faith.
6. (Describe two. Student response.)
7. (List two:) They may disagree about the time, money, and effort the religious spouse should devote to religious concerns. They may react differently to conflicts and stress in their lives. They may confuse their children by teaching them different beliefs and values.

Student Activity Guide
Activity D, *Mate Selection Puzzle.*

Teacher's Resource Guide

					¹F	A	M	I	L	I	E	S			
				²S	I	M	I	L	A	R	I	T	Y		
			³A	T	H	E	I	S	T						
				⁴V	A	L	U	E	S						
						⁵S	I	B	L	I	N	G	S		
⁶C	O	M	P	L	E	M	E	N	T	A	R	Y	N	E	E	D	S
							⁷L	E	I	S	U	R	E	T	I	M	E
				⁸R	O	L	E	S							
				⁹E	D	U	C	A	T	I	O	N			
		¹⁰P	A	R	E	N	T	I	M	A	G	E			
			¹¹P	R	O	X	I	M	I	T	Y				
			¹²C	O	S	M	O	P	O	L	I	T	A	N	
				¹³I	N	T	E	R	F	A	I	T	H	

Chapter 12 Test

1. E	11. T	21. D
2. D	12. F	22. B
3. F	13. T	23. C
4. C	14. T	24. A
5. H	15. F	25. C
6. A	16. T	26. D
7. J	17. T	27. A
8. I	18. T	28. C
9. B	19. F	29. A
10. G	20. T	30. D

31. (Student response.)
32. (Student response. See page 293 of text.)

Finding Mr./Ms. Right

Name____ **Date** _______________ **Period**______________

Read the following statements about engagement and marriage issues. Circle *A* if you agree with the statement and *D* if you disagree with the statement. Then complete the statement below.

A   D   1. There is one and only one person in this world to whom I could be happily married.

A   D   2. I am more likely to marry someone who lives and works over 500 miles away than someone who lives and works near me.

A   D   3. If I am basically content with my life, I am likely to be happier if I choose a spouse whose family is from the same social class as that of my own family.

A   D   4. My concept of the ideal spouse is unaffected by how I perceive my parent of the opposite sex.

A   D   5. Opposites attract–therefore, if I find I enjoy sharing common interests with my date, I should drop him or her immediately.

A   D   6. Opposites attract–therefore, a person who is moody and excitable may be attracted to someone who seems strong and steady and vice versa.

A   D   7. Opposites attract–therefore, a person who is confident and even conceited may be attracted to someone who is shy and lacks self-esteem and vice versa.

A   D   8. Opposites attract–therefore, I would be happiest with someone whose values are totally different from mine.

A   D   9. I should not consider a parent's opinion of my girlfriend or boyfriend when deciding whether the relationship should become more serious.

A   D   10. In our society most people view interracial marriages the same way they view non-interracial marriages.

A   D   11. If I married a person of a different religious faith, I would insist that my spouse convert to my religion.

A   D   12. If I married a person of a different faith, I would willingly convert to his or her religion.

A   D   13. If I married a person of a different religious faith, I would be willing to adhere to his or her customs and beliefs regarding food, holidays, and attendance at religious services.

A   D   14. If I married a person of a different religious faith, I would be willing to adhere to his or her beliefs about birth control and abortion.

A   D   15. If I married a person of a different religious faith, I would actively support the instruction of our children in my spouse's faith.

I strongly (agree/disagree) with statement ______ because _______________________________________

____

____

____

____

____

____

____

Spouses' Educational Backgrounds

Name _______________________________________ **Date** ______________ **Period**______________

Respond to the following statements concerning the educational backgrounds of marriage partners. Tabulate the answers of all class members. Discuss ways in which the answers from your class may differ from the answers of students in other countries or from 40 years ago.

______ Male   ______ Female

Level of education I plan to complete:

______ High school

______ Vocational school

______ Community college

______ College (4 years)

______ Graduate school

Level of education I would like my spouse to complete:

______ High school

______ Vocational school

______ Community college

______ College (4 years)

______ Graduate school

Read the following questions. Circle *A* if you agree with the statement and *D* if you disagree with the statement.

A   D   1. It is important for both a husband and wife to have equal educational backgrounds.

A   D   2. A wife should have more formal education than her husband.

A   D   3. A husband should have more formal education than his wife.

A   D   4. A wife should be willing to postpone her education in order to earn money and put her husband through college.

A   D   5. If a couple marries before college graduation, both the husband and wife should continue classes part time and work part time.

A   D   6. A couple should not marry unless their parents are willing to support them until graduation.

A   D   7. People with either a master's or doctoral degree can share and communicate more easily with spouses who have at least a college degree.

A   D   8. Educational background makes no difference in a marriage based on true love.

A   D   9. Education should be a lifelong process for both spouses.

A   D   10. Couples with similar levels of education are more likely to have a greater number of conversational topics of mutual interest.

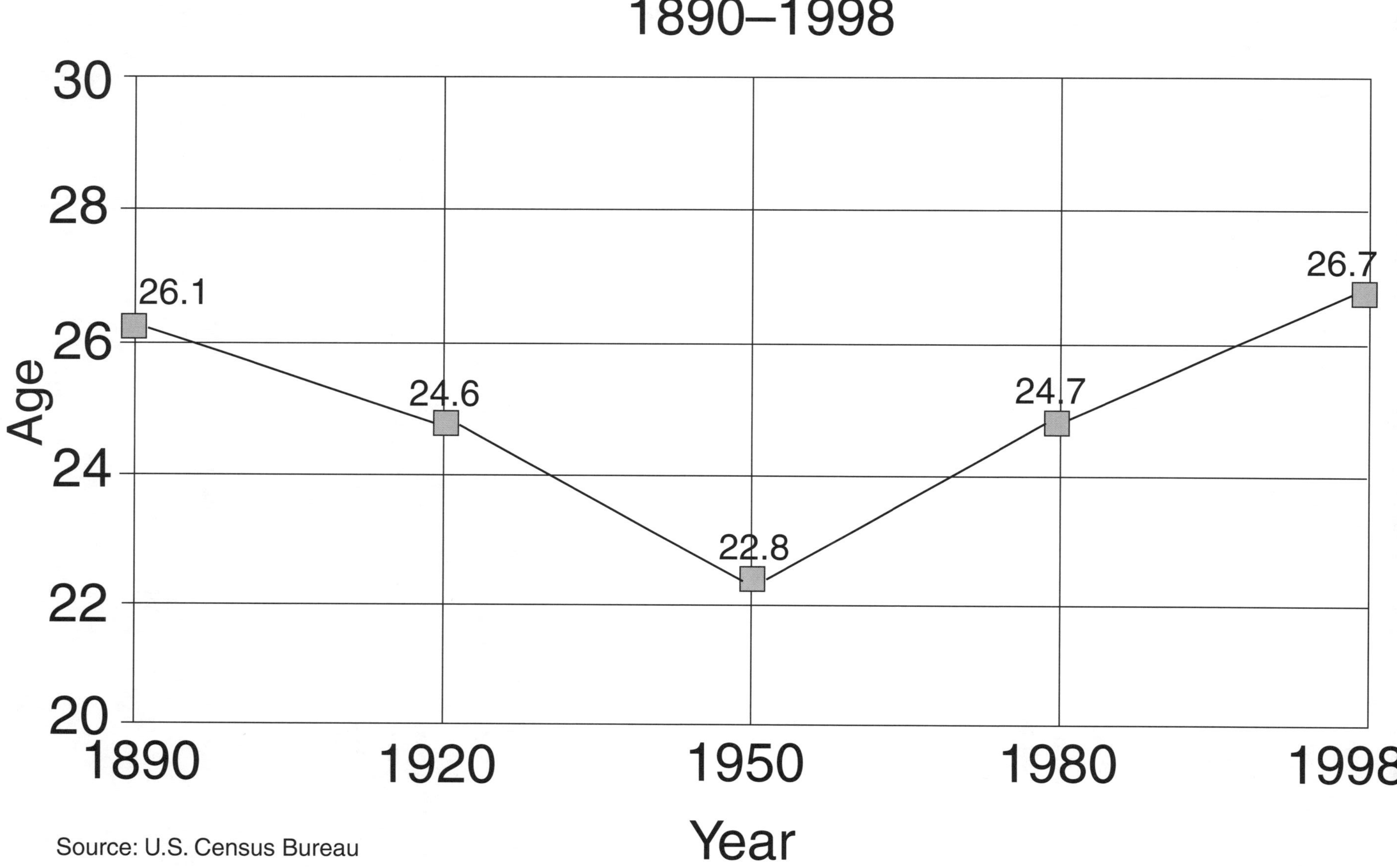

Men's Age at First Marriage
1890–1998
30
28
26
24
22
20
Age
26.1
24.6
22.8
24.7
26.7
1890
1920
1950
1980
1998
Year
Source: U.S. Census Bureau

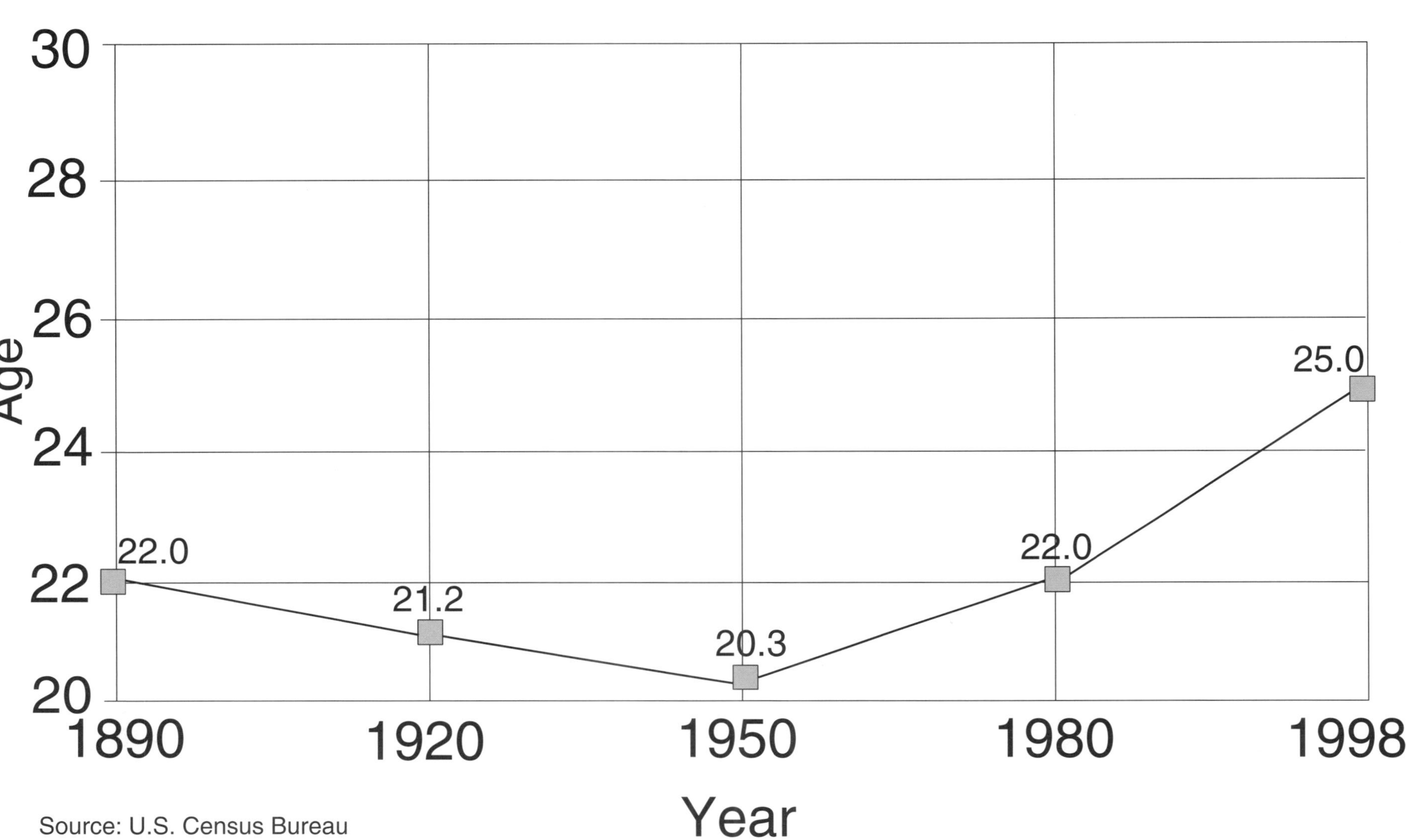

Women's Age at First Marriage
1890–1998
Age
30
28
26
24
22
20
25.0
22.0
21.2
20.3
22.0
1890
1920
1950
1980
1998
Year
Source: U.S. Census Bureau

Choosing to Marry

Name ____

Date _________________________________ **Period** ___________ **Score** ___________

Chapter 12 Test

Matching: Match the following terms and identifying phrases.

_____ 1. A force in mate selection in which couples seek partners who make up for areas in which they feel weak.

_____ 2. One who denies the existence of a god.

_____ 3. A force in mate selection in which couples seek partners with qualities similar to those of their parents.

_____ 4. Type of marriage in which the partners are of different races.

_____ 5. Describes a society composed of people from a variety of countries around the world.

_____ 6. Type of marriage in which the partners have different religious backgrounds and beliefs.

_____ 7. Beliefs about the tasks and responsibilities that a spouse should perform.

_____ 8. Type of mixed marriage in which the spouses come from different countries.

_____ 9. Force in spouse selection emphasizing the nearness of two prospective spouses to one another.

_____ 10. One who believes a god exists.

A. interfaith
B. proximity
C. interracial
D. atheist
E. complementary needs
F. parent image
G. theist
H. cosmopolitan
I. international
J. role expectations
K. similarity

True/False: Circle *T* if the statement is true or *F* if the statement is false.

T F 11. Spouses can share many roles in a marriage.

T F 12. Generally, couples who spend much of their leisure time together have weak marriages.

T F 13. Usually, the biggest problem facing an interfaith marriage with children is the question of the children's religious training.

T F 14. In general, marriages have a greater chance of success when parents approve of them.

T F 15. Generally, a couple who have had similar levels of education share and communicate less than couples with dissimilar levels of education.

T F 16. Mixed marriages involve partners of different countries, races, or religious faiths.

T F 17. Partners in international marriages must blend different cultural backgrounds and traditions.

T F 18. The older you are when you marry, the less likely you are to divorce.

(Continued)

T   F   19. Experts encourage situations in which one spouse drops out of school in order to work so the other spouse can stay in school.

T   F   20. If you have been raised in a loving home with high ethical standards, you will tend to seek a spouse with whom you can create a similar home.

Multiple Choice: Select the best response. Write the letter in the space provided.

_______ 21. Derrick and Patrice dated in high school. After graduation, Derrick began working for an oil company and Patrice became a flight attendant. Although they dated others, they always kept in touch with each other. Five years passed before they began dating each other more often and discussing marriage. Both recognized the differences in their careers, but they felt more comfortable thinking about marriage with someone who had grown up in the same hometown. They became engaged and were married. This represents which force of mate selection?
  A. role conflict
  B. complementary needs
  C. education
  D. proximity

_______ 22. Dominic was an active person. He liked to dominate conversations and dictate decisions. He married Janice, a woman who was quietly efficient, stable, and easygoing. After his hectic days, Dominic looked forward to peaceful evenings at home with Janice. Which force in mate selection does this represent?
  A. role conflict
  B. complementary needs
  C. parent image
  D. similarity

_______ 23. William knew when he met LaTosha that she would be a perfect wife for him. She had a way of putting others at ease, just like his mother. He had always thought that his father had found the only woman like that. He was happy when LaTosha agreed to marry him. Which mate selection theory does this represent?
  A. similarity
  B. complementary needs
  C. parent image
  D. proximity

_______ 24. Kevin and Tricia lived in the same small town and had dated for three years. They were both members of the same religion and voted for the same political party. Both dressed conservatively and shared the same interest in spectator sports. They felt comfortable with each other. Their friends felt they would have a successful marriage. Which theory does this represent?
  A. similarity
  B. complementary needs
  C. parent image
  D. role conflict

_______ 25. People who marry at very young ages are more likely than older couples to _______.
  A. have completed their education
  B. have happy, long-lasting marriages
  C. have financial problems
  D. have the emotional maturity necessary to take on the responsibilities of marriage

(Continued)

_____ 26. Shared leisure-time activities allow a couple to _____.
    A. live more creative, abundant lives
    B. grow and improve their relationship
    C. experience companionship
    D. All of the above.

_____ 27. Marriages are more likely to be happy if the couple _____.
    A. share similar values
    B. have widely different social backgrounds
    C. experience severe role conflict
    D. are unaware of their complementary needs

_____ 28. A theist-atheist marriage is one in which _____.
    A. the couple come from different racial backgrounds
    B. the couple come from different countries
    C. one spouse believes in God and the other spouse does not
    D. one spouse has a college degree and the other does not

_____ 29. In today's society family members' roles _____.
    A. are becoming more varied
    B. are becoming more traditional
    C. are unnecessary
    D. have been eliminated

_____ 30. Compared to less healthy people, persons who are mentally and physically healthy tend to _____.
    A. communicate less well
    B. be more influenced by the parent image theory
    C. be more influenced by the force of complementary needs
    D. have an easier time resolving areas of marital stress

Essay Questions: Provide complete responses to the following questions or statements.

31. Which force affecting spouse selection do you think is the most important? Explain the reasons for your choice.

32. Briefly discuss the influence of parental approval in spouse selection, noting possible problems that might arise when parents do not approve of the marriage.

Chapter 13
Engagement and Marriage

Objectives

After studying this chapter, students will be able to
- describe the purpose of the engagement period.
- identify issues for themselves and a future spouse to discuss prior to marriage.
- recognize the legal and moral commitments in beginning a marriage relationship.
- assess wedding plans as they affect total commitments and goals in marriage.

Bulletin Boards

I. Title: "The Wedding–Beginning Life Together"
Post photos of different types of wedding attire and wedding settings. Have students bring in family wedding pictures to add to the bulletin board.

II. Title: "Wedding Customs Around the World"
Create a bulletin board illustrating wedding and engagement customs from different countries. (*National Geographic Magazine* is one good source for pictures.) You might also ask foreign exchange students in your school for information and illustrations.

Teaching Materials

Text, pages 302-324
Terms to Know, To Review, To Do, and *To Think About*

Student Activity Guide
    A. *Communication During Engagement*
    B. *Career Goals in Marriage*
    C. *Marriage Law Crossword*
    D. *Planning a Wedding*

Teacher's Resource Guide/Binder
    A Personal Commitment, reproducible master, 13-1
    Purposes of Engagement, transparency master, 13-2
    The Engagement Period, reproducible master, 13-3
    Marriage Laws in Your State, reproducible master, 13-4
    What's in a Name? transparency master, 13-5
    Chapter 13 Test

Teacher's Resource Binder
    Revealing the Past, color transparency, CT-13A
    Functions of a Wedding, color transparency, CT-13B

Introductory Activities

1. *A Personal Commitment,* reproducible master, 13-1. Ask students to react to questions concerning engagement and marriage that will be covered in this chapter. Divide the class into small groups. Assign specific questions for each group to discuss. Ask group members to share key discussion points with the class.

2. Instruct each student to list issues couples should discuss and attempt to resolve before marriage. Students should share items from their lists as you write issues on the board. Determine with students which issues most students listed and reasons for their significance.

Strategies to Reteach, Reinforce, Enrich, and Extend Text Concepts

Engagement

3. **RT** *Purposes of Engagement,* transparency master, 13-2. Use this transparency to discuss with students the purpose of the engagement period in our culture. Ask students which purpose they feel is most important as well as least important.

4. **ER** Investigate customs of other cultures that occur before a couple marries (similar to engagement). If possible, ask students representing other cultures to explain customs to the class.

Communication during Engagement

5. **RF** *Communication During Engagement,* Activity A, SAG. Instruct students to indicate how important it is to discuss the listed topics during the engagement period.

6. **RF** Ask students to review the questions under the "Personality Traits" section. Students should answer the first part of each question individually and evaluate their personal readiness for marriage.

7. **RF** *Career Goals in Marriage,* Activity B, SAG. Students should indicate their opinions about balancing career goals with family obligations.

8. **RT** Discuss in-law relationships with students. Cite cultural conditions that may contribute to in-law problems (in-law jokes, TV shows, etc.). Ask students to identify positive ways to handle in-law problems.

9. **ER** Students should identify factors to consider when planning future living arrangements. If both partners own homes or condos, how might they decide where to live? What is the most popular housing choice for young couples today?

10. **RF** Instruct students to form small groups and discuss how friends can affect marriages in both positive and negative ways. Students in one group should cite possible problems and ask members of another group for solutions. You may then reverse the process.

11. **RT** *Revealing the Past,* color transparency, CT-13A. Use this transparency to discuss with students information that a couple considering marriage are obligated to reveal to each other. What might be the consequences of withholding or never revealing such information?

12. **RF** *The Engagement Period,* reproducible master, 13-3. Divide the class into four groups. Assign one of the case histories of engaged couples to each group. Instruct group members to discuss the questions listed on the reproducible master. Members should share their responses in class.

13. **ER** Invite a marriage counselor to speak to the class about the importance of good communication during the engagement period.

Breaking Engagements

14. **RF** Discuss with students reasons why breaking an engagement is difficult. Ask students what they would do if they felt incompatible with a future spouse? How would they handle the responsibility of initiating a breakup? If they were on the receiving end of a breakup, how would they handle these feelings? Do they think a marriage "on the rebound" has much chance for success? Ask students to explain their reasons.

15. **RT** Ask students how they would handle a breakup that makes them the target of verbal abuse (such as prank phone calls) or physical abuse. Point out the existence of shelters and

the importance of not prolonging an abusive relationship with frequent reconciliations, etc.

Marriage Laws

16. **RF** *Marriage Law Crossword,* Activity C, SAG. Instruct students to complete the crossword puzzle.
17. **ER** *Marriage Laws in Your State,* reproducible master, 13-4. Students should research your state's marriage laws and answer the questions. You may instruct them to interview a judge or a lawyer or to invite a guest speaker on this subject.
18. **EX** A group of legislators in one state has proposed adding the following warning about domestic abuse to marriage license applications: "Neither you nor your spouse is the property of the other. The laws of this state affirm your right to enter into this marriage and at the same time to live within the marriage free from violence and abuse." Write this statement on a transparency or on the board and solicit students' opinions. Is it wise to add this phrase to a marriage license application? Why or why not?
19. **EX** *What's in a Name?* transparency master, 13-5. Use this transparency to discuss the various alternatives couples can consider when deciding on their married names. Point out that about 10 percent of married U.S. women have opted for surnames other than their husbands', and that this trend is growing. Why are some couples dissatisfied with the traditional system under which the wife takes her husband's surname? Can innovative solutions make genealogies more difficult to trace? Ask for a show of hands to indicate preferences regarding the most common options. (Keep records so you can track trends over the years and compare students' preferences.)

Weddings

20. **ER** Review U.S. marriage customs, then divide students into small groups to research marriage customs in other countries. Ask each group to present an oral report about their research.
21. **RT** *Functions of a Wedding,* color transparency, CT-13B. Refer to this transparency as you discuss with students the primary functions the wedding ceremony serves. Ask students which function they believe to be most and least important.
22. **RF** *Planning a Wedding,* Activity D, SAG. Divide the class into six groups. Ask each group to research different aspects of a wedding. Instruct each group to prepare a detailed written report as well as a brief oral report. Estimate the costs of various types of weddings. As each group reports, students should record cost-related information on the "Wedding Costs" chart provided. Discuss the wide variety of costs involved and the importance of careful planning and budgeting.
23. **ER** Research variations of wedding procedures for unusual situations, such as ways to handle divorced parents, widowed parents, second marriages, stepchildren, etc.
24. **ER** Have students research current honeymoon customs. Find out how far in advance honeymoons should be planned, how long the average honeymoon lasts, and how much the average honeymoon costs.
25. **ER** Bring bridal magazines to class and find honeymoon-related advertisements. Discuss the availability of honeymoon resorts, the most popular places for honeymoons, etc.
26. **ER** Ask a bridal consultant to speak to your class concerning wedding planning.

Answer Key for Chapter 13

Text
To Review, pages 322-323.

1. false
2. (List four:) The doctor will be able to determine the general state of health of each person. The doctor will review their medical histories and warn them of any hereditary conditions that may cause problems. They will have the chance to ask questions about sex roles in marriage. They will have the chance to get contraceptive information. They will have established doctor-patient relationships, which may be helpful later.
3. (Student response. List two. See pages 309-310.)
4. (List one positive and one negative influence.) Positive: Friends can add variety to the spouses' lives, broaden their range of experiences, help them keep in touch with the world, and provide a source of support in

time of need. Negative: Friends may cause conflict if they expect the married person to remain their friend with no strings attached.

5. A previous marriage, problems that would affect having children, a history of severe health problems, a criminal or prison record, and debts or similar obligations that might handicap the marriage.

6. false

7. (Student response. List one example of each type of marriage.) *Consanguineous marriages* are marriages of persons related by blood, such as brothers and sisters. *Marriages of affinity* are marriages of persons related by marriage, such as stepparents and stepchildren.

8. Certain judicial and public officials, such as judges and justices of the peace. A minister, rabbi, or priest officiates at ceremonial weddings.

9. false

10. true

Student Activity Guide

Activity C, *Marriage Law Crossword.*

Across and down answers filled in the crossword grid:
AFFINITY, CIVIL, CONSANGUINEOUS, ELOPEMENT, CEREMONIAL, BIGAMY, LICENSE, OFFICIATE, CLERGYMAN, MONOGAMOUS

Teacher's Resource Guide

Chapter 13 Test

1. E	11. T	21. D
2. F	12. T	22. D
3. B	13. T	23. A
4. I	14. F	24. B
5. G	15. T	25. A
6. J	16. F	26. D
7. H	17. T	27. B
8. A	18. F	28. A
9. D	19. F	29. B
10. C	20. T	30. D

31. It serves as an announcement to family, friends, and society of a couple's intentions to marry. It gives the couple time to plan the wedding ceremony. It is a testing period during which the couple can evaluate their relationship and make plans for their future.

32. (Student response.)

33. (List three. Student response.)

A Personal Commitment

Name _______________________________________ **Date** _______________ **Period**_______________

Read the following questions about engagement and marriage issues. Check *Yes* or *No* to indicate how you would handle each situation.

Yes   **No**

_____   _____   1. If you did not like certain qualities about your future partner, would you plan to change them once you were married?

_____   _____   2. If you noticed a tendency to disagree with your future mate in certain areas, would you discuss this and try to resolve the differences before marriage?

_____   _____   3. Do you think a marriage relationship should be fifty-fifty on all matters?

_____   _____   4. Do you think it is important that you and your future mate are comfortable with each other's parents?

_____   _____   5. If you believed that friends of your future mate were demanding too much time from, or negatively influencing, your future mate, would you bring this to his or her attention?

_____   _____   6. Do you feel it is important that you both have the same attitudes about spending and saving money?

_____   _____   7. Do you feel it is important that you both agree on plans for children?

_____   _____   8. If your future mate did not want to have children, would you be able to go along with this decision?

_____   _____   9. If you have differing religious backgrounds, should you discuss those differences before marriage and reach some type of compromise?

_____   _____   10. If you married a person of another faith, would you maintain your own religious faith, even if your partner did not want to change to your faith?

_____   _____   11. If your partner was of a different faith, would you be willing to adhere to customs regarding food, birth control, and holidays of this faith?

_____   _____   12. Would you be willing to raise your children in a religious faith different from your own?

_____   _____   13. Do you think the engagement period should last at least six months?

_____   _____   14. Do you feel that a person's attitude toward divorce affects his or her attitude toward marriage?

_____   _____   15. If laws made it more difficult to obtain a divorce, would marriages be stronger?

Purposes of Engagement

- ♥ Announcing intentions to marry

- ♥ Testing compatibility and planning for the future

- ♥ Planning the wedding

The Engagement Period

Couples should use the engagement period to identify any problems they may need to resolve before marriage. Many of these problems relate to career goals, education, personalities, religion, finances, friendships, and families. Read the case histories of the engaged couples below and answer the following questions for each:

- Describe the background of each of the partners.
- Describe the anticipated strengths of each marriage.
- What conflicts might arise in their marriage?
- Should the couples marry as planned, or would you advise them to postpone, or even cancel, their marriage plans?

Brad and Carrie

Carrie, 23, is engaged to Brad, 27. Carrie is studious, quiet, and friendly. A college senior, Carrie would like to continue her education and earn a master's degree. Her parents live in Arkansas. Brad is extremely outgoing and ambitious. He has completed his business degree and secured a high-paying job in Boston. He is from Boston, and his parents still live there. Neither Brad nor Carrie have brothers or sisters. They are both conservative. Brad is not religious, but his parents are Protestant. Carrie is Baptist. Carrie and Brad plan to rent a townhouse in Boston. Brad has lots of friends there, but Carrie is not always comfortable around them. Brad has been able to save some money. Carrie has a student loan to repay.

Robert and Serena

Robert, 20, is a foreman in a warehouse and Serena, 19, works as a clerk in an office supply store. They recently became engaged. Robert lives with good friends from his active social circle. Serena, who is much quieter, lives with her aunt and has few close friends. Both sets of parents live out of town. Robert has no savings and owes money on his car. He often runs short of cash before payday arrives. Serena, through careful budgeting, has managed to save a small amount of money. When she suggests to Robert that he should try to save more, he becomes angry. They plan to find an apartment close to Serena's aunt. They are both Catholic.

Susan and George

Susan, 32, is assertive, strong, and independent. She married when she was 17 and had a baby within a year. Her husband left her shortly after their daughter was born. She didn't have any job skills, but she was able to work as a waitress while she earned an accounting degree. Eventually, Susan secured a good job and bought a townhouse. Although her monthly earnings disappear quickly, she has managed to stay out of debt. She has joined a Methodist church near her home. Her friends are mainly business associates. George has just asked Susan to marry him. He is 36 and lives with his parents. He has worked in his family's construction business all his life and has been able to save quite a bit of money. George, who is quiet and sometimes moody, is very close to his family and participates in Jewish customs and holidays.

Luther and Shenshell

Luther and Shenshell are engaged to be married. Luther, who is going to medical school, is outgoing and intense. Shenshell is a fashion buyer for a local department store. She, too, is outgoing and friendly. She began working as a sales clerk in the store right out of high school and worked her way up to a buyer. Shenshell is making good money now at age 32, and she spends it freely. She was recently able to buy her own condominium, where she frequently entertains friends and family. Luther, an only child, has had to struggle to pay for medical school ever since his father died. He has always had to work to get through school and lives modestly in a small apartment. He is 27.

Marriage Laws in Your State

Name _______________________________ **Date** _____________ **Period** _____________

Marriage laws vary from state to state. Research the laws in your state, or interview a lawyer or judge to answer the following questions.

1. What are the age requirements for marriage?

   Male______ Female______

2. Is parental consent required, and if so, under what circumstances? _______________________

   ____

   ____

   ____

   ____

3. Is a blood test required? For how long is it valid? For what diseases are couples tested? __________

   ____

   ____

   ____

   ____

4. Is a physical examination by a physician required? _______________________________________

5. Does your state have laws concerning sound mind? If so, explain. _________________________

   ____

   ____

   ____

   ____

6. Are certain couples prohibited from marrying in your state (consanguineous marriage, marriages of affinity)? Explain. ____

   ____

   ____

   ____

(Continued)

Name ____

7. How does a couple obtain a marriage license? _________________________________

   ____

   ____

   ____

   ____

   ____

8. How much does a marriage license cost? ______________________________________

9. How long is the waiting period between the time a couple applies for a license, obtains a license, and participates in the marriage ceremony? _______________________________

   ____

10. Who can legally officiate at a marriage in your state? ________________________

    ____

    ____

• LORI • LENARD • VALERIE • DANIEL • ROBERT • TACINA • MARC • ED •

WHAT'S IN A NAME?

Options for married couples include:

1. Husband and wife each keep their own name.
   Maria Lynn Lewis and John Allen Jackson

2. Wife uses maiden name and new surname.
   Maria Lewis Jackson

3. Wife and husband combine surnames.
   Maria and John Lewis Jackson
   Maria and John Jacksonlewis

4. Husband and wife use a surname based on middle names.
   Maria and John Allyn

5. Wife and husband agree on a new surname.
   Maria and John Harmony

6. Other options?_______________________________

LEAR • JONES • JOHNSON • BOYD • MARQUEZ •

ABBOTT • BARRIOS • FLORES • FRANKLIN • O'LEARY •

RAUL • DANA • KAROLL • TYBRELL • TAMMY • PRISCILLA • ANTONIO •

Engagement and Marriage

Name _______________________________________

Date _______________________________________ **Period** _____________ **Score** _______________

Chapter 13 Test

Matching: Match the following terms and identifying phrases.

_______ 1. Basis for lawsuits in earlier years when an engagement was a legally binding contract.

_______ 2. Relationship involving one wife and one husband.

_______ 3. A crime in which a person enters a second marriage before the first one is dissolved.

_______ 4. Marriages of people related by marriage.

_______ 5. Valid for a limited time in most states.

_______ 6. An outgrowth of our early history resulting from the fact that officiates were not readily available.

_______ 7. Marriages of people related by blood.

_______ 8. Traditional wedding performed by a minister, priest, or rabbi.

_______ 9. Wedding performed by a judicial or public official.

_______ 10. The person who performs the wedding.

A. ceremonial wedding
B. bigamy
C. officiate
D. civil wedding
E. breach of promise
F. monogamous
G. license
H. consanguineous
I. affinity
J. common-law marriage

True/False: Circle *T* if the statement is true or *F* if the statement is false.

T F 11. Many states no longer view engagement as a legally binding contract.

T F 12. Spouses need not agree on everything in order to be happy.

T F 13. Sexual adjustment in marriage tends to be interrelated with all other areas of adjustment.

T F 14. All states allow persons 17 years of age and older to marry without parental consent.

T F 15. When a disappointed lover quickly marries someone else following a broken engagement, this is known as *marrying on the rebound.*

T F 16. Polygamous marriages are legal in some states.

T F 17. If people are found to have certain communicable diseases, particularly some STDs, they cannot marry until they are cured.

T F 18. A long, extended honeymoon is often recommended by marriage counselors.

T F 19. Parents who were united in a marriage of affinity run a heightened risk of producing children with disabilities.

T F 20. Most states have laws prohibiting the marriage of people who are unable to understand the act of getting married.

(Continued)

Multiple Choice: Select the best response. Write the letter in the space provided.

_______ 21. A premarital medical exam and counseling _____.
   A. should be done early in the engagement period
   B. provides the couple with a chance to ask about contraception, if they wish
   C. gives the physician the opportunity to review both partners' medical histories and family backgrounds and to discuss any hereditary conditions
   D. All of the above.

_______ 22. People of what faith can be legally married without an officiate?
   A. Catholic
   B. Methodist
   C. Muslim
   D. Quaker

_______ 23. Marriage between a father and a daughter is an example of a _____.
   A. consanguineous marriage
   B. marriage of affinity
   C. conflict-habituated marriage
   D. civil marriage

_______ 24. The most common reason couples give for eloping is that _____.
   A. they lack money for a wedding
   B. their parents object to the marriage
   C. they want to avoid all the "show and pomp" of a ceremonial wedding
   D. they cannot get a marriage license

_______ 25. The most common complaint couples make about in-laws is that their in-laws _____.
   A. interfere and meddle
   B. refuse to aid the couple financially
   C. spoil the couple's children
   D. are thoughtless and unappreciative

_______ 26. What information should a person reveal during the engagement period?
   A. A prison record.
   B. A previous marriage.
   C. A history of serious health problems.
   D. All of the above.

_______ 27. Common-law marriages _____.
   A. are illegal in all states
   B. may begin when a couple makes a declaration of informal marriage in court
   C. involve only people who are related to one another
   D. can be legally dissolved without legal divorce procedures

_______ 28. The distinguishing factor between common-law marriages and living together is _____.
   A. the couple's intent to be considered as husband and wife
   B. the couple's degree of compatibility
   C. the presence of children
   D. the quality of relationships with in-laws

_______ 29. Which of the following statements is true?
   A. Marriage is one of the least successful legal arrangements in the U.S.
   B. The state views itself as the third party in any marriage.
   C. Marriage laws are the same in every state.
   D. All of the above.

(Continued)

     Contemporary Living Teacher's Resources

_______ 30. Which of the following is a function of a wedding?
      A. It signifies the start of the couple's new life together.
      B. It announces the marriage to the public.
      C. It satisfies the legal requirements of the state.
      D. All of the above.

Essay Questions: Provide complete responses to the following questions or statements.

31. Name the three major purposes of the engagement period.

32. Discuss reasons why it is important for engaged couples to discuss career goals in marriage.

33. Identify three typical marriage laws and discuss the importance of each.

Chapter 14
Building a Marriage

Objectives

After studying this chapter, students will be able to
- recognize factors related to happiness and success in marriage.
- analyze five techniques for handling marital disagreements.
- distinguish between productive and destructive quarreling.
- recognize the normalcy and function of conflict in marriage.
- assess the resources available to help couples resolve conflict.

Bulletin Boards

I. Title: "A Sense of Humor–An Essential Part of Marriage"

Instruct students to collect a variety of cartoons about married life. Students should mount the cartoons behind a variety of frame shapes and sizes cut from colored construction paper.

II. Title: "Scenes from Marriage"

Each person takes into marriage certain expectations of what married life will be like. Create a bulletin board illustrating the various aspects of married life. Divide it into sections labeled *Housing, Transportation, Careers, Recreation, Children, Activities, Religious Participation,* and *Education.* Illustrate each section with magazine pictures that depict the various options available, or ask students to sketch options they might choose.

Teaching Materials

Text, pages 326-348
Terms to Know, To Review, To Do, and *To Think About*

Student Activity Guide
A. *Making Marital Adjustments*
B. *Conflict in Marriage*
C. *Who Will Lead?*

Teacher's Resource Guide/Binder
Handling Marital Disagreements, reproducible master, 14-1
Marriage Matchup, reproducible master, 14-2
Questions in Marriage Counseling, transparency master, 14-3
Could I Be a Marriage Counselor? transparency master, 14-4
Chapter 14 Test

Teacher's Resource Binder
Humor, color transparency, CT-14A

Forms of Adjustment in Marriage, color transparency, CT-14B

Software for Contemporary Living
Chapter Review Game

Introductory Activities

1. Ask students to respond to the open-ended statement "Happiness in marriage is...." Discuss their responses. Do they include both emotional and material expectations for marriage? Are the expectations realistic?
2. Give each student a sheet of newsprint and a marking pen. On the top half of the sheet they should sketch a scene from their future home shortly after they are married. On the bottom half they should sketch a scene from their home 20 years later. Ask students to explain their sketches. Post them on the bulletin board.

Strategies to Reteach, Reinforce, Enrich, and Extend Text Concepts

Happiness in Marriage

3. **RT** Ask students to accept or reject the statement "Self-esteem is necessary to achieve happiness in marriage."
4. **RF** Trivial behaviors often cause problems in a marriage. Discuss how the following behaviors can create problems in a marriage and indicate ways to handle them.
   - Squeezing the toothpaste tube in the middle
   - Throwing clothes on the floor
   - Putting feet on the furniture
   - Eating too much junk food
   - Leaving drawers and closet doors open
   - Leaving lights on
   - Not calling when returning home late
   - Starting projects but never finishing them
   - Not showing affection
5. **ER** *Humor,* color transparency, CT-14A. Discuss with students positive and negative types of humor in marriage. Ask class members to provide examples of each type.

Adjustments in Marriage

6. **RF** *Forms of Adjustment in Marriage,* color transparency, CT-14B. Refer to this transparency as you discuss the five basic ways married couples can approach disagreements.
7. **RF** Each of the following examples illustrates one of the five forms of adjustment in marriage. Read the examples to the class after discussing the forms of adjustment. Refer to the transparency as students identify the forms of adjustment.
   A. Sam and Elaine are buying a car. Sam believes that Elaine knows more about cars than he does, so he leaves the final decision up to her. (Concession)
   B. Emilio and Tomasina both want to spend the upcoming holiday with their own relatives, who live in different cities. They continue to argue and never reach a decision. They end up staying home alone during the holiday. (Hostility)
   C. Susan is a Democrat and Laird is a Republican. They recognize their differences. They go to the polls together and vote, neither trying to change the other's opinion. (Accommodation)
   D. Olivia is afraid of water and hates to go fishing. Nevertheless, she goes along with her husband's vacation plans every summer, hating the days spent in a smelly fishing camp. (Martyrdom)
   E. Joseph and Shalonda are of different faiths. They decide the best way to solve their problem is to give up both religions and seek an entirely new faith together. (Compromise)
8. **RF** Show how all five types of adjustments can be used to deal with one marital problem. Divide students into five groups. Ask each group to use a different type of adjustment to deal with the same problem and report to the class. Judge which solution would work best. (Sample problem: Dan and Cornelia have two weeks of summer vacation. Dan wants to camp in Colorado. Cornelia wants to visit relatives in New York.)
9. **EX** Divide the class into five groups. Assign one method of adjustment to each group. Ask each group to role-play a solution to the same marital problem. Evaluate the solutions to see which ones work best. (Sample problem: Troy and Mandy have received their income tax refund check of $500. Mandy wants to buy a

new kitchen table and chairs. Troy wants to save the money and use it later on to buy a new car.)

10. **EX**   Instruct students to role-play the following conflict situations using any of the five forms of adjustment. Divide the class into groups of two or three students each. Ask each group to select a number between 1 and 6. This will determine the scene they will play. Allow 10 minutes for the groups to set up the role-play. Each group will select an adjustment form to portray. The class will try to identify the adjustment form being used in each scene.
    (1) One spouse leaves clothes all over the house.
    (2) Both spouses work and a school-age child becomes sick.
    (3) Both spouses work and the car breaks down and needs to be repaired.
    (4) One spouse talks on the phone every evening for hours.
    (5) The party behavior of one spouse disturbs the other.
    (6) One spouse watches too much television.

11. **RF**   *Making Marital Adjustments*, Activity A, SAG. Instruct students to identify the adjustment form used to resolve typical disagreements in marriage.

12. **RF**   Discuss postponing the resolution of marital problems. Compare this with handling problems as soon as possible. Accept or reject the adage "Never let the sun go down on your wrath."

Functions of Conflict

13. **RF**   *Conflict in Marriage*, Activity B, SAG. Students are to indicate whether they agree or disagree with statements concerning conflict in marriage.

14. **RF**   *Handling Marital Disagreements*, reproducible master, 14-1. Have students complete the sentences and answer the questions on how they would handle marital disagreements. Share responses and discuss.

15. **RF**   *Who Will Lead?* Activity C, SAG. Instruct students to write their reactions to situations concerning who will lead in marriage.

16. **EX**   Review the characteristics of productive and destructive quarreling described in the text. Ask students to role-play the conflicts in Strategy 10, first in a destructive manner and then in a productive manner. Compare situations.

17. **RF**   *Marriage Matchup*, reproducible master, 14-2. Students should use this activity to review chapter concepts and terms.

Marriage Counseling

18. **RF**   *Questions in Marriage Counseling*, transparency master, 14-3. Refer to this transparency as you discuss with students questions that people may commonly ask marriage counselors.

19. **ER**   Instruct students to research sources for marriage counseling in your area. Determine costs, services available, and specializations.

20. **ER**   Students should research counseling methods marriage counselors may use, such as pet peeve lists, role reversal, etc. They then should judge which methods best suit certain types of problems.

21. **ER**   Invite married couples to serve on a panel to discuss how they resolve marital problems. Students should prepare beforehand and pose problems to the couples, then ask how they would solve them. Ask the panel to discuss the pros and cons of dealing with problems as early as possible in a marriage.

22. **ER**   Invite a qualified, highly regarded marriage counselor to speak to the class about the role of the counselor in handling problem areas in marriages. Ask the speaker to include background information on the education and training of licensed marriage counselors as well as on counseling techniques.

23. **EX**   *Could I Be a Marriage Counselor?* transparency master, 14-4. Refer to this list of attributes as you introduce this career field to students. How are these attributes similar to those needed for jobs in social work or psychiatry?

Answer Key for Chapter 14

Text
To Review, page 347.

   1. C
   2. C
   3. false
   4. A. accommodation. B. martyrdom. C. ongoing hostility. D. accommodation. E. concession. F. martyrdom.

5. (Student response. See pages 341-342.)
6. (Name two of each type.) Good sources: Ministers, educators, psychologists, psychiatrists, social workers, physicians, counselors provided by employers, counselors recommended by professional organizations. Questionable sources: Friends, relatives, incompetent and unqualified counselors.
7. (Student response. Describe two methods.)

Student Activity Guide
Activity A, *Making Marital Adjustments.*

1. A. M. B. OH. C. AC. D. CP. E. CC.
2. A. CP. B. CP. C. CC. D. M. E. OH.
3. A. CP. B. OH. C. M. D. CC. E. AC.
4. A. CP. B. CC. C. AC. D. M. E. OH.
5. A. OH. B. CP. C. CC. D. AC. E. M.

Teacher's Resource Guide
Marriage Matchup, reproducible master, 14-2.

1. C	7. J
2. I	8. B
3. E	9. F
4. L	10. A
5. G	11. H
6. K	12. D

Chapter 14 Test

1. D	11. T	21. D
2. H	12. F	22. B
3. B	13. F	23. C
4. I	14. T	24. B
5. G	15. F	25. A
6. J	16. T	26. C
7. F	17. F	27. B
8. E	18. F	28. D
9. C	19. T	29. A
10. A	20. F	30. D

31. Spouses who have high self-esteem do not need to seek constant attention and approval from their mates. They are able to focus on the "we" feeling rather than the "I" feeling. Also, if two people feel secure, they can better withstand each other's anger and deal with it effectively.
32. (Student response.)
33. (Describe two of the following:) Lists of each other's faults and good points; checklists of personality traits; checklists of wants and needs; open-ended questions; techniques for role-plays.

Handling Marital Disagreements

Name_______________________________ **Date** _____________ **Period**____________

How would you handle marital disagreements? Complete the following sentences and answer the questions below. (There are no right or wrong answers.)

During an argument:

1. If my mate started to cry, I would ____

____

2. If my mate started yelling at me, I would____________________________________

____

3. If my mate stormed out of the room, I would _________________________________

____

4. If my mate suddenly stopped talking to me, I would ____________________________

____

5. If my mate was always set on having his or her own way, I would___________________

____

6. If one mate is better informed on the issue being debated, the other mate should ___________

____

Answer the following questions.

7. If your mate always felt he or she was correct, what would your reaction be? ___________

____

____

8. Would you have trouble accepting your mate's point of view if you strongly believed in an opposite
   view? ____

____

9. If you believed in something that was really important to you, would you stand fast no matter how
   hard your mate tried to change your mind? ___________________________________

____

____

10. Explain the adage "Live and let live." How does it apply to marriage? ________________

____

____

____

Marriage Matchup

Name _______________________________________ **Date** _______________ **Period**_______________

Match the following terms and identifying phrases.

_______ 1. Love can fade and then reappear. This is called the _______ of love.

_______ 2. Type of adjustment in which both partners give in and find a solution that is satisfactory for both.

_______ 3. Type of adjustment in which one partner avoids trouble at all costs by always giving in.

_______ 4. Type of quarreling that is limited to the issue in question, clarifies issues, and can strengthen a marriage.

_______ 5. Type of adjustment in which one partner wins all in a disagreement and the other loses all.

_______ 6. Two kinds of humor that should be avoided in marriage are sarcasm and _______.

_______ 7. Type of adjustment in which partners agree to disagree.

_______ 8. The shattering of unrealistic ideas.

_______ 9. A feeling of liking yourself, also known as _______, is needed for a successful marriage.

_______ 10. Type of quarreling in which partners attack each other's self-esteem.

_______ 11. The type of adjustment in which quarreling and bickering are constant is called *ongoing* _______.

_______ 12. When you have _______, you can understand how your partner feels without sharing those same feelings at the same time.

A. destructive

B. disillusionment

C. intermittency

D. empathy

E. martyrdom

F. self-esteem

G. concession

H. hostility

I. compromise

J. accommodation

K. ridicule

L. productive

Questions in Marriage Counseling

- **How can I communicate better?**

- **Are my expectations reasonable?**

- **How can I stop my problematic behavior?**

- **How can I deal with my feelings?**

- **How can I handle problems?**

- **Am I doing the right thing?**

Could I Be a Marriage Counselor?

Am I

- sensitive?
- insightful?
- empathetic?
- a good listener?
- people oriented?
- a good communicator?
- willing to receive education and training?
- able to set aside my problems and help others with theirs?

Building a Marriage

Name ____

Date ______________________________________ **Period** _____________ **Score** _______________

Chapter 14 Test

Matching: Match the following terms and identifying phrases.

_____ 1. Form of adjustment in which the spouses "agree to disagree."

_____ 2. Form of adjustment in which the winner is happy and the loser can look forward to winning at another time.

_____ 3. Form of adjustment in which neither partner has to make a great sacrifice to give in to the other.

_____ 4. Form of adjustment in which quarreling and bickering are continuous.

_____ 5. Form of adjustment in which one person gives in constantly so the other always wins.

_____ 6. Leads to a secure foundation in a relationship that contains no anxiety or apprehension.

_____ 7. Conferring with one another to arrive at a settlement of a matter.

_____ 8. The shattering of unrealistic ideas.

_____ 9. The ebb and flow of feelings of love.

_____ 10. Involves honest expressions of feelings and careful listening on both sides resulting in the clarifying of issues.

A. productive quarreling

B. compromise

C. intermittency

D. accommodation

E. disillusionment

F. negotiation

G. martyrdom

H. concession

I. ongoing hostility

J. trust

True/False: Circle *T* if the statement is true or *F* if the statement is false.

T F 11. High self-esteem is different from selfishness.

T F 12. If you are in a bad mood, it is best if you try to hide this fact from your spouse rather than communicating it.

T F 13. Accommodation as a form of adjustment means refusing to talk to a spouse for prolonged periods of time.

T F 14. Taking turns and flipping a coin are two methods of settling conflict by concession.

T F 15. Conflict does not occur in a good marriage.

T F 16. If one spouse in a troubled marriage refuses to see a marriage counselor, the other spouse often can still benefit from individual sessions with a qualified professional.

T F 17. In the martyrdom form of adjustment, spouses take turns giving in to one another.

T F 18. In destructive quarreling, the quarrel focuses on the issue rather than being allowed to wander off into other topics.

T F 19. Empathy allows you to understand how your partner feels without necessarily sharing those feelings at the same moment.

T F 20. Productive quarreling attacks the self-esteem of the persons involved.

(Continued)

Name ____

Multiple Choice: Select the best response. Write it in the space provided.

_______ 21. Which of the following statements is true?
   A.   Even in a successful marriage spouses should not expect to be happy all of the time.
   B.   When you enter marriage, you have three different personalities–what you are, what you think you are, and what your mate thinks you are.
   C.   If you have self-esteem, you have confidence in yourself.
   D.   All of the above.

_______ 22. The primary emotion couples hope to feel and display in marriage is _______.
   A.   hostility
   B.   affection
   C.   adventure
   D.   power

_______ 23. Conflict can help _______.
   A.   solve problems
   B.   release tensions
   C.   Both of the above.
   D.   None of the above.

_______ 24. Which of the following statements about conflict is true?
   A.   Once a couple face conflict, their marriage will never be as happy as it was before the conflict arose.
   B.   If a marriage has no conflict at all, the relationship may exist only on the surface, without real feelings of involvement between the spouses.
   C.   A great deal of conflict will have a positive effect on the relationship.
   D.   The best solution to conflict is having one spouse take over the complete responsibility for making decisions.

_______ 25. Which of the following statements applies to accommodation as an adjustment form?
   A.   Differences continue to exist but they do not hinder the relationship.
   B.   Tension and antagonism occur frequently and are expressed destructively.
   C.   Both partners must be willing to gamble on a win or lose outcome.
   D.   The final adjustment contains some elements of both spouses' wishes.

_______ 26. If spouses are quarreling about how they are going to use a $100 tax refund check and the wife says, "You decide this year and I'll decide next year," which adjustment form are they using?
   A.   Accommodation.
   B.   Ongoing hostility.
   C.   Concession.
   D.   Martyrdom.

_______ 27. In destructive quarreling, _______.
   A.   the couple remains focused on the problem issue
   B.   spouses may verbally attack relatives, cherished values, or prized possessions
   C.   all available information is used to find a solution
   D.   both spouses experience increased feelings of love, trust, and self-esteem

_______ 28. In productive quarreling, _______.
   A.   the quarrel often extends beyond the original issue
   B.   the self-esteem of the personalities involved is attacked
   C.   the marriage relationship is damaged by the effects of the quarrel
   D.   a solution can be reached without hurting either spouse's feelings

(Continued)

                                    Contemporary Living Teacher's Resources

_______ 29. Which of the following statements is true?
   A.   Most marriage counselors try to help people establish good patterns of communication.
   B.   Most qualified marriage counselors make no attempt to help people develop healthy ways of finding their own solutions to problems.
   C.   All states have strict licensing requirements to ensure that marriage counselors are comprehensively trained and carefully screened for character flaws.
   D.   A qualified marriage counselor will ignore unhealthy behaviors that add to the couple's problems.

_______ 30. Marriage counseling is more likely to succeed if both spouses are _______.
   A.   committed to the relationship
   B.   willing to make changes within themselves for the sake of the marriage
   C.   honest and open-minded enough to reveal their true emotions
   D.   All of the above.

Essay Questions: Provide complete responses to the following questions or statements.

31.   Why is a marriage stronger if both spouses have high self-esteem?

32.   Explain the importance of a sense of humor and appreciation in marriage.

33.   Describe two techniques marriage counselors use to reopen communication lines between marriage partners.

Part 5
Dimensions of Families

Chapter 15 ■ ■ ■ ■ ■ ■ ■ ■ ■ ■ ■ ■ ■ ■
Family Life Today

Objectives

After studying this chapter, students will be able to

- analyze the factors contributing to the changing family.
- identify the three functions of the family.
- explain the relationship between family roles and responsibilities.
- list characteristics of strong families.
- identify six common family structures.
- describe the five stages of the family life cycle.

Bulletin Boards

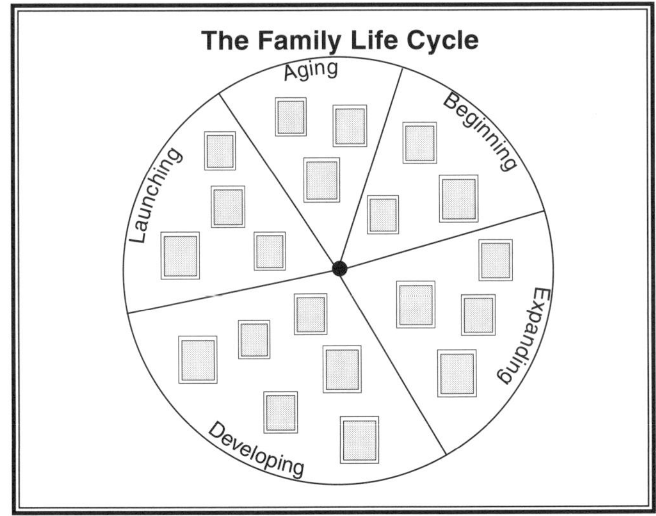

I. Title: "Family Life Cycle"

Mount a large circle on the bulletin board. Label sections of the circle as each stage of the family life cycle as shown. Then ask students to bring in family photos or photos clipped from magazines illustrating each stage of the family life cycle.

II. Title: "Functions of the Family"

Cut out forms of a family standing by a house. Next to them, list the following phrases: *To provide for the physical needs of the family*, *To provide for the socialization of the children*, and *To provide for the psychological well-being of all family members*.

Teaching Materials

Text, pages 352-373

Terms to Know, To Review, To Do and *To Think About*

Student Activity Guide

A. *Family Roles and Responsibilities*
B. *Identifying Family Structures*
C. *Understanding Family Structures*
D. *The Family Life Cycle*

Teacher's Resource Guide/Binder

What Makes a Family Strong? reproducible master, 15-1

Family Structures Are Unique, transparency master, 15-2

Understanding the Family Life Cycle, reproducible master, 15-3

The Beginning Stage, reproducible master, 15-4

Chapter 15 Test

Teacher's Resource Binder

The Family Life Cycle, color transparency, CT-15

Software for Contemporary Living

Chapter Review Game

Introductory Activities

1. Distribute index cards and ask students to write what they think makes a family strong. Ask them to give an illustration or example. Do not have them sign the cards. Have students pass them to the front of the room. Then read the cards and discuss.
2. Ask students to relate one favorite story about their family that has been passed down from their grandparents. Ask them to discuss if this could be a strength that could be passed on to their future family. Discuss.

Strategies to Reteach, Reinforce, Enrich, and Extend Text Concepts

What Is a Family?

3. **RT**   Ask students to respond to the question, "What is a family?"
4. **ER**   Ask a family therapist to discuss with students the concept of "family."
5. **RT**   Ask students to list as many different types of families as they can.

The Changing Family

6. **RT**   Ask students to discuss how families have changed. Discuss how technology has provided some reasons for the changes. Ask students to discuss other factors contributing to changes in the family and how families are developing strengths to meet these changes.
7. **ER**   Ask students from various ethnic backgrounds to discuss how the American family may differ from the family that represents their own ethnic backgrounds.

Functions of the Family

8. **EX**   Ask students to cite activities and organizations within their community that provide assistance to families by fulfilling family functions, such as a school breakfast program, community organizations, church groups, etc.
9. **ER**   Ask students to compare the functions of the family today with those of families 50 years ago. (They may want to talk with older people to gain information.) Are the functions still the same or have they been modified? What were the problems of the families then as compared to the problems of families today?

Roles and Responsibilities of Family Members

10. **RT**   Ask students to discuss the responsibilities of families to provide for the physical needs of their children in reference to the vast increase of social programs which, in essence, take over responsibilities of parents in providing for their children.
11. **RT**   Ask students to respond to the statement, "Roles are defined by responsibilities." In news stories, we hear of many parents who are not fulfilling basic responsibilities of providing for their families. Ask students to react by discussing what should be done to instill accountability in our society for fulfilling responsibilities.
12. **RF**   Ask students to define a "dysfunctional family." Discuss what happens when a family member does not fulfill his or her responsibilities. What happens when a teen rebels? How can this create problems for the entire family?
13. **RF**   *Family Roles and Responsibilities*, Activity A, SAG. Many responsibilities must be carried out by various family members in performing the basic functions of a family. These responsibilities are often defined by a person's role in the family. Students are asked to list the various responsibilities that are performed in their families. They are then asked to indicate whose role it is to fulfill each responsibility.

Characteristics of Strong Families

14. **RT**   *What Makes a Family Strong?* reproducible master, 15-1. Ask students to review the characteristics that make a family strong. Ask them to add other characteristics they think should be included.

Family Structures

15. **RF**   *Identifying Family Structures*, Activity B, SAG. Have students identify family structures and record characteristics of each. Cite examples of family structures from TV shows, movies, literature, or history. Discuss, noting the positive and negative characteristics of each.

16. *Understanding Family Structures*, Activity C, SAG. Have students describe each family structure. Then, in small groups, have them discuss some of the problems found in each structure, as well as the strengths of each.

17. **RT**   Divide the class into small groups and ask them to discuss this statement: "The word for families today is options." What do they feel this statement means? Do they agree with this statement? Do they see this as a help or a hindrance in strengthening families in our society?

18. **ER**   Special project. Ask each student to select a family structure to research. Ask them to find out if this structure is becoming more or less common and why, the advantages and disadvantages of this structure, and the effects of the structure on the children. Report back to class and discuss.

19. **RT**   *Family Structures Are Unique*, transparency master, 15-2. Use the transparency to review the characteristics of each family structure. Note the main interests, goals, primary needs, and possible stresses faced by members of each structure.

20. **RF**   Divorce and separation account for an increasing number of single-parent families. Why does this pose a double emotional burden (loss of a mate at the same time the responsibilities of being a single parent increase)? What types of support are available for these families?

21. **RT**   Ask students to discuss the emergence of an increasing number of family structures headed by an unwed parent. Ask students to cite the reasons for this increase.

22. **RT**   Ask students to respond to this statement: "The blended family can be described in one word—complicated." Discuss the factors that support this statement. Are these factors always negative? Positive? A combination of the two?

23. **ER**   Ask a family counselor to speak to the class concerning problems and strengths of blended families. Ask questions regarding jealousy, sibling acceptance, uniform discipline, pressures of finances, time, energy, and acceptance.

24. **RF**   Ask students to interview blended families and cite the special challenges and joys they have experienced. Report back to class and discuss.

25. **ER**   Ask students to interview members of an extended family. Have them discuss the reasons several generations live together, and the problems as well as the strengths extended families encounter.

26. **ER**   Ask a speaker from a foster family program to speak to the class regarding foster families. Have students prepare a list of questions in advance.

27. **ER**   Ask a speaker from an adoption agency to speak to the class concerning adoptions.

The Family Life Cycle

28. **RF**   *The Family Life Cycle*, Activity D, SAG. Ask students to use this activity to project their own anticipated family life cycle. They will shade in the squares on the chart indicating the years they will spend in each stage. They will then answer questions concerning their family life cycle plans. Ask each student to comment on the projected plan.

29. **RT**   *Understanding the Family Life Cycle*, reproducible master, 15-3. Students are asked to plot the stages of the family life cycle on a circle and answer questions related to the stages of the family life cycle.

30. **RF**   *The Beginning Stage*, reproducible master, 15-4. Divide the class into small groups to discuss the situations given on the master or have the class, as a whole, discuss each case. Have students answer the questions.

31. **EX**   Ask class members to project ahead and discuss what they hope they will be doing 50 years from now, including work or retirement, relationships, financial position, travel, charity work, etc. Ask them to discuss how their present life may impact on their aging years.

32. **RT**   *The Family Life Cycle*, color transparency, CT-15. Use this transparency to illustrate the family life cycle. Ask students to give examples of events that often occur during each stage of the life cycle.

Answer Key for Chapter 15

Text
To Review, page 372.

1. A group of two or more persons, related by blood, marriage, or adoption, who reside together in a household. (Student response for student's own definition of family.)

2. (Name four. Student response.)

3. The family provides the environment for nurturing the social skills of children. This equips them to move out into the world. The family guides children as they learn right from wrong. Children learn about the culture of the society in which they live. Families teach by example what is acceptable and what is not acceptable so that children can take their place as productive members of society.

4. The role of a son or daughter is a given role that you acquire when you are born into a family. You may also have the given roles of brother or sister. When you marry, you will assume a chosen role as husband or wife. You may also choose to assume another chosen role—that of father or mother.

5. In a functional family, all family members fulfill their roles and responsibilities. If one family member does not fulfill his or her responsibility, the structure is out of balance, or may become dysfunctional.

6. (List four. Student response.)

7. A. two-parent family. B. adoptive family. C. foster family. D. blended family. E. single-parent family. F. extended kinship family.

8. School-age children.

9. (Name three. Student response.)

Teacher's Resource Guide
Chapter 15 Test

1. I	11. T	21. D
2. F	12. T	22. D
3. A	13. F	23. D
4. H	14. T	24. B
5. J	15. T	25. C
6. C	16. T	26. A
7. B	17. T	27. A
8. D	18. F	28. C
9. G	19. T	29. D
10. E	20. F	30. B

31. (Student response.)
32. (Student response.)
33. (Student response.)

What Makes a Family Strong?

Name _______________________________ **Date** _____________ **Period** ___________

1. Briefly describe the characteristics that you think make a family strong.

   ____

   ____

   ____

2. Does communication help strengthen a family or hinder family growth? Give three examples of
   how good communication can strengthen a family.

   ____

   ____

   ____

3. How can family members support each other?

   ____

   ____

   ____

4. How can parents instill a sense of right and wrong in their children?

   ____

   ____

   ____

5. How does sharing humor help to strengthen families?

   ____

   ____

   ____

6. How can families make a contribution to their communities?

   ____

   ____

   ____

7. Write a paragraph describing a family that you feel is strong or write a paragraph describing a future
   family you might have that would exhibit the strengths that you consider to be important.

   ____

   ____

   ____

   ____

   ____

Family Structures Are Unique

Two-Parent
Family

Single-Parent
Family

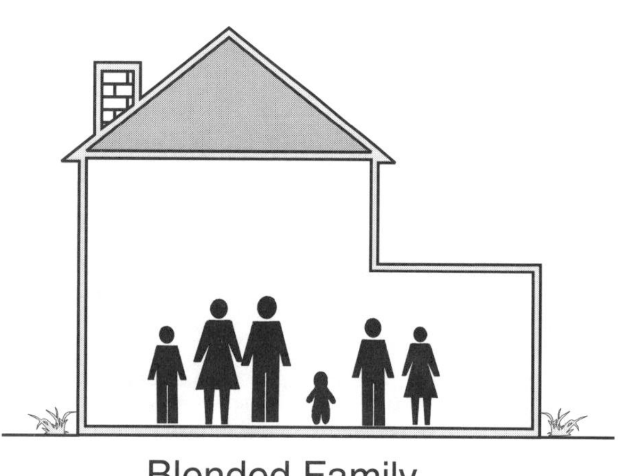

Blended Family

Extended Kinship
Family

Understanding the Family Life Cycle

Name_________________________________ **Date** ____________ **Period**____________

Divide this circle into the five stages of the family life cycle. Label each stage. Then answer the questions on the following page.

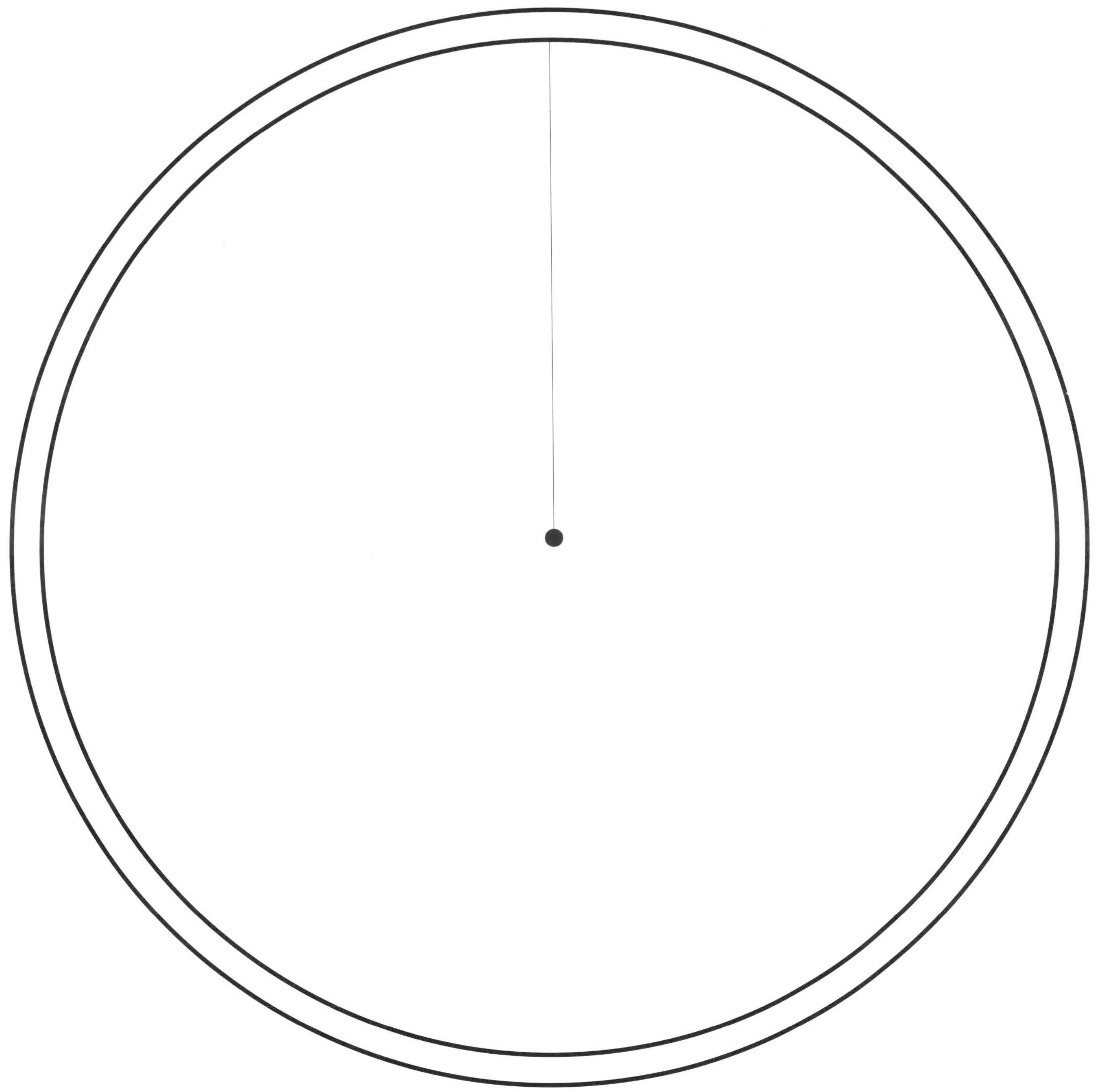

(Continued)

Name _______________________________________

1. How does the family change in size through the stages? _______________

   ____

   ____

   ____

   ____

2. About how many years would a typical family be in each stage? _______________

   ____

   ____

   ____

3. How do the roles of various family members change as they proceed through the life cycle?

   ____

   ____

   ____

   ____

   ____

4. Describe the major goals of each stage in the life cycle. _______________

   ____

   ____

   ____

   ____

   ____

   ____

5. What major adjustments must be made within each stage? _______________

   ____

   ____

   ____

   ____

   ____

   ____

   ____

The Beginning Stage

The following couples are in the beginning stage of the family life cycle. Read each case situation below and then discuss the following questions:

   a.   Has this couple established a secure first stage in their marriage?

   b.   What are the strengths of this marriage?

   c.   What might be some problem areas in this marriage?

   d.   Is this couple ready to enter the next stage of the family life cycle?

   e.   What problems should be resolved before they have children?

Case Situations

1. Molly and Anton dated all during college and were married the summer after they both graduated. Molly doesn't know if she wants to work or start a family. Anton wants a family, but knows they are not yet financially able to do so. Anton works long hours, and Molly gets upset that he is never home.

2. Shelley and Keith married when Keith was 30 and Shelley was 28. They both have excellent jobs. They enjoy their evenings and weekends together when they can travel and be with friends. Shelley is advancing in her career and is very involved with her work. Keith is very secure in his career and would like to think about starting a family. Shelley always puts off talking about children.

3. Estelle and Vincent married right out of high school. Vincent works in the produce department of a supermarket. He has moved up to assistant manager, and feels he can advance even further in the store. Estelle is working as a beautician and would like to have her own shop someday. They work hard, are saving to buy a home, and look forward to starting a family as soon as they can.

4. Cheryl and Noah married after a whirlwind courtship. Cheryl was divorced, and Noah had been engaged to a girl from home. They met, married, and are still learning about each other. Cheryl makes good money as a model and travels on assignments. Noah is a junior law partner and has to put in long hours. They have not yet talked about having children.

Family Life Today

Name ____

Date _________________________________ **Period** _____________ **Score** ______________

Chapter 15 Test

Matching: Match the following terms and identifying phrases.

_______ 1. When the family system does not fulfill its responsibilities and it becomes out of balance.

_______ 2. Stages the typical family goes through beginning with marriage.

_______ 3. Family structure in which several generations of a family live together.

_______ 4. Stage where the husband and wife refocus on their relationship.

_______ 5. Family structure in which either or both spouses may have been married before and have one or more children from the previous marriage.

_______ 6. This family structure is sometimes called the two-parent structure.

_______ 7. Role you acquire when born into a family.

_______ 8. When you make a choice and acquire another role.

_______ 9. When all members in the family fulfill their roles and responsibilities.

_______ 10. Your roles are defined by this.

A. extended kinship
B. given role
C. nuclear
D. chosen role
E. responsibilities
F. family life cycle
G. functional
H. launching
I. dysfunctional
J. blended family
K. foster family

True/False: Circle *T* if the statement is true or *F* if the statement is false.

T F 11. The family is probably the most influential factor in shaping a person's personality.

T F 12. Throughout history, families have had to adapt to varying economic and social pressures.

T F 13. Dysfunctional families operate as a system or team.

T F 14. A little over one-third of American families consist of married couples with children.

T F 15. The single-parent family is growing faster than any other family form.

T F 16. Relationships in blended families may be complicated.

T F 17. Foster family homes are evaluated and licensed according to state requirements.

T F 18. During the expanding stage of the family life cycle, the major focus is adjustment to married life.

T F 19. Parents with young children often experience role conflicts.

T F 20. Parenthood during the adolescent years calls for increased control as children become more independent.

(Continued)

Contemporary Living Teacher's Resources

Multiple Choice: Select the best response. Write the letter in the space provided.

_____ 21. Which of the following is a basic function of families in our society?
  A. To provide physical care for children.
  B. To nurture personality growth of children.
  C. To meet emotional needs of all members.
  D. All of the above.

_____ 22. Families are changing in our society because _____.
  A. of an increasing number of divorces
  B. more women working outside the home
  C. couples are having fewer children
  D. All of the above.

_____ 23. Which of the following is a current trend?
  A. Marriage is based more on love and affection.
  B. Men and women share the wage earner role.
  C. Parents are beginning to value time as highly as money.
  D. All of the above.

_____ 24. The unwed parent and his or her child can have full and satisfying lives if the parent _____.
  A. wants to keep the baby just to have someone to love
  B. truly wants to raise his or her child and is willing to accept all the responsibilities
  C. wants to escape an unhappy home life
  D. All of the above.

_____ 25. When several generations of a family share a residence, the family structure is called _____.
  A. nuclear
  B. foster
  C. extended kinship
  D. blended

_____ 26. During the beginning stage of the family life cycle, _____.
  A. individuals must adjust to life with the other person while still maintaining his or her own individuality
  B. children leave the family home to pursue education and career goals
  C. the family is reorganized to fit the expanding world of school-age children
  D. Both A and C.

_____ 27. During the expanding stage, _____.
  A. the new roles of father and mother are added to the roles of husband and wife
  B. the primary focus remains the relationship of the couple
  C. parenthood is postponed
  D. interpersonal relationships decrease

_____ 28. During the developing stage, _____.
  A. the major goal is to tighten the control of the family
  B. parents need to give less freedom to the children
  C. the main goal is reorganization of the family to fit the expanding world of school-age children
  D. parents need to tighten family ties and give more discipline

(Continued)

_______ 29. During the launching stage, _______.
    A. the child leaves home—but may return
    B. husband and wife refocus on their relationship
    C. parents may face responsibilities for both parents and children
    D. All of the above.

_______ 30. During the aging stage, _______.
    A. all people retire from active work
    B. travel and friendships can add enjoyment
    C. people live a very limited life
    D. grandparenting roles are less meaningful

Essay Questions: Provide complete responses to the following questions or statements.

31. Families change as society changes. What trends do you see taking place today?

32. List five characteristics of a strong family and briefly discuss how this helps the family.

33. Choose one stage of the family life cycle. Describe the major focus of this stage and describe what usually occurs during this stage.

Chapter 16
The Parenting Decision

Objectives

After studying this chapter, students will be able to

- describe the role and responsibilities of parenthood.
- describe the sharing of parenting responsibilities in families today.
- identify several factors involved in the decision to become parents.
- explain the human reproductive process in females and males.
- describe methods of planning or preventing pregnancy.
- recognize alternatives available when a couple cannot achieve a pregnancy.
- assess the importance of genetic counseling and testing.

Bulletin Boards

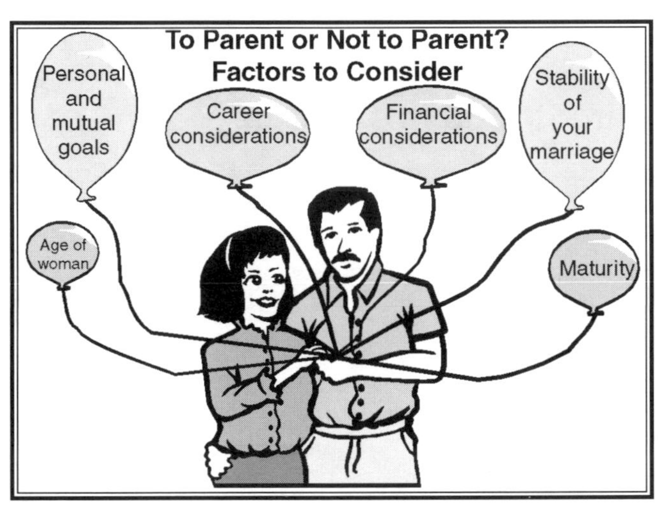

I. Title: "To Parent or Not to Parent? Factors to Consider"

Cut out pictures or silhouettes of a couple. Then cut out "balloons" with the various decision factors printed on them. Attach the balloons to yarn and to the couple's hands.

II. Title: "Parents Need a Sense of Humor"

Collect cartoons from magazines and newspapers that depict the many times a sense of humor is involved in the role of parenting. Cut frames for each cartoon out of construction paper. Vary the frames in size, shape, and color.

Teaching Materials

Text, pages 374-394

Terms to Know, To Review, To Do, and *To Think About*

Student Activity Guide

    A. *Views on Parenthood*
    B. *Deciding About Parenthood*
    C. *The Human Reproductive System*
    D. *Methods of Preventing Pregnancy*

Teacher's Resource Guide/Binder

Roles Expand Geometrically When You Become a Parent, reproducible master, 16-1

Parent Interview, reproducible master, 16-2

Reasons for Having Children vs. Reasons for Not Having Children, transparency master, 16-3

Costs of Having a Baby, reproducible master, 16-4

Chapter 16 Test

Teacher's Resource Binder

Parenthood Choice Sequences, color transparency, CT-16

Introductory Activities

1. Ask each student to write one sentence on an index card stating what he or she feels is the main responsibility of being a parent. Gather the cards and read them to the class. Check for duplicate responses and then have students rank them according to priority of importance.
2. Ask students to accept or reject the statement, "Young husbands and wives today have more responsibilities, more career opportunities, and more choices." Compare today's young couples with couples 50 years ago. Were their responsibilities the same or greater? In what area? How do career choices compare with today's young couples? If you believe young couples have more choices, does this enhance their lifestyle or create complications when they are considering a parenting choice?

Strategies to Reteach, Reinforce, Enrich, and Extend Text Concepts

Parental Roles and Responsibilities

3. **RT** When couples marry, they may have different goals. Some will have individual goals, intent on enhancing their individual careers. Some will be mate-oriented, intent on enhancing their marriage, while some will be parent-oriented, intent on enhancing their role as parents in a family. Compare the three.
4. **RF** *Views on Parenthood*, Activity A, SAG. Students are asked to complete a checklist of statements concerning parenthood. Tabulate the results and discuss.
5. **RT** Have students accept or reject the statement, "A couple should want to have a child and should view parenting as a positive expansion of their lives before starting a family."
6. **RT** What is meant by the statement, "The most important responsibility of parenting is the nurturing of the personality of each child." How can parents fulfill this basic responsibility?
7. **RT** How can parents instill the virtues of honesty, responsibility, trust, loyalty, courtesy, and mutual respect in their children? Can this best be taught by setting rules to follow, by examples of the parents, or by a combination of these?
8. **RF** One of the responsibilities of parents is to encourage independence in their children. Compare situations where parents are very protective and instances where parents allow their children opportunities to develop independence, while still guiding them. Which is the best approach?

Sharing Parenting Responsibilities

9. **RT** *Roles Expand Geometrically When You Become a Parent*, reproducible master, 16-1. Ask students to cite examples of how roles expand when people become parents.
10. **ER** *Parent Interview*, reproducible master, 16-2. Ask each student to interview a parent selected from the list on the master. One of each type of parent should be selected, but some types may be repeated. Have the parents answer the questions listed on the master. Report the results of the interviews. Note the similarities and differences in the responses received.
11. **ER** Some couples reverse the traditional parenting roles. In these cases, the father stays home and cares for the children and the mother works outside the home. Do you think this arrangement could work for you?
12. **RF** Ask students to list roles and responsibilities of parents they would consider in their future marriage and parenthood roles. Have students compare their responses.
13. **RF** Ask students to complete the following statement: "In today's families, the father's role has...." Compare responses.

Parenthood is a Choice

14. **RF** Ask students to complete one of the following sentences, "Someday, I want to be a parent because....", or, "I never want to be a parent because...." Compare responses.
15. **RF** Ask students if they think it is important for a couple to discuss their individual and mutual choices for parenthood before they marry. If one doesn't want children and the other spouse does, would this create a problem in marriage?

16. **RT** *Parenthood Choice Sequence,* color transparency, CT-16. Use this transparency as a basis of discussion about various alternatives couples have regarding their future goals. Ask students to consider their own life goals and describe which parenthood choice sequence would match their goals in life. Ask students to describe other sequences that are not illustrated on the transparency.

17. **RF** Compare attitudes toward parenting that might result if a couple "just happens" to have a baby or if a couple plans to have a baby. Discuss how attitudes in either case may influence their parenting role.

18. **RF** *Deciding About Parenthood,* Activity B, SAG. Ask students to complete the activity and discuss the different responses. Ask boys to read the girls' responses and girls to read the boys' responses. If they were to marry someone with these responses, would they find any problems or strengths?

19. **EX** *Reasons for Having Children vs. Reasons for Not Having Children,* transparency master, 16-3. Use this master to record students' views as they debate reasons for having children vs. reasons for not having children.

Other Factors to Consider in the Parenting Decision

20. **RT** Pregnancy during the teen years may pose health risks. Discuss what these risks may be and how the health of both mother and baby may be affected.

21. **RF** Today many couples are delaying starting their family, thus pushing back the "biological clock" of the woman. Discuss what this means and how this might create problems in their ability to become pregnant.

22. **RF** Discuss the interrelationship between home life and work life. How might parenting impact work? Have students list parenting situations that might come up that would impact a parent's job. Discuss how these situations could be resolved. Also discuss career demands that might impact parenting, and discuss how these might be resolved.

23. **ER** Ask students to research the basic costs of a layette and equipment when a baby is born. Prices may be found in advertisements or by going to businesses that sell baby clothes and equipment and resale shops that handle baby items.

24. **ER** *Costs of Having a Baby,* reproducible master, 16-4. Ask students to research the costs of having a baby. Stress to students that these costs are only the beginning in raising a child to adulthood.

25. **RF** Ask students to react to the following: "Your satisfaction as a marriage partner and parent will be influenced by the sense of accomplishment you feel in your career. Likewise, your career success will be greatly enhanced if you feel your marriage and parenting goals are also being achieved." Discuss the interdependency of these goals.

26. **ER** Research costs of child care in your area. How does this cost impact parents' financial situation if both continue working. If a previously employed parent chooses to stay home to care for their child, how does this impact on their financial situation?

27. **RT** Discuss how couples should determine the number and spacing of their children. Consider the mother's health, sibling relationships, and the financial aspects involved. Discuss the pros and cons of couples having just one child.

28. **RF** Spacing children three or four years apart is recommended if possible. List the reasons why authorities consider this the best spacing.

29. **EX** Couples who choose to have only one child are often criticized, and an only child is often described as spoiled and uncooperative. How has this view been challenged by psychologists and family-planning experts? What do they cite as positive factors of "onlies."

Planning a Pregnancy

30. **RF** *The Human Reproductive System,* Activity C, SAG. Use this activity to review the terms related to human reproduction.

31. **RF** *Methods of Preventing Pregnancy,* Activity D, SAG. Students are asked to fill in the crossword puzzle using terms related to birth control.

If a Couple Cannot Have Children

32. **ER** Have students research recent medical advances in solving infertility problems. Report on artificial insemination, in vitro fertilization, and other methods.

33. **ER** Ask a doctor to speak to the class about causes of infertility and possible treatments.
34. **RT** Discuss adoption as an option for couples who are unable to conceive.

Genetic Counseling

35. **RT** Define genetic counseling and discuss the benefits of it. When should a couple consult a genetic counselor?
36. **ER** Research amniocentesis and ultrasound examinations. Are there any dangers associated with these tests?

Answer Key for Chapter 16

Text
To Review, page 393.

1. (Describe three. Student response.)
2. Parents share more of the parenting responsibilities today than they did in the past due to the increased employment of women outside the home.
3. (Student response.)
4. (List three:) This amount of spacing allows parents to have greater interaction with each child. It helps the mother to maintain better health. It allows the financial impact of the children to be spread over a longer period of time. It lessens the chances of sibling rivalry due to competition.
5. A. ovaries. B. fallopian tubes. C. uterus. D. cervix. E. testes. F. semen. G. vas deferens. H. epididymis.
6. abstinence
7. The rhythm method is based on abstinence during the period of the female reproductive cycle when the egg is available for fertilization. The woman determines when she ovulates and has no sexual intercourse for a few days before and after this occurs.
8. Norplant
9. vasectomy
10. Tubal ligation.
11. Artificial insemination and in vitro fertilization.

12. The doctor studies the medical histories of both prospective parents' families. The doctor may also examine the prospective parents for possible disease conditions.

Student Activity Guide
Activity C, *The Human Reproductive System.*

Male:
1. E
2. F
3. A
4. D
5. B
6. G
7. C

Female:
8. A
9. C
10. D
11. B
12. E
13. F

Activity D, *Methods of Preventing Pregnancy.*

1	2	3	4	5	6	7	8	9	10	11	12	13	14	15	16	17	18	19	20	21	22	23
																		W[1]				
						C[2]						T[3]						I				
						O						U			R[4]	H	Y	T	H	M		
						N						B						H				
			D[5]			D[6]	I	A	P	H	R	A	G	M				D				
			E			O						L						R				
		S[7]	P	E	R	M	I	C	I[8]	D	A	L	V	A	G	I	N	A	L			
			O						U			I						W				
N[9]	O	R	P	L	A	N	T		D			G						A				
			R									A						L				
			O				V[10]	A	S	E	C	T	O	M	Y							
			V									I										
			E									O										
			R			O[11]	R	A	L	C	O	N	T	R	A	C	E	P	T	I	V	E
			A																			

Teacher's Resource Guide

Chapter 16 Test

#		#		#	
1.	E	10.	T	19.	B
2.	A	11.	T	20.	A
3.	D	12.	F	21.	C
4.	B	13.	T	22.	B
5.	F	14.	T	23.	A
6.	T	15.	T	24.	C
7.	F	16.	F	25.	B
8.	T	17.	T	26.	C
9.	F	18.	F	27.	B

28. (Student response. See pages 377-378.)
29. (See pages 378-384 of the text.)
30. (See pages 384-385 of the text.)

Roles Expand Geometrically When You Become a Parent

Parenthood is the beginning of a journey involving growing relationships, both within the immediate family and outside the family. Family size may vary, and the number of years in each stage of the family life cycle may vary. Review the chart below and note the following:

- How the roles may expand throughout each stage.
- How the family starts out with two people. Then, in the aging stage, it shrinks to two and then one.
- How the number of interpersonal relationships within the family expands as roles expand.

	Beginning Stage	Expanding Stage	Developing Stage	Launching Stage	Aging Stage
Possible Family Size	2	3-4	4-5+	5-2	2-1
Interpersonal Relationships within Family	1	3-8	8-14	14-1	1-0
Roles in the Family	husband wife	husband-father wife-mother son-brother daughter-sister	husband-father- grandfather wife-mother- grandmother son-brother- uncle daughter- sister-aunt	husband-father- grandfather wife-mother- grandmother son-brother- husband- father-uncle daughter- sister-wife- mother-aunt	husband-father- grandfather- wife-mother- grandmother son-brother- husband- father-uncle daughter- sister-wife- mother-aunt

Parent Interview

Name_______________________________________ **Date** _______________ **Period**_______________

Select one of the following parents to interview: a married parent, a single parent who has never been married, a divorced parent, a parent whose spouse has died, a stepparent, a foster parent, a parent of an adopted child, a parent with school-age children, a parent of teenagers, a parent whose children are on their own, or a grandparent. Ask the parent to respond to the following questions. Compare responses with those of your classmates.

Type of parent: _______________________________   Sex of parent: _______________________________

Approximate age of parent: _______________   Age(s) of child or children:_______________

1. What do you think is the most rewarding part of being a parent?_______________________________

____

____

____

2. What do you think is the most difficult part of being a parent? _______________________________

____

____

____

3. What do you believe are the primary responsibilities of parenthood? _______________________________

____

____

____

4. What do you think are the most important personality traits a parent should display? _______________

____

____

5. What are the most important qualities parents can help their children develop? _______________

____

____

____

6. What do you think is the most important thing parents should do in raising their children? _______

____

____

____

7. How do you think young people can prepare themselves to become good parents?_______________

____

____

Reasons for Not Having Children

VS

Reasons for Having Children

Costs of Having a Baby

Group members: _______________________________

____

____

_______________________________ **Date** ___________ **Period** ___________

Having a baby involves financial considerations. In small groups, research the cost of the following items in your area. (Note that these are merely the costs of having a baby. Raising a child to adulthood entails a far greater financial commitment for which parents should be prepared.)

Pregnancy

Maternity wardrobe (five outfits) _______________

Obstetrician's fee _______________________________

Additional costs for tests, etc. _______________

Delivery

Obstetrician fee for delivery _________________

Hospital costs for room and services __________

Nursery charges for baby ____________________

Doctor's fee for baby_______________________

Baby's Layette

Clothing(four nightgowns, four knit shirts, three sweaters, cap, four socks, bibs) _______________

Bedding (two sets of crib sheets, two blankets, bumper pad)_______________________________

Diapers (three dozen) _______________________

Baby Care Supplies __________________________

Nursery furniture (crib, dresser, changing table)

____

Feeding Costs

Nursing clothing items for mother ____________

Equipment for bottle-feeding ________________

Formula cost for one week____________________

Additional Items

Car seat ___________________________________

Stroller___________________________________

Other _____________________________________

TOTAL __________

The Parenting Decision

Date _______________________ Period ____________ Score ______________

Chapter 16 Test

Matching: Match the following terms and identifying phrases.

_______ 1. A process where a physician places sperm directly in the upper part of the woman's uterus or in the fallopian tubes.

_______ 2. Sound waves used to provide an outline or "picture" of the fetus inside the mother.

_______ 3. A process in which an egg is removed from a woman's ovary and fertilized in a glass dish.

_______ 4. A process in which a long, thin needle is inserted into the uterus and part of the fluid surrounding the fetus is drawn out and analyzed for abnormalities.

_______ 5. Advice given by a physician to prospective parents on matters of heredity.

A. ultrasound examination
B. amniocentesis
C. hereditary disease
D. in vitro fertilization
E. artificial insemination
F. genetic counseling

True/False: Circle *T* if the statement is true or *F* if the statement is false.

T F 6. The decision-making process regarding if and when to have children is often overlooked.

T F 7. The most important responsibility of parents is to give their children everything they want.

T F 8. Parents will have fulfilled their responsibilities when their children become self-sufficient adults who accept responsibility for their own decisions.

T F 9. Children benefit most when the mother assumes most of the family roles.

T F 10. The best time for a woman to have children is when she is in excellent physical health.

T F 11. Raising a child from birth to adulthood includes expenses that add up to many thousands of dollars.

T F 12. Only children are often spoiled, lonely, and uncooperative.

T F 13. Spacing children three or four years apart is recommended if possible.

T F 14. Couples who want to plan their families need to know the basics of human reproduction.

T F 15. The only sure way of preventing pregnancy is abstinence.

T F 16. Sterilization brings a temporary end to fertility.

T F 17. About 10 percent of all married couples are infertile.

T F 18. The best time to seek genetic counseling is after conception.

(Continued)

Multiple Choice: Select the best response. Write the letter in the space provided.

_____ 19. Which of the following store and mature eggs, and produce hormones?
A. Testes.
B. Ovaries.
C. Fallopian tubes.
D. Vas deferens.

_____ 20. The _____, the lining of the uterus, becomes thick and spongy and ready to accept a fertilized egg each month.
A. endometrium
B. semen
C. epididymis
D. scrotum

_____ 21. Which of the following is part of the female reproductive system?
A. Vas deferens.
B. Scrotum.
C. Cervix.
D. Ejaculatory ducts.

_____ 22. Which of the following is part of the male reproductive system?
A. Vagina.
B. Testes.
C. Fallopian tubes.
D. Uterus.

_____ 23. When the nucleus of the sperm joins the nucleus of the egg, _____ occurs.
A. conception or fertilization
B. ovulation
C. ejaculation
D. intercourse

_____ 24. One teaspoon of semen contains about _____ million sperm.
A. 3
B. 30
C. 300
D. None of the above.

_____ 25. Which of the following methods of birth control is based on abstinence during the period of the female reproductive cycle when the egg is available for fertilization?
A. Withdrawal.
B. Rhythm method.
C. Vasectomy.
D. Tubal ligation.

_____ 26. Which of the following is a male contraceptive that fits over the erect penis and traps semen so no sperm enter the vagina?
A. Cervical cap.
B. Diaphragm.
C. Condom.
D. Intrauterine device (IUD).

(Continued)

Contemporary Living Teacher's Resources

_______ 27. Which of the following is a contraceptive injection that prevents pregnancy for three months?
   A. Norplant.
   B. Depo-Provera.
   C. Tubal ligation.
   D. None of the above.

Essay Questions: Provide complete responses to the following questions or statements.

28. Describe the sharing of parenting responsibilities in families today in contrast with earlier times.

29. List six factors a couple should consider when deciding to become parents.

30. Explain how the number and spacing of children affect both the marriage and the entire family.

Chapter 17
A Baby Is Born

Objectives

After studying this chapter, students will be able to
- identify signs of pregnancy.
- describe the changes that occur during pregnancy.
- summarize important health practices for pregnant women.
- explain the process of childbirth.
- describe methods of childbirth.

Bulletin Boards

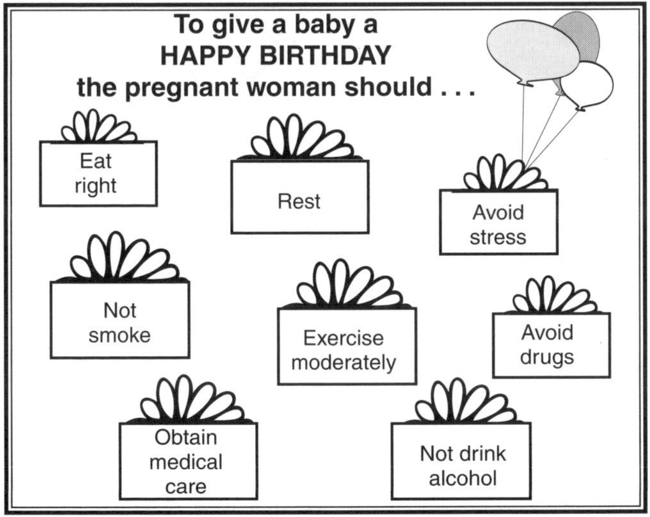

I. Title: "To give a baby a HAPPY BIRTHDAY the pregnant woman should..."

Decorate the bulletin board with birthday party-type decorations, such as balloons and crepe paper streamers. Then cut "presents" out of construction paper or gift wrap and add bows and the words shown above or other ways a woman can take care of herself to assure a healthy pregnancy.

II. Title: "Becoming a Family"

Mount pictures of a husband, wife, and baby showing different aspects of becoming a family. Try to find different types of pictures to depict both the joys and the challenges of becoming a family.

Teaching Materials

Text, pages 396-415

Terms to Know, To Review, To Do, and *To Think About*

Student Activity Guide
- A. *Diet During Pregnancy*
- B. *Health Practices of the Mother-to-Be*
- C. *Stages of Labor*
- D. *Methods of Childbirth*

Teacher's Resource Guide/Binder

Signs of Pregnancy, transparency master, 17-1
Pregnancy, transparency master, 17-2
Caring for Baby Before Birth, reproducible masters, 17-3A and 17-3B
Substances to Avoid During Pregnancy, transparency master, 17-4
Chapter 17 Test

Teacher's Resource Binder

Abdominal Changes During Pregnancy, color transparency, CT-17

Software for Contemporary Living

Chapter Review Game

Introductory Activities

1. Compare the following scenarios. How do the emotions compare? What are the negative aspects that Gresha and Brad have to look at? Compare a pregnancy that "just happens" to one that is planned.
   A. Gresha is a junior in high school, and she has been dating Brad, a senior, for over a year. At first they had made a vow not to become sexually active, but they broke this vow about two months ago. Her menstrual period is three weeks overdue and she feels nauseated. A home pregnancy test indicates she is pregnant. When she told Brad, he looked at her and said, "Oh, no! How did this happen? This is going to spoil all our plans."
   B. Allison and Frank, both 33, have successful careers, but they feel they want to start their family. They have been trying for a year, so when Allison felt she was pregnant and her doctor confirmed it, she was so excited. She told Frank, "We're pregnant! We're going to have a baby!" Frank picked her up and exclaimed, "A family! This is a dream come true!"

2. In the past, most of the information concerning pregnancy has focused on what a pregnant woman should do to assure that she will give birth to a healthy baby and that her health will be maintained. Today, health authorities are focusing on the importance of the health of the mother prior to pregnancy. By the time the woman determines she is pregnant, much of the development of the baby has occurred. During the first three months of pregnancy, all of the baby's organs are formed, and the health habits of the mother are extremely important. The March of Dimes is promoting a program called "Think Ahead," and the focus is on teens. Ask a March of Dimes speaker to come to class to speak on this subject, stressing the importance of a healthy lifestyle.

Strategies to Reteach, Reinforce, Enrich, and Extend Text Concepts

Evidence of Pregnancy

3. **RT** *Signs of Pregnancy*, transparency master, 17-1. Use this master as a basis of discussion as you describe the various signs of pregnancy.

4. **RT** For those who want to become pregnant, the symptoms of pregnancy may also be apparent, even though pregnancy has not occurred. Discuss reasons, other than pregnancy, that might cause a woman to miss a period.

5. **RT** What is "morning sickness?" Does it always occur in the morning? How long does it usually continue during pregnancy? How can a woman deal with it effectively?

6. **RT** *Abdominal Changes During Pregnancy*, color transparency, CT-17. Use this transparency to illustrate the changes a woman's body undergoes during pregnancy. Ask a physician or nurse to discuss other changes that occur during pregnancy.

7. **RT** When "quickening" occurs for the first time, a pregnant woman may not be aware of it. Briefly describe the feeling as given in the text. What causes this to occur?

8. **RT** Some women have scars or "stretch marks" on their abdomens after they give birth. What causes these, and what can a woman do to prevent these from appearing? Once they appear, will they go away?

9. **ER** Ask an obstetrician to come to class and set up a typical first-visit scenario. Outline what information the doctor will need and what questions the woman might want to ask.

10. **RT** What might be the effects of delaying medical attention during pregnancy? Cite the dangers to the mother and baby.

11. **ER** Research the various tests that might be done during pregnancy. What does ultrasound reveal and how is this done? (See Chapter 16.)

12. **EX** Suzanne tells her doctor that the first day of her last menstrual period was July 21. Using the formula for determining birth date, what will be the approximate due date for the baby? Give students other dates and allow them to figure the due dates.

The Developing Baby

13. **RF** Ask students to number from one to nine on a sheet of paper. Write down one or two developments in each of the nine months. Discuss how quickly the baby's organs develop.

14. **RF** Show a film on prenatal development.

15. **RT** *Pregnancy,* transparency master, 17-2. Use this master to illustrate and identify various terms associated with pregnancy.
16. **RT** *Caring for Baby Before Birth,* reproducible masters, 17-3A and 17-3B. Use these masters to allow students to test themselves on their knowledge of caring for a baby before birth. They can check the accuracy of their responses by using the answer sheet (17-3B).

Care of the Mother

17. **ER** Ask a community health nurse to speak to the class about health care available to pregnant women in your area. Ask class members to prepare a list of questions before the speaker comes. Record the responses.
18. **RF** *Diet During Pregnancy,* Activity A, SAG. Ask students to plan a diet for a pregnant woman for a week using the suggestions for foods in the different food groups.
19. **RF** *Health Practices of the Mother-to-Be,* Activity B, SAG. Ask students to work in small groups to research a list of topics related to health practices of the mother-to-be and her baby. Students are asked to prepare a report to share with the class.
20. **RF** Weight control is very important during pregnancy. Discuss the problem of gaining too much weight, why this might happen, and what can be done to control this. Discuss also the concern of gaining too little weight.
21. **RT** Should a pregnant woman have her teeth examined during pregnancy, and should any major work be done at that time? What precautions need to be taken?
22. **ER** Exercise during pregnancy is beneficial, but what precautions should be followed? Ask a doctor to describe exercises that a pregnant woman can do and those that should be avoided.
23. **ER** Research several large businesses, a school district personnel office, and an airline to discover regulations and conditions for employment for a woman who is pregnant. Do you think women should be allowed to work in any type of job? What precautions should be followed? What liability would be involved if a pregnant woman was injured while working?
24. **RT** Discuss the impact of smoking and drinking during pregnancy on the health of the mother and the baby. How does smoking affect the weight of the baby? Are there other problems that might result when a pregnant woman smokes? What are the doctor's reasons for advising a pregnant woman not to drink during pregnancy? What may result if an alcoholic woman gives birth?
25. **EX** Ask students to obtain current articles describing the effects of using illegal drugs during pregnancy. What dangers exist for the child and how does society bear the burden for the care of these children?
26. **RT** Discuss the dangers of using prescription drugs or over-the-counter drugs during pregnancy. What should a pregnant woman do before she uses these drugs?
27. **RT** *Substances to Avoid During Pregnancy,* transparency master, 17-4. Use this master as you discuss the various substances to avoid during pregnancy. Ask students to describe the harmful effects of each of the substances discussed and write their responses on the transparency.
28. **RT** What does the term "miscarriage" mean? Why do miscarriages occur?

Time for Delivery

29. **ER** Ask students to talk to young parents, and have them tell how they knew it was time to go to the hospital for the birth.
30. **RT** Define lightening. Describe what happens and why it is called this. When is lightening most likely to occur with the first delivery and with subsequent deliveries?
31. **RF** *Stages of Labor,* Activity C, SAG. Ask students to complete the activity and discuss what happens during labor and delivery.
32. **RF** *Methods of Childbirth,* Activity D, SAG. Ask students to complete the descriptions of different methods of childbirth, listing what they believe to be the pros and cons of each method.
33. **ER** Ask a nurse to speak to the class about the different methods of childbirth, the advantages and disadvantages of each, the number of days the mother spends in the hospital with each, and what the parents-to-be need to do concerning preparation for childbirth.
34. **ER** Ask a Lamaze instructor to come to class to describe the Lamaze method of childbirth.
35. **ER** Ask students to research the positive aspects of using family-centered childbirth and discuss.
36. **RF** Cesarean sections are used when a surgical birth is needed. How does a cesarean section compare to a normal delivery? Why is

it sometimes needed?

37. **ER**   Ask students to read articles pertaining to bonding. Why do medical authorities feel it is important for this to occur between baby and mother and father?

38. **RT**   Define lactation, and briefly describe how the mother's body prepares to nurse the baby. Define colostrum, and discuss how this forerunner of milk assists in providing for the baby during the hours just after birth.

39. **RF**   Ask students to draw a line through the center of a page. Label one column "Breast-Feeding" and the other column "Bottle-Feeding." Under each heading, ask students to list advantages and disadvantages.

Answer Key for Chapter 17

Text
To Review, page 414.

1. (List three:) Cessation of menstruation; breast changes; frequent urination; nausea; quickening; abdominal changes.
2. Quickening
3. Keeps the fetus at an even temperature; cushions the fetus against possible injury; provides a medium in which the fetus can move around easily; assists in the birth of the baby.
4. ninth
5. Between 25 and 35 pounds.
6. Children of alcoholic mothers are sometimes born with a pattern of defects known as fetal alcohol syndrome. Common defects are growth deficiencies and limited mental capacities. The children usually have narrow eyes, low nasal bridges, and short upturned noses. Many are jittery and poorly coordinated with short attention spans and behavioral problems.
7. True labor pains vary in intensity, are spaced evenly apart, and return in a rhythmical pattern. False labor pains remain equal in intensity, are spaced irregularly, and are not rhythmical in pattern.
8. Lamaze method.
9. bonding
10. (Name two advantages of each.) Breast-feeding: More economical than bottle-feeding. For some it is more convenient. It supplies human milk which is the ideal food for newborns. It is sweeter than cows' milk. It is easier to digest. Bottle-feeding: Husband and

wife can share experience of feeding the child. Formula is always consistent in composition. There is always enough to satisfy the baby's needs. It is less tiring to the mother. The mother may have an easier time controlling her recovery. It allows the mother to return to work shortly after delivery.

Student Activity Guide
Activity C, *Stages of Labor.*

1. dilation
2. It begins with the first uterine contraction.
3. It ends when the baby's head is in the birth canal.
4. about nine hours
5. A, C, E, G
6. expulsion
7. It begins when the cervix is fully dilated and the baby's head is in the birth canal.
8. It ends when the baby is born.
9. 45 minutes
10. Steps: B, D, H, I, K, L
11. afterbirth
12. 10 to 15 minutes
13. Steps: F, J

Teacher's Resource Guide
Chapter 17 Test

1. I		11. O		21. T	
2. J		12. G		22. T	
3. N		13. D		23. D	
4. A		14. B		24. A	
5. F		15. T		25. D	
6. H		16. F		26. B	
7. K		17. F		27. D	
8. C		18. F		28. A	
9. M		19. F		29. C	
10. E		20. T		30. B	

31. Note the first day of the last normal menstrual period. Count back three months from this date. Add seven days. This will be the approximate birth date.
32. (Student response.)
33. (Student response. List two advantages for each.)

Signs of Pregnancy

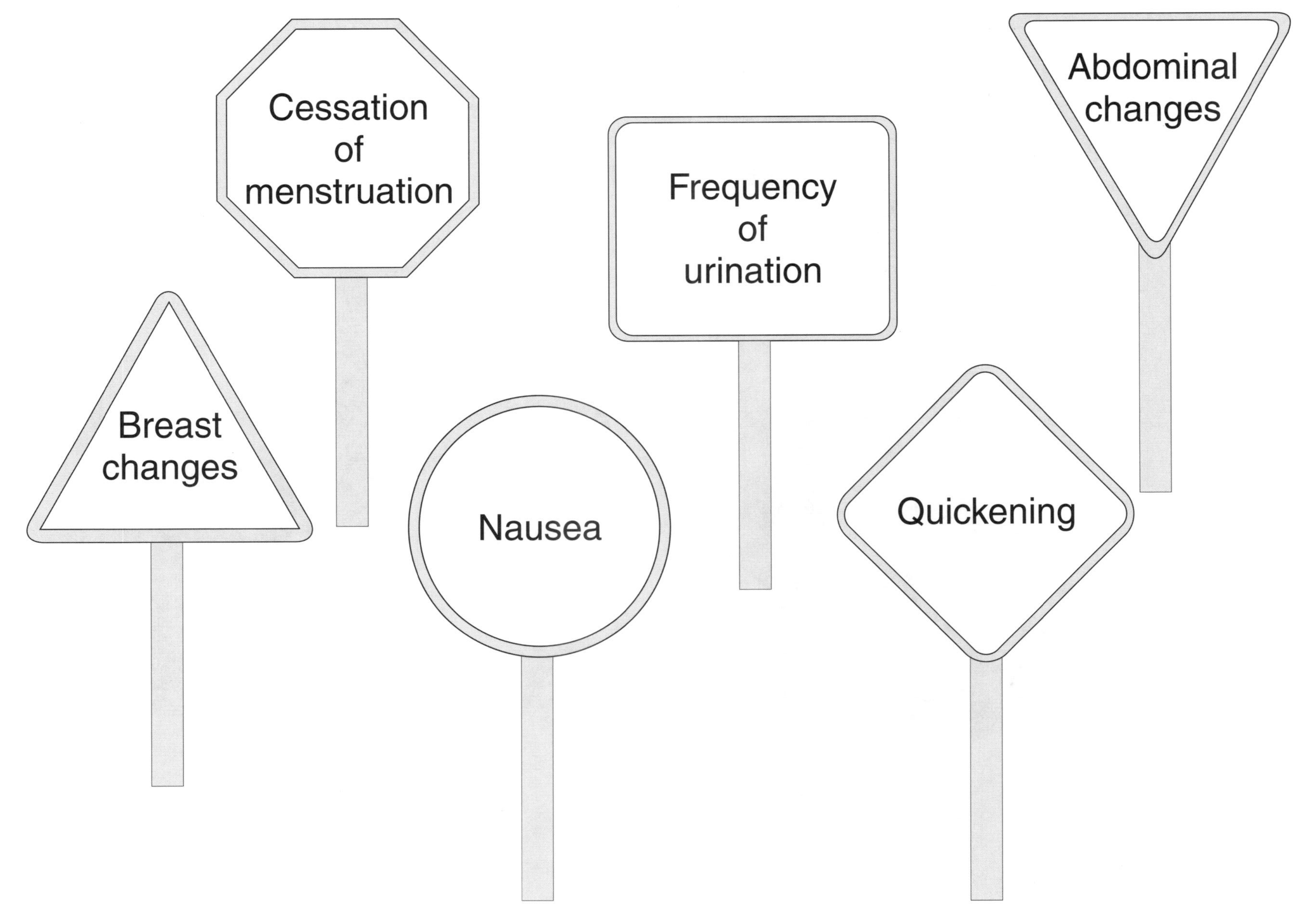

Pregnancy

Uterus
Pacenta
Umbilical
Cord
Fetus
Amnio-Chorionic
Fluid
Amniotic
Fluid

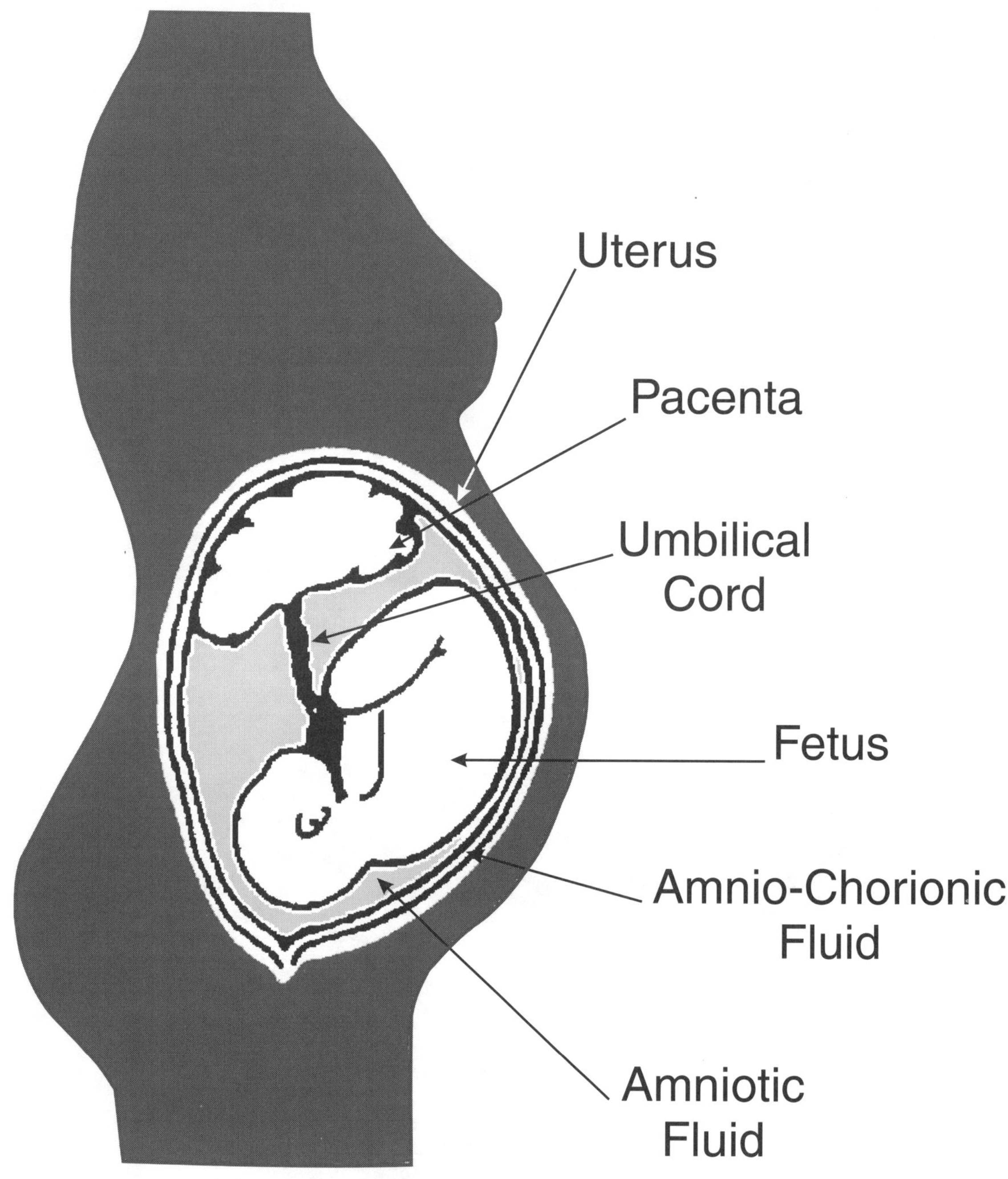

Caring for Baby Before Birth

Name _______________________________   **Date** ________________   **Period** __________

Answer the following questions. Circle *T* if the statement is true or *F* if the statement is false.

T F   1. It's not necessary for a woman to see a health care provider until after she is pregnant.

T F   2. The most crucial stages of an unborn baby's development could occur even before the woman realizes that she is pregnant.

T F   3. A woman can help to prevent certain types of birth defects by including folic acid in her diet before she becomes pregnant.

T F   4. During pregnancy, a woman will need additional calories and nutrients to help her baby develop.

T F   5. A woman should not be concerned about her weight before pregnancy, since she'll be putting on a lot of pounds anyway.

T F   6. Certain medical problems are easier to manage during pregnancy if they are well-controlled before pregnancy.

T F   7. Smoking and drinking have little or no impact on the health of a baby.

T F   8. The lifestyle of the father has no impact on the health of his baby.

T F   9. Knowing the family history can help a person plan for a healthy pregnancy.

T F   10. Vaccinations are an important part of pre-pregnancy planning.

(Continued)

Caring for Baby Before Birth

Answer Key

1. *False.* It is a good idea for a woman to see a health care provider before she becomes pregnant. That way, she can plan for pregnancy. Planning can help her identify health risks and make lifestyle changes before she becomes pregnant.

2. *True.* In the first eight weeks of pregnancy, the brain, heart, and spinal cord begin to form. This process can begin even before a woman misses her period and knows that she is pregnant.

3. *True.* Studies show that the risk of certain birth defects of the spine and brain, called neural tube defects, can be reduced by taking 0.4 milligrams of folic acid every day before and in the early weeks of pregnancy. Most multivitamins contain the recommended amount. Folic acid also is found in green, leafy vegetables, liver, beans, citrus fruits, and whole grain foods.

4. *True.* During pregnancy most women need 300 extra calories per day. It's also important to get plenty of calcium and iron. Many women take a supplement recommended by their health care provider.

5. *False.* Women who begin pregnancy overweight are more likely to develop high blood pressure or diabetes during pregnancy. Underweight women are more likely to have a low-birthweight baby. A woman should discuss her ideal weight with her health care provider before becoming pregnant and start a program to achieve her optimal weight before she conceives.

6. *True.* Conditions such as diabetes, epilepsy, and high blood pressure can affect a pregnancy. However, if these problems are diagnosed and managed in advance, a woman will still have a good chance for a healthy pregnancy.

7. *False.* If a woman smokes heavily, she is more likely to have a miscarriage. Drinking alcohol excessively or taking drugs could cause her baby to be born with birth defects. It's best for a woman to choose a healthy lifestyle before she becomes pregnant.

8. *False.* Men who smoke around their pregnant partners may put their babies at risk from secondhand smoke. Men who are exposed to chemicals or radiation in the workplace may be more likely to have a baby with health problems.

9. *True.* If a family has a history of inherited disease, a couple may want to see a genetic counselor. Tests are not available for many serious disorders.

10. *True.* Infection with measles or rubella during pregnancy can cause birth defects. A woman should talk to her health care provider about immunity to these diseases before she becomes pregnant. For example, a simple blood test can determine if someone is immune to rubella. If not, the woman should get vaccinated before becoming pregnant, and then delay conception for three months after the vaccination.

Scoring:

Give yourself 10 points for each correct answer, and check your knowledge level below.

80-100: You already know a lot about what can be done before and during pregnancy to assure a healthy baby. Congratulations! You are well-informed about health care issues and pregnancy.

40-70: You're aware of some, but not all, of the factors that can influence the outcome of a pregnancy. Reading this chapter will help you learn more.

0-30: By taking this quiz, you've learned that there are many specific things a couple can do to improve their chances of having a healthy baby. Remember these health care practices as you make lifestyle decisions that will affect your future children.

By planning for pregnancy with a health care provider, a woman is more likely to give birth to a healthy infant.

Substances to Avoid During Pregnancy

Harmful Effects

-
-
-
-

A Baby Is Born

Name ____

Date _____________________________________ **Period** ______________ **Score** ______________

Chapter 17 Test

Matching: Match the following terms and identifying phrases.

_______ 1. The sticky precursor of milk that the baby receives when nursing until the third day after birth. It provides the infant with immunity to certain illnesses.

_______ 2. A special organ that functions as an interchange between the developing fetus and the mother.

_______ 3. The developing child from the ninth week of pregnancy through birth.

_______ 4. The birth of a baby before it has developed enough to live in the outside world.

_______ 5. The beginning of the formation of close emotional ties between the mother and her baby.

_______ 6. The secretion of milk from the breasts.

_______ 7. The "bag of waters."

_______ 8. Focuses on the birth experience of the baby. Its goal is to make the birth process less shocking and more comforting for the baby.

_______ 9. The developing baby from the implantation through the eighth week of pregnancy.

_______ 10. A surgical procedure in which the walls of the abdomen and uterus are cut and the baby is lifted out of the uterus.

_______ 11. Method of childbirth based on the theory that the pain of childbirth can be controlled by the woman.

_______ 12. The period of time following the delivery of the baby.

_______ 13. Method of childbirth based on the belief that birth affects the family as a unit as well as each individual family member.

_______ 14. This links the baby to the placenta.

A. miscarriage
B. umbilical cord
C. Leboyer method of childbirth
D. family-centered childbirth
E. cesarean section
F. bonding
G. postpartum period
H. lactation
I. colostrum
J. placenta
K. amnio-chorionic membrane
L. endometrium
M. embryo
N. fetus
O. Lamaze method of childbirth

(Continued)

True/False: Circle *T* if the statement is true or *F* if the statement is false.

T F 15. When an expected period of menstruation is missed by more than 10 days, under normal circumstances, pregnancy is likely.

T F 16. Breast changes during pregnancy will not be apparent until the last month of pregnancy.

T F 17. A blood test is used to determine if a woman is pregnant.

T F 18. By the end of the third lunar month, the fetus measures about 19 inches in length and weighs about 6 pounds.

T F 19. The baby will take what it needs from the mother so she doesn't have to pay attention to her diet.

T F 20. A total weight gain of between 25 and 35 pounds during pregnancy is often recommended.

T F 21. Mothers who smoke increase the risk of miscarriage or premature delivery.

T F 22. Most miscarriages occur because nature is trying to get rid of an imperfect embryo.

Multiple Choice: Select the best response. Write the letter in the space provided.

_______ 23. A woman may miss her period or cause it to be late because ______.
   A. of emotions
   B. of a change of climate
   C. she is pregnant
   D. All of the above.

_______ 24. The heart of the developing baby is pulsating by the end of the ______ month.
   A. first
   B. fourth
   C. fifth
   D. eighth

_______ 25. If the fetus is born by the end of the ______ month, it has a good chance of survival if cared for by skilled physicians.
   A. first
   B. third
   C. fifth
   D. seventh

_______ 26. Whenever an expectant mother is feeling ill, she should ______.
   A. take any prescription drugs prescribed to her before she became pregnant
   B. consult her physician
   C. take over-the-counter medications
   D. None of the above.

_______ 27. Fetal alcohol syndrome, which occurs when a pregnant woman drinks alcohol, may cause ______ in the baby.
   A. growth deficiency and limited mental growth
   B. narrow eyes, low nasal bridge, and a short upturned nose
   C. jittery and poor coordination with a short attention span
   D. All of the above.

(Continued)

_______ 28. The longest stage of labor is the _______ stage.
  A. dilation
  B. expulsion
  C. afterbirth
  D. last

_______ 29. During a normal birth, the placenta is expelled during _______ stage of labor.
  A. the first
  B. the second
  C. the third
  D. the expulsion

_______ 30. A period of _______ is required after childbirth for a woman's uterus and other pelvic struc-tures to return to their former condition before she was pregnant.
  A. six to eight days
  B. six to eight weeks
  C. six to eight months
  D. None of the above.

Essay Questions: Provide complete responses to the following questions or statements.

31. Describe how to estimate the birth date of a baby.

32. If you were expecting a baby, which method of childbirth would you choose? Explain why.

33. List two advantages of breast-feeding and two advantages of bottle-feeding.

Chapter 18
Your New Baby

Objectives

After studying this chapter, students will be able to

- describe how parenthood changes the roles of husband and wife.
- identify characteristics and abilities of newborns.
- describe scheduling, feeding, bath, and clothing needs of infants.
- summarize the physical, intellectual, social, and emotional growth and development of children during the first year.
- recognize the special needs of children with physical or mental disabilities.

Bulletin Boards

I. Title: "Needs of the Newborn"

Cover the bulletin board with cotton receiving blankets. Attach one of each item of clothing a newborn needs. Under each item, list the quantity needed, the approximate cost of each, and the total cost in the form of an equation (for example, 3 x $2.50 = $7.50). Include the following items: diapers (4 dozen), knit shirts (3), knit gowns or kimonos (3), stretch coveralls (3), sweaters (2), knit cap or hat (1), booties (2 pairs), socks (5 pairs), blanket sleeper or bunting (1), receiving blankets (3), heavy blanket (1), and bibs (4). The numbers in parentheses indicate the minimum number needed of each item. List the total cost of the wardrobe at the bottom of the bulletin board.

II. Title: "Who Are You?"

Ask students to bring in baby photos of themselves. Post these on the bulletin board. Have a contest to see who can identify the most babies correctly. Use this bulletin board to discuss the concept of physical development.

Teaching Materials

Text, pages 416-437

Terms to Know, To Review, To Do, and *To Think About*

Student Activity Guide

    A. *How Newborns Look and Act*
    B. *Observation of an Infant*
    C. *Interview a New Parent*
    D. *Meeting a Newborn's Needs*

Teacher's Resource Guide/Binder

Introduction of Solid Foods, transparency master, 18-1

Diaper Costs, reproducible master, 18-2

Dangers and Safeguards, reproducible master, 18-3

How to Explain a Disability, reproducible master, 18-4

Chapter 18 Test

Teacher's Resource Binder

Parenthood's New Roles, color transparency, CT-18

Software for Contemporary Living

Chapter Review Game

Introductory Activities

1. Ask a panel of new parents to come to class and share their experiences about what it was like during the first few months with their new baby.

2. Ask students to write a short paper stating what they hope to learn about babies in this class.

Strategies to Reteach, Reinforce, Enrich and Extend Text Concepts

Parenthood Brings New Roles

3. **EX**   Ask students to sit in a circle and write sentences on index cards stating what they feel will be their roles as parents. Gather the cards and then redistribute them to students. Ask students to read each card and discuss.

4. **RT**   *Parenthood's New Roles*, color transparency, CT-18. Use this transparency as the new roles associated with parenthood are discussed. Ask students to think of other roles that parents experience.

5. **RF**   How can parenthood, especially with the first baby, strengthen the husband-wife relationship? What stresses can parenthood create?

6. **RT**   Compare the attitudes of parents who look on parenthood as depriving them of freedom to those who look upon parenthood as the positive expansion of their family.

The Newborn

7. **RF**   *How Newborns Look and Act*, Activity A, SAG. Students are asked to write descriptive phrases at each point on a diagram to indicate how babies look at birth. They are then asked to complete a matching exercise.

8. **ER**   Have students cut out pictures of newborns and babies. Have students point out various aspects of the babies' appearance such as size of head, amount of hair, etc.

9. **RT**   Ask students to discuss what they feel is the most important ability newborn babies have.

10. **RT**   Explain how babies' reflexes help them adapt to their new environment.

11. **RT**   Describe how a baby's schedule can upset the routine of the household.

12. **EX**   Authorities say when a baby cries, parents should not hesitate to pick him/her up and try to decide what is wrong. Do you agree? Do you think this will "spoil" a baby?

13. **ER**   Ask students to demonstrate the proper way to hold a baby while bottle-feeding, when and how to "burp" the baby, and precautions to take when feeding.

14. **RF**   Ask students to discuss how to introduce a new food to a baby. What suggestions are given? What may be the baby's reactions?

15. **RT**   *Introduction of Solid Foods*, transparency master, 18-1. Use this transparency as you discuss the sequence of introducing new foods to babies.

16. **ER**   Ask students to set up a typical bathing scene. Have them use a life-size doll to show how to sponge bathe and tub bathe the baby. Gather the correct equipment for the bath and for dressing the baby following the bath.

17. **ER**   *Diaper Costs*, reproducible master, 18-2. Students are to compare various brands of disposable diapers.

18. **ER**   Ask students to practice folding a cloth diaper. Discuss the advantages and disadvantages of using cloth diapers.

19. **EX**   Ask students to contact a store that sells baby clothes. Ask to borrow a typical layette for a newborn and display the items along with their prices.

20. **ER**   Obtain several typical baby garments and ask students to examine the labels. Why is it important to check the labels concerning fabric content, washing instructions, and any safety precautions?

21. **RT**   Ask students to suggest ways to quiet a crying baby. Describe a hunger cry, indigestion cry, and pain or sick cry. Why should cries be checked out immediately?

22. **ER** *Observation of an Infant,* Activity B, SAG. Students are asked to observe an infant (under one year of age) and find out information listed on the form. (They may need to ask some questions of the infant's parents.) Have students compare their observations with those of other class members.
23. **ER** *Interview a New Parent,* Activity C, SAG. Students are asked to interview a new parent, or you can ask new parents to come to class to relate their experiences about when they first became parents. Answer the questions listed.
24. **RF** *Meeting a Newborn's Needs,* Activity D, SAG. Students are asked to complete sentences regarding the needs of newborns.

Growth and Development During the First Year

25. **ER** Ask a parent to bring his or her year-old baby to class to discuss development of the baby from birth through the first year, citing physical, intellectual, emotional, and social development.
26. **EX** Ask students to design play activities that would stimulate physical development of large muscles.
27. **RT** *Dangers and Safeguards,* reproducible master, 18-3. Have students review the safety precautions in the home and in the yard. Ask them to list dangers and how parents can prevent accidents.
28. **RF** View a video on the growth and development of children from birth to one year.
29. **RT** By one year, children's games are actually learning activities. What do various games, such as the game of peekaboo, reveal about development?
30. **ER** Ask students who babysit to relate episodes that depict how small babies respond to strangers.
31. **ER** Ask students to interview child care providers to discuss how they handle instances of separation anxiety. How do they reassure these children? What do they suggest parents do?
32. **RT** Why is it so important for small children to feel secure? If they don't feel secure with parents or child care providers, how may it affect them later in life?
33. **RF** Ask students to relate episodes revealing fears in children, such as noises (from a vacuum cleaner or airplane), pets, strangers, new experiences.

Children with Special Needs

34. **ER** Ask a special education teacher to talk with the class concerning children with disabilities. Have students prepare a list of questions in advance.
35. **RF** *How to Explain a Disability,* reproducible master, 18-4. Use this master as a handout to help students better understand how to relate to people with disabilities.
36. **ER** When a child with a disability is born, parents often may have emotions of guilt, self-pity, or fear. How can parents find assistance to help them understand the disability?
37. **ER** Ask students to call the United Way to locate organizations and community assistance programs for families with exceptional children.
38. **ER** Ask students to review the three groups of mental disabilities and to locate community resources for educable and trainable children.
39. **ER** Invite parents of mentally disabled children to come to class to discuss the special needs of their children.

Answer Key for Chapter 18

Text
To Review, page 436.

1. (Student response.)
2. rooting
3. Because the stumps of their umbilical cords have not yet healed.
4. Cotton fabrics are soft, absorbent, and easy to launder.
5. (List three:) Newborns cry when they are hungry, when they have indigestion, when they have wet or soiled diapers, when they do not feel well.
6. True.
7. Through their five senses: seeing, hearing, feeling, smelling, and tasting.
8. They learn that the person who disappears will reappear.
9. Separation anxiety is shown by babies when adults they love leave them for a short time. This often occurs when a parent leaves an almost one-year-old with a babysitter. Babies fear their parents will not return.

10. Those who are educable, those who are trainable, and those who have severe/profound mental disabilities.

Student Activity Guide

Activity A, *How Newborns Look and Act.*

Hair–varies from bald to quite a bit of hair; Shape of head–may be elongated; Neck–extremely short; Cheeks–fat; Nose–short and flat; Chin–receding; Eyebrows–hardly discernible; Eyelashes–hardly noticeable; Eye color–smoky blue; Chest–narrow; Shoulders–sloping; Average weight–7 1/2 pounds; Average length–20 to 21 inches; Body proportions–head looks too large; Skin–blotchy and wrinkled; Abdomen–large and protruding; Arms and legs–short and scrawny; Hands and feet–tiny; Bones–soft and flexible; Muscles–soft, small, and uncontrolled.

Reflexes:
1. E
2. C
3. A
4. D
5. B

Activity D, *Meeting a Newborn's Needs.*

1. 18, 20
2. six, four
3. night
4. leave the baby alone on a table or in a tub
5. Sponge

6. 3
7. towel
8. cloth, disposable. Disposable
9. Cotton
10. flammability
11. The baby is hungry. The baby has indigestion. The baby has wet or soiled diapers. The baby has an illness.
12. spoil
13. story
14. Separation anxiety
15. six

Teacher's Resource Guide

Chapter 18 Test

1. F	11. C	21. F
2. D	12. E	22. T
3. K	13. F	23. C
4. L	14. T	24. D
5. B	15. T	25. B
6. J	16. F	26. C
7. G	17. F	27. C
8. I	18. F	28. D
9. M	19. T	29. B
10. H	20. T	30. C

31. (Student response.)
32. (Student response.)
33. You will be better prepared to care for your children. You will be able to help your child proceed smoothly through the various stages of development.

Introduction of Solid Foods

Most doctors recommend a sequence like this one for the introduction of solid foods.

Approximate Timing	Foods to Be Introduced, One at a Time
At age 3 to 4 months	Baby cereal mixed with milk or formula.
2 weeks later	Strained or pureed fruits, such as applesauce, pears, peaches, and bananas.
2 weeks later	Strained or pureed vegetables, such as carrots, squash, green beans, and peas.
2 weeks later	Egg yolk mixed with cereal.
2 weeks later	Strained beef or lamb and soft scrambled egg.
4 weeks later	Finger foods, such as crackers, toast, and cheese.
8 weeks later	Table foods, such as ground meat, chopped foods, and cooked vegetables.

Diaper Costs

Name _______________________________________ **Date** _______________ **Period**_______________

Diapers are the major article of clothing for a baby. Therefore, they can be a big expense. Many parents use disposable diapers. Disposable diapers come in a variety of sizes, shapes, weights, and designs. Research the different types of disposable diapers available, and complete the chart below.

Type	Cost (per diaper)	Characteristics

Do you think disposable diapers are the best choice for parents? Why or why not? _______________

____

Extra credit: Research the other two options for diapers–cloth diapers and diapers from a diaper service. Discuss the costs, advantages, and disadvantages of these two options below. How do disposable diapers compare in convenience, cost, and cleanliness to cloth diapers?

Cloth diapers:____

____

____

____

____

Diapers from a diaper service:____

____

____

____

____

Dangers and Safeguards

Babies can move by kicking their feet and pushing their bodies, so they may fall off a flat surface. When babies are laid on a bed, barriers should be placed around them to prevent them from falling, and their position should be checked often.

Babies discover open doors and will travel where there might be danger. They also like to close doors and may close them on their fingers. All doors should be closed or doorways blocked with secure barriers.

Slats in cribs and playpens should be no more than 2 3/8 inches (6 cm) apart so a baby's head cannot be caught between the slats. If there is more than a two-finger space between the mattress and the side of the crib, the mattress is too small. An infant could suffocate by wedging his or her head in this gap.

Babies should never be left alone in the bathtub. They can drown in only a small amount of water. They can also scald themselves by turning on the hot water. In fact, parents may want to wrap a washcloth around a hot faucet to prevent babies from burning their waving hands.

When traveling in a car, babies should be securely fastened in a car restraint that has been approved by consumer protection groups. Babies should always ride in the backseat of a car. (If a baby is placed in the front of any vehicle equipped with a passenger-side airbag, the initial impact of the airbag could lead to serious head injury or death.)

Babies like to poke things into electrical sockets and pull cords. To prevent these dangers, covers should be placed over unused sockets. Lamps and appliances that are not used should be put away. The cords of lamps and appliances that are used need to be made inaccessible to a baby's reach.

Babies like to pull themselves up on any available furniture. Tables and chairs that are not stable should be removed while babies are in this stage.

Bottles propped in bottle holders should not be offered to small babies. Milk may flow too fast and cause choking or digestive problems. Instead, small babies should be held so the milk flow can be controlled.

How to Explain a Disability

The following are suggestions for explaining a disability to a child.

- *Communicate.*

  Explain as much as you can about the physical disability so that the child does not become frightened by the unknown.

- *Show compassion.*

  Show the child that you understand what a hurtful thing a disability can be.

- *Help the child comprehend.*

  Be very sure to convey the truth that the disability is never the child's fault.

- *Help the child realize the disability will not defeat him or her.*

  When talking with the child, convey the message that the disability may be very hard to deal with, but that the child will make progress and will learn to do new things.

Age	What to Say To a Child with a Disability	What to Say To a Nondisabled Child
2-4	"No one knows why, but sometimes children are born without everything their bodies need and that is what happened to you. This means you will have to work harder to learn and grow, and we are going to work hard to help you."	"Most children are born with everything they need, but sometimes children are born without everything they need. Sometimes they need crutches, or wheelchairs, or braces to help them walk and sit."
5-8	"I know it's really hard when your body can't do everything you want it to do. It's not fair that you have to work so hard to make your body do what you want. Everyone has some things that are easy for them, and some that they have to work harder to do. Sure, you have this problem, but you're lucky because you have lots and lots of talents, too."	"Kids are all different, and they have different things they can do well. They also have some things that are harder for them. Some things that are very easy for you to do would be very difficult for someone else. It takes a lot of courage for kids with physical disabilities, but this courage will help them keep trying and working at it."
9-12	"It's too bad you have a disability. That makes things harder for you, but remember, you have lots of abilities. You can work to strengthen them. It's natural to feel angry, but try not to give up."	"Whenever you see children with disabilities, remember that even though they are having a hard time, they're still kids who need friends and understanding."

Your New Baby

Chapter 18 Test

Matching: Match the following terms and identifying phrases.

_______ 1. Causes newborns to extend their toes when the soles of their feet are touched.

_______ 2. Causes newborns to close their hands tightly when their palms are touched.

_______ 3. Refers to development in the areas of perception, attention, association, and other aspects of the mind.

_______ 4. The process of learning to relate to other people.

_______ 5. When babies lie on their backs, they turn their heads to one side. If they turn to the right, their right hands extend outward, and their left arms extend upward. If they turn to the left, their left hands extend outward, and their right arms extend upward.

_______ 6. When babies handle objects using just their thumbs and index fingers.

_______ 7. Involves skills that use the muscles of the trunk, neck, legs, and arms.

_______ 8. When babies grab objects using the palm and fingers opposing the thumb.

_______ 9. Babies fear that parents will not return.

_______ 10. Involves skills that use the muscles of the hands, fingers, feet, and toes.

_______ 11. When newborns are touched on one of their cheeks, this reflex causes them to turn their heads in that direction and open their mouths.

_______ 12. When newborns are tapped on their abdomen or when their support is suddenly removed, this reflex causes them to spread their arms apart and then bring them together again in a bow. They perform the same motion with their legs.

A. fontanels
B. tonic neck reflex
C. rooting reflex
D. grasp reflex
E. startle reflex
F. Babinski reflex
G. large muscle development
H. small muscle development
I. mitten grasp
J. pincer grip
K. intellectual development
L. social development
M. separation anxiety

(Continued)

True/False: Circle *T* if the statement is true or *F* if the statement is false.

T F   13. At birth, girls are generally longer and heavier than boys.

T F   14. A newborn cries only when something needs to be done.

T F   15. A baby's growth and development will follow the same general pattern that all babies follow.

T F   16. A baby's physical growth will depend on only hereditary factors.

T F   17. Babies learn to walk before they sit up.

T F   18. Loud noises comfort young babies.

T F   19. Because child development is gradual and continuous, some of the stages overlap.

T F   20. As early as the ninth month, babies learn the meaning of a few specific words such as "no."

T F   21. Social contact is unnecessary for young babies.

T F   22. The cause of physical disabilities may be either hereditary or environmental.

Multiple Choice: Select the best response. Write the letter in the space provided.

______   23. When they first come home from the hospital, most babies sleep for about ______ hours a day.
  A. six to eight
  B. 10-15
  C. 18-20
  D. 22-24

______   24. Fabrics for baby clothes should be ______.
  A. soft
  B. absorbent
  C. easy to launder
  D. All of the above.

______   25. The most noticeable growth in infants during the first year is in the area of ______ growth.
  A. social
  B. physical
  C. intellectual
  D. emotional

______   26. Babies make their first deliberate sounds at about ______.
  A. two weeks
  B. one month
  C. three months
  D. eight months

______   27. Babies exhibit stranger anxiety (attachment to familiar persons and fear of strangers) at about ______.
  A. birth to three months
  B. three months to six months
  C. six to nine months
  D. nine to twelve months

______   28. Most authorities believe that ______.
  A. it is practically impossible to spoil a baby
  B. parents spoil a baby if they respond to his or her cries
  C. when babies' needs are reasonably met, they seldom display stress and frustration
  D. Both A and C.

(Continued)

                                                    Contemporary Living Teacher's Resources

_______ 29. Children who _______ can learn to be productive in a sheltered workshop setting, but they cannot get along by themselves in a community setting.
A. are educable
B. are trainable
C. have severe mental disabilities
D. have profound mental disabilities

_______ 30. Parents of a child who is mentally disabled should _______.
A. be ashamed of their child
B. regard the child as a hardship
C. treat the child as normally as possible, especially in the areas of discipline and love
D. never discipline the child

Essay Questions: Provide complete responses to the following questions or statements.

31. Pretend you are a parent. Which would you choose for your baby–disposable diapers, cloth diapers, or diapers from a diaper service? Explain why.

32. Choose one of the four main areas of child growth and development. Describe the changes that take place as a child progresses in that area.

33. What are the advantages of knowing the principles of child development?

Chapter 19
Helping Children Grow and Develop

Objectives

After studying this chapter, students will be able to

- describe a nurturing, healthy, and safe environment for children.
- summarize the physical, intellectual, social, and emotional growth and development of children from ages one through five years.
- explain parenting concerns related to the preschool years.
- evaluate different types of substitute child care.
- explain parenting concerns related to the school-age years.

Bulletin Boards

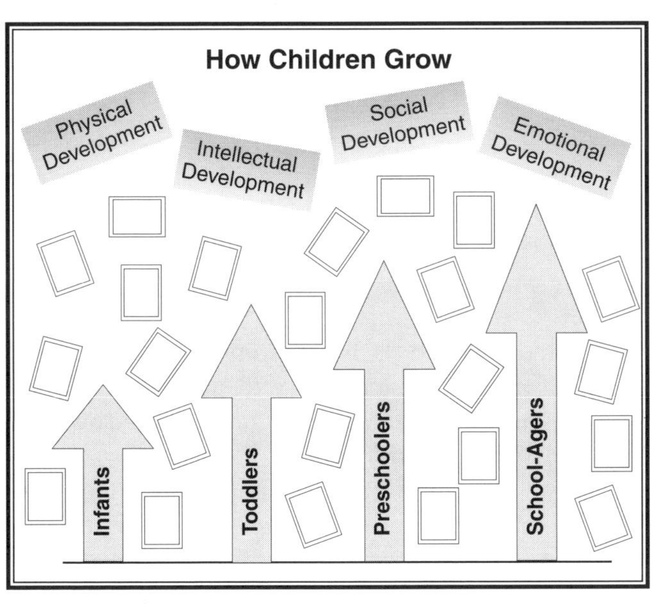

I. Title: "How Children Grow"

Write the following titles on construction paper and place them on the bulletin board below the main title: *Physical Development, Intellectual Development, Social Development,* and *Emotional Development.* Across the bottom of the bulletin board, create a time line marked as shown with the points *Infants, Toddlers, Preschoolers, School-Agers.* Students should bring to school four baby pictures of themselves–one as an infant, one as a toddler, one as a preschooler, and one as a school-ager. The pictures should illustrate either physical, intellectual, social, or emotional development. Have students mount their pictures on construction paper and write their names on the paper backing. Students should place pictures on the time line in the appropriate place.

II. Title: "Substitute Child Care"

Using one strip of colorful construction paper, divide a bulletin board in half horizontally. Use another paper strip to divide the board in half vertically. Place one of the following titles in each square: *In-Home Child Care, Family Child Care, Child Care Centers,* and *Day Care for Children Who Are Ill.* Students should write one- or two-word descriptions of the benefits of each type of substitute child care on squares of colored paper. (Students also should list the various types of child care centers in the third square.) Discuss these positive aspects of various forms of child care in class. During the discussion, ask students to define the drawbacks of each arrangement as well.

Teaching Materials

Text, pages 438-469
Terms to Know, To Review, To Do and *To Think About*

Student Activity Guide
A. *Keeping Children Safe*
B. *The Preschooler*
C. *When You Were a Child*
D. *Substitute Child Care*
E. *Checklist for a Child Care Center*

Teacher's Resource Guide/Binder
What Do You Know About Children? reproducible master, 19-1
Handling Parenting Decisions, reproducible master, 19-2
A Parent's Guide to Discipline, transparency master, 19-3
When a Child Is the First One Home, transparency master, 19-4
Chapter 19 Test

Teacher's Resource Binder
Does Child Care Measure Up? color transparency, CT-19

Software for Contemporary Living
Chapter Review Game

Introductory Activities

1. Form a circle of chairs and ask students to contribute to discussion topics. Explain that "to nurture" means to supply with nourishment. Ask students what "nourishment" children need in a home to feel loved. If a child feels loved, discuss with students how he or she will act as a person and within the family. As a comparison, discuss failure to thrive with students.

2. Ask students to identify 10 problems in society that they feel pose challenges for parents and children. List and number the problems on the chalkboard. Ask each student to draw a horizontal line across a sheet of paper. At one end of the line write *more important.* On the other end of the line write *less important.* Ask each student to consider the 10 problem areas the class has listed. Position them on the horizontal line on their paper indicating which they feel are more important and less important. Then draw a similar horizontal line on the chalkboard. As a class, students should decide where the problems should fall on the continuum. Is it

hard for students to reach a consensus? Ask how they can prepare themselves to face the challenges of parenting.

Strategies to Reteach, Reinforce, Enrich, and Extend Text Concepts

Creating a Nurturing Environment for Your Child

3. **EX** How can parents encourage children without pushing them? Ask students to suggest healthy ways for parents to encourage children. Can students recall positive ways parents encouraged them? Ask students to explain.

4. **RF** Why is it important for parents to expect realistic accomplishments of children? Ask students to cite examples of parents who have unrealistic expectations and how these expectations may affect children.

5. **RT** Discuss behavior modeling with students. What is modeling? How can modeling influence children's perceptions of how they should behave? How can parents model virtues of honesty, perseverance, and loyalty?

Creating a Safe and Healthy Environment for Your Child

6. **ER** Ask students to observe families in fast-food restaurants and discuss the nutritional value of the foods children eat. What are the healthful items listed on the menu? Do children choose these items?

7. **ER** Instruct students to research preventative health services available in the community. Are health clinics that serve children available? Do local communities offer immunizations for children? Discuss findings with students in class.

8. **EX** *Keeping Children Safe,* Activity A, SAG. Instruct students to evaluate the safety hazards listed. Students should describe the danger of each hazard and how to reduce the safety risk to children.

9. **RT** Discuss with students why teaching safety is an ongoing process for parents. Ask students to describe and give examples of how safety rules change for children as they

grow. How can parents let children know the importance of following safety rules they set?

10. **ER** Invite a shopping mall security guard or police officer to speak to the class about keeping children safe in shopping malls and other public places. How can parents ensure safety? If children are lost in a public place, how should parents react?

11. **EX** Discuss with students safety precautions parents must take at home when babies begin to walk.

Growth and Development during the Preschool Years

12. **EX** Ask students to observe the differences in physical abilities among children of different ages. Note hand dexterity; large muscle development; and the abilities to run, stop, swerve, skip, climb, jump, etc. Discuss with students in class.

13. **EX** Bradford is five years old and wants to help his mother with the yard work. Ask students to describe the tasks Bradford is able to handle.

14. **ER** Instruct students to observe a specific child in a nursery school setting. Students should note the child's age and list all the child's actions that relate to intellectual development. In class, students should compare the skills of various children observed. They also should compare children's intellectual development to Chart 19-7 in the text.

15. **EX** Discuss the influence of the family on a child's social development. How does the family contribute to positive social growth? Negative behavior patterns?

16. **ER** *The Preschooler*, Activity B, SAG. Invite students to learn about guidance techniques by interviewing a preschool child's parent. Discuss interview results in class.

17. **RF** Consider the statement "Play is a child's work." Discuss the different types of child's play. What is the difference between cooperative and parallel play? Discuss the benefits a child receives from play activities.

18. **ER** Instruct students to observe a specific child in a nursery school setting. Students should note the child's age and list all the child's actions that relate to emotional development. In class, students should compare the skills of various children observed. They should also compare children's emotional development to Chart 19-15 in the text.

The Preschool Years

19. **RF** *A Parent's Guide to Discipline*, transparency master, 19-3. Review with students these guidelines for healthy, effective discipline. Discuss with students the difference between discipline and punishment.

20. **EX** Ask students to respond to the following situation: Pretend you are a parent and your preschool child is afraid to go to bed in a dark room because he or she believes monsters live under the bed. How would you treat this fear? What would you say and do to reassure your child?

21. **EX** Ask students to cite situations where they have witnessed a child having a temper tantrum. What behaviors did the child exhibit? How did the parent react? If in a public place, how did people around the child react? How do authorities suggest parents handle temper tantrums? Why might these suggestions calm children?

22. **EX** Have students research ways children display the emotion of anger. Role-play scenes in which a child displays anger. Discuss with students common causes of children's anger. What possible long-term consequences might they experience if parents deal with children's anger in negative ways?

23. **EX** Discuss with students how a parent can prepare a first child to accept a new brother or sister. Have students role-play a father telling his son that he will soon have a new brother or sister.

24. **EX** *When You Were a Child*, Activity C, SAG. Ask students to respond to questions about situations they faced as children. Ask them how they feel about the situations now. How would they deal with similar situations as parents?

Substitute Child Care

25. **RT** Authorities state that the most ideal environment for a child is in the home with caring and loving parents. They suggest a child's parent should be the primary caregiver for at least the first three years of life. Ask students if they agree. If both parents must work, what do students feel is the best substitute child care arrangement for them?

26. **ER** Invite a panel of working parents who use different forms of substitute child care to discuss the pros and cons of their arrange-

ments in class. Leave time for questions at the end of the panel discussion.

27. **RF** Discuss with students why it is important for parents to visit and evaluate substitute caregivers and child care centers. What should parents pay attention to when choosing child care? List suggestions on the chalkboard.

28. **ER** In some states people who care for children in their homes are required to register their family child care business. Is this true in your state? Have students investigate the laws and what registering entails.

29. **EX** Instruct students to research how many employer-sponsored child care facilities operate in your area. What advantages do businesses who sponsor child care reap? What are the advantages for parents and their children? How are the costs handled?

30. **ER** Instruct students to research your community to see if a child care center that serves ill children is available. Discuss the services they offer in class. How are children with contagious diseases cared for?

31. **RF** *Does Child Care Measure Up?* color transparency, CT-19. Use this color transparency to discuss the importance of evaluating child care centers before selecting one. (You may use the transparency to introduce strategy 32.)

32. **EX** *Checklist for a Child Care Center,* Activity E, SAG. Instruct each student to select a child care center to visit and observe. They should use the checklist to evaluate the quality of the facility. Compare the results of their observations.

The School Years

33. **EX** Instruct students to write a short essay describing how they spend leisure time with family members. What activities do they enjoy together? How do family members make time for these activities? How does leisure time improve the family's well-being? If students do not spend leisure time with family members, ask them to list possible activities their family members could enjoy together. How could they make time for these activities? How would spending leisure time together improve their family life? How might they propose their leisure time plans to family members? Discuss essays with students in class.

34. **EX** Discuss with students how important friendships are to children. How can parents help children build healthy friendships? Did parents ever voice disapproval of students' friends? Did parents try to dissolve the friendships? Students should explain their reactions to the intervention. Would they have done the same if they had been the parent?

35. **EX** Children often exaggerate and tell tall tales. Cite how children "learn" to lie from parental examples and from their desire to please parents. When should a parent become concerned about these behaviors? What should parents do if they suspect children are telling tall tales? How might this reaction differ if children are telling serious lies?

36. **EX** Ask students to respond to the question "How might parents teach children to be responsible?" Have students recall episodes from their childhoods when parents taught them to accept responsibility. What did they gain from these lessons? What can parents do to help children develop responsibility? How does a sense of responsibility affect a person's behavior throughout his or her lifetime?

37. **RT** Ask students the following questions about how parents can teach children money management:
    - If parents give children an allowance, how much should they give to their 3-year-old, 5-year-old, 6-year-old, 8-year-old, 10-year-old?
    - If a child were spending his or her money foolishly, how should a parent react?
    - Should parents give children more per week than they need?
    - What are the positive and negative aspects of paying children for completing jobs at home?

38. **EX** *What Do You Know About Children?* reproducible master, 19-1. Instruct students to read each statement concerning young children. Students should indicate whether they agree or disagree with the statement and justify their reason.

After-School Child Care

39. **EX** *When a Child Is the First One Home,* transparency master, 19-4. Ask students to pretend they are working parents with school-age children they must leave alone for a few hours

each day after school. Have students suggest guidelines for each category listed that children should follow while home alone. Write student guidelines on the transparency in the appropriate block. Discuss with students how parents can determine whether children are mature enough to stay alone.

40. **ER** Instruct students to research support services that may care for and/or assist latchkey children. Share results in class.

41. **EX** *Handling Parenting Decisions*, reproducible master, 19-2. Instruct students to make parenting decisions by completing each sentence.

Answer Key for Chapter 19

Text
To Review, page 468.

1. (Student response.)
2. (Student response for example.)
3. (List five: student response.)
4. true
5. Young children are self-centered and play by themselves. As they grow older, they may prefer parallel play. In this form of play, children like to play next to their peers, but they do not play with their peers. They watch what others are doing and may copy their actions, but they do not interact. In cooperative play, the next stage, children choose to interact with one or more people during play.
6. Discipline is often equated with punishment. Punishment is one of many forms of discipline. There are many other forms of discipline that are more effective in guiding children's behavior, such as modeling and setting limits.
7. Fears can be useful in the lives of children. Learning that fires burn and that knives cut can protect children from harm. However, fears that prevent a child from meeting life normally can produce damaging habits and actions. Such negative responses to fear may create long-lasting problems.
8. (Describe four types: student response.)
9. Participating together in recreational activities helps to pull families together.

Communication is sometimes easier when family members are enjoying relaxing activities. Parents and children who find recreational activities they all enjoy are drawn together because of their mutual interests and enjoyment. This mutual interest can help to sustain a bond that will keep teens from drawing away from their parents.

10. Avoid telling lies yourself. Let children know you are aware of their lies and they will gradually have fewer reasons to lie. However, do not be too stern, for most children pass through a stage of lying. Reward children for telling the truth. Help them accept the fact that all people make mistakes. Let them know they will not be severely punished for making mistakes.
11. Give children an allowance. Assign a value to all household and yard tasks and pay for each job done. Give children money when they need it.
12. Latchkey children need to be trained in the skills of self-sufficiency and safety. Parents need to establish a safe environment for their children when they are home alone. They need to establish guidelines for the use of appliances and equipment. There should be ground rules for allowing other children or acquaintances into the home. Safety precautions concerning strangers should be discussed with the children, as well as proper use of the telephone.

Teacher's Resource Guide
Chapter 19 Test

1. F	11. T	21. C
2. H	12. T	22. A
3. E	13. F	23. B
4. G	14. T	24. A
5. I	15. F	25. C
6. B	16. T	26. D
7. J	17. F	27. C
8. A	18. F	28. A
9. C	19. F	29. B
10. D	20. F	30. D

31. (Student response.)
32. (Student response.)
33. (Student response.)

What Do You Know About Children?

Name ____**Date** _______________**Period**______________

Read each of the following statements concerning young children. Circle *A* if you agree with the statement and *D* if you disagree. Then write a brief reason for your answer. Discuss each statement in class.

A   D   1. Between the ages of two and seven, children think mostly about themselves and are concerned mainly with their own well-being.

____

____

____

A   D   2. If a preschooler wants to complete a task but is unable to do it well, the parent should intervene and do it for him or her.

____

____

____

A   D   3. Preschoolers are able to play cooperatively as soon as they start spending time with playmates.

____

____

____

A   D   4. A temper tantrum should be ignored as long as the child is not harming himself/herself or anyone else.

____

____

____

A   D   5. Children need to know they are loved, even when they have done something wrong.

____

____

____

A   D   6. Children will develop large muscle control before they develop fine muscle control.

____

____

____

A   D   7. One of the main reasons why children may tell lies is that they are very anxious for parental approval.

____

____

____

(Continued)

Name ___________________________________

A D   8. Paying children for household tasks may put a price on tasks that should be a part of family duties and may teach children to work only when they are paid.

____

____

____

A D   9. Parents can help children overcome fears by forcing them to do whatever it is they fear.

____

____

____

A D   10. Adults should give preschoolers limits so they will know what adults expect of them as well as what they cannot do.

____

____

____

Handling Parenting Decisions

Name ____**Date** ________________**Period**________________

How would you handle parenting decisions? Pretend you are a parent and read the following sentences, then write how you would handle each situation.

1. If my crawling baby broke an expensive vase by knocking it off the coffee table, I would ___________

   ____

   ____

   ____

2. If I saw my three-year-old looking at the cleaning products stored below the kitchen sink, I would

   ____

   ____

   ____

3. If my preschooler liked to wander away from me in the shopping mall, I would___________________

   ____

   ____

   ____

4. If my child had not started to walk by the time the chart in the doctor's office said he should have, I would ____

   ____

   ____

   ____

5. If my five-year-old named the colors of five flowers in the yard, I would respond by _______________

   ____

   ____

   ____

6. If my two-year-old did not like to share her toys, I would ______________________________________

   ____

   ____

   ____

7. If my five-year-old displayed over-aggressive behavior too often, I would ________________________

   ____

   ____

   ____

(Continued)

Name _______________________________

8. If my angry six-year-old told me he hated me, I would _______________________________

____

____

____

9. If I were about to have my second child, I would tell my three-year-old _______________

____

____

____

10. If I had to work and rely on substitute child care, I would choose _______________

____

____

____

11. If I did not like one of my nine-year-old child's closest friends, I would _______________

____

____

____

12. If my seven-year-old enjoyed telling tall tales, I would respond by _______________

____

____

____

13. If my ten-year-old regularly forgot to take her lunch money to school, I would help her remember by

____

____

____

14. If my preteen regularly overspent his weekly allowance and asked me for more money, I would respond by _______________

____

____

____

15. If my eleven-year-old was going to have to stay alone for two hours each day after school, I would prepare her or him by _______________

____

____

____

A Parent's Guide to Discipline

- Set limits.

- Be consistent.

- Use consequences.

- Stay calm.

- Use positive language.

- Listen closely to your child.

- Explain the rules clearly.

- Offer limited, specific, and acceptable choices.

- Provide alternative ways to express feelings.

- Use timeouts.

- Admit your mistakes.

- Praise positive behavior.

When a Child Is the First One Home

Guidelines for . . .

Entering the Home	Using the Phone
Answering the Door	Using Appliances
Handling Emergencies	Managing Time

Helping Children Grow and Develop

Name ____

Date ____ **Period** ____________ **Score** ______________

Chapter 19 Test

Matching: Match the following terms and identifying phrases.

_____ 1. Affectionate care and attention.	A. modeling
_____ 2. The achievement of control over movement of different parts of the body.	B. temper tantrum
	C. positive reinforcement
_____ 3. When a child plays next to peers but not with them.	D. latchkey child
_____ 4. When a child interacts with peers in play.	E. parallel play
_____ 5. The use of different methods and techniques to teach children self-control and limits.	F. nurturance
	G. cooperative play
_____ 6. Violent outburst of anger.	H. motor development
_____ 7. Moving a child away from others when his or her behavior is disruptive.	I. discipline
	J. timeout

_____ 8. Children learn by imitating behavior of people they admire.

_____ 9. A guidance technique that involves praising desired behavior.

_____ 10. Child regularly left without direct adult supervision before or after school.

True/False: Circle *T* if the statement is true or *F* if the statement is false.

T F 11. Toddlers and preschoolers need to sleep at least 10 hours a night.

T F 12. Five-year-old children can tie shoelaces.

T F 13. Two-year-olds may count to 10 or more.

T F 14. Parents should begin to discipline children at an early age.

T F 15. Fears are not useful in a child's life because they cause unnecessary stress.

T F 16. Care given in the home of a hired caregiver is the most common form of substitute child care.

T F 17. Cooperative child care centers offer lower tuition costs because they are part of colleges and universities.

T F 18. Children tell tall tales and lies because they have not learned to be responsible yet.

T F 19. Authorities feel the best way to teach children about money is to pay them for each job they perform around the house and yard.

T F 20. Children in self-care do well in school because they have a lot of quiet time to study.

(Continued)

Multiple Choice: Choose the best response. Write the letter in the space provided.

_____ 21. Failure to thrive is a condition in which babies who are below average in height and weight _____.
   A. grow up to be short, underweight adults
   B. do not react positively to people because they have not been around anyone but parents
   C. do not respond normally to people because they lack emotional interaction with parents
   D. do not get along with other children because they were overprotected as infants

_____ 22. Parents can meet the nutritional needs of young children by _____.
   A. giving them several small meals a day
   B. letting children eat their favorite foods
   C. making sure children get plenty of exercise
   D. Both A and C.

_____ 23. As children develop physically, they learn to _____.
   A. control their small muscles before they learn to control their large muscles
   B. control their large muscles before they learn to control their small muscles
   C. control their large and small muscles at the same time
   D. control their muscles at their own pace and follow no set pattern

_____ 24. Four-year-old children who develop motor skills at an average pace are able to _____.
   A. hop on one foot
   B. bathe themselves
   C. copy letters, numbers, and designs
   D. All of the above.

_____ 25. Two-year-old children who develop intellectual abilities at an average pace are able to _____.
   A. count to 10 or more
   B. name some colors
   C. remember events of the previous day
   D. give simple directions

_____ 26. Three-year-old children who develop social abilities at an average pace are able to _____.
   A. wait for their turn to talk
   B. choose special friends
   C. imitate a parent as they play dress up
   D. feel comfortable going places without parents

_____ 27. One-year-old children who develop emotional abilities at an average pace may _____.
   A. fear the dark
   B. dawdle while eating
   C. carry a favorite toy at all times
   D. be sensitive about being helped

_____ 28. Child care centers benefit children because _____.
   A. child care centers employ staff trained in child development
   B. children receive lots of personal attention
   C. parents are close by if children need them
   D. All of the above.

(Continued)

_______ 29. A parent should question his or her child's association with a certain friend if _____.
   A. the friend asks to borrow lunch money
   B. the friend hits the child
   C. the friend talks to the child too much in school
   D. the friend offers the child too much junk food

_______ 30. Parents can encourage children to develop responsibility by _____.
   A. pushing children to develop their intellectual skills
   B. using fear to keep children from disobeying
   C. making sure children attend a reputable child care center
   D. encouraging children to think about how to solve a problem

Essay Questions: Provide complete responses to the following questions or statements.

31. Briefly describe how parents can provide a nurturing environment for children.

32. Choose one of the four main areas of child growth and development. Describe the changes that take place as a child progresses in that area.

33. Explain how you would help your child develop responsibility.

Part 6
Families Face Change

Chapter 20
Balancing Family and Work Concerns

Objectives

After studying this chapter, students will be able to

- explain reasons why people work.
- evaluate various types of work and family arrangements and patterns.
- summarize the impact of work on families.
- describe ways that families are influencing the workplace.
- identify techniques for balancing family and work demands.

Bulletin Boards

I. Title: "Juggling Family and Work"

Draw and put up a figure made of construction paper with a clown face and outstretched arms, as if juggling. Above the clown arrange brightly colored circles of construction paper that are labeled as follows: *Quality Time, Job Deadlines, Meals, Child Care, Medical Care, Ill Family Members, Job Advancement, Grocery Shopping, Household Tasks.*

II. Title: "Balancing Career and Family Obligations"

Create a scale using black construction paper and marking pens on a white background. Cut out figures from a magazine representing family members, and place on one side of the scale. Cut out pictures of a man and a woman in demanding careers (doctor, police, religious leader) and place them on the other side of the scale. Refer to the bulletin board when discussing career goals in marriage.

Teaching Materials

Text, pages 472-491

Terms to Know, To Review, To Do, and *To Think About*

Student Activity Guide

    A. *Blending Employment with Family Life*
    B. *Job Sharing*
    C. *Setting Priorities*
    D. *Challenges for Employed Couples*

Teacher's Resource Guide/Binder

Family/Work Arrangements: Pros and Cons, transparency master, 20-1

Dollar Value of Household Chores, reproducible master, 20-2

Whose Role Is It Anyway? reproducible master, 20-3

The Glass Ceiling, transparency master, 20-4

Chapter 20 Test

Teacher's Resource Binder

Family/Work Arrangements, color transparency, CT-20A

Which Depicts Quality Time? color transparency, CT-20B

Software for Contemporary Living

Chapter Review Game

Introductory Activities

1. *Blending Employment with Family Life,* Activity A, SAG. Ask students to respond to statements concerning dual-career families. Use the responses as a basis for class discussion.
2. Poll class members to see how many live in families in which both parents work for pay. Do they prefer mothers to work for pay or to be full-time homemakers? How about fathers? How many students are planning to have a dual-career marriage? How many plan to continue working after children are born? After children are in school? After children have left the home?

Strategies to Reteach, Reinforce, Enrich, and Extend Text Concepts

Why Work?

3. **ER** Invite parents who are successfully blending family and work responsibilities to speak to students on the topic "Why Work?"
4. **ER** "The spouse who works for pay has greater financial independence than the spouse who is a full-time homemaker." Foster a student debate about this statement.

Changing Attitudes

5. **ER** Assemble a panel of people who perform occupations that are nontraditional for their gender. (For example, you may invite a female police officer and firefighter or a male nurse.) Ask them to describe their work. If they receive negative reactions to their occu-pational choices, ask them to describe how they deal with such responses.
6. **ER** Invite a personnel officer or employment attorney to discuss with students how to respond to illegal gender-based interview questions.

Types of Work and Family Arrangements

7. **RT** *Family/Work Arrangements,* color transparency, CT-20A. Use this transparency to review the four types of family/work arrangements described in the text. With which arrangements are students most familiar? Which arrangements do students hope to use in later life? Is it possible that one person may use all four arrangements at various times during a lifetime?
8. **RF** *Family/Work Arrangements: Pros and Cons,* transparency master, 20-1. Refer to this transparency as you discuss with students the pros and cons of various family/work arrangements. As the discussion progresses, write students' contributions in the "pros" and "cons" boxes as appropriate.
9. **EX** Compare single-earner and dual-career families. Describe how each family would settle the problems of overtime work, travel requirements, job transfers requiring a family move, entertaining, child care, and household chores.
10. **RF** Dual-career marriages have caused the roles of male and female spouses to change. Men are becoming more involved in home and child care and women are contributing to the family income. Discuss the pros and cons (if any) of these changes.
11. **ER** Ask persons in various types of careers to serve on a panel to discuss ways to balance family and career obligations. Discuss the importance of setting career goals before marriage.
12. **ER** Ask two dual-career couples to speak to the class. Discuss how they handle problems in a dual-career household.
13. **EX** Review problems of employed couples. Role-play scenes to show how each spouse's attitude toward the other's job can affect a marriage, how couples can resolve child care problems, how they can resolve problems of hurt pride when one spouse makes more than the other, and how couples may decide which spouse should control the spending.

14. **RF** *Dollar Value of Household Chores,* reproducible master, 20-2. Ask students to research the dollar value of household chores and to indicate how much a family would have to spend if they hired others to do these chores. Do students believe that full-time homemakers are appreciated enough for what they do?

15. **RF** *Whose Role Is It Anyway?* reproducible master, 20-3. Use this activity to help students see the various roles husbands and wives perform as married couples and ways their tasks can be divided. Read the activity instructions. After students have sorted their cards and arranged them in descending order of importance, ask them to indicate which cards they placed on the top and bottom of each stack. Discuss differences and similarities of opinion. Have students count the number of cards in each stack. What does this reveal? If both spouses are employed outside the home, how does this affect roles they perform? If one spouse does not work, what changes would the students make in their categories? Ask students to complete each of the variations included in the activity. Discuss changes they make in their role divisions.

Patterns of Work and Childbearing

16. **EX** Discuss in class how many students plan to have children? Of these, how many plan to have children in their twenties? Thirties? Forties? Discuss students' reasons for their choices.

17. **ER** Assemble a panel of working mothers, including one who had children in her early twenties, one who waited until age 30, and one who waited until age 40. Ask each to present the reasons for their choices. What does each mother see as the advantages and disadvantages of her situation?

18. **ER** Invite an obstetrician or nurse to address the class on the topic "Mothers Over 30: High-Risk Pregnancies?" Allow time for questions, answers, and discussion.

19. **ER** Ask three middle-aged professional women who had children later in life to address the class on the topic, "Why I'm Glad I Waited to Have Children." Allow time for discussion.

Impact of Work on Families

20. **ER** Present the following case study to students:

Tanya, a single, working mother, woke up one day with the flu and a fever. She had every reason to call in sick. However, her employer's on-site child care facility refused to accept Tanya's three-year-old that day unless Tanya came to work. Tanya decided to go to work. She reasoned that working while sick would be easier than staying home and taking care of a rambunctious three-year-old while sick.

Discuss with students why an employer-provided child care facility may refuse to accept children of absent employees. (Note: To reduce absenteeism.) How might this policy indirectly affect Tanya's health if she develops complications? How did Tanya's health affect the quality of her work? Discuss the situation of coworkers who were exposed to Tanya's illness.

21. **ER** Present the following case study to students:

Two-year-old Jeffrey woke up one morning with a bad cold. Both Jeffrey's parents had important meetings at the office that day and could not miss work. Instead of bringing Jeffrey to the doctor, his parents brought him to the child care center. Jeffrey's mother commented to her coworker, "Today was just one of those days when work had to come first."

How do you think Jeffrey felt? Was the parents' decision fair to Jeffrey and the children at the child care center? Discuss with students.

22. **EX** Ask students to research the child care policies and provisions of countries in northern and western Europe and report to the class. Why are some of these countries making a special effort to help young working parents combine their careers with parenting? Would students be willing to pay higher taxes in order to have the child care and career support these working European parents enjoy?

How Families Are Influencing the Workplace

23. **RF** *Job Sharing,* Activity B, SAG. Ask each student to imagine he or she is sharing a job with another person. Instruct each student to list the tasks each job sharer is responsible to complete. After students have completed the exercise, ask if they foresee any problems with the arrangement. How could the prob-

lems be avoided or resolved? What advantages to job sharing do students see? What persons other than part-time homemakers might be interested in job sharing? (Note: Someone wishing to start a business, write a book, recover from an illness, work at another part-time job, work part-time while retired, etc.)

24. **EX** Present the following case study to students:

    Julio's child care provider called early one morning to report that she was sick and couldn't take care of Julio that day. Though he had plenty of leave, Julio's father took Julio to the office and tried to be both a graphic artist and a father. The secretaries helped with child care and spent a lot of their work time playing with Julio.

    How does this case study illustrate how families are influencing the workplace? Are all the influences positive? Would more work have been accomplished at the office if Julio's father had taken a day of annual leave to stay home with the baby? Was Julio's father taking advantage of the secretaries by letting them help with child care? Would the secretaries have been justified in going ahead with their work instead of caring for Julio?

25. **EX** When Lori's mother was terminally ill 15 years ago, Lori had to quit her job in order to care for her mother. When Lori's father had a heart attack this year, however, Lori was able to take leave from her job under the Family and Medical Leave Act to care for him. Later, when her father's health improved, Lori returned to work. What general trends brought about the passage of the Family and Medical Leave Act? (Note: More women in the work force.) How does this example illustrate how families have influenced the workplace?

Realities of the Workplace

26. **RT** *The Glass Ceiling,* transparency master, 20-4. Refer to this transparency to illustrate the fact that although women represent 45.7 percent of the work force, they do not occupy many top management positions. Explore with students possible reasons for this glass ceiling.

27. **EX** Present the following case study to the class:

At first, Marco liked his new supervisor, and she seemed to like him. One day before a meeting, however, she told Marco she thought he was adorable. She asked him to turn around so that she and her female coworkers could get a better look at him. He played along with the request as the coworkers laughed and whistled at him. Marco pretended to laugh off the incident, but inside he felt humiliated.

What could Marco have said or done at the time to prevent this incident? What actions could he have taken later?

Techniques for Managing Family and Work

28. **RF** *Setting Priorities,* Activity C, SAG. Each student should assign a level of priority to a variety of tasks scheduled for a typical weekend. How do students feel after ranking the tasks? Frustrated because they could not realistically accomplish more? At peace because they had chosen to accomplish the most important tasks? Why is prioritizing important for busy couples?

29. **RF** *Challenges for Employed Couples,* Activity D, SAG. Instruct each student to identify what he or she feels is the greatest challenge facing a dual-career couple. Discuss with students how couples can best handle this challenge.

30. **RF** *Which Depicts Quality Time?* color transparency, CT-20B. Ask students to test their understanding of *quality time* by choosing the illustration in CT-20B that best depicts quality time. Use the transparency to discuss the importance of quality time. Why is it sometimes difficult for parents to spend quality time with children? Ask students to list possible ways parents can spend quality time with children.

Answer Key for Chapter 20

Text
To Review, page 489.

1. (List three:) Financial security, opportunities for self-expression, personal growth, satisfying relationships with coworkers, outside contacts and interests, increased purchasing power, financial self-sufficiency.

2. Dual-worker families, families with part-time workers, families with full-time homemakers, single-parent families. (Student response to describe one advantage and one disadvantage of each type.)

3. A displaced homemaker is a longtime homemaker whose supporting spouse has left or remarried and whose children have grown. A displaced homemaker usually loses support, insurance coverage, and other sources of financial security that a spouse had provided.

4. A couple can establish healthy patterns of family and work life without the added complications of children. Each spouse can complete his or her education and get started on a career. The couple also can gain a sense of themselves and each other as wage earners.

5. (Student response.)

6. The Family and Medical Leave Act entitles workers to 12 weeks of unpaid leave per year following the birth or adoption of a child. Equal time is also given to care for a seriously ill relative or a serious personal health condition. At the end of the leave period, a worker has the right to regain his or her former job or a comparable one.

7. Block scheduling: B. Job sharing: D. Employer-sponsored child care: A. Flextime: E. Employee-assistance programs: C.

8. false

9. Setting priorities helps family members accomplish the most important tasks each day.

10. *Quality time* refers to time a person spends giving full attention to another person or persons. Working parents who find quality time for children and each other usually have a more satisfying family life.

Teacher's Resource Guide
Chapter 20 Test

1. D	11. F	21. A
2. G	12. T	22. A
3. A	13. F	23. C
4. J	14. F	24. B
5. I	15. T	25. B
6. F	16. T	26. B
7. H	17. T	27. D
8. B	18. F	28. C
9. K	19. F	29. C
10. C	20. F	30. A

31. Work provides opportunities for self-expression, personal growth, and satisfying interaction with other workers. Work is the means by which the family supports itself. Working couples can share interesting work-related experiences and help each other deal with job pressures. They will still have one person's income even if the other spouse loses his or her job. Financial self-sufficiency gives people greater independence and more life choices.

32. Contented family members make more productive employees. A person having trouble at home may have trouble concentrating at work. Similarly, a bad day at work may mean a person is out-of-sorts with his or her family.

33. Priorities are influenced by values and standards. Priorities, values, and standards of individual families are unique to each family. (Student response for two examples.)

Family/Work Arrangements: Pros and Cons

Arrangement	Pros	Cons
Dual worker		
One full-time worker and one part-time worker		
One full-time worker and one full-time homemaker		
Single-parent family		

Dollar Value of Household Chores

Name ____**Date** _____________________**Period**_______________

Research the dollar value of household chores. Consult local want ads, consumer services, and employment agencies to find the average wages people earn for doing such chores. Indicate how much a family would have to spend each week for these services if they had to hire people to do them. Discuss in class.

Household Chore	Wage/Hour	Hours/Week	Weekly Cost for Family
Preparation of meals			
Kitchen management/cleanup			
Household cleaning			
Laundry			
Child care			
Household shopping			
Chauffeuring			
Family counseling			
Interior design/decoration			
Garment construction/repair			
Heavy household chores			
Minor household repairs			
Lawn and yard care			
Car maintenance			

Total weekly cost for family would be____________

Whose Role Is It Anyway?

Roles that must be performed by husbands and wives are listed on the following cards. List any additional roles you might think of on the cards marked *Other.* Cut the cards apart on the dotted lines. Predict which roles you and a future spouse will perform when you marry by sorting the cards into three categories: (1) roles the *husband* will perform, (2) roles the *wife* will perform, and (3) roles *both partners* will perform. Then arrange the cards within each category in descending order of importance. (Place the most important role at the top of the pile and the least important role at the bottom of the pile.)

Variations:
   a. Sort the cards as you believe a person of the opposite sex might arrange them. Did you change the order?
   b. Sort the cards as you believe your parents might arrange them. What changes, if any, did you make?
   c. Sort the cards as you believe your grandparents might arrange them. What changes did you make?
   d. When children are older, what roles might they perform? Place these cards in a separate category.

Arrange social activities with friends.	Repair and maintain the home.
Provide emotional support for partner.	Arrange for children's recreation and sports activities.
Provide income for family.	Care for hurt and sick children.
Responsible for interaction with parents and in-laws.	Participate in religious activities.
Plan recreational activities for the family.	Prepare meals for the family.
Attend children's school functions and conferences.	Maintain car.
Decorate the home.	Clean the house.

(Continued)

Discipline the children.	Clean up after meals.
Provide for the financial needs of the children.	Drive children to activities.
Arrange for savings and investments.	Pay the bills and keep financial records.
Supervise children's play.	Make beds and pick up around the house.
Decide when and where to move.	Select and purchase family car.
Provide for the religious training of the children.	Handle insurance policies.
Shop for groceries and other household items.	Select a place to live.
Mow the lawn and shovel snow.	Provide understanding and comfort for children.
Other:	Other:
Other:	Other:
Other:	Other:

The Glass Ceiling

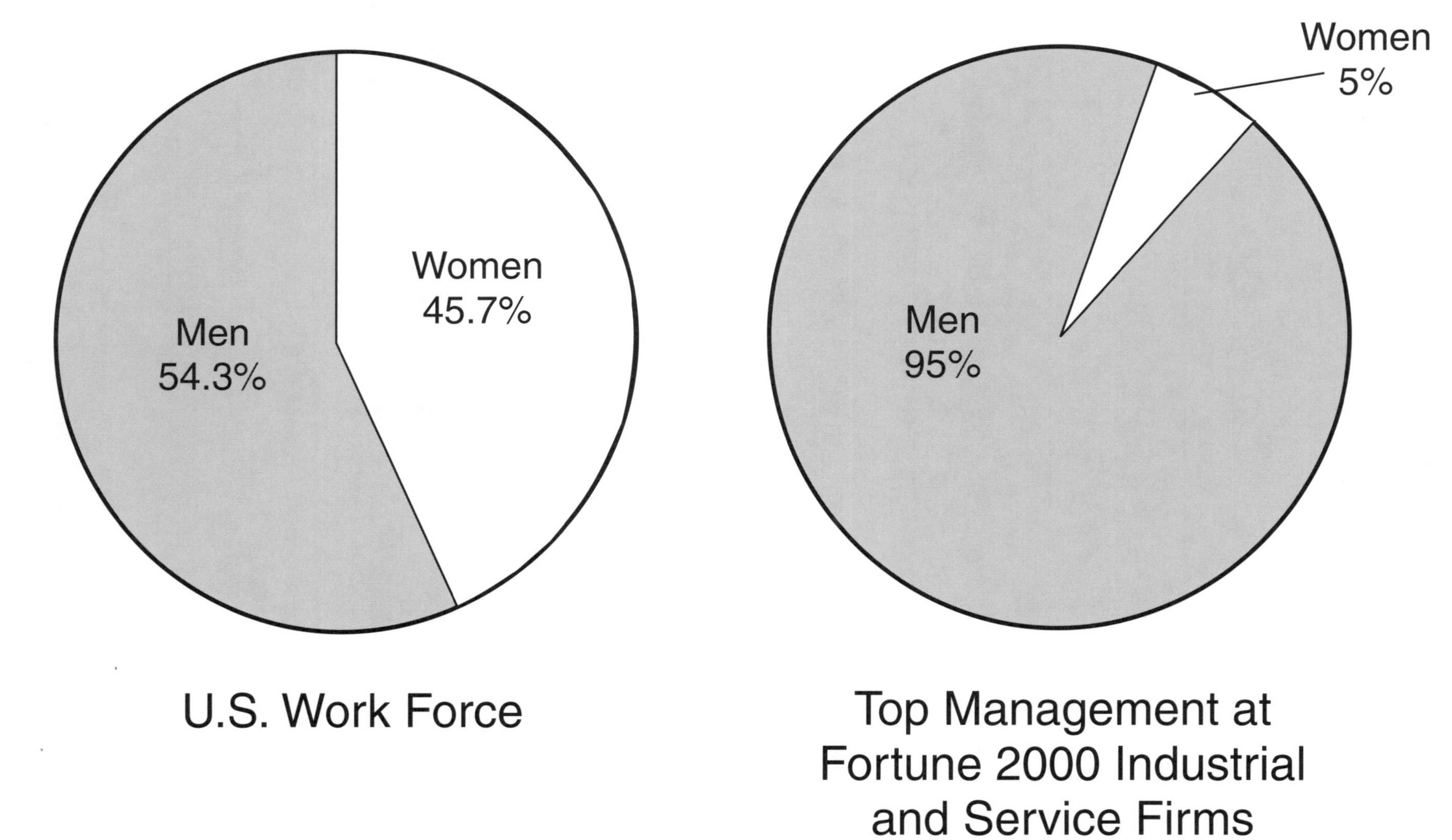

Sources: Census Bureau, Glass Ceiling Commission

Balancing Family and Work Concerns

Name ____

Date _________________________________ **Period** ______________ **Score** _______________

Chapter 20 Test

Matching: Match the following terms and identifying phrases.

_______ 1. Type of homemaker whose spouse has left or remarried and whose children have grown.

_______ 2. Workers choose their working hours, subject to certain rules.

_______ 3. Family in which both parents are employed.

_______ 4. Working 40 hours in three or four days.

_______ 5. Financial support from the breadwinning spouse following a divorce.

_______ 6. Requires that pregnant employees be treated the same as employees with temporary disabilities.

_______ 7. Entitles workers to 12 weeks of unpaid leave per year following the birth or adoption of a child.

_______ 8. Works less than a full work week and thus has more time to focus on raising children and managing the household.

_______ 9. Economical in terms of benefits yielded by money invested.

_______ 10. Arrangement in which two part-time workers handle the responsibilities of one full-time job.

A. dual-career
B. part-time worker
C. job-sharing
D. displaced
E. quality time
F. Pregnancy Discrimination Act of 1978
G. flextime
H. Family and Medical Leave Act
I. alimony
J. block scheduling
K. cost-effective

True/False: Circle *T* if the statement is true or *F* if the statement is false.

T F 11. Currently in the United States only 1 birth in 10 is to a mother over age 30.

T F 12. Currently in the United States nearly one woman in five in her late thirties has not yet had a child.

T F 13. Currently in the United States 8 families in 10 fit the traditional pattern of husband as full-time breadwinner, wife as full-time homemaker, and children at home.

T F 14. Currently in the United States it is legal for an employer to refuse to hire someone as a nurse because of his or her gender.

T F 15. To hold perfectionist standards in all areas can set a family up for feelings of frustration, stress, and failure.

T F 16. In a job interview it is illegal for a prospective employer to ask an interviewee about his or her marital status or child care arrangements.

T F 17. Homemakers provide many services that would otherwise have to be paid for or provided by other family members.

(Continued)

T F   18. If a homemaker decides to look for paid employment, a reliable prior work history is likely to be of little help in finding a job.

T F   19. Balancing family and work demands becomes less challenging during illness and times of family crisis.

T F   20. Currently in the United States the average age of first marriage for women is 20.3 years.

Multiple Choice: Select the best response. Write the letter in the space provided.

_______ 21. Compared to women in the year 1960, women today on average tend to marry _____.
   A. at a later age
   B. at an earlier age
   C. at the same age
   D. their childhood sweetheart

_______ 22. Compared to men in the year 1960, men today on average tend to marry _____.
   A. at a later age
   B. at an earlier age
   C. at the same age
   D. their childhood sweetheart

_______ 23. Delaying childbearing until after age 30 usually _____.
   A. means that the woman will be at somewhat lower risk for complications during pregnancy than if she had become pregnant in her twenties
   B. means that the couple have decided to have no children
   C. allows a couple to establish healthy patterns of family and work life without the added complications of children
   D. means that a spouse who stays home will be viewed as a servant

_______ 24. Currently in the United States couples on average are having approximately _____.
   A. one child
   B. two children
   C. three children
   D. four children

_______ 25. Compared to couples in the late 1950s, couples in the United States today are having their first child _____.
   A. earlier in their marriage
   B. later in their marriage
   C. at about the same time in their marriage
   D. at a younger age

_______ 26. A full-time homemaker whose marriage lasted only a brief time before a divorce occurred _____.
   A. is assured of receiving Social Security benefits based on the ex-spouse's employment
   B. may not qualify for any lifelong Social Security benefits based on the ex-spouse's employment
   C. will receive lifelong Social Security benefits if he or she worked hard as a homemaker during the marriage
   D. will receive lifelong Social Security benefits based on how well he or she raised children

_______ 27. Compared to older mothers, women who bear children in their early teens _____.
   A. are more likely to receive regular child support payments from the children's father
   B. are more likely to finish high school and go on to college
   C. are less likely to need public assistance (welfare)
   D. are at greater risk of living in poverty

(Continued)

_____ 28. Spouses who become displaced homemakers may find that they are dependent on their own resources for ______.
    A. financial support
    B. medical insurance coverage
    C. Both of the above.
    D. Neither of the above.

_____ 29. Currently in the United States a husband and wife are both employed in ______.
    A. one out of five marriages
    B. two out of five marriages
    C. three out of five marriages
    D. four out of five marriages

_____ 30. Compared to a financially dependent person, a person who is financially self-sufficient generally ______.
    A. has greater independence and more life choices
    B. has less independence and fewer life choices
    C. has more difficulty putting a bad marriage behind him or her and starting a new life
    D. is more likely to remain in a physically or emotionally abusive marriage

Essay Questions: Provide complete responses to the following questions or statements.

31. Identify and briefly discuss the primary reasons why people engage in paid work.

32. Explain how work can affect family life and how family life can affect work.

33. Explain the relationship between priorities, values, and standards. Provide at least two specific examples.

Chapter 21
Dealing With Family Crises

Objectives

After studying this chapter, students will be able to

- identify resources that can help people handle crises.
- explain how to cope with crises.
- describe specific types of family crises.

Bulletin Boards

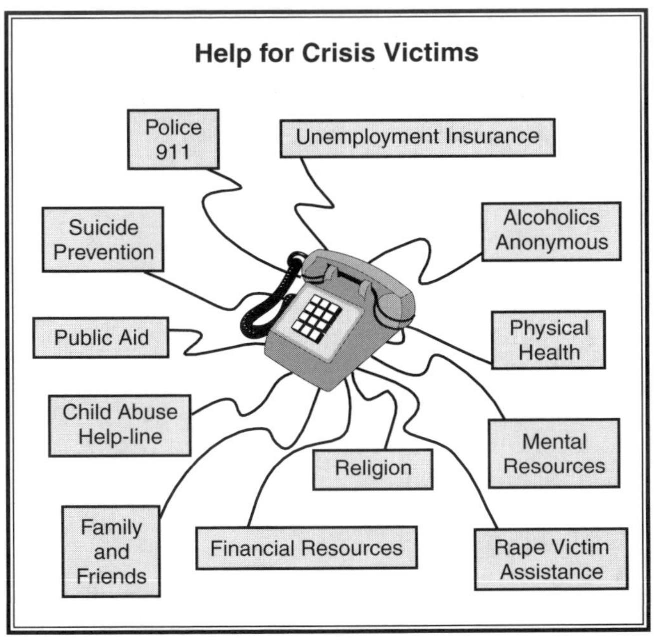

I. Title: "Help for Crisis Victims"

Cut out a large picture of a telephone from a magazine or draw a picture of one and place it in the center of the bulletin board. Around the outer edges of the bulletin board, post phone numbers for various agencies that can be contacted for help in crisis situations. Most of these numbers are listed in a telephone directory. Also mount pictures that depict the other resources discussed in this chapter, such as family members, friends, mental and financial resources, and physical health. Draw a curly line depicting a telephone cord from the phone to each resource and phone number.

II. Title: "Resources for Handling Crises"

Divide the bulletin board into six sections. Label the sections with the following: *mental resources, physical health, family relationships, friends, financial resources,* and *community resources.* Find newspaper and magazine articles that illustrate the use of these various resources in handling crises. Advertisements for insurance, investments, and banking services can be used for financial resources. Students may bring in articles they find. Mount the articles and ads in the appropriate categories.

Teaching Materials

Text, pages 492-526

Terms to Know, To Review, To Do, and *To Think About*

Student Activity Guide

   A. *Dealing with Crisis*
   B. *Crisis Crossword*
   C. *The Crisis of Alcoholism*
   D. *Teenage Gambling*
   E. *Missing Children*
   F. *Teen Suicide*

Teacher's Resource Guide/Binder

How Would You Handle the Crisis? reproducible master, 21-1

Steps to Follow in Coping with a Crisis, transparency master, 21-2

Domestic Violence, reproducible master, 21-3

Child Abuse and Neglect, reproducible master, 21-4

Chapter 21 Test

Teacher's Resource Binder

Resources for Handling Crises, color transparency, CT-21

Software for Contemporary Living

Chapter Review Game

Introductory Activities

1. Have your students experience a "small crisis" with the following activity. When your students arrive for class, ask them to get out a piece of paper and put all their books away. You're going to give them a pop quiz. When everyone appears to be ready, ask them to write down the feelings they are now experiencing with the announcement of the quiz. Do they feel you are taking advantage of them? Do they feel ready to take the test? Do they think their classmates are ready? How can they vent their displeasure?

   This is an example of a "small crisis." Discuss with students how they felt and how they reacted to the crisis. Compare this small crisis to a major one which they may have experienced. What were their physical reactions? What were their emotional reactions?

2. *How Would You Handle the Crisis?* reproducible master, 21-1. Have the students in your class work in small groups on this assignment. Each group will have a different crisis to "handle" while this chapter is being studied. Make photocopies of the reproducible masters; then cut the cards apart. Each group of students will draw a card to determine their assignment. Allow at least a week for them to work on their projects.

   Each group is to devise a plan to handle their crisis situation. Be certain that they explain how each of the resources to help deal with crises can be utilized in handling their situation. These include mental resources, physical health, family members, financial resources, friends, and community resources.

They should also answer the additional questions included on their cards. Students may need to interview persons in community and government agencies who are trained to handle such crises. Library or Internet research may be necessary. When the projects are completed, have the students prepare reports for the class and discuss.

Strategies to Reteach, Reinforce, Enrich, and Extend Text Concepts

Resources to Help Withstand Crises

3. **RT** *Resources for Handling Crises,* color transparency, CT-21. Use this transparency to review the various resources available to help withstand a crisis.

4. **RF** *Dealing with Crisis,* Activity A, SAG. Students are given a list of crises and are to rank them according to the impact they would have on a young adult. Given another list of crises, they are to rank them according to the impact they would have on a marriage. They are to then discuss how various resources can be called upon to help deal with a crisis situation.

5. **RT** Ask students to cite types of crises that young people may face. Discuss how the way they handle these crises can affect their future.

6. **RF** From newspapers and magazines, have students collect articles that describe crises. Identify what resources could be utilized to meet each of the crises.

7. **ER** Ask students to research incidences where individuals in crisis situations have been able to perform with increased strength. Explain how the body responds to the need.

8. **RF** The old adage, "Save for a rainy day," is a simple formula for building financial reserves in case of a crisis. How important is this, and what are the ways individuals and families can develop and protect financial resources?

9. **RF** Roles in a family can change due to a crisis. Ask students to cite how roles may change for the various members of a family in the following situations: a school-age child is diagnosed with juvenile arthritis; father is injured and will be off work for a year; mother has a nervous breakdown; teenage

son has a car accident and requires hospital care and physical therapy.

10. **RF** Parents may try to shield children from knowing about a family crisis. Should children be informed? If they are not informed, what problems may occur? In what ways might children help during a crisis?

11. **ER** Businesses are recognizing that workers are more productive if they are not bothered by personal problems. Have students research local businesses to see how many provide counseling services as a fringe benefit for their employees. Describe how these work.

12. **ER** Many people have faced crises in their lives and have gained greater strength because of their experiences. Cite examples of famous people from history, such as Helen Keller and Beethoven. Ask students to give examples of people who have recently been in the news and have dealt with crises.

13. **RF** Family members and neighbors were the main support during a crisis in the early years of our country. How has this changed?

14. **EX** Have students research community resources that are available for families who face crises. Have students contact city and county offices and obtain copies of directories that list community resources for dealing with crises. Ask groups of students to contact each of the resources to secure more information. Record the name, phone number, address, and contact person, along with a brief description of the services offered. File the information and make it available to all students.

15. **RF** How can telephone hotlines help individuals and family members in a crisis situation? What hotlines are available in your area?

16. **RF** If intervention is needed, how does a family find a trained professional to handle the intervention? What is the goal of this process? How do families cooperate in achieving this goal?

17. **RF** How can support groups be of benefit to family members facing a particular crisis? Research those available in your area.

Coping with Crises

18. **RT** *Steps to Follow in Coping with a Crisis,* transparency master, 21-2. Use this transparency to review the steps to follow in coping with a crisis.

19. **RT** Discuss why it is sometimes difficult for families or individuals to recognize that they do have a crisis.

20. **EX** How might a family go about identifying alternative solutions? Have students role-play a family conference where solutions to a crisis are sought.

21. **EX** Discuss how goals may need to be adjusted due to such crises as the following: teen is arrested for drug use; serious illness of a family member; teen becomes pregnant; wage earner dies; wage earner becomes unemployed. Have students give other examples of crises and how goals might need to be adjusted.

Seeking Stability in Crisis

22. **RF** *Crisis Crossword,* Activity B, SAG. Use this activity to review students' understanding of terms used in this chapter.

Unemployment

23. **EX** Have students role-play the following situation involving unemployment: Mr. Matthews has been laid off. His children are resentful because they know they will have to do without some things they want to buy.

24. **EX** Have students look in the classified ad section of a local newspaper. Determine which types of jobs are in demand. List five jobs which require specific training. If the markets in those areas are low, what happens to people trained in those areas? List five jobs which require general training. What alternatives does a person with general training have when looking for a job? What are the pros and cons of general and specific training?

25. **EX** Discuss how family members can support each other when a wage earner loses his or her job. How can teens offer assistance to family members at this time?

Frequent Moves

26. **EX** Ask students to research the number of times the average family moves. Also have students take a poll in your school to determine the number of times students have moved, what problems they faced, and what positive benefits they derived. Discuss how

students in elementary school, middle school, and high school can be made to feel welcome when they enter a new school at midyear.

27. **EX** Ask students to role-play the following: Father is being transferred to a new location. Mother is upset about leaving her home, and the children worry about leaving friends. Discuss what the family can do to make the move more appealing to all family members. Research community agencies that help families who are moving into your community.

Addictions to Alcohol and Other Drugs

28. **EX** *The Crisis of Alcoholism,* Activity C, SAG. Students are to review several statements concerning alcoholism. Then they are to work in small groups and discuss their reactions to the statements. Combine the best ideas and write the group's reactions to three of the statements.
29. **RF** Ask students to accept or reject the statement, "Alcohol causes alcoholism." Does this put the responsibility on the individual?
30. **EX** Ask a drug abuse counselor to speak to the class about addiction to alcohol and drugs. Have students formulate a list of questions prior to the speaker's visit.
31. **RF** Discuss how a teen's drug addiction affects the entire family. How are children affected when a parent is addicted? What resources are available for children?
32. **RF** How does a family member become an enabler for an addict? Cite typical behaviors.
33. **EX** Investigate the resources available for individuals and families affected by alcohol and drug addiction. Cite both private and community agencies, the costs of their services, their methods of treatment, etc. Assemble a file of information that will be available to all students.

Compulsive Gambling

34. **EX** *Teenage Gambling,* Activity D, SAG. Students are to answer questions concerning gambling among teens.
35. **RT** Review the four phases that the compulsive gambler goes through. How can a person get hooked on gambling?
36. **RT** What is chasing? Bailout? How do these serve to create an even more serious crisis?

37. **EX** Research how state governments have added to the gambling problem by sponsoring state lotteries and legalizing gambling in specific locations. How has this benefited the general population? How has this harmed individuals and families? How has this affected crime rates?

Depression

38. **EX** Ask a psychiatrist to speak to the class about depression. Have students prepare a list of questions.
39. **RF** Review what you should do if you suspect a family member or friend is suffering from depression.
40. **RF** Discuss the incidence of depression among teenagers. Is this an adult illness or can it occur at any age?

Suicide

41. **EX** *Teen Suicide,* Activity F, SAG. Students are to read the statements about teen suicide and indicate whether they think each statement is a myth or a truth. They can then turn to the back of the page to check their responses. Use the statements as a basis for class discussion.
42. **RF** Ask students the following: If a friend hinted of suicide, what would you do? When a person feels depressed, why is it important to talk with someone?
43. **EX** Assemble a file of resources available in your community for dealing with the problems of depression and suicide. Cite both private and community resources, the types of services they offer, the costs of their services, the time required for treatment, etc. Make the file available for students.

Criminal Attack

44. **RF** Ask students to describe precautions young persons can take to prevent criminal attack in their homes, in public areas, at work, and when driving. Draw up a safety code and post on the bulletin board.
45. **ER** Research incidences of criminal attack reported in newspapers. Try to analyze the victims' actions that may have led to the attacks and what precautions they might have taken to prevent the attacks. Discuss the

probable outcomes of the cases if charges were filed.

46. **RF** Discuss community efforts to prevent the incidence of criminal attack, such as local police protection, neighborhood patrol groups, "safe homes" for children walking to and from school, increased lighting in parking lots, etc.

47. **RF** Discuss the two kinds of rapists, and what seems to be the focus of their feelings when they commit this violent act.

Violent Behavior in Families

48. **EX** *Domestic Violence*, reproducible master, 21-3. Use this master to lead the class in a discussion of the factors that contribute to domestic violence. Either make a transparency or give each student a copy of the master. First ask students to identify contributing factors in each of the four categories. Some factors are discussed in the text, but you may want students to read other references for additional factors and record their findings on this form. Factors to include might be the following:

Culture–male as authority figure is generally accepted; boys are encouraged to be aggressive and girls are to be passive; in some cultures the wife and children are regarded as property of husband.

Society–people lead more isolated lives; relatives may be far away; availability of help is limited; violence in media is familiar and accepted.

Individual–abuser may feel need to demonstrate physical dominance; abuser and/or victim may have witnessed or experienced abuse as a child; abuser may be having difficulties in other aspects of life and take out anger at home.

Families–male/female roles are changing; family problems involving finances, children, etc., may lead to abuse.

Following a discussion of the factors contributing to domestic violence, ask students to suggest solutions related to each of these areas. Record ideas on a new form or transparency.

49. **RF** Review the cycle of violence. How can escalation following a triggering event, which brings on violence, be stopped through conflict resolution, as described in Chapter 10?

50. **RF** Review the legal rights of victims of domestic violence in the civil court as discussed on page 517 of the text. Since rules vary from state to state, find out what the rules are in your state and share with the class. Aggravated battery charges may be brought against an abuser, but this must be done in a criminal court. Review procedures for making a criminal charge.

51. **RF** Discuss the three phases of spouse/partner abuse. Why do victims of spouse/partner abuse often stay or return? What is often the result?

52. **RF** Review the three ways the elderly might be abused. How can they defend themselves? Who can help them? What are the pressures that sometimes lead a person to abuse an elderly person?

53. **EX** Have students research how child abuse is handled by the authorities in your area. Find out what procedures are followed in approaching the parents, what charges can be brought, what counseling assistance is made available, etc.

54. **EX** Ask class members to collect newspaper and magazine articles concerning child abuse and neglect. Post these on a bulletin board and use them as the basis for class discussion. Evaluate the situations as to the possible causes of the abuse, types of abuse, how the abuse was revealed, the condition of the children, and who the active and passive abusers were.

55. **RF** Ask students to accept or reject the statement, "Child abuse and neglect are not planned." If this is true, what causes child abuse to occur? What can be done to help eliminate the conditions that bring on the abuse?

56. **EX** Ask a person from a child welfare or protection agency to speak to the class about child abuse. Have students prepare a list of questions before the speaker arrives.

57. **RF** Discuss how a person should report a suspected case of child abuse. What is the role of the schools? What is the role of the doctor who suspects child abuse? How is this information being gathered nationally? What is being done in your local community to reduce the incidence of child abuse? Are there any group therapy programs available locally for parents who may suspect they have child abuse tendencies and want help before they harm their children?

58. **EX**   Assemble a file of information concerning child abuse and neglect. Make the file available to all students.
59. **RT**   *Child Abuse and Neglect,* reproducible master, 21-4. Use this activity to review terms related to child abuse and neglect and to evaluate students' understanding of procedures to follow in the case of suspected child abuse.

Missing Children

60. **EX**   *Missing Children,* Activity E, SAG. Students are to indicate whether they agree or disagree with statements concerning the issue of missing children. Discuss their responses in class.
61. **RF**   Authorities stress to parents that it is not just the stranger, but the situation that should be feared. Discuss how parents can teach their children to protect themselves from being abducted, including situations where the child knows the abductor.
62. **ER**   Have students research the laws that have been passed dealing with missing children, such as the Missing Children Act of 1982. How is information about missing children handled?
63. **ER**   Have students research agencies that assist in finding missing children. Write to the *National Center for Missing and Exploited Children,* 2101 Wilson Boulevard, Suite 550, Arlington, VA, 22201, or call (800) 843-5678 for information about the problem of missing and exploited children, and for a list of groups located throughout the country organized to assist children and their parents.
64. **EX**   New techniques for identification of children are being used by parents. Ask students to find out if the following methods are available in your area and how helpful they feel each method would be.
    - Fingerprinting: Helpful if a child is injured or is abducted.
    - Dental technology: A microfilm disk or a stainless steel data wafer, containing vital information about the child, can be bonded to the back side of a tooth, visible only to an examining dentist. In addition, a national computer bank of dental information can be accessed.
    - ID tags: Tags can be attached to shoelaces.
65. **ER**   Ask a speaker from the police department to speak on the problem of missing persons. What procedures are followed when a child is reported missing? How often does parental kidnapping occur?

Runaways

66. **EX**   Discuss running away from home–the causes and effects. Consider the reasons cited for running away, and analyze how problems could be handled in other ways. Where do runaways find refuge, and how safe are these places? Discuss the telephone service called "Operation Peace of Mind." Do students agree with its premise?
67. **EX**   Ask volunteers to role-play a family situation in which a teenager has run away. Reveal the effects this has on the father, mother, sister, and brother. Discuss the feelings of everyone involved.

Answer Key for Chapter 21

Text
To Review, page 524.

1. false
2. An intervention is a means of forcing a person to look at his or her behavior without the mask of denial. The aim of intervention is to convince the individual, such as an addict or alcoholic, that he or she needs help before he or she "hits bottom." This is done by bringing together family members and other important people in the person's life. These people speak truthfully, out of love, confronting the addict with specific details of his or her problem. The outcome in successful intervention is that the person admits the problem and voluntarily enters treatment.
3. Recognize the existence of a crisis. Seek alternative solutions to the crisis. Look to each other for support. Resume efforts to achieve personal and family goals.
4. When the security of their home is threatened, a feeling of vulnerability surrounds the entire family. They are not sure what the future will hold.
5. (Student response.)
6. (Student response.)
7. Once the gambler begins losing, he or she attempts to get back what was lost. He or she uses savings or money needed for necessities to try to win back losses–to chase the losses.

8. Sleeping problems, loss of appetite, decline in energy, feelings of worthlessness, and a general feeling of hopelessness.
9. Persons who commit suicide impulsively, those who complain constantly and feel that life is not worthwhile, those who are seriously ill, and those who have lost loved ones.
10. (List three. Student response.)
11. Phase one: Tension builds over a series of small incidents. Phase two: Violence occurs involving physical abuse. Phase three: The honeymoon stage when the abuser realizes his or her mistake and asks for forgiveness.
12. physical neglect
13. false
14. A breakdown of family communications.

Student Activity Guide

Activity B, *Crisis Crossword.*

Across:
1. DIVORCE
3. UNEMPLOYMENT
8. ABUSE
9. NEGLECT
10. ALCOHOLIC
13. RUNAWAY
14. INTERVENTION
15. SHELTERS
16. ELDER
17. INCEST

Down:
1. DEPRESSION
2. COMPULSIVE
4. MOVES
5. HOTLINE
6. BAILOUT
7. SUICIDE
10. ABDUCTED
11. SPOUSE
12. ENABLER
13. RAP

Teacher's Resource Guide

Child Abuse and Neglect, reproducible master, 21-4.

1. Child abuse.
2. Physical abuse.
3. Physical neglect.
4. Sexual abuse.
5. Emotional abuse.
6. Passive abuse.
7. Cycling effect.
8. Immature.
9-14. (Student response.)

Chapter 21 Test

1. J	13. F	25. T
2. K	14. T	26. A
3. I	15. T	27. C
4. C	16. F	28. D
5. G	17. F	29. A
6. E	18. T	30. B
7. B	19. F	31. D
8. D	20. T	32. D
9. A	21. F	33. A
10. H	22. F	34. C
11. F	23. F	35. D
12. F	24. T	

36. (List four:) Mental resources, physical health, family relationships, financial resources, friends, community resources. Student response for an example of how each resource can be used during a crisis. (See pages 494-499 of text.)
37. Recognize the existence of a crisis.
Seek alternative solutions to the crisis.
Look to each other for support.
Resume efforts to achieve personal and family goals.
38. (Student response to briefly describe each of the phases:) Phase 1: Tension-Building Stage. Phase 2: Violent Incident. Phase 3: "Honeymoon" Stage.
39. (Name four: Student response.)

How Would You Handle the Crisis?

Various crises are described on the cards that follow. Cut the cards apart on the dotted lines. Have students work in small groups. Each group of students will draw a card and devise a plan to handle the crisis. They should explain how mental resources, physical health, family relationships, financial resources, friends, community services, and government agencies can all be called upon to help in dealing with the crisis. Students should also answer the questions listed on their cards. Have the students work on their projects while the class studies the chapter (or allow one week). Then have them share their reports with the class and discuss.

. . . .

Unemployed

George works as a foreman in a steel mill. Nina, his wife, has always done volunteer work in the community. Pat is a senior in high school and plans to go to college when he graduates. Pam is a freshman in high school. They have $20,000 in a savings fund.

Crisis: George comes home with a "pink slip." He has lost his job.

How can the family sustain their mental and physical health?

How can they meet daily living expenses?

Should temporary work be sought by George?

Should George research the job market and seek additional training?

How can family debts be consolidated?

Will Pat have to change his plans?

Will Nina have to seek a paying job?

Can the family collect unemployment benefits?

. . . .

A Family Moves

Lyle has worked as a salesman for many years. His wife, Vicky, got a job last year as an elementary school teacher. They have three children: Jon, 14, Penny, 10, and Shenice, 4.

Crisis: Lyle has been promoted to regional sales manager. He will have to move immediately from the west coast to Cleveland, Ohio.

How might this news affect mental and physical health of family members?

What are the negative and positive aspects of this move?

Should Vicky's job be a factor in the decision to move?

How can the children's fears and concerns about the move be alleviated?

What school and medical records need to be obtained for the children?

How will the house be sold? How can a house be found in the new location?

How is a moving company contracted? Who packs?

. . . .

(Continued)

Alcoholism

Debra and Charles have been married for 10 years. They have two children. Danielle is eight and Peter is seven. Charles must travel frequently on company business. Debra works part time, and changes jobs often.

Crisis: Charles is concerned that Debra is becoming an alcoholic.

How might Debra's ability to care for her children be affected by her drinking problem?

How might the children feel?

How might Debra's job be affected?

How can Charles help Debra to recognize that she has a problem?

What resources can they seek in helping them both and their children?

Compulsive Gambling

Michelle and Larry have been married for eight years and are trying to save money to buy a home. They both are employed. They have put all of their savings into stocks and mutual funds. Recently, however, Michelle has had trouble paying their household bills.

Crisis: Michelle finds a statement from their broker indicating that all of their stocks and mutual funds have been sold. When Michelle confronts Larry, he confesses that he has used all of their savings to pay off gambling debts. He told her he started gambling because he thought he could raise the money for a home faster that way. Larry told Michelle that at first he gambled only with a part of his weekly paycheck. After awhile, he started dipping into their savings.

How can Michelle help Larry to recognize that he has a problem?

Can anyone make Larry see the fallacy of trying to win "big" money?

Can Michelle talk to anyone about how she should respond to her husband's gambling problem?

Where can they go for help with their financial problems?

Can they both seek help from self-help groups?

Suicide

Mike is worried about his best friend, Shawn. Ever since Mike has known him, Shawn has wanted to be the best in everything he did. He always wanted to get the best grades, be the best athlete, have the lead in school plays, and date the most popular girl in school. Now that they both will soon be graduating from high school, Shawn wants to attend the best college in his field. Last week he received a letter of rejection from the college he wanted to attend. Then, Saturday night, his girlfriend said she wanted to stop seeing him.

Crisis: Shawn has hinted to Mike that he no longer has anything to live for.

What should Mike do?

What could Mike say to Shawn?

Considering Shawn's background, what might have led to this crisis?

What resources might be sought in order to help Shawn?

(Continued)

Criminal Attack

Camille lives in an apartment in a large city. The neighborhood in which she lives has been the site of several criminal attacks recently. Camille leaves her apartment unlocked when she runs down to the laundry room of the basement, knowing she'll be gone only a few minutes.

Crisis: Camille returns to her apartment and is attacked and robbed.

What immediate help must Camille seek?

What procedures do police follow in an assault case?

If the attacker is caught, can Camille be reimbursed for her medical expenses and financial losses?

What can neighbors and friends do to assure greater security in the area?

What precautions should Camille take so that this will not happen again?

How can Camille's emotional health be restored?

. . . .

Sexual Assault

Cindy was in training for the high school track team. She frequently went jogging in the park. One evening, a man came running up behind her. When they neared some bushes, he grabbed her and pulled her into the bushes. She tried to fight back, but he was too strong.

Crisis: Cindy was attacked and raped. The man fled. She struggled to pull her clothes back on and walked to the nearest house. Her parents were called.

What should Cindy and her parents do first?

How can the rape be reported?

Why is it important to call the police right away?

What medical examinations are needed?

What precautions should Cindy have taken that might have prevented this crime?

What general precautions should people take to prevent being raped by a stranger?

What resources are available in most communities to help rape victims?

. . . .

Spouse Abuse

When Alice met Owen, she was impressed with his masculine strength and "take-charge" attitude. She soon discovered he also had a violent temper, but she never thought he would use it against her. He always treated her like a princess, and didn't even want her to have to work. After they were married, everything began to change. They had three children right away. Owen's job was very demanding, yet he wanted very much to be a success. He began taking his frustrations out on Alice by slapping her around. After each incident, Owen felt guilty and asked Alice for forgiveness.

Crisis: Owen is fired. He beats Alice, blaming her for all of their problems.

What immediate help should Alice seek?

What long-term help should Alice seek?

Identify the three phases of spouse abuse as they relate to this couple.

Why do you think Alice didn't do anything about the abuse when it began?

What factors might have led to the violence?

How might the children be affected?

Should Alice seek a divorce?

. . . .

(Continued)

Child Abuse

Holly and Powell have two small children. Powell's sister stops by their home once a week for a visit. She has become concerned with frequent "accidents" that have harmed the children, but she has said nothing.

Crisis: The three-year-old child has been taken to the hospital emergency room with a broken arm and bruises to the head. The doctor suspects child abuse.

What can the doctor do to help the family?

Should the doctor report what he suspects?

What legal action might be taken?

How can the children be protected from further abuse?

What could Powell's sister have done? What can she do now?

What community resources are available to help both the children and their parents?

. . . .

Missing Children

Celeste and Howard have two young children. Celeste takes them with her to the shopping mall. Philip, age six, wants to stay in the toy department of the department store while Celeste takes the two-year-old with her to shop for clothes. Celeste tells Philip to stay in the toy department until she returns.

Crisis: When Celeste returns to the toy department, Philip is nowhere in sight.

What procedures should Celeste follow?

What procedures do the police follow in the case of a missing child?

What can parents do to protect their children from abduction?

What new programs are available to parents to help locate and identify their children if an abduction should occur?

. . . .

Steps to Follow in Coping with a Crisis

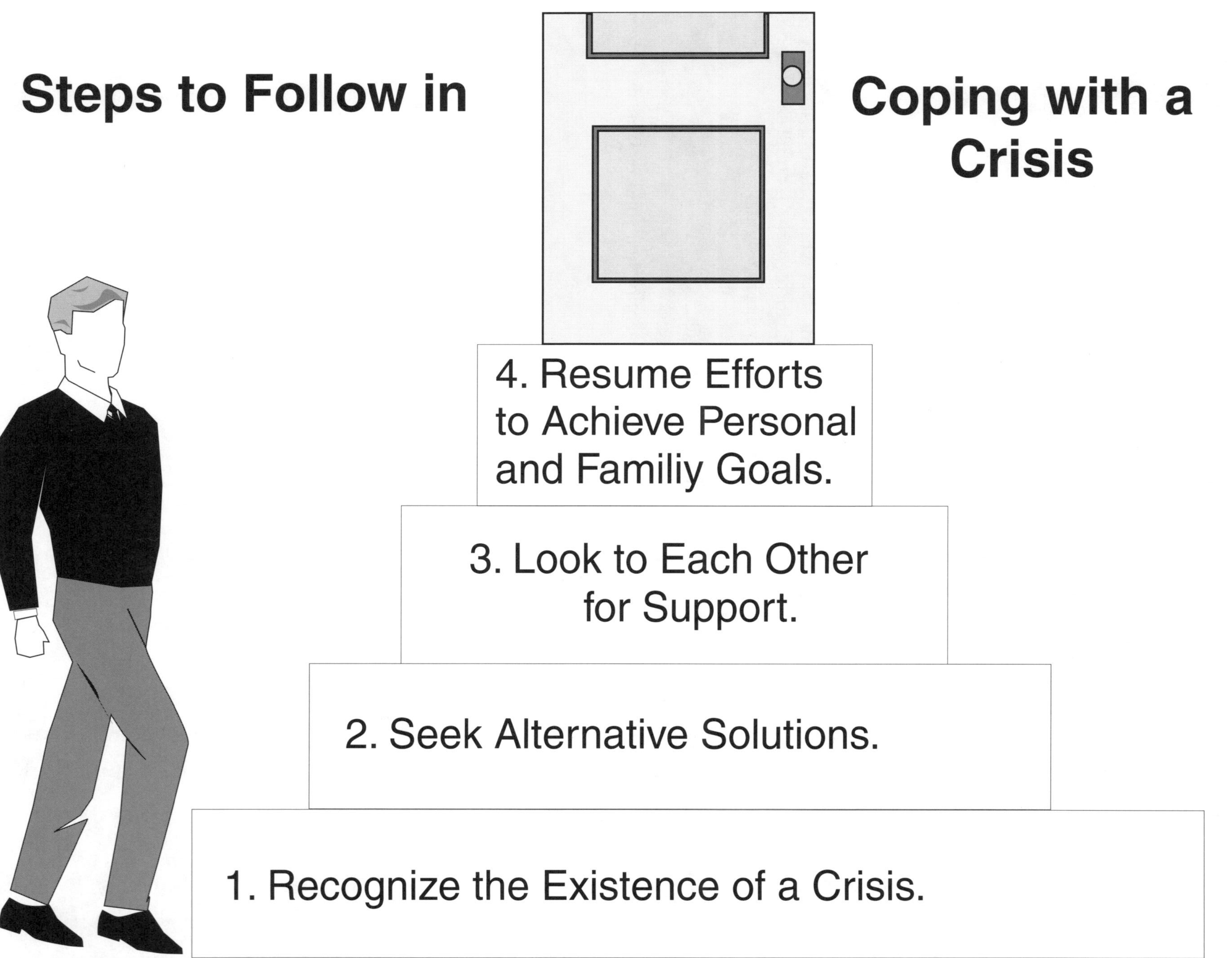

Domestic Violence

Causes: Cite factors that contribute to domestic violence in each of the following categories.

Solutions: How can cultural influences be altered to help reduce domestic violence? What can society, individuals, and families do to reduce domestic violence?

Culture	Society

Individuals	Families

Child Abuse and Neglect

Name _________________________________ **Date** ______________ **Period** ______________

Read the following case situation and fill in the blanks with the correct terms. Then answer the questions that follow.

Dawn and Gus live near Dawn's brother, Kurt, and his wife, Beth. Kurt and Beth have two children. Dawn and Gus are becoming concerned about how they treat their children. Dawn has begun to do some research into the problem of child abuse. She and Gus want to be careful they don't accuse the parents falsely of such a serious offense. Dawn has learned that any physical or mental injury, sexual abuse, negligent treatment, or maltreatment of a child under age 18 by a person who is responsible for the child's welfare may be defined as _________(1)_________.

1. _______________________

Dawn and Gus have seen Kurt discipline Troy several times. His strong slaps to the face and wringing of the boy's arms could be described as _________(2)_________.

2. _______________________

Dawn also remembers a neighbor of Beth's telling her that the children often come to her house asking for food. This could be a form of _________(3)_________. Dawn also read that forcing a child to engage in sexual activities was called _________(4)_________, although they have no reason to suspect this is occurring. They have seen Kurt continually and severely criticize his daughter for failing to live up to his standards. This could be referred to as _________(5)_________. Dawn and Gus have never seen Beth physically harm the children, but she stands by when Kurt is punishing them and does nothing to protect them. This is evidence of _________(6)_________.

3. _______________________

4. _______________________

5. _______________________

6. _______________________

Dawn remembers that Kurt was often hit and verbally reprimanded by their father. This would indicate a _________(7)_________ which is often found in cases of child abuse. Kurt married Beth when they were both quite young to escape his father's wrath. Beth got pregnant right away and they were perhaps too _________(8)_________ to handle the demands of parenthood.

7. _______________________

8. _______________________

9. What should Dawn and Gus do? ____

____

____

10. Where should they go to report their suspicions? _______________________________

____

____

(Continued)

Name ____

11. What procedures will be followed? ____

____

____

12. How can doctors detect signs of repeated child abuse and what can they do about it?_______________

____

____

____

13. What might happen if Dawn and Gus suspected abuse, but did nothing about it? _______________

____

____

____

14. What might happen if Dawn and Gus suspected abuse, reported it, and it was determined that no abuse was occurring? ____

____

____

____

Dealing with Family Crises

Date ____ Period ____________ Score ______________

Chapter 21 Test

Matching: Match the following terms and identifying phrases.

_______ 1. Forcing a person to engage in sexual activities.

_______ 2. A set of unhealthy behaviors learned by family members in order to survive great emotional pain and stress.

_______ 3. When parents continually make demands that their children are incapable of meeting, followed by criticism and humiliation.

_______ 4. A crucial time or event that causes a change in a person's life.

_______ 5. Failure to provide children with love and affection.

_______ 6. A gambler's attempts to win back what he or she lost.

_______ 7. Means of forcing an addict to honestly look at his or her behavior.

_______ 8. Failure to provide sufficient food, clothing, shelter, medical care, education, guidance, and supervision for a child.

_______ 9. Someone who unknowingly acts in ways that contribute to an addict's drug use.

_______ 10. The infliction of physical injury.

A. enabler
B. intervention
C. crisis
D. physical neglect
E. chasing
F. bailout
G. emotional neglect
H. physical abuse
I. emotional abuse
J. sexual abuse
K. codependency

True/False: Circle *T* if the statement is true or *F* if the statement is false.

T   F   11. When a family has a crisis, it means the end to happiness and achievement.

T   F   12. The majority of personal bankruptcies are the result of gambling, which creates a large monetary need.

T   F   13. Telephone hotlines operate only during normal business hours.

T   F   14. Support groups are made up of persons or family members who have experienced a similar crisis situation.

T   F   15. In some cases, a crisis might not be immediately recognizable.

T   F   16. When a person becomes unemployed, creditors ask for immediate payment of outstanding bills.

T   F   17. When a family is told they have to move, family members feel a sense of excitement.

T   F   18. Those who begin abusing drugs usually start with marijuana.

T   F   19. When family members "help" an alcoholic with his or her problem, the addiction generally ends sooner.

(Continued)

Contemporary Living Teacher's Resources

T F 20. Gambling has been legalized in many states to raise revenues, but it has actually had the opposite effect.

T F 21. Chronic depression lasts for only a few months.

T F 22. In the last 25 years, the rate of suicide among teenagers has decreased dramatically.

T F 23. If, when you return home, you find your door open or unlocked, go in and call the police.

T F 24. A sexual assault by a stranger is more likely to be violent in nature.

T F 25. A child who is abused is more likely to grow up to be an abusive parent.

Multiple Choice: Choose the best response. Write the letter in the space provided.

______ 26. When a family experiences a crisis, ______.
   A. children usually want to help their family
   B. children should not be told because they would not understand
   C. the family is usually pulled apart
   D. the roles of family members remain stable

______ 27. Following a crisis, all personal and family goals ______.
   A. will have to be forgotten
   B. can be attained as planned
   C. can be achieved, but some may need to be adjusted
   D. will no longer be needed

______ 28. Which of these tactics is recommended for family members of an alcoholic?
   A. Bribe the alcoholic to stop drinking by making a deal with him or her.
   B. Handle the responsibilities the alcoholic is unable to fulfill.
   C. Call in sick for the alcoholic if he or she is unable to go to work.
   D. Stop any enabling behaviors and get professional help.

______ 29. Select the true statement concerning compulsive gambling.
   A. Once a gambler begins losing, chasing often begins.
   B. Family members and friends should help the gambler by offering a bailout.
   C. Compulsive gamblers are not as prone to commit other crimes.
   D. A compulsive gambler can quit at any time.

______ 30. Depression ______.
   A. affects only the mind
   B. is usually treated with a combination of medication and psychological therapy
   C. cannot be treated
   D. has very specific and easily recognized symptoms

______ 31. If a friend has hinted about suicide, you should ______.
   A. ignore the comment to prevent him or her from thinking any more about it
   B. give your friend advice on handling the problem
   C. ignore the comment because most people who talk about suicide never commit it
   D. suggest to your friend that he or she should seek professional help

______ 32. If your car stalls, you should ______.
   A. leave the car immediately and walk to the nearest house to call for help
   B. get out and raise the hood. Then return to the car and lock yourself inside. Turn on the flashing hazard lights and wait for help
   C. wait until someone comes. Then get out of the car and show the person what is wrong
   D. stay in the car. Do not raise the hood, but do turn on the flashing hazard lights

(Continued)

_____ 33. Select the true statement concerning sexual assault.
   A. Younger rape victims are more often raped by relatives or acquaintances.
   B. In all cases of sexual assault, sexual gratification is the primary motivation.
   C. A rapist is always easy to spot.
   D. Sexual assaults are usually reported to the authorities.

_____ 34. Select the true statement concerning domestic violence.
   A. Most domestic violence is committed by husbands.
   B. Verbal abuse is not considered a form of domestic violence.
   C. Anger and frustration are the emotions that form the core of most domestic violence.
   D. Experts agree that violence at home does not lead children to act violently outside the home.

_____ 35. Select the true statement concerning child abuse.
   A. The abusive parent usually does not seek medical attention for the injured child.
   B. Almost all abused children are under age four.
   C. When child abuse occurs in a family with two parents, usually only one parent is abusive.
   D. Child sexual abusers generally use bribes and threats instead of physical force.

Essay Questions: Provide complete responses to the following questions or statements.

36. Name four resources that help people withstand crises. Give an example of how each resource can be used during a crisis.

37. List the four steps to follow in coping with a crisis.

38. Briefly describe the three phases of spouse or partner abuse.

39. Name four precautions parents can take to prevent their children from being abducted.

Chapter 22
Divorce and Remarriage

Objectives

After studying this chapter, students will be able to
- explain possible reasons for the high rate of divorce in the United States.
- summarize the differences between annulment, legal separation, and divorce.
- list the basic procedures, grounds, defenses, and terms of agreement typically used in divorce proceedings.
- explain the adjustments faced by divorced persons.
- describe the challenges faced by blended families.

Bulletin Boards

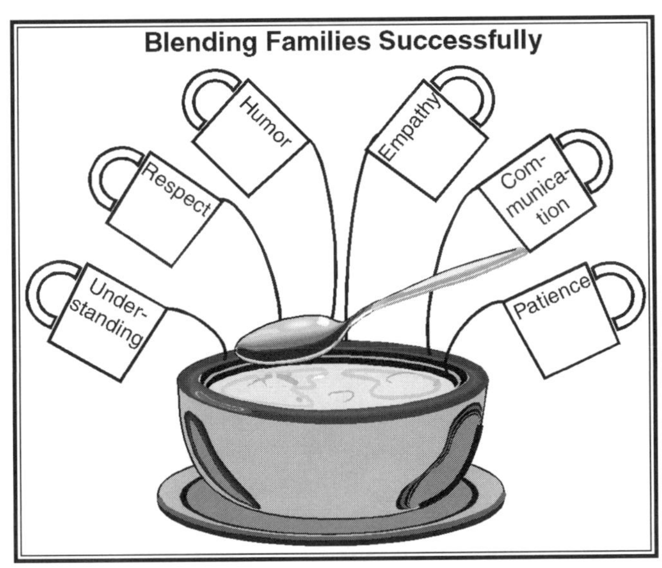

I. Title: "Blending Families Successfully"

Draw on brightly colored construction paper a mixing bowl with a spoon handle protruding from it. Cut it out and place it on a bulletin board. Use strands of brightly colored yarn to connect the top of the bowl with construction paper shapes labeled as follows: *Understanding, Respect, Humor, Empathy, Communication, Patience.*

II. Title: "Divorce Issues"

Tear in half vertically a magazine photo of a couple on their wedding day. Place the two pieces in the center of the bulletin board on a white background. Use strands of black yarn to connect the picture with paper rectangles surrounding the picture. Label rectangles as follows: *Child Custody, Visitation Rights, Child Support, Property Settlement, New Living Arrangements, Emotional Adjustments, Counseling, Legal Expenses.*

Teaching Materials

Text, pages 528-543

Terms to Know, To Review, To Do, and *To Think About*

Student Activity Guide

    A. *Views on Divorce*
    B. *Legal Termination of Marriage*
    C. *Divorce Issues*
    D. *Blending Families*

Teacher's Resource Guide/Binder

U.S. Divorce and Marriage Rates, 1940-1995, transparency master, 22-1

Divorce Rates in Selected Industrialized Countries, 1960-1990, transparency master, 22-2

Divorce Laws in Your State, reproducible master, 22-3

Financial Aspects of Divorce, reproducible master, 22-4

Outwitted, transparency master, 22-5

Divorce Facts: Review Cards, reproducible master, 22-6

Chapter 22 Test

Teacher's Resource Binder

Marital Status of the U.S. Population Ages 25-44, 1960 and 1998, color transparency, CT-22A

Custody Arrangements, color transparency, CT-22B

Software for Contemporary Living

Chapter Review Game

Introductory Activities

1. *U.S. Divorce and Marriage Rates, 1940-1995,* transparency master, 22-1. Use this graph to point out the remarkable increase in the divorce rate since 1940. Ask students to name a few reasons for this increase (Availability of more effective birth control, women's greater financial independence). Ask students to speculate why the rate seems to have reached a plateau in recent years (Fewer divorces are associated with the current aging population).

2. *Divorce Rates in Selected Industrialized Countries, 1960-1990,* transparency master, 22-2. Use this graph to illustrate the increases in divorce rates experienced by selected industrialized countries since 1960. Discuss with students reasons why the divorce rates in other countries are lower than in the United States (Greater social stigma associated with divorce; greater tolerance of extramarital relationships; lower marriage rates).

3. Ask students to name three issues that could pose challenges in a remarriage without children and three more issues that could pose challenges in a remarriage with children from one or more previous marriages.

Strategies to Reteach, Reinforce, Enrich, and Extend Text Concepts

Divorce Trends and Issues

4. **EX** *Views on Divorce,* Activity A, SAG. Ask students to complete the checklist, indicating their opinions about divorce. Use the responses as the basis for a class discussion.

5. **RF** If a couple goes into marriage thinking, "If it doesn't work out, we can always get a divorce," how can this attitude affect their marriage? On the other hand, if divorce were not an option in our society, how many couples do you think would still marry?

6. **RT** *Marital Status of the U.S. Population Ages 25-44, 1960 and 1998,* color transparency, CT-22A. Use this graph to point out the differences in marital status among today's young adults and those of 1960. Discuss reasons why more young people today are not married.

7. **EX** The following statements indicate possible causes for the rising divorce rate in our country. Write the statements on the board and instruct each student to write a brief reaction paper to one of them. Do the students agree with the statements? Can or should the trends be changed?

   - The changing roles of women have caused changes in the financial earnings and balance of power in many marriages.

   - Divorce no longer carries a stigma in our society.

   - Individuals no longer need a partner to give them an identity.

   - There is a great emphasis on personal freedom and independence in our society.

   - The role of religion in keeping marriages together has changed in our society.

   - Because of the permissive mood that began in the 60s and 70s, most couples no longer view marriage as a lifetime commitment.

   - People often expect marriage to provide complete fulfillment and solve all personal problems.

Legal Termination of Marriage

8. **ER** *Divorce Laws in Your State,* reproducible master, 22-3. Ask students to research divorce laws in your state and answer the questions. You may wish to arrange for them to interview a judge or a lawyer, or to have someone speak to the class on this subject.

9. **EX** Set up an imaginary divorce court and role-play divorce actions of various couples. Ask one class member to serve as the judge and others to serve as lawyers and persons

seeking divorce. In each case the judge should hand down a decision based on his or her views. Students should assess each decision.

10. **EX** *Divorce Issues,* Activity C, SAG. Instruct students to write their reactions to statements concerning divorce issues and settlements. Discuss responses.

11. **RF** *Financial Aspects of Divorce,* reproducible master, 22-4. Duplicate and distribute this activity and use it as a basis for class discussion. Stress the importance of looking into marriage before "leaping" into it.

12. **RF** Discuss monetary settlements in divorce actions, including the settlement of community and separate property claims, alimony, child support, and division of outstanding debts. What basis do the courts use for arriving at settlements? What financial problems may divorced people encounter? Do ex-spouses always pay child support? Can ex-spouses use legal action to enforce payment?

13. **RT** Divorce affects people of all ages and creates different concerns among the people involved. Discuss the concerns the following individuals might have: a middle-aged parent whose child is divorcing, an elderly parent whose child is divorcing, a young adult who is divorcing, a teenager whose parents are divorcing, a young child whose parents are divorcing, and a young couple with children who are divorcing.

14. **RF** Divide the class into small groups. Ask each group to develop a list of questions children might have when they learn that their parents are divorcing. Questions listed might include the following:
    * What will happen to me?
    * Is it my fault?
    * Who will feed me?
    * Can I get them back together?
    * Who will give me lunch money?
    * Will I ever see my parent again?

    Compare lists and discuss how parents should answer these questions.

15. **RF** Discuss how preschool, school-age, and adolescent children might react differently to the news of an impending parental divorce. For instance, they might deny the reality of the divorce, lie to conceal the divorce from friends, take the blame themselves, become angry or violent, run away from home, etc.

16. **RF** *Legal Termination of Marriage,* Activity B, SAG. Students can use this crossword puzzle to review terms found in this chapter.

17. **ER** Ask a divorce lawyer to speak to your class concerning divorce laws in your state. Ask questions about filing dates, procedures, residency requirements, contested and non-contested rules, grounds, alimony, and child support rulings.

18. **ER** Arrange for students to visit a divorce court and view divorce action proceedings. (Make arrangements with the court, judge, school administrators, and parents.)

19. **RT** *Custody Arrangements,* color transparency, CT-22B. Use this transparency to foster discussion of the four types of custody arrangements. Which type do students think is best for the average family?

20. **ER** Invite a family counselor to speak to your class about the effects divorce has on all members of a family. Ask him or her to discuss trends in child custody cases and the success of dual-custody cases. How do changes in financial and social matters generally affect fathers, mothers, young children, and teenage children.

21. **ER** Invite a marriage counselor to speak to students about divorce. Ask the counselor to explain how divorce affects family members. How can family members make the situation more bearable? What resources are available to help family members cope?

22. **ER** Invite a panel of divorced persons to talk to students about some of the problems they encountered during the divorce process.

23. **RF** *Divorce Facts: Review Cards,* reproducible master, 22-6. Photocopy and place the listed review questions on index cards. In small groups, students should quiz each other before the chapter test to review divorce information.

Remarriage

24. **RF** Statistics show that remarriages in which only one partner has been divorced are less likely to end in divorce than remarriages in which both partners have been divorced. Discuss with students possible reasons for this.

25. **RT** Discuss with students reasons why many counselors advise recently divorced persons to wait at least two years before remarrying.

26. **RT** Members of recently blended families often need to negotiate rules of behavior for their situations. For example, in Jan's previous marriage her teenage children were not expected to do household chores because Jan was a full-time homemaker. The same was true for the teenage children from her husband Ted's previous marriage. To make ends meet now, however, Jan must work full time in a job with considerable overtime. What new rules must Jan, Ted, and their children agree to? Students should list reasonable expectations for the teens and parents in this situation.

27. **EX** Ask students to discuss how they would feel if they suddenly had to share their home and family with new stepbrothers or stepsisters. What other issues would need to be resolved? What are some solutions?

28. **RT** One characteristic of blended families is that people who have been raised with different sets of values and rules must learn to live together. Discuss with students reasons why tolerance and understanding are especially important during the adjustment period.

29. **EX** *Outwitted*, transparency master, 22-5. Project this poem on the screen and read it aloud. Ask students to explain the basic message of the poem. How might it apply to members of newly blended families? Students should give examples of activities that could draw others into a family circle.

30. **EX** *Blending Families*, Activity D, SAG. Instruct students to read and respond to these case studies in writing. Discuss case studies and responses in class.

31. **EX** Research suggests that a remarried couple's difficulties with children of previous marriages are, on average, the greatest barriers to the success of their marriage. Why do you think this is so?

32. **RF** A common problem for children in blended families is building love for new parents and siblings without feeling guilty about taking love away from natural parents. Discuss this problem with students and brainstorm possible solutions.

33. **RF** How can blended families build new family traditions without upsetting previous traditions? Should new families drop old traditions? Discuss with students the importance of creating new family traditions.

Answer Key for Chapter 22

Text
To Review, page 542.

1. *Annulment,* which is a court order that states that a legal marriage never took place. *Divorce,* which is a legal dissolution of the marriage contract.

2. Moral decline, changing opportunities for women, a more urban society, less social stigma related to divorce, and greater emphasis on personal happiness.

3. A, B, and D.

4. A *legal separation* does not end a marriage but it does end a marriage relationship. A couple no longer lives together, but none of the marital rights and obligations are changed. The partners make a legal agreement to live apart, to divide their property, and to provide for their children. A *divorce* ends a marriage contract. The spouses consult lawyers and go through the legal issues of deciding property settlements and child custody. Spouses are free to marry again.

5. *No-fault divorces* eliminate the need for proving one partner guilty. They allow the couple to end the marriage by mutual agreement. This makes the divorce less bitter and less expensive.

6. A. incompatibility. B. separation. C. cruelty. D. drug or alcohol addiction.

7. *Condonation* means that once the "guilty" party has been condoned or forgiven for a certain action, that action cannot be the grounds for divorce. *Connivance* can be used as a defense when one person is guilty of causing the condition used as grounds for the divorce. *Collusion* occurs when a couple want a divorce but have no legal grounds, so they set up necessary grounds for divorce. They work together to plan a scheme that would make one partner appear guilty of something like desertion or adultery.

8. *Alimony* is the money paid by the primary wage earner to the other marriage partner during and after the divorce. *Child support* is money the non-custodial parent is required to pay toward the financial support of the children until the children are 18 years old.

9. Each former spouse must set up a separate household. Each needs a place to live, a car,

and furniture. If there are children, the custo-dial parent must meet the additional costs of the children's food, clothing, and special needs as they grow. The other parent may be responsible for child support and/or alimony.

10. (Describe two. Student response.)

Student Activity Guide

Activity B, *Legal Termination of Marriage.*

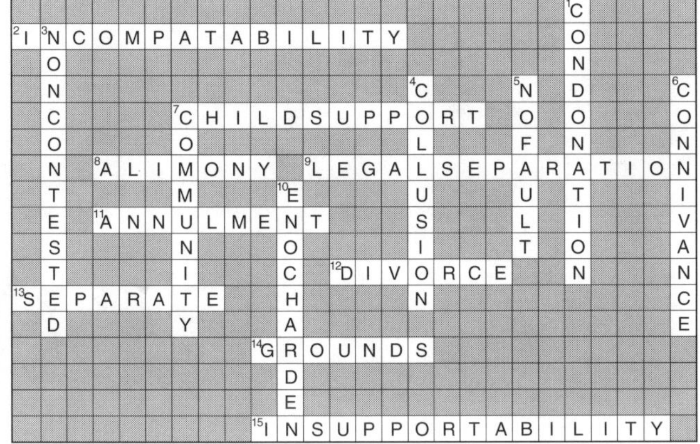

Teacher's Resource Guide

Financial Aspects of Divorce, reproducible master, 22-4.

1. T	6. T
2. T	7. F
3. T	8. T
4. F	9. F
5. T	10. F

Chapter 22 Test

1. B	13. J	25. T
2. G	14. M	26. D
3. L	15. O	27. B
4. A	16. T	28. A
5. E	17. F	29. D
6. F	18. F	30. C
7. I	19. F	31. D
8. C	20. T	32. D
9. N	21. T	33. D
10. H	22. T	34. C
11. K	23. F	35. B
12. D	24. F	

36. The parent with custody may wish to place conditions on visiting privileges of the other parent. Children may be used as pawns in negotiations. One parent may ask the child for information about the other parent's household. Children may feel they should choose sides, though they may not want to.

37. Most children of divorced persons retain relationships with their natural parents. Past and present family relationships become complex because there are so many of them. Family members' expectations of one another may be unclear and confusing.

38. Newly divorced people may have to find and furnish new living spaces; adjust to being single again; adapt to changes; accept new roles, rebuild self-esteem; and develop new, fulfilling relationships. If they have children, parents must find ways to maintain close parent-child relationships.

U.S. Divorce and Marriage Rates, 1940-1995

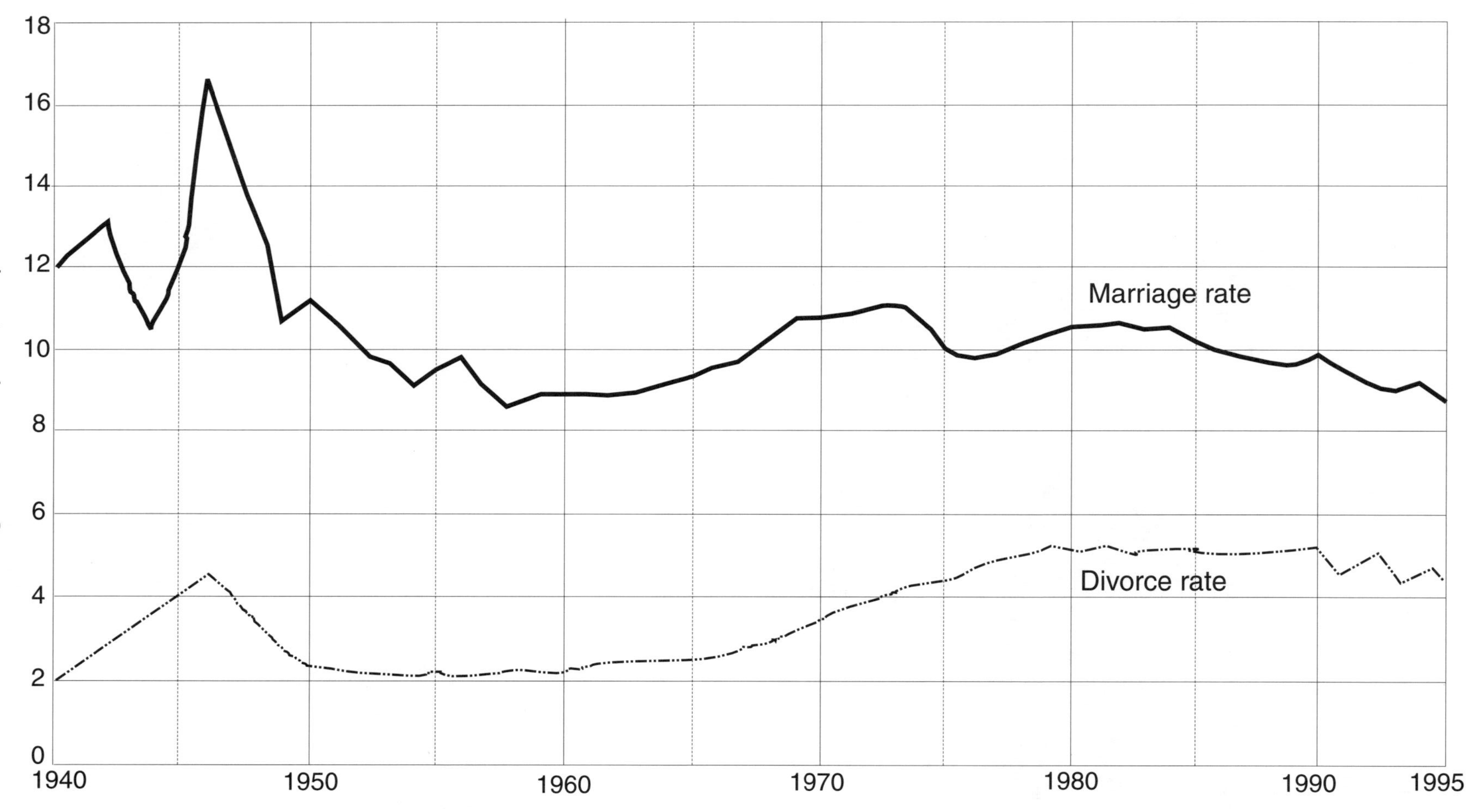

Source: National Center for Health Statistics, *Monthly Vital Statistics Report, Population Reference Bureau, Inc.*

Divorce Rates in Selected Industrialized Countries, 1960-1990

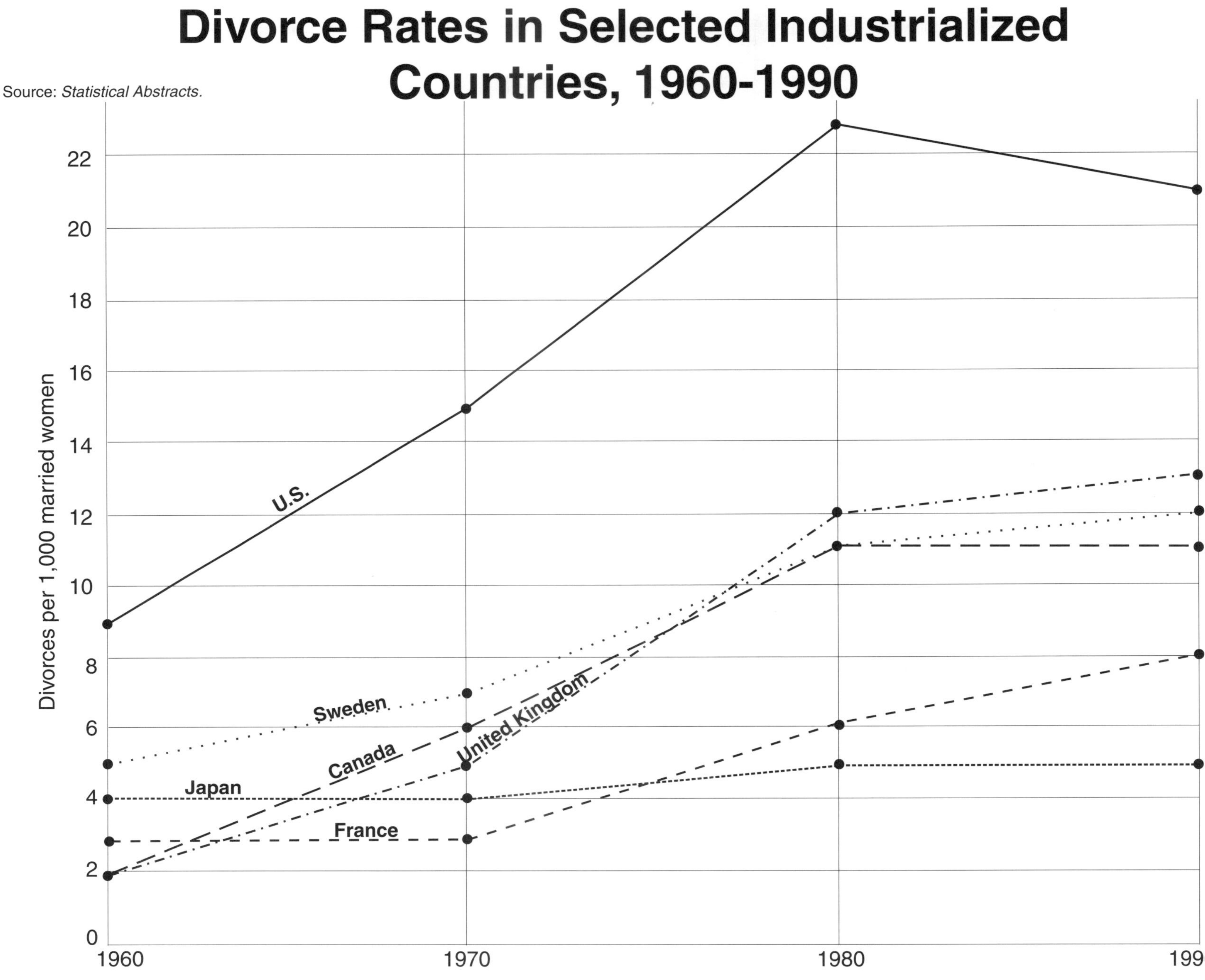

Divorce Laws in Your State

Name_______________________________________**Date**_____________________**Period**________________

Divorce laws vary from state to state. Answer the following questions by researching the laws in your state or interviewing a lawyer or judge.

1. List ways a marriage can be legally terminated in your state. _______________________________

____

____

____

____

____

2. List five grounds for annulment in your state. ____

____

____

____

____

____

____

3. List five grounds for divorce in your state. ____

____

____

____

____

____

4. What is a *no-fault divorce?* Is it allowed in your state? __________________________________

____

____

____

____

____

____

____

(Continued)

Name ____

5. What provisions for alimony, child custody, child support, and property divisions exist under the laws of your state? How are the amounts of each determined? ____

____

____

____

____

____

____

____

6. List the community property states and explain what community property means in relation to divorce settlements. ____

____

____

____

____

____

____

Financial Aspects of Divorce

Name______________________________________**Date**________________**Period**______________

Read the following questions about the financial aspects of divorce. Circle *T* if the statement is true or *F* if the statement is false.

T   F   1. Your spouse can withdraw all the money from your joint checking account.

T   F   2. Separated people can be charged with adultery.

T   F   3. One spouse can use the other's fear of losing the children to frighten him or her into a less favorable financial settlement.

T   F   4. Most divorcing partners become more generous and understanding as divorce negotiations continue.

T   F   5. Your spouse may be entitled to as much as one-half of your retirement pension in the event of divorce.

T   F   6. A spouse may quit his or her job in order to reduce the child support required of him or her.

T   F   7. To save money it is a good idea to let your family attorney represent both you and your spouse during divorce.

T   F   8. A divorced spouse is no longer required to pay alimony if the spouse receiving alimony remarries.

T   F   9. A divorced spouse is no longer responsible for child support if the spouse receiving child support remarries.

T   F   10. A divorced parent is responsible for child support even if the ex-spouse remarries and the children are legally adopted by their new stepparent.

Outwitted

He drew a circle that shut me out–

Heretic, rebel, a thing to flout.

But Love and I had the wit to win:

We drew a circle that took him in.

–Edwin Markham, 1852-1940

Divorce Facts: Review Cards

Place the questions below on index cards and write answers on the back of each card. Make several sets and distribute to students in small groups. Instruct students to quiz one another before the chapter test to review this material.

Q: A defense to prevent a divorce in which the person suing for divorce has forgiven the spouse for a certain action prior to the divorce case. A: Condonation.	Q: A ground for divorce in which the two people are no longer able to support a continuing relationship of marriage is called _____. A: insupportability.
Q: A defense to prevent divorce in which the person suing for divorce is found guilty of causing the condition used as grounds for the divorce. A: Connivance.	Q: If a spouse has disappeared for a stated period of time, usually five to seven years, what kind of divorce may be granted? A: Enoch Arden divorce.
Q: A situation in which a couple want a divorce but have no legal grounds to obtain one, so they set up a scheme to create grounds for the divorce. A: Collusion.	Q: A divorce in which one party files an answer to a summons and tries to prove no grounds exist, or files against the other spouse. A: Contested divorce.
Q: A divorce to which both spouses agree is called a _____. A: noncontested divorce.	Q: Any property acquired through the labors of either spouse during their marriage is considered to be owned by both. What is it called? A: Community property.

(Continued)

Q: When one of the spouses moves to a separate residence, but the spouses remain married it is called _____.

A: informal separation.

Q: Name the law that requires you to live in a state for a certain amount of time before you can file for a divorce.

A: Residency requirement or law.

Q: When a couple is legally separated and the court awards one partner continued financial support it is called _____.

A: separate maintenance.

Q: Property that was owned prior to the marriage or acquired as a gift or inheritance is called _____.

A: separate property.

Q: A ground for divorce that states the two spouses are unable to live together peaceably or in harmony is called _____.

A: incompatibility.

Q: When the court rules that a couple was never legally married, what legal action can terminate the marriage?

A: Annulment.

Q: What type of divorce eliminates the need for proving one partner guilty?

A: No-fault divorce.

Q: When the partners make a legal agreement to live apart it is called _____.

A: legal separation.

(Continued)

Q: When an annulment is granted, what happens to the property?

A: Each regains his or her property and divide joint property.

Q: Money paid by the primary wage earner to the other marriage partner during and after divorce is called ______.

A: alimony.

Q: When a couple (or one party) go to another country and secure a divorce in a short time, what is this type of divorce called?

A: A "quickie" divorce.

Q: What is the name of the court order that informs a spouse that a divorce action has been brought against him or her?

A: Summons.

Q: Money that one parent pays the other parent for support of the children is called ______.

A: child support.

Q: The legal dissolution of a marriage is called ______.

A: divorce.

Divorce and Remarriage

Name _______________________________________

Date _________________________________**Period**_______________**Score** ________________

Chapter 22 Test

Matching: Match the following terms and identifying phrases.

_______ 1. Divorce in which both parties agree to the divorce.

_______ 2. Situation in which a couple want a divorce but have no legal grounds, so they work together to plan a scheme that would give them grounds for the divorce.

_______ 3. Inability of the couple to support a continuing relationship of marriage.

_______ 4. Divorce that may be granted if a married person disappears for a stated period of time and it can be determined that an effort was made to locate that person.

_______ 5. Money paid by the primary wage earner to the other marriage partner during and after a divorce.

_______ 6. Divorce defense in which the person suing for divorce has forgiven the spouse for a certain action prior to the divorce case and thus, that action cannot be used as grounds for divorce.

_______ 7. Any property acquired through the labors of either spouse during their marriage.

_______ 8. Means by which the defendant is notified that a divorce action has been brought against him or her.

_______ 9. Legal termination of a marriage relationship in which the court rules that the couple were never legally married.

_______ 10. Money that one separated or divorced parent pays the other parent to support the couple's children until the children reach the age of 18.

_______ 11. Legal agreement made by marriage partners to live apart.

A. Enoch Arden divorce
B. noncontested divorce
C. summons
D. separate property
E. alimony
F. condonation
G. collusion
H. child support
I. community property
J. contested divorce
K. legal separation
L. insupportability
M. connivance
N. annulment
O. divorce

(Continued)

_______ 12. Property that can be positively shown to have been owned prior to marriage or acquired during marriage by gift or inheritance and retained separately.

_______ 13. Divorce in which one party files for divorce and the other party files an answer and tries to prove no grounds exist or files a summons and complaint against the other spouse.

_______ 14. Divorce defense that can be used when one person is guilty of scheming to cause the condition used as grounds for the divorce.

_______ 15. Legal dissolution of the marriage contract.

True/False: Circle *T* if the statement is true or *F* if the statement is false.

T F   16. Increased divorce rates in recent decades have been experienced not only by the United States but by other industrialized countries as well.

T F   17. Divorce carries more social disapproval today than in the earlier part of this century.

T F   18. Divorce was more common earlier in this century than it is today.

T F   19. Most Americans believe that it is wrong for unhappily married couples to divorce.

T F   20. Incompatibility as grounds for divorce means two spouses are unable to live together peaceably.

T F   21. No-fault divorce eliminates the need for proving one partner guilty.

T F   22. Under some circumstances, children of annulled marriages may be considered legally illegitimate and may lose their right to inheritance.

T F   23. A large majority of divorces are contested.

T F   24. The more young children a divorced woman has at home, the greater her chances are of remarriage.

T F   25. Blended families are families in which one or both spouses may have been married before and may have one or more children.

Multiple Choice: Select the best response. Write the letter in the space provided.

_______ 26. Most social scientists believe the divorce rate in the United States is higher today than it was early in this century because _______.
   A. the success of a marriage today is viewed more in terms of personal happiness than it was early in this century
   B. the social stigma attached to divorce has decreased in recent decades
   C. opportunities for women to become financially sufficient in careers outside the home have increased in recent decades.
   D. All of the above.

(Continued)

Contemporary Living Teacher's Resources

_____ 27. *Desertion* refers to _____.
    A. a legal agreement that provides for a couple's desire to live separately but to share responsibilities for raising their children
    B. abandonment of the marital partner
    C. legal proof that the marriage contract was entered into under fraudulent circumstances
    D. the refusal of a spouse to abide by a premarital agreement

_____ 28. Under the split-custody arrangement _____.
    A. one or more of the divorced couple's children live with one parent and the rest live with the other parent
    B. the responsibility for caring for the children of a divorced couple is given to one parent only
    C. custody of the divorced couple's children is given to an individual outside the family
    D. neither divorced parent is responsible for the children

_____ 29. A common ground(s) for annulment is (are) _____.
    A. concealment of disease
    B. financial misrepresentation
    C. concealment of a previous marriage or divorce
    D. All of the above.

_____ 30. Legal dissolution of a marriage contract is _____.
    A. emotional divorce
    B. legal separation
    C. divorce
    D. desertion

_____ 31. A divorce can be granted on which of the following ground(s)?
    A. Incompatibility.
    B. Separation (living apart for a specified time).
    C. Alcohol or drug addiction.
    D. All of the above.

_____ 32. *Condonation* refers to _____.
    A. living apart from one's spouse
    B. a commonly used method of birth control
    C. a form of bigamy
    D. None of the above.

_____ 33. Legal divorce occurs when _____.
    A. the couple realize their marriage relationship is not going well.
    B. the couple consult a marriage counselor.
    C. the couple stop speaking to one another.
    D. None of the above.

_____ 34. Which of the following is used to set the amount of alimony?
    A. The couple's standard of living.
    B. The primary wage earner's income.
    C. Both of the above.
    D. Neither of the above.

(Continued)

_______ 35. *Rehabilitative alimony* refers to ______.
      A. lifelong support of one former spouse by the other former spouse
      B. temporary support provided by one former spouse to enable the other former spouse to update or upgrade his or her job skills and ability to earn a living
      C. physical therapy to regain the use of a paralyzed limb after a disabling injury
      D. child support payments

Essay Questions: Provide complete responses to the following questions or statements.

36. Why is child visitation often a source of stress and conflict for divorced parents and children alike?

37. Why is role stress often magnified in blended families?

38. List adjustments that newly divorced people must make.

Chapter 23
Aging, Fulfillment of Life, and Death

Objectives

After studying this chapter, students will be able to
- recognize the fact that our society, as a whole, is growing older.
- describe the young adult years and the challenges of this stage of life.
- describe the middle-age stage and the added responsibilities of intergenerational caregiving during this stage.
- summarize the emotional, physical, and financial aspects of aging.
- describe various types of housing for the elderly.
- explain hospice care.
- list the stages of dying and the stages of grieving.
- identify the problems of the survivors.
- define terms related to the legal issues of death.

Bulletin Boards

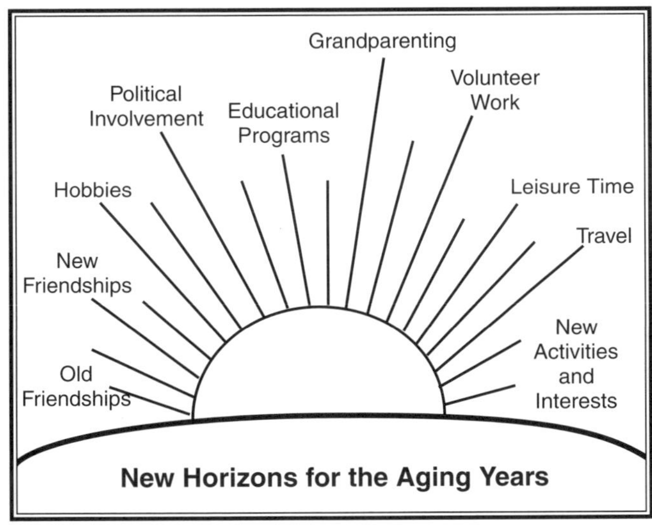

New Horizons for the Aging Years

I. Title: "New Horizons for the Aging Years"

Depict the sun rising on the horizon using green, orange, and yellow construction paper. Use a yellow or orange marking pen to draw beams radiating from the sun pointing to various activities older adults enjoy.

II. Title: "Your Life 50 Years from Now"

Mount the scenes sketched by your students in learning activity three.

Teaching Materials

Text, pages 544-566

Terms to Know, To Review, To Do, and *To Think About*

Student Activity Guide

   A. *How the Human Body Ages*
   B. *Stages of Dying and Grieving*
   C. *Terms Related to Death and Dying*
   D. *Survey of Funeral Costs*

Teacher's Resource Guide/Binder

Myths of Aging, reproducible masters, 23-1A and 23-1B

Intergenerational Caregiving–A Case Study, reproducible master, 23-2

The Positive Side of Aging, transparency master, 23-3

Aging Brings Change, reproducible master, 23-4

Chapter 23 Test

Teacher's Resource Binder

The "Sandwiched" Generation, color transparency, CT-23

Software for Contemporary Living

   Chapter Review Game

Introductory Activities

1. *Myths of Aging,* reproducible masters, 23-1A and 23-1B. Many people have misconceptions about the elderly. This activity lists some of these myths about aging. Have your students read these statements and decide which are facts and which are myths. The myths are explained on the reproducible master, 23-1B. You may want to reproduce only the first page of the activity, and then read the explanations to your class as you discuss their responses. In the second part of the activity, your students are to write their own reactions to statements about aging. These also can be used as a basis for class discussion.
2. Have students form a circle and ask each person to respond to the statement, "Growing old to me means..."
3. Ask students to sketch scenes which they think will depict their lives 50 years from now. Have them include as many visual keys as possible to portray the scenes. Then ask each student to write a brief descriptive paragraph under the sketch to help interpret the scene. Display the sketches and use as a basis for class discussion.

Strategies to Reteach, Reinforce, Enrich, and Extend Text Concepts

4. **RT** Ask your students if they agree that middle age begins at 45 and old age begins at 65. Do they know people who are 50 and act "old" or are 70 and act "young"?
5. **RT** Ask your students to think about the fact that they will spend almost half their lives as middle-aged and elderly people. How do they feel about this?

Young Adulthood

6. **ER** Ask students to interview persons in their early 20s to age 45. (Record the interviews, if they agree.) Prepare a list of questions, such as the following: What are the joys of this stage of life? What are some of the problems?
7. **RF** Ask students to describe instances when young adults may require help from their parents. Identify the kinds of help parents may need to provide. Then ask the students if they would call upon their parents if they were in any of these situations.

Middle Age

8. **RF** Ask students what problems may need to be resolved if adult children "return to the nest." Brainstorm potential problems and possible solutions.
9. **RF** *The "Sandwiched" Generation,* color transparency, CT-23. Use this transparency to illustrate the burdens often faced by middle-aged couples who must care for parents, children, and grandchildren.
10. **EX** *Intergenerational Caregiving–A Case Study,* reproducible master, 23-2. Students are to respond with possible solutions to meet the needs of three generations living in one household.
11. **RF** Ask students to examine the emotional challenges middle-aged persons face today. Some middle-aged persons may lead very hectic lives. Others may be alone for the first time in their lives.
12. **EX** Have students research community resources that are available for care of older family members, such as social service agency nurses, day-care for the elderly, etc.

Old Age

13. **RF** Discuss the impact the growing population of older adults will have on our country–on social security, employment, health care, families, politics, housing, recreational facilities, etc.
14. **RF** Discuss fears that a shrinking work force of younger people may be hard pressed to pay for programs that support an ever-growing older population. Do students share this concern? What can be done?
15. **EX** The elderly are playing a more active role in politics, and they will likely become more influential as their numbers grow. Have students research the influence they have had on legislation in this country. Report on activities of the Gray Panthers and the AARP (American Association of Retired Persons).
16. **EX** There is a growing trend for older persons to return to the workforce because there

are fewer young people available to work. Ask students to interview employers who employ older adults. What are the positive and negative factors involved?

Aspects of Aging

17. **RF** *The Positive Side of Aging,* transparency master, 23-3. Use this transparency to review the positive aspects of growing old.
18. **EX** Interview an elderly person who is active and seems to view life in positive terms. Record the interview, if permission is given. Play the tape for the class and discuss.
19. **RF** Many people feel the key to aging is to remain mentally active. Discuss the resources and activities available for older citizens to keep them mentally stimulated.
20. **RF** *How the Human Body Ages,* Activity A, SAG. Given a drawing of a person, students are to cite the physical changes that occur as the person ages.
21. **EX** Ask students to find magazine and newspaper articles dealing with nutrition and exercise for older persons. What recommendations are given in the articles? What resources in your community help elderly persons receive the medicine, food, and exercise they need?
22. **EX** Investigate food and medicine gimmicks that are designed primarily for the elderly. Ask interested students to research Alzheimer's disease and report to the class.
23. **EX** Financial planning for the aging years should be started early in life. What can individuals do to assure they will have financial security? Why is it important for individuals to take personal responsibility for their financial security rather than count on government programs? How can this be done?
24. **EX** Ask students to research the benefits provided by Social Security, Medicare, and Medicaid.
25. **EX** Have students research the businesses and service organizations that offer reduced rates to senior citizens. Also note any special services or programs designed specifically to meet the needs of senior citizens.
26. **EX** Investigate programs for planning financial security during retirement. Compare programs available from private industries, school systems, life insurance companies, etc.
27. **EX** Ask students to list the different types of housing available in your area for the elderly (own home, living with children, retirement community, nursing home, subsidized housing, condominium, etc.) Divide the class into small groups and have each group investigate one type. Ask each group to report on availability, application procedures, types of services offered, types of living arrangements available, health care provided, and costs. Prepare reports for the class.
28. **EX** Plan a field trip to a nursing home. Find out about the different levels of care provided (self-care, modified self-care, and total nursing care), costs, availability, etc.
29. **ER** Have students role-play the following scene: A married couple is discussing with an elderly parent the need for nursing home care. Depict possible approaches. Discuss the likely outcomes of each. Which will lead to the best adjustment by the elderly parent?

New Horizons in Aging

30. **ER** Have students interview grandparents about their attitudes toward their roles as grandparents. How have they seen the role of grandparenting changing during the last decade? What do the students see as being important in their relationship with their grandparents? Ask them to project the role they hope to play in the lives of their grandchildren someday.
31. **ER** Ask students to bring in pictures from magazines that depict grandparents. Do they sense that grandparenting today offers more independence than in past years?
32. **RF** Discuss how grandparents contribute to the development of their grandchildren. What problems sometimes occur when grandparents become too involved in the lives of their grandchildren?
33. **RF** Ask students what they think the word "retirement" means? Should there be a mandatory retirement age? How can people plan for a satisfying retirement?
34. **RF** Ask students to consider the statement, "People need something to retire to–not from." What would be the difference between "to" and "from"?
35. **ER** Role-play some typical scenes of a couple adjusting to retirement. Consider how time schedules, activities, finances, and friendships influence the adjustment.

36. **EX** Have students research the organizations and services that are available for retired people in your community. Also research volunteer opportunities for retired persons.

37. **RF** *Aging Brings Change*, reproducible master, 23-4. In the areas listed (emotional, physical, financial, housing, and retirement), students are to list the changes that are likely to occur during the later years of life. Indicate those changes that are negative and those that can be positive.

Accepting Death As a Reality of Life

38. **ER** Ask a person familiar with hospice-type care to speak to the class about this type of care. How do people specifically trained for hospice care comfort the dying and the families left behind?

39. **EX** *Stages of Dying and Grieving*, Activity B, SAG. Students are to identify the five stages of dying and grieving and to give examples of typical behaviors, statements, or feelings that a person might have at each stage.

40. **ER** Have students research the death customs and traditions of various cultures. Present oral reports to the class, using visual aids if possible. Discuss the differences that cultures display in the acceptance of death.

41. **RF** Discuss how death customs have changed in our culture. Cite the change from dying in homes to dying in hospitals and to the more recent move to hospice care.

Those Left Behind

42. **ER** Have students research how people learn to accept the death of a loved one. Read books and articles which tell how persons have accepted the death of a child, a spouse, a parent, etc. Discuss.

43. **EX** Review suggestions for telling children about death. Have each student write a short scene in which a parent is telling a young child about the death of a grandparent.

44. **EX** Discuss how widows and widowers accept the death of their mates and what they do to adjust to their new lives. Investigate wise decisions they make as well as unwise decisions, such as investing in fraudulent schemes, spending money foolishly, being taken in by persons as they seek companionship.

Legal Issues of Death

45. **RF** *Terms Related to Death and Dying*, Activity C, SAG. Use this activity to review students' understanding of vocabulary terms related to death and dying.

46. **ER** Have students interview a medical examiner about the laws in your state concerning death. Report back to class.

47. **ER** Ask a lawyer to speak to the class about making out a will. How can individuals make out their own wills? How can wills be changed? How can they be broken? What happens if an individual dies without a will? How does a person make a living will? How do people arrange for donations of body parts to organ banks? Also ask the lawyer to summarize inheritance laws in your state.

48. **EX** *Survey of Funeral Costs*, Activity D, SAG. Take a field trip, or ask students to research the information in this activity. They will need to interview a funeral home director, a cemetery director, and a monument dealer to find out about the many costs related to death. The class can be divided into small groups to conduct the interviews and then share their findings with the rest of the class.

49. **ER** Ask a funeral director to outline the many decisions that have to be made when someone dies.

Answer Key for Chapter 23

Text
To Review, page 565

1. About 76 years.
2. The couple is often "sandwiched" between caring for their children and caring for their parents at a time when they would really like more time for themselves.
3. (Student response.)
4. C
5. When persons are alone, they may skip meals because they have no social contacts.
6. menopause; climacteric
7. Start planning for retirement long before reaching this stage. Investigate pre-retirement programs that are available. Develop outside interests or leisure-time activities. Maintain relationships with friends.
8. A medical facility designed for people who have only a few weeks or months to live.

Emphasis is placed on pain management and maintenance of a peaceful, supportive environment in a homelike atmosphere.

9. Stage two–anger.
10. Stage five–acceptance.
11. false
12. false
13. living will
14. Having a legal will enables a person to designate how property will be distributed after his or her death. A will can name legal guardians for minor children. Having a will saves the survivors from many extra problems.

Student Activity Guide

Activity A, *How the Human Body Ages.*

Hearing–Sensory problems most often begin with a hearing loss. Sight–May gradually diminish. Skin–Loss of elasticity results in wrinkling. Bones–Become weaker and more fragile. Heart–Muscles of the heart may become less efficient. Blood vessels–May become narrower. Reproductive system–Women: menopause; Men: climacteric. Maximum size and strength of body framework reached at about age 25.

Activity B, *Stages of Dying and Grieving.*

Stages are denial, anger, bargaining, depression, and acceptance. (Student response for examples of each for dying and grieving.)

Activity C, *Terms Related to Death and Dying.*

1. I	8. L
2. A	9. D
3. B	10. J
4. E	11. N
5. M	12. G
6. K	13. F
7. H	14. C

Teacher's Resource Guide

Chapter 23 Test

1. H	11. F	21. B
2. K	12. F	22. C
3. F	13. T	23. B
4. G	14. T	24. D
5. I	15. T	25. A
6. B	16. F	26. C
7. J	17. F	27. B
8. C	18. F	28. D
9. E	19. T	29. D
10. A	20. F	30. A

31. To form an independent household; to form meaningful relationships, often involving engagement, marriage, and parenting; and to establish oneself in a career.
32. (Student response.)
33. The five stages are: denial, anger, bargaining, depression, and acceptance. (Student response for brief descriptions of each stage.)
34. (Student response.)

Myths of Aging

Name ____ **Date** ______________ **Period** ______________

In the following activity, decide which of the statements are facts about aging and which are myths. Then respond to the statements at the bottom of this page.

Fact **Myth**

________ ________ 1. Most old people are poor.

________ ________ 2. Most old people want to move in with their children.

________ ________ 3. Most old people live in nursing homes.

________ ________ 4. Most elderly people have lost touch with their children and grandchildren.

________ ________ 5. Intelligence declines with old age.

________ ________ 6. All elderly people are senile.

________ ________ 7. The elderly have no interest in sex.

________ ________ 8. Older people lose interest in politics.

________ ________ 9. People are unable to keep up with the working world after age 65 and should retire.

________ ________ 10. Aging starts suddenly in the human body and moves very rapidly.

________ ________ 11. The first physical sign of aging is loss of teeth.

________ ________ 12. As people age, they actually need more calories to provide them with increased needs for energy.

What comes to your mind when you think of aging? ____

____

____

____

How old is old? ____

____

____

What do you think you will be doing 50 years from now?_______________________________________

____

____

What concerns you most about growing old? ____

____

____

What will you look forward to as you grow old?____

____

____

Answers for *Myths of Aging*

1. Myth. While income may be reduced due to retirement, only 14 percent of the elderly in our country live below the poverty line. Many elderly have retirement pensions or have planned financially for their aging years. They also benefit from Medicare, receive special tax treatment, and enjoy senior discounts.

2. Myth. About 75 percent of elderly people own their own homes. When possible, most elderly people prefer living on their own, even if it means bearing some hardships.

3. Myth. Less than five percent of the elderly live in nursing homes or other institutions.

4. Myth. Studies reveal that over 75 percent of elderly people see their children or grandchildren once a week. Grandparents who live away from their children frequently travel to visit them.

5. Myth. Studies show that in healthy individuals there is no decrease in intelligence of people between 60 and 75 years of age. Elderly people often expand their interests and abilities during the retirement years.

6. Myth. Only eight percent of people over 65 suffer from senility, a characteristic of Alzheimer's disease. Others who sometimes seem to have lost mental function are actually suffering from depression, low self-esteem, hearing or vision problems, or loneliness.

7. Myth. Sexual interest does not cease as people age, but it may diminish somewhat.

8. Myth. Older people as a group are politically active. Many belong to the Gray Panthers, an advocacy group of older citizens who keep informed of legislation and programs which affect the elderly.

9. Myth. Many elderly people continue working into their 70's, or retire at 65 and begin a second career.

10. Myth. Aging actually starts around age 25 and continues very slowly over the years.

11. Myth. One of the first visible signs of aging is the skin, which becomes wrinkled due to a loss of elasticity. Loss of teeth depends on health factors, and many older people have most of their own teeth.

12. Myth. As people grow older they need fewer calories, but they continue to need a well-balanced diet that includes a variety of foods.

Intergenerational Caregiving–A Case Study

Name ____ **Date** _______________ **Period** _______________

Read the following case study of a couple involved with intergenerational caregiving. As each problem arises, suggest possible solutions for this extended family.

Case Study: Myra and Don are a middle-aged couple with a 22-year-old son, Mark, a 17-year-old daughter, Cindy, a 10-year-old son, Adam, and an 8-year-old daughter, Melissa. Don's widowed mother is in poor health. She cannot afford a nursing home, so she is moving in with them. They have a four-bedroom home.

Melissa is giving up her room for Grandmother and moving in with Cindy. Cindy resents having to share her room, but she doesn't want to hurt Grandmother's feelings. What can be done to make sharing a room easier? ____

____

____

____

Myra is returning to her bookkeeping job to help pay for Grandmother's medical bills and to save money for Cindy's college tuition next year. Who will take care of Grandmother during the day? _______

____

____

____

The family has decided to look into a community day care service for Grandmother. Grandmother is frightened by new experiences. What can the family do to help her adjust to this change? _____________

____

____

____

Cindy wants to visit one of the colleges she is thinking about attending next year. Myra and Don want a few days off to take her. What arrangements could be made so they can make this trip? _________

____

____

____

Grandmother gets upset when Adam has his friends over. She complains that the music is too loud, and they leave soda cans sitting around. She thinks they are undisciplined. What can Myra and Don do to resolve the problem for both Adam and Grandmother? ____

____

____

____

____

(Continued)

Name ____

Mark shows up. He has lost his job and can't afford to keep his apartment. He has to move back home until he can find work. Where can he stay? How might his presence help the family? How might his presence add to the family's burdens?____

____

____

____

____

____

Myra and Don both realize this may be a trying time for them and their children, but they want to focus on the positive benefits of having three generations living in one household. What kinds of activities might they try to enhance the situation for all of them? ____

____

____

____

____

____

____

The Positive Side of Aging

Aging Brings Change

Name _______________________________ **Date** _____________ **Period** _____________

At each stage of life, there are gains and there are losses. For example, aging persons may lose some strength or physical vigor, but they may gain new leisure-time interests. In the areas listed below, list the changes that are likely to occur during the later years of life. Indicate those changes that are negative and those that can be positive.

Emotional Aspects	
Negative	Positive

Physical Aspects	
Negative	Positive

Financial Aspects	
Negative	Positive

(Continued)

Name ____

Housing	
Negative	Positive

Retirement	
Negative	Positive

Aging, Fulfillment of Life, and Death

Name ____

Date _____________________________________ **Period** _____________ **Score** _______________

Chapter 23 Test

Matching: Match the following terms and identifying phrases.

_______ 1. Sociologists name for middle-aged couples who provide care for their children as well as their elderly parents.

_______ 2. An oral will.

_______ 3. Medical facility designed for people who have only a few weeks or months to live.

_______ 4. Care provided for members of one generation by members of another.

_______ 5. Dying without a will.

_______ 6. Arrangements are made for body parts of a deceased person to be held for medical science.

_______ 7. Parents feel useless and depressed after their children leave home.

_______ 8. Allows people to choose whether or not they want to be kept alive when there is apparently no hope for them to recover.

_______ 9. A will written in the handwriting of the person making the will.

_______ 10. Detailed physical examination of a dead body.

A. autopsy
B. organ bank
C. living will
D. beneficiaries
E. holographic will
F. hospice
G. intergenerational caregiving
H. sandwich generation
I. intestate
J. empty nest syndrome
K. nuncupative will

True/False: Circle *T* if the statement is true or *F* if the statement is false.

T F 11. Today's young adult children generally require less help from their parents than previous generations.

T F 12. Every adult will experience a mid-life crisis.

T F 13. As a whole, the older population has been growing at a rate much faster than the general population.

T F 14. A human reaches physical maturity at about age 25.

T F 15. The climacteric in men is a less pronounced change than menopause in women.

T F 16. Many older persons list housing arrangements as their greatest worry.

T F 17. It is unusual for a grieving spouse to be angry at the deceased.

T F 18. When a death occurs in the family, children should not experience the mourning.

T F 19. People can choose whether or not they want to be kept alive on life support systems.

T F 20. All states require that an autopsy be performed on a dead body.

(Continued)

Multiple Choice: Choose the best response. Write the letter in the space provided.

______ 21. For most people, one of the earliest visible signs of aging is ______.
    A. a loss of hearing
    B. wrinkling of the skin
    C. a loss of vision
    D. weakening of the bones

______ 22. Which of the following statements is *false*?
    A. Most elderly persons need to reduce the number of calories they consume.
    B. The bones of elderly persons do not change in size, but they do change in chemical composition.
    C. Elderly persons should not exercise because they will become too tired.
    D. Loss of elasticity in the skin results in wrinkles.

______ 23. Which of the following statements is *false*?
    A. During menopause, biological changes occur that trigger both psychological and emotional changes.
    B. When a woman is between 45 and 50 years old, the production of the sex hormone increases.
    C. The imbalance of hormones in a woman's body during menopause may cause her to have hot flashes.
    D. Production of the male sex hormone peaks at about age 20.

______ 24. Which of the following statements is *true*?
    A. About half of the elderly persons in the United States live in nursing homes.
    B. Retirement communities are the perfect solution for the housing problems of elderly persons.
    C. If elderly persons move in with their children, they should assume the responsibility for making all the major decisions for the family.
    D. If an elderly person's home is convenient, safe, and comfortable, the person would probably be wise to continue living there.

______ 25. Which of the following statements is *false*?
    A. The nuclear family system in our society has strengthened the ties between grandparents and grandchildren.
    B. Many middle-aged people are grandparents.
    C. During the retirement years, persons should not give up all their friends to stay home with their mates.
    D. Retirement planning should begin early in life and should take financial matters, housing possibilities, and leisure activities into consideration.

______ 26. The stage called ______ is occurring when a dying person mourns past losses, things not done, and wrongs committed. Then the person enters a state of preparatory grief, growing quiet and wanting no visitors.
    A. anger
    B. denial
    C. depression
    D. acceptance

______ 27. When a loved one dies suddenly, the first stage of grieving is often ______.
    A. bargaining
    B. denial
    C. acceptance
    D. depression

(Continued)

_____ 28. When someone you love dies, you should _____.
    A. talk out your grief and cry
    B. remember the good times you had with the deceased
    C. delay any major decisions until you can think clearly
    D. All of the above.

_____ 29. What is the best way to tell a young girl that her grandfather has died?
    A. "Grandfather has gone on a long journey."
    B. "God took Grandfather away because He wants Grandfather in heaven with Him."
    C. "Grandfather has just gone to the hospital."
    D. First, talk about how flowers and pets die. Once the child knows that death is a normal part of life, she will be able to accept the death of her grandfather more easily.

_____ 30. A _____ is a watch held over the body of a dead person before burial.
    A. wake
    B. cremation
    C. funeral
    D. autopsy

Essay Questions: Provide complete responses to the following questions or statements.

31. List the three tasks typically faced by persons during the years of young adulthood.

32. Discuss the impact of the growing population of older adults on our society.

33. Briefly describe the five stages of grieving. .

34. Explain hospice care.

Part 7

Managing Family Living

Chapter 24
Providing for the Family's Physical Needs

Objectives

After studying this chapter, students will be able to
- list factors affecting consumer decisions.
- recognize wise consumer choices.
- interpret information provided on food labels.
- evaluate the pros and cons of renting or buying a home.
- identify transportation alternatives.
- describe the costs of buying and maintaining a car.
- list ways in which leisure-time activities can add to family life.

Bulletin Boards

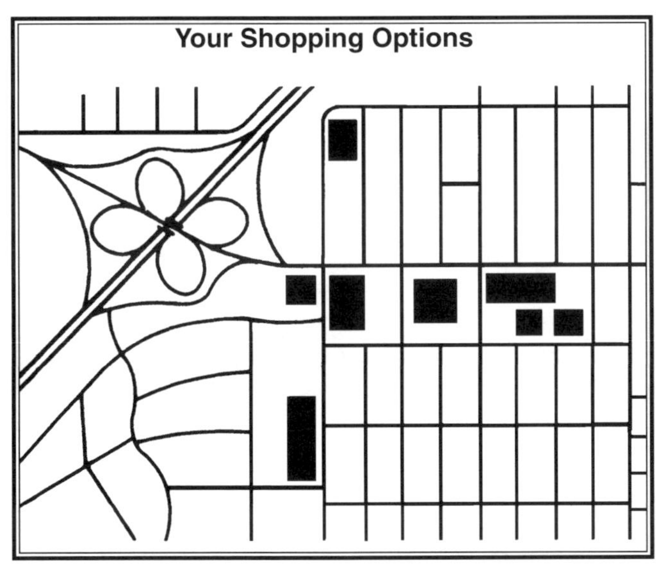

I. Title: "Your Shopping Options"

Cover the bulletin board with a map of your community. Cut out various store shapes from colored construction paper. Attach these to the map to highlight store locations in your community. Feature the variety of shopping options available today, such as outlet stores, warehouse clubs, stores that feature bulk merchandise, resale shops, discount stores, department stores, specialty shops, sample shops, convenience stores, etc.

II. Title: "Should You Buy or Rent?"

Divide the bulletin board into two sections. At the top of one half of the board, place the words *Should You Buy?* On the other half, place the words *Should You Rent?* Under each section, place pictures of various homes and housing options available. Attach real estate ads listing houses for sale and apartments for rent. List the advantages and disadvantages of each option and post under each section.

Teaching Materials

Text, pages 570-598
Terms to Know, To Review, To Do, and *To Think About*

Student Activity Guide
    A. *Consumer Terms*
    B. *Nutrition Label Analysis*
    C. *Product Survey*
    D. *Making Housing Decisions*

Teacher's Resource Guide/Binder
Consumers and Advertising, reproducible master, 24-1

Advertising: Pros and Cons, transparency master, 24-2

Food Choices, transparency master, 24-3

What's in a Lease? reproducible master, 24-4

Chapter 24 Test

Teacher's Resource Binder

The Food Label, color transparency, CT-24A

Food Safety Tips, color transparency, CT-24B

Software for Contemporary Living

Chapter Review Game

Introductory Activities

1. *Consumers and Advertising,* reproducible master, 24-1. Show students three examples of magazine advertising. Show one ad that is informational, one that plays on hidden needs, and one that promotes a harmful substance. Discuss with students ways consumers may respond to the ads. Then ask students to respond to the items in *Consumers and Advertising.* Discuss their responses.

2. Ask each student to predict the amount of money they will need to live on at age 25. Then have them look at newspaper ads for jobs for which they are currently qualified that pay this salary. Were they able to find jobs that pay the salary they think they will need? If not, discuss the advantages of further education and training.

Strategies to Reteach, Reinforce, Enrich, and Extend Text Concepts

What Needs Must Be Met?

3. **RT**   Ask students to describe ways in which their goals might change 5 years from now, 10 years from now, etc. How might their goals change following marriage? Following parenthood?

4. **RF**   Discuss the meaning of the term *limited resources.* Explain that learning to manage resources is even more important when resources are limited. Illustrate on the chalkboard the ways people can use different resources or combinations of resources to reach goals.

5. **EX**   Ask each student to identify a human resource that might go unrecognized and

unused in a family. Have them write a paper explaining how this resource could be developed and how it could help a family satisfy needs and/or reach goals.

Factors Affecting Consumer Decisions

6. **ER**   Study the importance of the teenage market to our economy. Poll students to see how much money they spend and what items account for most of their spending. Have students clip from magazines examples of advertisements aimed at the teenage market.

7. **RF**   *Advertising: Pros and Cons,* transparency master, 24-2. Use this transparency as the basis for a discussion of advertising and its benefits and disadvantages for the consumer. Following the discussion, ask students to write a brief reaction paper stating their conclusions concerning advertising.

8. **RT**   Consumers unconsciously seek to satisfy hidden needs when making purchasing decisions. Advertisers structure their ads to appeal to these needs. Instruct students to locate ads that meet the hidden needs listed in the text. Mount the ads on the bulletin board and number them. Then ask class members to determine the hidden need appealed to in each ad.

9. **ER**   Ask students to count the number of advertisements they encounter during one day. Discuss the possibilities: radio spots, television commercials, billboards, newspaper and magazine ads, direct mail appeals, signs on buses and cabs, etc.

10. **EX**   Find magazine and newspaper ads that depict the caveat emptor and caveat venditor attitudes in advertising. Plan a bulletin board with these ads and ask class members to evaluate them.

11. **RF**   *Consumer Terms,* Activity A, SAG. Students can use this activity to review terms related to advertising.

12. **ER**   Ask students to research the consumer protection agencies that are available to the consumer. Outline the steps that a consumer should follow when seeking help from any of these agencies.

Environmental Responsibility

13. **RT**   Ask students to list 10 ways in which families can use their energy dollars more efficiently.

14. **ER** Invite an extension educator or representative of a community environmental organization to address the class on the topic "Environmental Responsibility in the Household." Allow time for students' questions and discussion.

15. **ER** Invite a city official to address the class on the topic "Environmental Challenges Our City Faces." Allow time for discussion of ways students can help address these challenges.

Food Decisions

16. **ER** Ask students to investigate various types of stores that sell food in your area. Draw a map of the area and pinpoint the location of these stores, using a key to show independently owned stores, nationally owned chain stores, locally owned chain stores, discount stores, convenience stores, etc. Post the map and key on a bulletin board.

17. **RT** *The Food Label*, color transparency, CT-24A. This transparency is an enlarged version of Figure 24-10 in the text. Refer to it as you discuss with students the basic features of the food label. Ask students the following questions:
    - Why is the serving size provided in both household and metric measures?
    - Do most of today's U.S. consumers need to worry about consuming too much (rather than too little) fat, cholesterol, and sodium?
    - How are the Percent Daily Values helpful? (Lists nutrients on the same scale so consumers trying to eat more healthfully will no longer have to remember what number is low for fat, saturated fat, cholesterol, and sodium. They simply can look for five percent or less on an individual food.)

18. **RT** *Food Choices*, transparency master, 24-3. The average American family eats too much fat. Use this transparency to illustrate ways in which the family menu planner can promote the family's health by choosing low-fat instead of high-fat versions of various foods.

19. **RF** *Nutrition Label Analysis*, Activity B, SAG. Ask students to read food labels on three types of breakfast cereal to determine the most healthful choice.

20. **RF** *Product Survey*, Activity C, SAG. Groups of students should select a particular product, such as paper towels, coffee, canned peaches, milk, etc. Instruct students to visit a store and survey every variation of that product. They will record the information on the chart and report to the class.

21. **ER** Using the map in Strategy 16, ask groups of students to go to one of each kind of store in your area and price a typical food list. Give each group the same list, naming container sizes, grades, brands, etc. The following day, post the results on a large graph. Determine the store with the lowest prices for the list of items.

22. **ER** To illustrate the concept that the same menu can vary widely in cost, divide the class into six groups. Each group should prepare a market order for the following menu: steak, potato, green beans, tossed green salad, rolls, coffee, and ice cream. Ask two groups to interpret the menu as a low-cost menu, two groups to interpret the menu as medium cost menu, and two groups to interpret the menu as a high-cost menu. Have the groups list the ingredients they will need to serve four people. Students then should visit a store to find the items they will need and the prices of these items. Compare the three cost levels for serving the same menu. Which items ranged the most in price? What was the cost of the most expensive menu? The least expensive menu? Which form of a food product (fresh, frozen, canned, convenience) was least expensive? Most expensive?

23. **ER** Instruct students to investigate supermarket gimmicks used to entice shoppers to buy. Consider the product's position on the shelf, color appeal, store atmosphere, sample availability, purchase offer, etc. Students should list marketing strategies they notice. Discuss in class consumer pressures in the supermarket.

24. **ER** Discuss with students the use of coupons to obtain discounts. What are their advantages and disadvantages? Bring samples of coupons and read the small print outlining restrictions.

25. **RT** *Food Safety Tips*, color transparency, CT-24B. Refer to this transparency to emphasize the importance of food safety in preparing food or teaching others to prepare food.

Clothing Decisions

26. **ER** Discuss ways in which the consumer can save money on clothing purchases.

Consider seasonal sales, sample shops, discount stores, outlet stores, resale shops, online shopping, and mail-order catalogs. Ask different groups to select one clothing item, such as a man's pullover knit shirt, and to price a comparable item at each type of clothing source. Report back to class and discuss.

27. **RF** Discuss new trends in shopping, such as the following: warehouse clubs, outlet shops and malls, stores that feature bulk merchandise, home shopping, resale shops, online shopping, direct mail, and mail-order catalogs. Also discuss the fact that store hours have been extended to accommodate shoppers.

28. **EX** Ask students to research the times during the year when department stores and other stores have major sales. When are the best bargains available? Can you save by buying out-of-season clothing and/or holiday gift items on sale? Is there a good time of year to stock up on household linens? When is jewelry often on sale?

Housing Decisions

29. **ER** Make a list of all the types of housing available in your area. Record desirable and undesirable characteristics of each. Indicate the approximate cost of each. What limitations are there in some of these housing units? Find pictures and make a bulletin board display depicting types of housing available today.

30. **ER** Poll class members to see whether they want to rent or buy their first dwelling. What are the advantages and disadvantages of each option? Discuss with students different situations of individuals and couples and why it would be best for each to rent or to buy.

31. **RF** *What's in a Lease?* reproducible master, 24-4. Students may find lease agreements difficult to read. This master will help them interpret the legal language found in standard lease agreements. Have students try to obtain copies of lease agreements by visiting rental properties.

32. **RF** *Making Housing Decisions*, Activity D, SAG. Instruct students to visit a rental property in their community and complete the checklist. If possible, they should obtain a copy of the lease and answer the questions concerning the rental agreement. Have students compare the various rental properties they visited in their community.

33. **ER** Instruct students to use the classified section of a Sunday newspaper or go online to research rental costs of apartments, mobile homes, and houses. Students should make a chart showing the approximate high and low costs and the features that are included.

34. **ER** Discuss the hidden costs of renting an apartment for the first time. These costs may amount to hundreds of dollars and must be paid before a renter can move into the apartment. They include security deposits and deposits required by gas companies, electric companies, and telephone companies. Ask students to check with companies to find out their requirements, then report findings to the class. Find out whether deposits are returned or credited and whether they earn interest.

35. **ER** Investigate the costs of buying a house or condominium. Make a list of the costs involved. What is the average interest rate for mortgages in your area? How can a one-half percent increase in an interest rate affect the total cost of a dwelling? Use different interest rates, different down payments, and different pay-back periods to see how the cost of buying the same dwelling can vary.

Transportation Decisions

36. **ER** Ask students to research the EPA fuel-economy ratings of various brands of cars and report to the class. Give examples of cars with top, medium, and low ratings.

37. **ER** If you live in an urban area, outline a typical commuter's route on a map. Then ask students to research the actual costs of various transportation alternatives available (car, bus, subway, carpooling) to make this commute. Assume that use of an individual car involves costs of 32 cents per mile (for gas, depreciation, etc.). Which transportation option is the most economical? Which is best for the environment?

38. **ER** Ask a reputable auto dealer to discuss with students the best way to purchase a new car. How can consumers save money? What time of year is best to buy a car?

Leisure-Time Decisions

39. **ER** Ask students to list their top five favorite leisure-time activities. What personal tastes and values do these activities reflect? How many of these activities involve interaction with other family members? What additional uses of their leisure time might students like to explore?

40. **ER** Ask students to compile a list of activities that families of all ages can enjoy together. Why is it important for families to engage in some activities together?

Answer Key for Chapter 24

Text
To Review, page 597.

1. Caveat emptor; Caveat venditor.
2. A. Consumer Product Safety Commission. B. Food and Drug Administration. C. Federal Trade Commission. D. Better Business Bureau.
3. E
4. A feeling of personal accountability for protecting the environment.
5. C
6. B. Department stores.
7. (List five. Student response.)
8. A security deposit is a sum of money, usually one month's rent, paid to the landlord before moving into a rental unit. It insures the landlord against financial loss in case the tenant damages the unit or fails to pay the rent.
9. mortgage
10. (Name five. Student response.)
11. true

Student Activity Guide

Activity A, *Consumer Terms.*

1. E
2. B
3. I
4. A
5. G
6. H
7. C
8. D
9. J
10. F

Activity B, *Nutrition Label Analysis.*

1. 1 cup; 1 cup; 1/2 cup
2. A, C
3. A, C
4. A and B; C
5. B and C; A
6. B; A
7. C; B
8. A
9 B (Student response for reasons and reservations.)

Teacher's Resource Guide

Chapter 24 Test

1. H	11. T	21. B
2. C	12. F	22. A
3. K	13. F	23. C
4. A	14. F	24. A
5. D	15. T	25. B
6. G	16. F	26. A
7. E	17. T	27. A
8. J	18. F	28. D
9. I	19. F	29. C
10. F	20. T	30. D

31. Home ownership may provide a sense of independence, security, and stability. It is an investment that will probably bring a return when sold. Home ownership involves certain tax deductions. Renting offers flexibility. Renters do not need a large sum of money for a down payment. Their housing costs are more predictable.
32. Personal costs include: purchase price; auto insurance; driver's license; annual registration and tag renewal; residential parking stickers (in urban areas); gasoline; maintenance. Environmental costs: Burning gasoline means using a nonrenewable natural resource; fumes from auto exhaust are a major source of air pollution.
33. (Student response.)

Consumers and Advertising

Name ____ **Date** _______________ **Period** _______________

Read the statements below. Circle *T* if the statement is true or *F* if the statement is false.

T F   1. Advertising is essential in our free enterprise system.

T F   2. The government should do more to regulate advertising in order to protect the consumer.

T F   3. Teenagers are not influenced by brand names when they buy products.

T F   4. Advertising motivates consumers to buy items they really do not need.

T F   5. Most advertising misrepresents the product.

T F   6. Consumers would be better off if there were no advertising.

T F   7. Consumers are becoming better informed and are less likely to be influenced strongly by advertising.

T F   8. Just as ads for illegal, harmful substances like crack are banned, so too should ads for other harmful substances like tobacco and alcohol be banned.

T F   9. I immediately forget musical "jingle" advertisements after I have heard them.

T F   10. Advertising has no influence on my purchasing behavior.

Advertising: Pros and Cons

Pros	Cons
Advertising can help the consumer learn about new products and services.	Advertising often irritates and insults the consumer's intelligence.
Advertising can help the consumer discover new ways to use a product.	Advertising often fails to give a true picture of the product being sold.
Advertising provides useful shopping information, such as warranties and guarantees.	Advertising often provides little useful information to help consumers in their buying decisions.
Advertising allows the consumer to compare prices and values of various products.	Advertising encourages consumers to buy products they may not need, want, or be able to afford.
Advertising tells the consumers where to find a particular product or service.	Advertising can cause consumers to feel their current products (particularly clothes) are out of date.
Advertising can help the consumer make specific consumer decisions.	Advertisements are sometimes directed at children who are unable to resist irrational appeals.
Advertising helps businesses sell their product. Sales help the economy to grow.	People shown in advertisements are seldom representative of people in real life.
Advertising is an important source of financial support for the mass media (newspapers, magazines, television, and radio).	Advertising often increases the price of the product it promotes.

Food Choices

Lower Fat	Calories	Fat (g)	Higher Fat	Calories	Fat (g)
Baked potato	120	1	French fries	225	14
Whole wheat bread (1 slice)	60	1	Croissant	230	12
Baked chicken, skinless	160	6	Fried chicken, with skin	220	11
Broccoli, steamed	25	0	Broccoli with cheese sauce	111	7

Source: U.S. Department of Agriculture

What's in a Lease?

A lease can be very difficult to read. First, the forms are usually long and the print quite small. Second, they are often written in legal language which is difficult for the average person to understand. For these reasons, tenants often sign leases thinking that what is written in the lease is legal and binding. They think that they have no choice but to sign if they wish to rent the unit.

Though it is true that leases are binding once they are signed, landlords may make changes in the lease agreement if the requests are reasonable. But these changes must be made in writing on the lease form and initialed by the landlord.

Listed below are typical clauses which may appear in lease forms. To the right is an interpretation of what the clause means to a tenant. Becoming familiar with the language of leases before you sign can save you a lot of grief later on.

If the lease states:	It means:
1. *Security deposit.* "Lessor may apply all or any portion of the security deposit in payment of any amounts due from Lessee."	Some landlords refuse to return deposits claiming unusual wear and tear or extra cleaning costs regardless of the condition of the apartment. Renters have little protection against unfair withholding of security deposits short of legal action.
2. *Condition of premises.* "Lessee has examined and knows the condition of premises and has received the same in good order and repair except as herein otherwise specified."	You have agreed the apartment is in fine shape. If you're satisfied that the apartment is OK as is, the landlord won't have to do anything to improve it. If you find later that the dishwasher doesn't work, the landlord may or may not bother to repair it.
3. *Limitation of liability.* "Except as provided by (state) statute, Lessor shall not be liable for any damage occasioned by failure to keep premises in repair, and shall not be liable for any damage done or occasioned by or from plumbing, gas, water, steam, or other pipes, snow or ice, ..."	The landlord is protected from his own negligence—you won't hold the landlord responsible for anything. If a pipe bursts and floods your apartment, you have agreed that you won't make the landlord pay for damages.
4. *Subletting.* "The Lessee will not assign this lease or sublet the premises without the written consent of the Lessor."	You can sublet the unit to others, in case you move before the period of the lease is up, but the landlord must give written consent. The landlord has the right to approve or disapprove a prospective tenant.
5. *Subletting.* "The premises shall be occupied only by the tenant and the members of the immediate family of the tenant . . . ."	The landlord, in this case, will not permit the apartment to be sublet. If you wish to move before the lease is up, you may be stuck paying rent until your lease ends.
6. *Repairs.* "Lessee agrees to repair all damage resulting from misuse or neglect. Upon Lessee's failure to make such repairs, after reasonable notice by Lessor, Lessor may make such repairs and Lessee shall be liable for any reasonable expense incurred."	In this case, the renter will pay for damage he or she causes. Some leases make the renter responsible for all repairs. Be certain the lease clearly states who is responsible for paying for repair.

(Continued)

If the lease states:	It means:
7. *Payment of costs.* "Lessee will pay and discharge all reasonable costs, attorney's fees and expenses that shall be made and incurred by Lessor in enforcing the covenants and agreements of this lease."	You agree to pay the landlord's legal fees if you should be taken to court. You pay the costs of being sued!
8. *Holding over.* "If the Lessee shall continue to occupy the premises after the expiration date, then the Lessor may at Lessor's option serve written notice on the Lessee within 30 days indicating that such holding over constitutes a renewal of the lease at double the rental.	If you stay in the apartment after the end of the lease term, this can be regarded by the landlord as a renewal of the lease. Some lease forms specify that the rent can double! Also watch for an automatic renewal clause that sets a date before which the landlord must be notified if the lease is to be terminated. Failure to notify the landlord by such a date might hold you to another year's rent!
9. *Default by Lessee.* "If the Lessee defaults in payments, as set forth in the lease, or in any agreement contained herein, it shall be lawful for Lessor or his representative to declare the term of this agreement ended, to re-enter the premises and to expel or put out the Lessee and any other persons occupying the premises, using such force as he may deem necessary and again repossess the premises."	If the renter does not pay the rent (or otherwise violates the lease), the landlord can enter the apartment and remove the renter and his or her belongings using appropriate force.
10. *Right of entry.* "Lessee will allow Lessor free access to premises at all reasonable hours for the purpose of inspecting the premises, or to make any needful repairs . . . ."	The landlord can enter your apartment for any reason at all reasonable hours. What is a reasonable hour? You may want to specify this in the lease, or request 24 hour notice to be given.
11. *Waiver of jury trial.* "The respective parties hereto shall waive trial by jury in any action or counterclaim brought by either party . . . ."	If involved in legal action with your landlord, you will not be able to seek a jury trial. A judge will make the decision.
12. *Illegality of provisions.* "If any clause, phrase, provision, or portion of this lease shall be invalid or unenforceable under applicable law, such event shall not affect invalid or unenforceable the remainder of this lease."	Just because part of the lease might be found to be illegal, that doesn't make the legal parts less valid and binding.

Providing for the Family's Physical Needs

Chapter 24 Test

Matching: Match the following terms and identifying phrases.

_______ 1. A renter rents a property to someone else.

_______ 2. Type of advertising designed to stimulate a person's subconscious mind.

_______ 3. The re-use of materials to produce new products.

_______ 4. Someone who buys goods and services.

_______ 5. Investigates complaints about the safety of food, drugs, and cosmetics.

_______ 6. Promotes advertising and selling practices that are fair to both businesses and consumers.

_______ 7. Protects consumers from unfair trade practices and false advertising.

_______ 8. Decomposes by natural biological processes.

_______ 9. Type of food that has been partially or fully prepared in order to save time.

_______ 10. A written, legally binding rental agreement.

A. consumer

B. mortgage

C. subliminal

D. Food and Drug Administration

E. Federal Trade Commission

F. lease

G. Better Business Bureau

H. sublet

I. convenience

J. biodegradable

K. recycle

True/False: Circle *T* if the statement is true or *F* if the statement is false.

T F 11. The term *condominium* refers to a type of housing ownership rather than a specific type of housing structure.

T F 12. The Percent Daily Values are based on a 3,000-calorie diet.

T F 13. If you are buying tomatoes to use to make chili, you will save money if you choose fancy whole tomatoes rather than canned stewed tomatoes.

T F 14. In the United States housing costs are the same from region to region.

T F 15. A new car depreciates in value as soon as the new owner drives it out of the dealer's lot.

T F 16. A styrofoam cup is an example of a biodegradable item.

T F 17. Wool is an example of a natural fiber.

T F 18. The purpose of the Consumer Product Safety Commission is to design new, safe products and to sell them to consumers as a way of raising money to pay off the national debt.

T F 19. Mortgage interest rates do not vary from one financial institution to the next.

T F 20. A declaration of ownership provides a listing of the special rules and regulations of a condominium.

(Continued)

Multiple Choice: Select the best response. Write the letter in the space provided.

_____ 21. *Caveat emptor* means _____.
A. let the seller beware
B. let the buyer beware
C. that each person should be taxed according to his or her ability to pay
D. that each person should be supported according to his or her level of need

_____ 22. Assigning a lease means that the tenant _____.
A. transfers the entire unexpired portion of the lease to someone else
B. assigns responsibility for finding a new tenant to the rental agent
C. authorizes someone else to receive the security deposit refund
D. has filed a grievance with the Better Business Bureau concerning the legality of the lease

_____ 23. Discount stores generally _____.
A. provide convenience for people who like to shop at home
B. carry clothes and accessories in various styles, sizes, qualities, and price ranges, and provide many customer services
C. provide lower quality goods at low prices, with few customer services
D. provide used clothing

_____ 24. When a business advertises a product at a low price to get you to visit the store, then tries to sell you something more expensive once you are inside, this business is using which approach?
A. Bait-and-switch.
B. Subliminal.
C. Puffery.
D. Environmental responsibility.

_____ 25. A winter coat in a cold climate is an example of a _____.
A. want
B. physical need
C. resource
D. psychological need

_____ 26. _____ is the science of relationships between living things and their environments.
A. Ecology
B. Ecosystem
C. Environmental responsibility
D. Recycling

_____ 27. The clothing characteristic of garment durability is most important for clothes and accessories that the consumer will wear _____.
A. frequently and over a number of years
B. as "fad" items
C. once a year
D. at a costume party

_____ 28. Before you sign a lease you should be aware of _____.
A. the interest rate on the mortgage
B. the amount of the down payment
C. the amount of the annual property tax
D. how the security deposit will be handled

(Continued)

_______ 29. Which one of the following practices does *not* help drivers reduce the amount of gasoline they are using?
A. Accelerate slowly.
B. Observe speed limits.
C. Idle the engine for long periods of time.
D. Choose a car with a good rating for fuel economy.

_______ 30. Which of the following is a nonrenewable resource?
A. Wood.
B. Cotton.
C. Fruit.
D. Gasoline.

Essay Questions: Provide complete responses to the following questions or statements.

31. Discuss the comparative advantages of owning a home versus renting a home.

32. Identify and describe the personal and environmental costs of buying and owning a car.

33. List and discuss ways that consumers can save energy (heating fuel, electricity) and reduce energy costs.

Chapter 25
Protecting the Family's Resources

Objectives

After studying this chapter, students will be able to
- identify different types of life and health insurance.
- describe various types of auto and homeowner's insurance.
- list the advantages and disadvantages of various types of life, health, auto, and homeowner's insurance.
- appraise their family's needs for life, health, auto, and homeowner's insurance.

Bulletin Boards

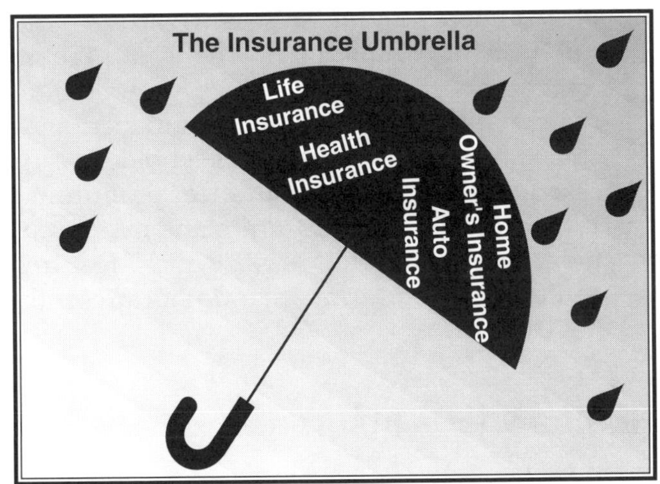

I. Title: "The Insurance Umbrella"

Make an umbrella from pieces of colorful construction paper and pin it to the bulletin board. On each sector of the umbrella pin a paper rectangle labeled as follows: *Life Insurance*, *Health Insurance*, *Auto Insurance*, and *Homeowner's Insurance*. Decorate the rest of the board with raindrops, either drawn or cut out of construction paper.

II. Title: "Your Insurance Shield"

Make a shield from pieces of colorful construction paper and attach it to the bulletin board. On the shield, pin or tape pictures (cut from magazines) of (1) an executive carrying a briefcase, (2) an ill person or a person receiving a checkup, (3) a home, and (4) an automobile. Label each picture as follows: (1) *Life Insurance*, (2) *Health Insurance*, (3) *Homeowner's Insurance*, and (4) *Auto Insurance*.

Teaching Materials

Text, pages 600-614
Terms to Know, To Review, To Do, and *To Think About*

Student Activity Guide
    A. *Insurance Opinions*
    B. *Insurance Crossword*
    C. *Insurance Decisions*

Teacher's Resource Guide/Binder
Mortality in the United States, transparency master, 25-1
Fastest-Growing Disability Insurance Claims, transparency master, 25-2
Auto Insurance Risks, reproducible master, 25-3
Careers in Insurance, reproducible master, 25-4
Chapter 25 Test

Teacher's Resource Binder
What's Insurable? color transparency, CT-25

Introductory Activities

1. *Mortality in the United States,* transparency master, 25-1. Use this transparency to inform students that Americans are vulnerable to certain illnesses and accidents. Discuss with students the importance of insurance and the roles sensible eating and living habits play in protecting against such diseases.
2. *What's Insurable?* color transparency, CT-25. Use this transparency to show students how various individuals try to protect against misfortune through insurance. Explain that most people probably have a home, personal property, an auto, health, and an income that they should insure in case of disability.
3. *Insurance Opinions,* Activity A, SAG. Ask students to complete this opinion inventory. Use their answers as the basis for a discussion and overview of insurance issues.

Strategies to Reteach, Reinforce, Enrich, and Extend Text Concepts

Life Insurance

4. **EX**   Review the reasons why people buy life insurance. Have students apply information to their life insurance needs now, 5 years from now, and 10 years from now.
5. **ER**   Invite a life insurance agent to speak to the class on "What Most Families Expect from Life Insurance."

Health Insurance

6. **ER**   Have students investigate different health insurance policies. Compare costs, benefits, coverage, cancellation practices. Ask students to give an oral report explaining the advantages of different types of health insurance, such as hospital expense, major medical, income replacement, etc.
7. **EX**   Compare in class deductible and coinsurance clauses in health insurance policies. Use a sample situation and figure what costs would be covered with each type of policy.

8. **RT**   Discuss with students categories of individuals who have difficulty getting health insurance. What is a pre-existing condition? Is it fair for high-risk individuals to be denied health insurance coverage? Would the average policyholder be willing to pay higher rates so that higher-risk individuals could be insured?
9. **RT**   *Fastest-Growing Disability Insurance Claims,* transparency master, 25-2. Use this transparency to discuss with students the types of claims that have increased the fastest in the last several years. Call students' attention to the fastest-increasing claim, carpal tunnel syndrome.
10. **ER**   Invite representatives from various health insurance plans in your area to discuss in class the types of insurance they sell. Allow time for a question-and-answer session.

Auto Insurance

11. **ER**   Instruct students to investigate different types of car insurance. What happens if a car is involved in an accident and the driver does not have insurance? What are the laws concerning car insurance in your state?
12. **RT**   *Auto Insurance Risks,* reproducible master, 25-3. Instruct students to complete this activity, then discuss insurance risks in class. Do students feel it is fair for high-risk individuals to be denied standard insurance coverage? Should individuals whose behaviors put their own lives and those of others in jeopardy have to pay higher rates in a high-risk pool?
13. **ER**   Students should research various auto safety features. Instruct students to prepare an oral report on their findings. Can the safety features help people secure auto insurance coverage? Can they help policyholders earn discounts on their insurance premiums? Which of the features are standard equipment in late-model cars? Which features could be added to cars that do not presently have them?

Homeowner's Insurance

14. **RT**   Discuss with students homeowner's and personal property insurance. Who needs this coverage? Why do apartment dwellers need property insurance? What does it cover? How much does it cost?

15. **ER**   Discounts on homeowner's insurance may be available if certain safety features are present in a house. Ask students to guess what some of these features may be. (Note: burglar alarms, deadbolt locks, fire extinguishers, smoke alarms.)

16. **ER**   Invite an insurance agent to speak to students about young people's insurance needs, including life insurance and homeowner's/personal property insurance.

17. **RF**   *Insurance Decisions*, Activity C, SAG. Use the scenarios in this exercise to stimulate small-group discussion on insurance issues.

Re-evaluating Your Insurance Needs

18. **EX**   Review the basic stages in the family life cycle with students. How may a family's insurance needs change at each stage?

19. **ER**   Invite an insurance agent to address students on the topic "Insurance Needs at Different Stages of Life."

20. **EX**   *Careers in Insurance*, reproducible master, 25-4. Ask students to research insurance careers using this activity. Students may wish to interview insurance agents for additional career information.

21. **RF**   *Insurance Crossword*, Activity B, SAG. Use this activity to review insurance-related vocabulary terms.

Answer Key for Chapter 25

Text
To Review, page 613.

1. term; premium; beneficiary; face amount
2. D, E, F
3. Catastrophic
4. A deductible clause states that the insured will pay an agreed-upon portion of the total expense, which may be the first $250, $500, or even $1,000 of the bill. The insurance company will pay the balance. A coinsurance clause states that the policyholder will pay a certain percentage of the costs, perhaps 20 to 25 percent, while the insurance company pays the remaining portion of the costs.
5. (Student response.)
6. (List five:) Amount of coverage you want. The year, make, and model of your car. Your driving record. The region in which you live. Your age, sex, and marital status. Driver education. Good grades.
7. Bodily injury liability insurance pays for damages and legal defense if you or a member of your family injures others while driving. Medical payments insurance pays for the medical expenses resulting from accidental injury. Protection against uninsured motorists applies to bodily injuries caused by an uninsured motorist or a hit–and–run driver. Property damage liability insurance pays for legal defense and the damages your car causes to the property of others. Comprehensive physical damage insurance protects you against financial loss caused by something other than another vehicle. Collision insurance protects you against financial loss when your car is damaged by collision with another vehicle or object or as a result of turning over.
8. Replacement cost. With this coverage, you will be able to replace what you have lost with items of similar value at today's prices. With the actual cash value, the value of items is depreciated according to their age, so the insurance company would pay you a lesser amount.

Student Activity Guide

Activity B, *Insurance Crossword.*

1 POLICY
2 FACE
3 PROPERTY
4 DAMAGE
5 VARIABLE
6 BENEFICIARY
7 COINSURANCE
8 WHOLE
9 COLLISION
10 INJURY
11 DEDUCTIBLE
12 TERM
13 NO FAULT
PREMIUM
COMPREHENSIVE

Teacher's Resource Guide

***Auto Insurance Risks,* reproducible master, 25-3.**

1. L	6. H	11. L
2. L	7. H	12. H
3. H	8. H	13. H
4. H	9. H	14. H
5. L	10. H	15. H

Chapter 25 Test

1. F	11. F	21. A
2. C	12. T	22. D
3. E	13. T	23. C
4. J	14. T	24. B
5. I	15. T	25. B
6. B	16. T	26. B
7. A	17. F	27. A
8. H	18. T	28. D
9. G	19. F	29. D
10. D	20. F	30. D

31. (Student response.)
32. (Student response.)
33. (Student response.)

Mortality in the United States

Leading Causes of Death in the U.S., 1994

- Heart disease

- Cancer

- Stroke

Principal Types of Accidental Deaths in the U.S., 1994

- Motor vehicle accidents

- Falls

- Poisonings

- Drownings

- Fires, burns

- Ingestion of food, objects

- Firearms

Fastest-Growing
Disability Insurance Claims

- Carpal tunnel syndrome

- Epstein-Barr virus

- Back and disk pain

- Psychiatric problems

- AIDS

Auto Insurance Risks

Name ____ **Date** _______________ **Period**_______________

To learn more about auto insurance risks and safety features, research and rate the risk levels below.

Risks

Assume that you are an auto insurance agent evaluating an insurance application. Rate the risk level for each driver characteristic below by circling *H* for higher risk or *L* for lower risk.

H L 1. Driver is a married, middle-aged female.

H L 2. Driver lives in a rural rather than urban area.

H L 3. Driver has been convicted of driving while intoxicated.

H L 4. Driver has lost license for speeding.

H L 5. Driver uses car to travel less than 10 miles per week.

H L 6. Driver is 19 years old and has no driving history–positive or negative.

H L 7. Driver has never had auto insurance before applying for it now.

H L 8. Driver uses car to commute 100 miles to work daily.

H L 9. Driver has been treated for frequent episodes of suicidal depression.

H L 10. Driver has a new red sports car in a make and model that has a high rate of theft.

H L 11. Driver has never had a car accident.

H L 12. Driver has had license suspended for playing "chicken" with another driver on a highway late at night.

H L 13. Driver's car is an expensive, late-model luxury car with all the optional features.

H L 14. Driver must take medication for narcolepsy.

H L 15. Driver is head of a household that includes an 18-year-old male who will drive the family car on weekends.

Careers in Insurance

Name ____ **Date** _____________ **Period** _____________

The insurance industry offers many careers in life, health, automobile, and homeowner's insurance. To learn more about them, research and answer the questions below.

1. Name at least five different careers in the insurance industry.

   a. ____

   b. ____

   c. ____

   d. ____

   e. ____

2. What education and training are needed for these careers?

   a. ____

   b. ____

   c. ____

   d. ____

   e. ____

3. What special aptitudes, if any, are needed for these careers?

   a. ____

   b. ____

   c. ____

   d. ____

   e. ____

4. Of the careers you have identified, name the two you think you would enjoy most. Give at least three reasons for each choice.

   a. ____

   ____

   ____

   ____

   ____

   b. ____

   ____

   ____

   ____

   ____

Protecting the Family's Resources

Name ____

Date ____ **Period** ______________ **Score** ______________

Chapter 25 Test

Matching: Match the following terms and identifying phrases.

_____ 1. Covers the costs of intensive care, heart surgery, or long illness.

_____ 2. The person designated to receive the benefits of a life insurance policy upon the insured's death.

_____ 3. The amount of money the policyholder receives if the policy is surrendered before death or when the policy matures.

_____ 4. May offer either replacement cost or actual cash value for damaged items.

_____ 5. A type of life insurance that offers both protection and savings and in which the two parts are clearly separated.

_____ 6. Payment made by the policyholder for insurance.

_____ 7. A type of auto insurance coverage that pays for medical expenses resulting from accidental injury.

_____ 8. Generally pays for hospitalization and medication; may also pay for some services such as X rays and lab tests.

_____ 9. Type of flexible life insurance that allows the insured to alter the coverage as the need for protection and the ability to pay for it change.

_____ 10. Health insurance that ensures that the company cannot cancel your policy just because you submit many claims.

A. medical payments insurance
B. premium
C. beneficiary
D. guaranteed renewable
E. cash value
F. catastrophic insurance
G. adjustable
H. basic medical insurance
I. universal
J. homeowner's insurance

True/False: Circle *T* if the statement is true or *F* if the statement is false.

T F 11. The face amount of an insurance policy is the amount of money a person pays for insurance.

T F 12. Term life insurance covers the life of the insured for a specified period of time.

T F 13. Whole life insurance is designed to cover a person's entire life and to build a cash value.

T F 14. Stop-loss protection in a health insurance policy limits the policyholder's out-of-pocket coinsurance medical expenses.

T F 15. Disability income insurance protects a person or family from loss of income due to a disabling illness or injury.

T F 16. No-fault auto insurance eliminates the need for a legal process proving who is at fault in an auto accident.

(Continued)

T F 17. Collision insurance pays for legal defense and the damages the policyholder's car causes to the property of others but does not cover the policyholder's car.

T F 18. Most homeowner's insurance policies include liability insurance to cover the medical costs of someone injured on the policyholder's property.

T F 19. The replacement cost of an item of personal property is likely to be lower than its actual cash value.

T F 20. Renters never need insurance on their personal property.

Multiple Choice: Select the best response. Write the letter in the space provided.

______ 21. The total sum of money that is paid to the beneficiary when a life insurance policyholder dies is equal to the ______ of the policy.
  A. face amount
  B. universality
  C. premium
  D. deductible

______ 22. The type of life insurance that offers protection but does not build cash value is ______.
  A. universal
  B. adjustable
  C. whole life
  D. term

______ 23. In a health insurance policy the type of clause that states that the policyholder will pay a certain percentage of the costs while the insurance company pays the remaining portion is a ______.
  A. stop-loss protection clause
  B. deductible clause
  C. coinsurance clause
  D. right-to-transfer clause

______ 24. In a health insurance policy the type of clause that gives you the right to continue your group policy even if you leave the group is a ______.
  A. guaranteed renewable clause
  B. right-to-transfer clause
  C. coinsurance clause
  D. deductible clause

______ 25. The type of insurance that pays for damages and legal defense if you or a member of your family injures others while driving is called ______.
  A. medical payments insurance
  B. bodily injury liability insurance
  C. property damage liability insurance
  D. comprehensive physical damage insurance

______ 26. Which of the following is a characteristic of HMOs?
  A. The insured is free to choose any physician.
  B. The insured uses physicians associated with the HMO.
  C. The insured usually has a deductible and a coinsurance payment.
  D. The insured does not pay a set fee on a regular basis.

(Continued)

_______ 27. A maximum benefits clause _______.
    A. sets a limit on the benefits the insured can collect over a lifetime
    B. gives the policyholder the right to continue the policy even after he or she leaves the participating group
    C. is designed to begin paying when basic coverage stops
    D. All of the above.

_______ 28. Disability income insurance coverage _______.
    A. is available to disabled people only
    B. usually provides for a lifetime income even in cases in which the disabled person recovers and goes back to work
    C. reimburses the policyholder on a fee-for-service basis
    D. guarantees the continuation of the wage earner's salary during the time he or she is unable to work

_______ 29. Auto insurance rates may vary according to _______.
    A. the policyholder's age and gender
    B. the year, make, and model of the policyholder's car
    C. the policyholder's driving record
    D. All of the above.

_______ 30. Insurance coverage for bodily injury caused by a hit-and-run driver is provided by _______.
    A. bodily injury liability insurance
    B. medical payments insurance
    C. property damage liability insurance
    D. protection against uninsured motorists insurance

Essay Questions: Provide complete responses to the following questions or statements.

31. Describe a good insurance program for a person who graduated from college two years ago. This person is single, is in good health, owns a car, and rents an apartment.

32. Describe a good insurance program for a family consisting of one breadwinner, one full-time homemaker, two young children, and a home with a mortgage.

33. Explain the basic differences between an HMO and a PPO.

Chapter 26
Using Banking Services

Objectives

After studying this chapter, students will be able to
- differentiate between gross income and net income.
- identify the types of payments that typically are collected through payroll deductions.
- compare various types of financial institutions and the services they provide.
- describe the use of a checking account.
- summarize ways to save and invest money.

Bulletin Boards

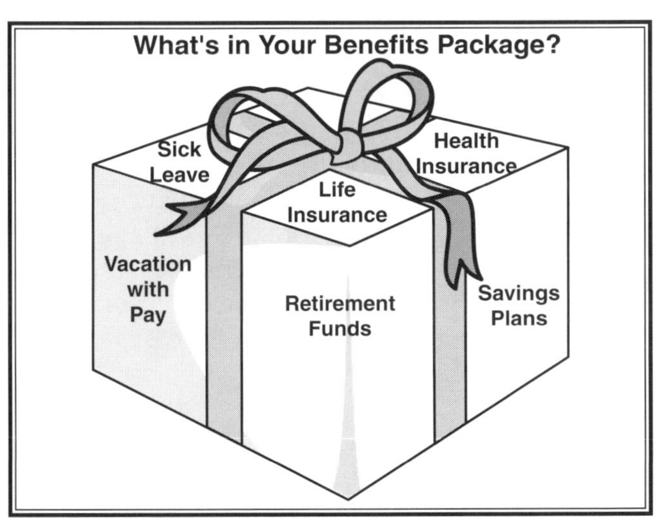

I. Title: "What's in Your Benefits Package?"

Design a large package tied with a bow as the background for this bulletin board. Then divide the "package" into sections marked as follows: *Sick Leave, Vacation with Pay, Savings Plans, Retirement Funds, Health Insurance,* and *Life Insurance.*

II. Title: "Social Security Benefits"

Label a brightly colored piece of construction paper *Social Security Benefits* and place it in the upper center of the bulletin board. Under this paper place three smaller rectangular pieces of paper labeled *Disability, Retirement,* and *Death.* Place magazine pictures depicting each situation under each label. Use brightly colored yarn to connect the labels with the larger paper.

Teaching Materials

Text, pages 616-636

Terms to Know, To Review, To Do, and *To Think About*

Student Activity Guide
- A. *Survey of Financial Institutions*
- B. *Monetary Pyramid*
- C. *Writing Checks*
- D. *Financial Decisions*

Teacher's Resource Guide/Binder

Banking, Taxes, and Saving, reproducible master, 26-1

Managing a Checking Account, reproducible master, 26-2

24-Hour Telephone Banking, transparency master, 26-3

The Bank Statement, transparency master, 26-4

Chapter 26 Test

Teacher's Resource Binder
U.S. Savings Bonds: Education Tax Benefit, color transparency, CT-26A
"Squirreling Away" Cash: Typical CD Rates, color transparency, CT-26B

Software for Contemporary Living
Chapter Review Game

Introductory Activities

1. Introduce the topic of banking services by asking students to complete the following statements:
   When I receive payment for something, I feel. . .
   When I go into a bank, I feel. . .
   People who frequently overdraw their checking accounts are. . .
   When I retire, I would like to. . .
   If I had $100 to save, I would. . .
   Briefly discuss these statements in the context of chapter subject matter.
2. *Banking, Taxes, and Saving,* reproducible master, 26-1. Use this activity to stimulate class interest and discussion of concepts related to banking, taxes, and saving. Explain that students' attitudes toward certain topics (such as the importance of saving for retirement) may change as they move through the family life cycle.

Strategies to Reteach, Reinforce, Enrich, and Extend Text Concepts

Your Income

3. **RF**   Ask students who work to bring in paycheck stubs that list various deductions. List these deductions on the chalkboard. Identify what any abbreviations stand for and discuss the purpose of each deduction. Define the terms *gross income* and *net income.*
4. **EX**   Using current income tax forms, compute the income tax for particular situations, such as: (a) single person, no children, earns $20,000; (b) married couple, filing jointly, no children, working spouse earns $25,500; (c) married couple, filing jointly, three children, working spouse earns $29,000; (d) married couple, filing jointly, no children, one spouse earns $20,500, the other spouse earns $16,000;

(e) married couple, filing jointly, no children, but elderly parents of wife to support, one spouse earns $34,000, the other spouse earns $28,000; and (f) married couple, filing jointly, four children, one spouse earns $39,000, the other spouse earns $20,000.

5. **RF**   Refer to the sample W-4 and W-2 forms on pages 620 and 625 of the text. Discuss the purposes of each form as well as how to fill out a W-4 form. Explain that students may claim an exemption from withholding if they do not expect to owe any federal income tax.
6. **ER**   Discuss with students the purposes of social security and the misconception that social security is the only retirement income a person needs. Discuss benefits received when a worker's earnings end due to disability or death.
7. **EX**   Social security taxes are figured as a percentage of gross income and are computed on annual earnings up to a maximum amount. Congress determines the percentage rate and the maximum earnings limit. Find out the current percentage rate and maximum limit and have students compute the FICA taxes that people would have to pay at various income levels.

Financial Institutions

8. **RT**   Discuss with students the major differences among the various types of financial institutions.
9. **ER**   *Survey of Financial Institutions,* Activity A, SAG. Instruct students to compare the services (passbook savings, five-year CDs, money market accounts, checking accounts) of three local financial institutions. Students also should indicate the best checking account choices for young married couples.
10. **RT**   Refer to illustration 26-9 on page 627 of the text. Discuss with students how banking and financial institutions use the information on checks to help people in cases of lost checks, stolen checks, etc.
11. **RT**   *U.S. Savings Bonds: Education Tax Benefit,* color transparency, CT-26A. By the year 2008, a college education is projected to cost between $17,000 and $37,000 per year. To encourage low- and middle-income families to save for their children's education, the federal government offers a tax benefit for interest earned on U.S. Savings Bonds.

Refer to this transparency while explaining how this benefit works and how impressively savings can accumulate if young parents start saving early for their children's education.

12. **RT** *"Squirreling Away" Cash: Typical CD Rates,* color transparency, CT-26B. Refer to this transparency to illustrate interest rates for certificates of deposit held for various lengths of time.

Checking Accounts

13. **RF** Discuss with students how to endorse checks and what methods of endorsement banks recognize.
14. **RF** Discuss how to fill out deposit tickets–the information needed, how the information should be recorded, and what to do with deposit receipts.
15. **RF** *Managing a Checking Account,* reproducible master, 26-2. Students can use this master to practice filling out a deposit slip, writing a check, balancing a checkbook, and checking a bank statement against a check register.
16. **RF** Explain when it may be necessary to use a cashier's check, a certified check, a money order, and traveler's checks.
17. **ER** Invite someone from the Social Security Administration to speak to the class. Ask questions about the objectives of the social security program, how social security can assist persons in many situations, and the future of the nation's social security program.
18. **ER** *24-Hour Telephone Banking,* transparency master, 26-3. Use this transparency to illustrate the trend toward automated routine banking transactions. How much time might bank customers save each month by using this service? Also discuss banking online.
19. **RF** *The Bank Statement,* transparency master, 26-4. Use this transparency to show students what an actual bank statement looks like. You also may use the transparency as a reference when reviewing how to balance a statement.
20. **RF** *Monetary Pyramid,* Activity B, SAG. Instruct students to read the definitions of banking services and to write the term names in the pyramid's corresponding spaces.

21. **RT** *Writing Checks,* Activity C, SAG. Students should complete this activity to review check writing information.

Saving and Investing Money

22. RT Discuss with students the different plans for saving and/or investing money. Also discuss the guidelines for choosing each.
23. **RF** Discuss the pros and cons of saving methods for a newly married couple. Indicate how the attitudes of both partners can affect the overall savings program.
24. **EX** Instruct students to compare interest rates using Chart 26-13 on page 632 of the text. Students should compute how much a couple could save in the following situations: saving $10 a month at six percent interest for 15 years; saving $50 a month at seven percent interest for 20 years.
25. **EX** *Financial Decisions,* Activity D, SAG. Instruct students to read the case studies and to write conclusions based on chapter information. Students should share their financial solutions in class.

Answer Key for Chapter 26

Text
To Review, page 634.

1. (List four:) Sick leave, vacations with pay, savings plans, pension and retirement funds, health and life insurance.
2. false
3. false
4. (List five: Student response.)
5. IRS: D. FDIC: B. NCUA: A. FICA: C.
6. Employees, their employers, and self-employed persons pay social security taxes. These taxes are used to pay benefits to eligible people. When a worker's earnings stop or are reduced because of disability, retirement, or death, monthly cash benefits are paid to replace part of the earnings the family has lost.
7. Contact your bank immediately.
8. true
9. Savings accounts: C. U.S. savings bonds: A. certificates of deposit: D. money market accounts: E. retirement accounts: B.
10. false

Student Activity Guide

Activity B, *Monetary Pyramid.*

```
                    1. W  4
                   2. N  E  T
                  3. F  I  C  A
                 4. G  R  O  S  S
                5. M  U  T  U  A  L
               6. S  A  V  I  N  G  S
              7. P  O  S  T  D  A  T  E
             8. C  E  R  T  I  F  I  E  D
            9. E  X  E  M  P  T  I  O  N  S
          10. C  R  E  D  I  T  U  N  I  O  N
         11. S  A  V  I  N  G  S  B  O  N  D  S
        12. F  R  I  N  G  E  B  E  N  E  F  I  T
       13. S  O  C  I  A  L  S  E  C  U  R  I  T  Y
      14. I  N  T  E  R  N  A  L  R  E  V  E  N  U  E
     15. J  O  I  N  T  B  A  N  K  A  C  C  O  U  N  T
    16. R  E  T  I  R  E  M  E  N  T  A  C  C  O  U  N  T
   17. M  O  N  E  Y  M  A  R  K  E  T  A  C  C  O  U  N  T
  18. W  A  G  E  A  N  D  T  A  X  S  T  A  T  E  M  E  N  T
 19. C  E  R  T  I  F  I  C  A  T  E  O  F  D  E  P  O  S  I  T
```

Activity C, *Writing Checks.*

1. (Student writes a check.)
2. (Student writes a check.)
3. A. Your legal signature.
   B. The end opposite the dollar amount.
4. Pay to the order of Joe Kim. Then write your signature.
5. (List five rules. See pages 625-627 of text.)

Teacher's Resource Guide

Managing a Checking Account, reproducible master, 26-2.

Making a deposit: Total deposit is $92.43.

Filling out a check register: After recording the deposit and the check, the balance should be $497.20

Balancing worksheet: Closing balance is $419.77.

Total of deposits not shown on statement is $92.43.

Total of outstanding checks is $15.00.

Final balance is $497.20.

Chapter 26 Test

1. F	11. T	21. B
2. I	12. F	22. A
3. B	13. F	23. C
4. H	14. T	24. D
5. K	15. T	25. B
6. D	16. T	26. B
7. A	17. F	27. C
8. E	18. T	28. D
9. C	19. F	29. A
10. G	20. T	30. B

31. Listing and description of any two of the following types of deductions: sick leave, vacation with pay, savings plans, retirement funds, health insurance, life insurance.
32. Identification and discussion of any three of the following types of financial institutions: commercial bank, savings and loan association, mutual savings bank, credit union.
33. Identification and discussion of any three of the following alternatives to a personal check: cashier's check, certified check, money order, traveler's check.

Banking, Taxes, and Saving

Name _______________________________________ **Date** _______________ **Period** _______________

Read each statement concerning banking and saving. Circle *A* if you agree with the statement or *D* if you disagree with the statement. Discuss each statement in class.

A D 1. When you go on a long trip, it is smart to carry a lot of cash rather than wasting time converting some of your cash to traveler's checks.

A D 2. Precious documents like deeds, titles, and savings bonds should be hidden somewhere in the house or apartment.

A D 3. It is silly to request overdraft protection at the bank because if you keep good records you will rarely, if ever, overdraw your checking account.

A D 4. People are only human and sometimes make mistakes. Therefore, overdraft protection is a good idea and worth any extra cost.

A D 5. Paying income tax is the responsibility of every income-earning citizen.

A D 6. Income tax is necessary to help government fulfill functions that citizens would otherwise have trouble fulfilling themselves (for example, the cost of defense).

A D 7. I would rather have my employer withhold too much rather than too little from my paycheck so that I will receive an income tax refund.

A D 8. I would rather have my employer withhold too little from my paycheck so I can save extra dollars and earn interest on them until tax time.

A D 9. Social security provides benefits only for retirement.

A D 10. If I could, I would withhold my contributions to social security and instead invest the money myself for my retirement.

A D 11. If I contribute steadily to social security throughout my working life, I will need no other savings for retirement.

A D 12. People who receive social security benefits should pay income tax on those benefits.

A D 13. It's a good idea to save for a "rainy day."

A D 14. It is pointless to save up a "nest egg" because the future is totally beyond our control.

A D 15. People do not need to start thinking about saving for retirement until after age 35.

A D 16. People who begin early to save for retirement have the peace of mind that comes with preparing for the future.

Managing a Checking Account

Name _______________________________ **Date** _______________ **Period** _______________

Managing a checking account involves several procedures. Pretend that you are Amy Nelson and that you have a checking account at South Holland Trust and Savings Bank. Make out a sample deposit slip and also write a check on your account. Enter your transactions in the check register on the next page.

Make out a deposit slip. You want to deposit your paycheck for $82.43 and $10.00 in currency you received for baby-sitting. The date is June 30.

Write a check for $15.00 to pay for a haircut at The Hair Hut. The date is June 30.

(Continued)

Name ____

Record your deposit and check for a haircut in this check register. Balance your checkbook.

RECORD ALL CHARGES OR CREDITS THAT AFFECT YOUR ACCOUNT

NUMBER	DATE	DESCRIPTION OF TRANSACTION	PAYMENT/DEBIT (-)	√ T	FEE (IF ANY) (-)	DEPOSIT/CREDIT (+)	BALANCE $ 276 90
220	6/2	Phone Company	$ 36 25		$	$	
221	6/4	Drug Store	5 50				
	6/5	Deposit				250 00	
222	6/10	Sports Haven (tennis shoes)	42 38				
223	6/18	Dan Hardy (pay back loan)	9 00				
224	6/20	Computer Palace (payment on computer)	26 00				
	6/25	Deposit				60 00	
225	6/28	Brown's Store for Men (sweater for Dad)	48 00				

REMEMBER TO RECORD AUTOMATIC PAYMENTS / DEPOSITS ON DATE AUTHORIZED.

You received the following bank statement at the beginning of July.

BANK STATEMENT   For Period Ending: 6/30/9x

BALANCE LAST STATEMENT	DEPOSITS AND CREDITS		CHECKS/WITHDRAWALS AND DEBITS		BALANCE THIS STATEMENT
	NO.	TOTAL AMOUNT	NO.	TOTAL AMOUNT	
276.90	2	310.00	6	167.13	419.77

CHECKING ACCOUNT TRANSACTIONS

DATE	DEBITS	CREDITS	DESCRIPTION
06/05		250.00	DEPOSIT
06/25		60.00	DEPOSIT

CHECKS

DATE	CHECK NO	AMOUNT	DATE	CHECK NO	AMOUNT
06/04	220	36.25	06/20	223	9.00
06/05	221	5.50	06/20	222	42.38
06/20	224	26.00	06/29	225	48.00

(Continued)

Name ____

The deposit you made and the check you wrote earlier in this activity are not shown in the bank statement. However, you did record them in your check register. Check the accuracy of your record keeping against the bank statement by filling in the worksheet below. The balance on the worksheet should be the same as the balance on your check register.

BALANCING WORKSHEET

Balance shown on
  BANK STATEMENT . . . . $_______________________

Add Deposits
  Not on Statement . . . . + $_______________________

  ____

  ____

  Sub-Total . . . . $_______________________

	Subtract Checks
Check	Issued But
No.	Not on Statement

_____________ $ _______________________

_____________   _______________________

_____________   _______________________

_____________   _______________________

_____________   _______________________

_____________   _______________________

_____________   _______________________

_____________   _______________________

_____________   _______________________

_____________   _______________________

_____________   _______________________

_____________   _______________________

      Total . . . . – $ _______________________
      BALANCE . . . . * $ _______________________

*The above balance should be the same as the up-to-date balance in your checkbook.

24-Hour Telephone Banking

Allows you to instantly:

- receive bank statements by mail or fax.

- confirm cleared checks.

- transfer money between accounts.

- receive your balance.

- know about current rates.

- reorder checks.

The Bank Statement

National Bank   **Statement**

STATEMENT PERIOD 08-25-00 THROUGH 09-27-00

_________________ **CHECKING SUMMARY** _________________

OPENING BALANCE	2,184.68	ACCOUNT #	93-302-717
+DEPOSITS	4,778.42	# OF ENCLOSURES	0
- CHECKS AND DEBITS	3,549.21	AVERAGE BALANCE	1,798.75
=NEW BALANCE	3,413.89		

_________________ **CHECKING ACTIVITY** _________________

DEPOSITS	DATE	AMOUNT	DEPOSITS	DATE	AMOUNT
DEPOSIT	09-02	1,368.00	DEPOSIT	09-26	3,410.42

CHECKS	DATE	AMOUNT	CHECKS	DATE	AMOUNT
680	09-07	410.00	REF 01	08-29	300.00
*682	09-14	77.11	REF 01	09-07	300.00
683	09-13	950.00	REF 01	09-13	300.00
684	09-22	400.00	REF 02	09-14	18.00
685	09-15	321.68	REF 01	09-16	400.00
*687	09-26	68.42	REF 03	09-27	4.00

REFERENCE DESCRIPTION

*DENOTES A BREAK IN CHECK SERIAL NUMBER SEQUENCE
REF 01 ELECTRONIC CASH WITHDRAWAL
REF 02 RESEARCH FEE/PHOTOCOPY
REF 03 SC/MAINTENANCE FEE

_________________ **CHECKING BALANCES** _________________

08-24	2,184.68	09-13	1,292.68	09-22	75.89
08-29	1,884.68	09-14	1,197.57	09-26	3,417.89
09-02	3,252.68	09-15	875.89	09-27	3,413.89
09-07	2,542.68	09-16	475.89		

Using Banking Services

Chapter 26 Test

Matching: Match the following terms and identifying phrases.

_______ 1. Form that tells your employer how many exemptions you are allowed and therefore how much of your income should be withheld from your paycheck for taxes.

_______ 2. Owned by stockholders and operated for profit.

_______ 3. The income a person accumulates before deductions are made.

_______ 4. Federal agency that handles matters related to income taxes.

_______ 5. United States savings bonds that earn a market-based variable rate or a minimum guaranteed rate if they are held at least five years.

_______ 6. Form that states how much money the federal government withheld from your paychecks the previous year.

_______ 7. Amount of income left after deductions are taken from a paycheck.

_______ 8. Occurs when a person writes a check with insufficient funds.

_______ 9. Sources or amounts of income that are not taxed.

_______ 10. A nonprofit financial institution owned by and operated for the benefit of its members.

A. net income
B. gross income
C. exemptions
D. W-2 Form
E. overdraft
F. W-4 Form
G. credit union
H. IRS
I. commercial bank
J. deductions
K. Series EE

True/False: Circle *T* if the statement is true or *F* if the statement is false.

T   F   11. Many jobs have fringe benefits like sick leave, vacation with pay, retirement funds, and life insurance.

T   F   12. A certified check is a check drawn by a bank on its own funds and signed by a bank officer.

T   F   13. A mutual savings bank is owned by the federal government.

T   F   14. A money order is an order for a specific amount of money payable to a specific payee.

T   F   15. Net income is sometimes called *take-home pay.*

T   F   16. The main differences among the many types of financial institutions are ownership and insurance.

T   F   17. The actual amount of income tax a person pays is based upon his or her gross income.

T   F   18. U.S. citizens who earn money pay taxes based on a graduated income scale.

(Continued)

T F   19. In most savings and loan associations deposits are not insured.

T F   20. Health insurance is an example of a deduction that can be made from a paycheck.

Multiple Choice: Select the best response. Write the letter in the space provided.

______ 21. Which of the following is an example of a retirement account?
  A. Twentieth-century fund.
  B. Keogh plan.
  C. Market-based fund.
  D. Currency exchange plan.

______ 22. If you wish to invest in a certificate of deposit, you ______.
  A. must have money you can deposit for a set period of time
  B. must belong to a credit union
  C. will be free to withdraw your money without penalty at any time
  D. will not be able to get your money back until after retirement, no matter what the circumstances

______ 23. A cashier's check ______.
  A. can be purchased at a post office
  B. can be purchased at a public library
  C. is drawn by a bank on its own funds and signed by a bank officer
  D. is actually a personal check with the bank's guarantee that the check will be paid

______ 24. Deposits to most credit union accounts are insured up to a specified limit by the ______.
  A. Internal Revenue Service
  B. Federal Deposit Insurance Corporation
  C. American Savings and Loan Association
  D. National Credit Union Association

______ 25. When writing a check for a purchase, it is important to remember to ______.
  A. postdate checks written on Sundays or holidays
  B. always use the same signature that you use for writing other checks
  C. leave a generous space between the dollar sign and the numerals
  D. sign it but leave the space for the amount blank so that the store clerk can fill in the correct amount

______ 26. If you make out a check to someone and it is lost or stolen ______.
  A. no action needs to be taken
  B. it is wise to report this immediately to the bank so payment on the check can be stopped
  C. you can mark the check "void" in your check register because it cannot be cashed
  D. None of the above.

______ 27. A NOW account ______.
  A. can be opened only by stockholders in a financial institution
  B. earns no interest
  C. earns interest if a balance is maintained at a specified minimum level
  D. cannot be accessed with an automated teller machine

______ 28. To avoid being a victim of theft, users of automated teller machines should ______.
  A. share their personal identification numbers only with family members and good friends
  B. continue their transaction even if they feel they are being observed by others
  C. write down their personal identification numbers and keep them only in their wallets
  D. avoid using the machines late at night or in dark or isolated places

(Continued)

_____ 29. If a person overdraws his or her checking account frequently, this person ______.
      A. will typically be charged a penalty fee by his or her bank for each "bad" check
      B. should not expect to hear from creditors demanding payment
      C. can expect his or her credit rating to remain unaffected
      D. has no need to consider automatic overdraft protection

_____ 30. Money invested in a retirement account earns interest that usually ______.
      A. is taxed as it accumulates during the investor's working years
      B. is not taxed until it is withdrawn
      C. is never taxed
      D. is put into a trust fund for all retirees investing in this type of account

Essay Questions: Provide complete responses to the following questions or statements.

31. List and briefly describe at least two deductions that typically are made from people's paychecks.

32. Identify three kinds of financial institutions and briefly discuss the differences between them.

33. Identify three means of payment that can be used in place of personal checks. Briefly discuss the differences between them.

Chapter 27
Managing Your Finances

Objectives

After studying this chapter, students will be able to
- describe types of arrangements that couples may use to handle family finances.
- design a budget for managing income and expenses.
- identify various types of credit.
- evaluate various sources of credit.
- recognize benefits and pitfalls of credit use.

Bulletin Boards

I. Title: "Buy Now! Pay Later. . . and Later"

Find a picture in a magazine of someone enjoying a vacation. Also find a picture of someone looking sad or upset (or sketch such a picture). Place sample bills and debt notices around the second picture, illustrating the overuse of credit.

II. Title: "A Balancing Act"

Using the scales in the bulletin board in Chapter 20, depict how income and spending need to balance. Create equal stacks of money on each side of the scale using play money. Label one side of the scales *Income* and the other side of the scales *Spending*.

Teaching Materials

Text, pages 638-653

Terms to Know, To Review, To Do, and *To Think About*

Student Activity Guide
- A. *How Well Do You Manage Money?*
- B. *Saving vs. Spending*
- C. *Budget for a Young Married Couple*
- D. *Love and Money*

Teacher's Resource Guide/Binder

The Family Life Cycle, transparency master, 27-1

Checking Account Arrangements, transparency master, 27-2

Who Will Write the Checks? reproducible master, 27-3

Your Financial Plan, reproducible master, 27-4

Chapter 27 Test

Teacher's Resource Binder

Define Your Budget Goals! color transparency, CT-27

Software for Contemporary Living

Chapter Review Game

Introductory Activities

1. *The Family Life Cycle,* transparency master, 27-1. Ask students to identify stages in the life of a typical family when money is likely to be plentiful. In which stages will money be scarce? How can families manage their money so it can help them through the lean times?
2. *How Well Do You Manage Money?* Activity A, SAG. Have students evaluate their current money management practices by answering the questions in this activity.
3. *Saving vs. Spending,* Activity B, SAG. Students should respond to statements concerning saving and spending as part of family financial management.

Strategies to Reteach, Reinforce, Enrich, and Extend Text Concepts

Handling Your Money

4. **RF** *Checking Account Arrangements,* transparency master, 27-2. Ask students to describe the four options couples have to set up checking accounts.
5. **RF** *Who Will Write the Checks?* reproducible master, 27-3. Use this activity to reinforce students' understanding of alternatives in controlling spending and setting up banking records.
6. **ER** Ask a family finance specialist to address the class on "How Families Handle Checking Accounts."

Budgeting

7. **RF** *Define Your Budget Goals!* color transparency, CT-27. Use this transparency to discuss with students the importance of goal-setting and to explore the typical goals of young couples.
8. **RF** Discuss with students the advantages of following a budget. Indicate stages of the life cycle when budgeting is especially important. Describe how budgets are influenced by attitudes like "A penny saved is a penny earned," "Don't be a penny pincher," "Live for today and don't borrow tomorrow's troubles," and "Buy now and pay later."
9. **EX** Instruct students to investigate different budgeting systems. Students should evaluate the usefulness of various budget books available in stationery stores and from financial institutions.
10. **EX** Consider with students the information given in the text suggesting percentages of net income to be spent for food, housing, transportation, clothing, savings, and miscellaneous items. Would these percentages apply to families in your community? How can these percentages be changed to meet different needs and wants?
11. **RF** *Budget for a Young Married Couple,* Activity C, SAG. Ask students to fill out a budget form for a young couple by identifying fixed and flexible expenses. Students should answer questions about the budget and suggest ways to revise it to fit the couple's changing circumstances.
12. **RF** *Your Financial Plan,* reproducible master, 27-4. Students can use this activity to plan a weekly budget for themselves. They can then record their expenses for the week on the chart and answer the questions at the end of the activity.

Using Credit

13. **EX** Instruct students to research types of credit available to consumers today. They should compare installment and noninstallment credit. What are the conveniences of revolving credit plans? How can these types of credit help people to spend money wisely? How can they trap people into spending too much?
14. **EX** Investigate sources of credit and compare the pros and cons of each source. Decide which credit source would be best in each of the following situations: (a) young married couple, want to buy a new car, both are employed, have little savings, credit line is established, no major debts; (b) college student, foreclosure threatened on car, owns valuable baseball card collection, has possible source of income in one month; (c) middle-aged couple with extensive savings in three savings and loan associations, desire to purchase condominium; and (d) young person, wants to buy first car, has no credit line or savings account, works 30 hours per week as a salesperson in a clothing store.
15. **EX** Instruct students to investigate the varying costs of credit. Use the following example: A family must use credit to buy a $1200

computer. Find the best source of credit for them to use. First have students list the various sources of credit available in the community (such as a retail store, commercial bank, savings and loan association, credit union, finance company, and credit card). Then have students list the factors they will need to compare in order to make the best choice (such as the down payment required, annual percentage rate, total finance charge, and total cost of the item). Divide the class into pairs or small groups to research each source. Instruct students to report their findings in class. Record the information on a large chart or the chalkboard and discuss the pros and cons of each source.

16. **RF** *Love and Money,* Activity D, SAG. Use these problem situations as a basis for small-group discussion of financial management within the context of family relationships.

17. **ER** Invite a speaker from the local credit bureau to explain the best way for a young person to establish credit.

18. **ER** Ask a financial planner to speak to your class about the need for financial planning.

Answer Key for Chapter 27

Text
To Review, page 652.

1. (1) A joint bank account both spouses share that allows them to make deposits and withdrawals at will. (2) Separate accounts the spouses maintain individually. Spouses pay bills by dividing expenses. (3) Two accounts managed separately but controlled by one spouse. (4) All spending managed by one spouse.

2. (List three:) A budget will help you use your income to meet your needs and reach your goals. A budget assures you that you can meet your expenses. A budget helps you and your spouse to gain confidence in each other as financial partners. A budget helps you recognize where you are spending money. A budget helps you reach both short- and long-terms goals.

3. (Name five:) Food, transportation, housing, clothing, health care, savings, and miscellaneous items.

4. A revolving credit plan allows you to make purchases up to a specified amount. You pay a percentage of the balance each month plus carrying charges to keep the account "revolving." You can continue to

charge on this account as long as you pay the carrying charges and the total bill remains within the agreed limit.

5. true

6. (List five:) Yourself, credit union, financial institutions, store dealer financing, finance companies, pawnbrokers, family and friends.

7. false

8. Credit bureaus collect information on the credit practices of individuals and make this information available to businesses. This protects stores and businesses from phony or misleading applications.

9. true

10. Protect your credit rating by keeping the promises you made when you signed the credit contract. Make your payments on time and in the correct amount. If for some reason you must miss a payment, contact the creditor at once to make special arrangements.

Teacher's Resource Guide

***Who Will Write the Checks?* reproducible master, 27-3.**

1. D	3. A
2. B	4. C

Chapter 27 Test

1. I	11. T	21. B
2. D	12. T	22. A
3. J	13. F	23. B
4. C	14. T	24. D
5. F	15. T	25. C
6. K	16. F	26. B
7. A	17. T	27. D
8. H	18. F	28. C
9. B	19. T	29. A
10. G	20. F	30. D

31. (Student response.)

32. You may be able to borrow from yourself with a passbook loan. With this transaction you can borrow money from your bank and use your savings as collateral. You may be able to borrow from your life insurance.

33. (List two of each.) Advantages: Convenient, eliminates the need to carry a lot of cash, allows you to pay bills once a month by check, provides a record of payment. Disadvantages: It is easy to overspend, cards can be stolen or lost, you may be held responsible for purchases made on lost or stolen cards, stores charge more to cover the costs of credit.

The Family Life Cycle

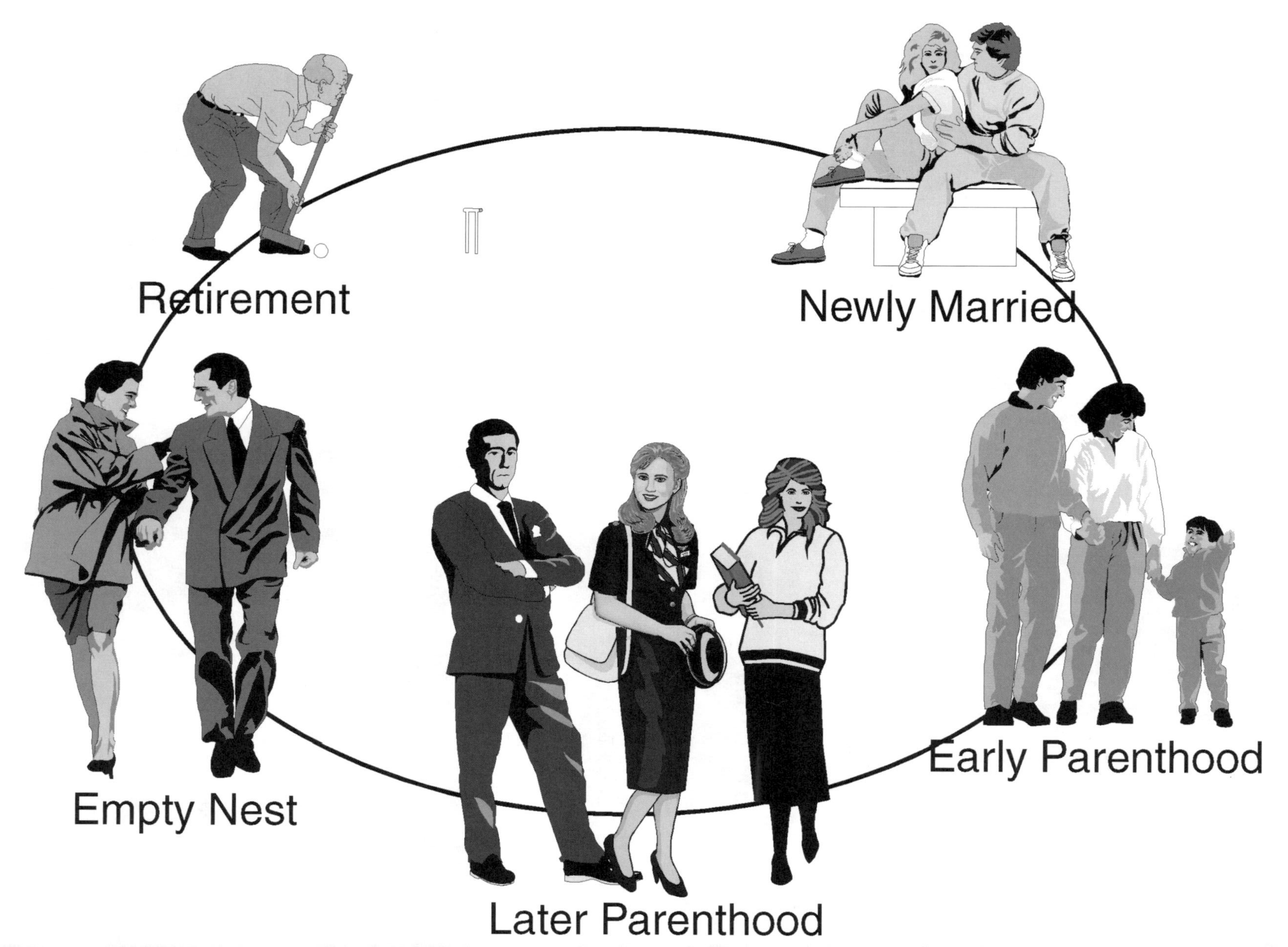

Checking Account Arrangements

 Joint bank account

 Separate bank accounts

 Two accounts funded by one spouse

 One account funded and controlled by one spouse

Who Will Write the Checks?

Name _______________________________________ **Date** _______________ **Period** _______________

Read the following case situations in which couples must decide how to control spending and set up banking records. Choose the alternative from the list below that you believe will best suit each couple's individual situation. Briefly explain your choice.

Alternatives:

A. Joint bank account

B. Separate bank accounts

C. Two accounts both funded by one spouse

D. One account funded and controlled by one spouse

1. Pamela is a figure skater who is training intensively for the Olympics. Her husband Antonio is a wealthy real estate developer who is devoted to Pamela and very generous. Pamela finds that when she is "on the road" she does not need to carry much money because Antonio receives and pays her bills. She does not want to think about depositing or writing checks, keeping a running checkbook balance, or balancing monthly bank statements. She only wants to eat, sleep, and train for the Olympics. Which type of account would be best for the couple at this time? Why?_______________

____

____

____

____

____

____

2. Before they met and married, both Marla and Mark were single and financially independent for many years. They are both in their late forties, employed, and accustomed to handling their own finances. Their incomes are similar. They presently have a joint banking account but dislike this arrangement. Marla says, "I never know if I can write a check because Mark may be planning to write one and then we will overdraw. We are constantly getting in each other's way. Also, Mark often forgets to record his checks in the checkbook." Which type of account might Marla and Mark try? How would it work? Why might it be more satisfactory?_______________

____

____

____

____

____

____

(Continued)

Name ____

3. Bill and Kathleen are a retired couple. Bill has been the sole breadwinner and has controlled all the finances during their 30-year marriage. Kathleen managed her own account sensibly for years before they were married. Recently Bill had major surgery for a life-threatening illness, and doctors say he may not live another year. He is hooked up to machines in the hospital and cannot write checks. The bills are piling up, and Kathleen has no way of paying them. The law in their state of residence does not require that joint assets be frozen in case of death. Which type of checking account might best suit this couple now? Why? ____

____

____

____

____

4. Mitch and Eloise both worked outside the home and managed their finances independently for several years. Their daughter Abigail was born a few months ago. Now they have agreed that Mitch will support the family and Eloise will be a full-time homemaker until Abigail is school age. They have tried using a joint checking account, but Eloise says she "feels suffocated" by it. She wants to have an account that she alone controls. Mitch wants the same type of account. Which type of checking account is best for them? Why? ____

____

____

____

____

____

Your Financial Plan

Name _______________________________________ **Date** _______________ **Period** _______________

Do you ever run short of cash before the end of the week? Do you sometimes wonder where all your money goes? Have you made any financial plans for reaching long-range goals, such as paying for a new car or a college education? Learning to use a budget may help you solve these problems. A financial plan or budget will help you control your money more efficiently. The activity below will get you started.

Plan a budget for a week. List your income, fixed expenses, flexible expenses, and savings. If some bills are paid monthly, average the cost on a weekly basis by dividing by four. Then keep track of your spending for a week. Record your expenditures on the chart. At the end of the week total the amounts you spent and determine if you went over or under your budgeted expenses. Then answer the questions at the end of this activity. (You may want to keep track of your expenses for several weeks, then prepare a budget for a month at a time.)

	Planned	Day 1	Day 2	Day 3	Day 4	Day 5	Day 6	Day 7	Actual	Amount Over/Under
Income:										
Allowance										
Wages										
Gifts										
Other:										
Total Income:										
Fixed expenses:										
Flexible expenses:										
Total Expenses:										
Savings:										

1. After keeping track of your income and expenses for a week, do you feel the need to revise your budget? Explain changes you would make. _______________________________________

____

____

2. Describe your long-range financial goals and how you plan to save for those goals. _______________

____

____

Managing Your Finances

Name ____

Date _______________________________________ **Period** _____________ **Score** _______________

Chapter 27 Test

Matching: Match the following terms and identifying phrases.

_______ 1. Type of credit in which the consumer is allowed to make purchases up to a specified amount and pays a percentage of the balance each month in addition to carrying charges.

_______ 2. Involves the spending of future income for goods and services received in the present.

_______ 3. Failure to pay on a loan.

_______ 4. Costs that fluctuate in amount and that may occur less regularly.

_______ 5. Type of credit in which the consumer agrees to pay for a purchase in several regular payments.

_______ 6. Is affected by how promptly a consumer who has previously had credit has paid his or her debts.

_______ 7. A plan for managing income and expenses.

_______ 8. Type of credit in which the consumer pays the full charge in one payment.

_______ 9. Costs that are predictable and that recur regularly.

_______ 10. The dollar amount that credit costs the consumer.

A. budget
B. fixed expenses
C. flexible expenses
D. credit
E. fiscal
F. installment credit
G. finance charges
H. noninstallment credit
I. revolving credit
J. default
K. credit rating

True/False: Circle *T* if the statement is true or *F* if the statement is false.

T F   11. When you use revolving credit, you agree to pay a percentage of the balance owed each month in addition to carrying charges.

T F   12. If you would like to set up a budget but have no idea of what your expenditures are, it is wise to keep records of your income and expenditures for a month or two before setting up the budget.

T F   13. A credit union collects information on the credit practices of individuals and makes the information available to businesses.

T F   14. Deliberately underspending in a budget category for several months may allow you to spend more at a later time.

T F   15. An advantage of a joint bank account is that money is available to either husband or wife if one spouse is unable to get to the bank.

T F   16. For the average American family the budget category requiring the least money is that of housing.

T F   17. Many life insurance policies accumulate a cash value, and policyholders may borrow against it.

(Continued)

T F   18. Loans from credit unions usually offer a comparatively high rate of interest.

T F   19. Using family or friends as a source of money can generate resentment and complicate relationships with them.

T F   20. Credit cards are the least common type of credit used in the United States.

Multiple Choice: Select the best response. Write the letter in the space provided.

_______   21. When you do not pay for an item or service as you receive it but pay the full charge in one payment, you are using _______.
A. installment credit
B. noninstallment credit
C. revolving credit
D. None of the above.

_______   22. Which of the following statements about separate checking accounts is true:
A. Conflict may arise if one of the partners feels the arrangement is unfair.
B. This arrangement allows for the maximum feeling of sharing.
C. If one spouse dies, the other will still have access to the account.
D. Each spouse must keep accurate running balances.

_______   23. When you set up a budget, you should try to save at least _____ percent of your monthly net income.
A. 5
B. 10
C. 20
D. 25

_______   24. A budget _____.
A. is a plan for evaluating income and expenses
B. should not require complicated math
C. serves as a record that can be helpful when figuring taxes
D. All of the above.

_______   25. To be successful your spending plan must _____.
A. follow advice given in financial periodicals precisely
B. be followed exactly and strictly, even in emergencies
C. be uniquely geared to your needs
D. not include a miscellaneous category

_______   26. If you are rejected for credit, you _____.
A. have no right to ask the credit bureau any questions about the matter
B. have the right to check your credit report for damaging information
C. cannot expect to ever qualify for credit in the future
D. have no way of getting false information out of the file kept by the credit bureau

_______   27. Which of the following is a possible source of credit?
A. Credit union.
B. Store dealer financing.
C. Bank.
D. All of the above.

(Continued)

_____ 28. If the borrower does not repay a loan to a pawnbroker within a stated time, the pawnbroker _____.
- A. will return the item to the borrower
- B. can take the borrower's car
- C. can sell the item that the borrower gave as collateral
- D. will lower the interest rate on the loan

_____ 29. A loan from a credit union _____.
- A. is available only to members of the credit union
- B. usually has higher interest rates than loans from finance companies
- C. must be repaid within six months
- D. must be repaid within two years

_____ 30. A disadvantage of credit cards is that _____.
- A. they can be lost
- B. they provide a temptation to overspend
- C. if someone steals and uses them, the credit card owner can be held responsible for part of the cost
- D. All of the above.

Essay Questions: Provide complete responses to the following questions or statements.

31. If you were married, how would you handle spending? How would you like to set up your checking and savings accounts with your spouse? Explain your choices.

32. Describe two ways you can be your own source of credit.

33. List two advantages and two disadvantages of the use of credit cards.